D1741825

SELECTED SERMONS OF ZACHARY BOYD

SELECTED SERMONS OF ZACHARY BOYD

edited by
David W. Atkinson

Published for the Scottish Text Society,
Aberdeen University Press
1989

© THE SCOTTISH TEXT SOCIETY 1989

ISBN 0 08 037000 4

Typeset from author-generated discs
and printed by AUP Glasgow/Aberdeen—A member of BPCC
Ltd.

CONTENTS

INTRODUCTION   ix
THE PUBLISHED AND UNPUBLISHED WORKS OF
    ZACHARY BOYD   xxxviii

I. ON SCRIPTURE AND PREACHING   1
    An Exposition of the Epistle of S. Paul   3

II. ON MATTERS THEOLOGICAL   17
    Christ Ovr Righteovsnesse   19
    The Christian His Pilgrimage   36

III. ON THE NEED FOR CHURCH REFORM   59
    The Cleansing of the Temple   61
    Mercy for Zion   77
    Zions Teares   87
    The Refvge of the Chvrch   107

IV. THE PURIFIED CHURCH   125
    Scotlands Hallelviah   127
    The Weapons of the Chvrch   144
    The Trivmph of the Chvrch   154

V. GENERAL DEVOTION   173
    A Sermon of Repentance   175
    The Worlds Condemnation   188
    The Danger of Carelesse Examination   199
    The Safetie of the Chvrch   214
    The Godly Man His Confidence   229

VI. OCCASIONAL SERMONS   243
    A Sermon for a Fast   245
    The Sick Man His Svte   260
    A Sermon Preached at the Excommunication of
    A Rebellious Adulterer   279

NOTES   301

ACKNOWLEDGEMENTS

I am deeply indebted to The University of Glasgow Library for allowing me access to the Boyd manuscripts. Thanks are especially due to Dr. Nigel Thorpe and the Special Collections' staff, who extended to me great assistance and courtesy on my many visits to Glasgow. I wish also to thank the staffs of the National Library of Scotland, the Mitchell Library, and Edinburgh University Library.

Special gratitude is extended to Dr. Roderick Lyall of the Scottish Text Society, who gave me valuable advice in completing the Boyd text; and to Dr. Elaine Petrie, who reviewed and commented on the manuscript. Thanks are also due to my colleagues at The University of Lethbridge, Dr. W.E. Aufrecht, Dr. T.F. Pope, and Mr. B.J. Smart.

While one is indebted to all one's teachers, I must make mention of Dr. R.H. Carnie and the late Dr. Anthony Petti, both of The University of Calgary, who encouraged me in my interests in the Scottish Reformation, and who, as my first instructors in paleography and bibliography, supplied me with my most basic tools.

The text could not have been produced without Ms Chris Lastuka, Ms Charlene Sawatsky, and Ms Karen Hardy, who did all the typing and were immensely patient throughout the editing process. I am also grateful to The University of Lethbridge for study leave to complete my work on Boyd. Above all, though, I must thank my wife, Terry, and my sons, Jonathan and Zachary, for their support in all my research endeavours.

Research for this selection of Boyd's sermons was conducted with the assistance of a grant from the Social Sciences and Humanities Research Council of Canada.

INTRODUCTION

Among seventeenth-century Scottish writers, Zachary Boyd is one of the most prolific, both as a poet and as a writer of religious prose. As well he is one of the most neglected, as few have had either the time or the inclination to work through his vast corpus of published and unpublished work. There is no question that Boyd was an uneven writer, as might be expected of one who wrote so much and whose primary interests were devotional and not literary. But this is not to say that Boyd did not write works as good as any of his day, for, as a preacher, who for over thirty-five years supplied spiritual guidance to the people of the Barony parish, Boyd stands as a major figure in the Protestant sermon tradition.

That Boyd was primarily a preacher is itself a major reason why he has been so ignored. While the sermons of such writers as John Donne and Jeremy Taylor have been given due recognition, this attention hardly matches the immense productivity of sixteenth and seventeenth-century preachers, who week after week, and year after year, poured out instruction, consolation, and spiritual comfort from their parish pulpits. Granted, their minds were on other things than what constitutes good literature, and the urgency of the moment often meant that their sermons never reached the "finished" stage. But this in no way explains why the sermon, the major literary product of a pious age, has never been recognised as a key to understanding a period in which Spenser, Donne, and Sidney were known to relatively few.

Why this is so is an intriguing commentary on the nature of the sermon. Although historians long ago gave up their preoccupation with kings, wars, and dynasties, they still ignore the sermon as an incisive barometer of the concerns of the ordinary person living in the sixteenth and seventeenth centuries. It is true that historians have looked at the sermons of the period as a source of social and political commentary. In doing so, however, they have not recognised sermon literature for what it is—a genre that deals with the ways of God, not men—and they have thereby not fully come to grips with the pervasive spirituality of the age, even while they might tacitly recognise its existence. For church historians, sermon literature is a source of frustration because it tends to provide little insight into the theological complexities of the Reformation. Doctrine and the theology derived from it aim to systematise what begins in religious experience. But the sermon, in addressing the personal relationship between God and the individual believer, is concerned with matters of devotion that, not only often conflict with doctrine, but in the everyday religious life of the Christian also take precedence over it. Consistently overlooked is how the sermon is a far more revealing statement of religiosity than a work of systematic theology could ever be, if for no other reason than it directly touches the religious life of those filling the church pews.

Literary critics have, as well, found little worthy of attention in the seventeenth-century sermon. The reasons for this are fairly obvious. In a period of remarkable literary accomplishment, the sermon seems for the most part deficient, except, for example, in the case of someone like Donne, where what is admired in his poetry also surfaces in his prose. It would be misleading to disclaim that many sermons are at best mediocre: that they are given to tedious repetition, commonplace imagery, and a generally dull, albeit workmanlike, prose. But here one crucial thing must be remembered: the sermon was never intended to be grist for modern literary criticism, and sermon writers never saw themselves as having to write for anyone other than their parishioners. It should be remembered, too, that sermons are intended to be heard and not read, and that what seems uninspired on the printed page may come alive with conviction and passion when read aloud. Only when heard can the plain style so popular among Protestant preachers be appreciated for the way its eloquent sincerity stands out in striking contrast to classical and metaphysical wit.

If Boyd's sermons are anything, they are typical of his age, and are important because they are so typical. Boyd wrote always with an eye to glorifying God, and with a concern for the immediate spiritual needs of the wayfaring Christian. His sermons are direct and couched in simple language, not only because the Christian message is itself simple, but also because Boyd's desire is to reach all persons. He therefore has little time for cleverness of expression, even while he possesses an awareness of language, which makes his sermons effective both as literature and as guides to devotional life. While Boyd's theology is that of a staunch Calvinist, and his sermons are not without theological meaning, Boyd does not speak as a theologian preoccupied with systematic exegesis, but as one concerned with bringing together God and the individual in a direct and immediate way. Specially called by God to this task, Boyd offers instruction on the fundamentals of Christian living, and thereby serves as God's instrument in opening Christian hearts to Him.

That Boyd wrote specifically with the intention of reaching as many persons as he could raises one further issue: why are his sermons written in English rather than Scots, which continued as the language of virtually all Scotsmen well into the seventeenth century? Here one must recognise a number of factors that led to increased English usage during the seventeenth century. First, there was increased interchange between Scotsmen and Englishmen during the seventeenth century, which came as the obvious result of having a Scottish king on the English throne. Second, Scottish letters were in an impoverished state generally in the seventeenth century, given that the institutions which maintained cultural life had largely disappeared with the removal of the court to London. This situation was exacerbated by having a Scottish Church, which, unlike its English counterpart, was no great supporter of letters. Finally, the English Bible had been in use in Scotland since at least 1560, and Scotsmen had therefore grown used to hearing English sermons drawn from an English Bible. Given this familiarity with Biblical English, as well as the absence of a truly Scottish literary culture, it is hardly surprising that English came to dominate all forms of expression, including that of religion and politics.[1] It is in this regard that Scotland produced a distinguished group of writers in English, including John Knox, James Melville, William Drummond, and Samuel Rutherford. That Boyd's prose can stand beside the works of these men affirms its place in the English prose tradition of seventeenth-century Scotland.

There is general agreement that Zachary Boyd was born in Kilmarnock, Ayrshire in 1585. His family background is not clear, although several nineteenth-century biographers assert that Boyd was a cousin of Andrew Boyd, Bishop of Argyle, and Robert Boyd of Trochrigg, and was connected with the Boyds of Pinkill, in Carrick, Ayrshire. Boyd received his early education in Kilmarnock, and then pursued his studies in the College of Glasgow, where he matriculated in 1601, and at St. Andrews from which he received the Master of Arts in 1607. Following a well established pattern for Scottish divines, Boyd then went to the Protestant College of Saumur in France to complete his education.[3] Boyd remained for sixteen years at Saumur where he enjoyed considerable success, being made Regent Professor in 1611 and offered the Principalship in 1615. The latter he declined, and in 1623, with increased Protestant persecution in France, he returned to Scotland. Upon his arrival back in Scotland, he lived for a short time in the household of Sir William Scott of Elie, and then in that of the Marquis of Hamilton. In due course, however, he was called to the Barony parish, a large district of 1,200 persons in the suburbs of Glasgow.[4] The Barony parish was to be Boyd's first and last, for he was to remain there until his death on March 3, 1653. Boyd was married twice, first to Elizabeth Fleming of Glasgow, who died in 1636, and then to Margaret Mure, who outlived him. Both marriages were childless.

Outside of his religious writing and his reputation as a preacher, Boyd is most remembered for his long-time association with Glasgow University. In 1631, Boyd was elected Dean of the Faculty, an office which made him responsible for the university's curriculum. The term of office was two years, and Boyd was re-elected in 1633 and 1635. In 1634 and again in 1635 and 1645 he was elected to the senior administrative position of Rector. Finally, in 1644, he was appointed Vice Chancellor, an honorary position he retained until his death. Boyd demonstrated his commitment to the university by his several generous financial gifts, which were used to assist students, acquire books for the library, and support various building projects.[5] As well, Boyd willed to Glasgow University assets of approximately twenty-thousand pounds Scots. The source of Boyd's wealth remains a mystery, although it is unlikely that it came from his income as a minister.[6]

Boyd's political affiliations are fairly well defined. As suggested by the dedication of *The Last Battell of the Sovle in Death* (1628), Boyd was at least a moderate royalist. Notwithstanding that it was common practice to dedicate one's works to important people, one should not discount that the first volume of *The Last Battell* is dedicated, first in English to Charles I, and then in French, to his consort Henrietta Maria; and the second volume is dedicated to Elizabeth, the Electress Palatine of Bohemia, daughter of James VI, as a "Balme of Comforts" on the death of her husband. Boyd also wrote a Latin oration in 1633 to welcome Charles to Holyrood. This *"Oratio Panegyrica"* is one of a number of works comprising *Academiae Glasguensis* ΧΑΡΣΤΗΡΙΟΝ, which was put together by various members of the university community as a tribute to their monarch.[7] It signalled, moreover, that Glasgow University was a centre of modest royalist support, as further revealed in the reluctance of many faculty to subscribe to the National Covenant of 1638.[8]

Most certainly Boyd was a member of this group, and indeed Robert Baillie describes Boyd as one of "the greatest opposites in the West to the subscription to the Covenant."[9] One must not, however, make too much of Boyd's royalist tendencies, for, along with just about everyone else associated with the university, he shortly did accept the prescripts of the Covenant. While Boyd remained an adherent to the Covenant for the remainder of his life, the degree of his commitment is difficult to ascertain. Certainly he did not pick up his musket when the king marched north to the Scottish border in the spring of 1639 and again in August, 1640. The best he could do was the poem, *The Battell of Newbvrne*, which celebrates in very bad verse how the *"Scots Armie obtained a notable victorie against the English Papists, Prelats, and Arminiens."*[10] Not without significance is how Boyd avoids describing the victory as one against the king. Equally suggestive is that Boyd, despite the praise he gives the Covenant in his sermons, supported the policy of the Scottish estates in their recall of Charles II to the throne.

Boyd's royalist tendencies must also be seen in the larger

context of a growing Scots concern with how events in England might effect Scotland. The Scottish presbyters saw in Cromwell and the Independents as much of a threat to the discipline and government of the reformed Kirk as they did in episcopacy. With the English Civil war turning against Charles I, and the Independents firmly in control of the army, the Scots aligned themselves with the king on the understanding that he would recognise the National Covenant and guarantee a Presbyterian church government in Scotland. Unfortunately for the Scots presbyters, they aligned themselves with the losing side. The results are well documented: a division of the Scots under Hamilton was routed by Cromwell in Lancashire, and then Cromwell turned north to defeat Leslie at the Battle of Dunbar on September 3, 1650.[11]

Significant, as well, is how Cromwell figures in an event of Boyd's life, although one must always pause over how much of the story is historical and how much apocryphal. While most of the magistrates and ministers fled Glasgow in the face of Cromwell and the English army, Boyd is said to have remained at his post.[12] So it was that when Cromwell and his officers appeared at the Cathedral Church in Glasgow, they were faced with the stalwart Boyd, who is said to have "railed on them all to their very face in the High Church." Cromwell did not do the expected thing, despite the advice that he "pistol the scoundrel,"[13] but invited Boyd for dinner, and the evening is said to have concluded with Cromwell and Boyd praying together into the small hours of the morning.

Little else is really known of Boyd's life, suggesting that for the most part he was removed from the thrust and parry of political events, committing himself instead to the needs of his Barony parish. Certainly Boyd seemed to know very early on where his strengths lay, as when he wrote from Saumur to his cousin Robert Boyd, "You know as well as I that I have not aspired after high things and choose rather to content myself with those that are lower."[14] Andrew Rivett confirms Boyd's self assessment in observing how Boyd's single ambition was "to bring himself under the yoak, in some honest and desirable place."[15] Boyd was totally committed to his pastoral responsibilities, and his works, by their number alone, underline his belief that "they who would doe this worke as they should must with earnest prayers, painefull reading, and serious meditation emptie their veines of blood till paleness . . . bee printed vpon their face."[16] Such commitment, it hardly needs saying, left Boyd with time for little else.

PUBLISHED WORK

A good deal of Boyd's published work is poetry, which appears in three separate collections. *The Garden of Zion* (1644), which is the work of his period in France, is a poetic retelling of Old Testament stories "from Adam unto the last of the Kings of Judah and Israel,"[17] from which are drawn "good uses" for the readers' edification. Written along the same lines are *The Psalms of David in Meeter* (1644) and *Scriptural Songs or Holy Poems* (1645). Boyd produced two other collections of verse, the *Four Evangels*, which, as its title suggests, retells the Gospels; and *Zion's Flowers or Christian Poems for Spiritual Edification*, which comprises nineteen dramatic poems dwelling on major Biblical events. Neither of these works has been published, except for four of the poems of *Zion's Flowers*, which the Edinburgh bibliophile, Gabriel Neil, brought out in 1855.

It is unfortunate that Boyd fancied himself a poet, and chose to publish more of his poetry than his prose. While Rivett could write how "Mr Boyd . . . labours *with* good fruit, and renders himself an excellent preacher,"[18] it is Boyd's reputation as a less than accomplished poet that has overshadowed his talents as a preacher. There were those, of course, who praised Boyd as a poet. Bailie Nicol Jarvie suggested to Frank Obald-stone, for example, that "Mr. Zachary Boyd's translation of the Scriptures . . . better poetry need nane to be."[19] In the "Preface to the Reader" of the 1686 *Spiritual Songs*, Boyd is praised for spurning "Quaint strains to please delicat ears," and supplying "spiritual Entertainment amidst the Toils and Sorrows" of life, which serve as an "Ordinance . . . of God ordered for His own glory."[20] Boyd is described as "not so much a Poet . . . as a Translater, studying all he can to keep his matter in the same Garb the Spirit of God hath left it in."[21] To be a writer of "holy Songs" was not enough, however, to guarantee Boyd's literary reputation. Thus in the preface to his *Mock Poem or Whigs Supplication* (1681), Samuel Colvil observed, "bad lines many times causeth more mirth than good ones. Where one laughs at the poems of *Virgil, Homer, Ariosto, Du Bartas* etc.[,] twenty will laugh at those of John Cockburn or Mr. Zacharie Boyd."[22] Equally disparaging was John Pinkerton, who regretted that Boyd's "just fame" as a "benefactor of learning has been obscured by that cloud of miserable rhymes."[23] And John Sleazer, in his *Theatrum Scotiae* (1693), even while arguing that Boyd's reputation as a bad poet is "grossly exaggerated," finds the best he can say of Boyd's poetry is that it is "unpolished."[24]

Boyd's reputation as a poor poet was not helped by his failure to have his metrical paraphrase of the Psalms accepted by the General Assembly to replace the version in use in Scotland since 1564. Although Boyd was apparently encouraged by the Assembly to present a text to the Commissioners in charge of determining a new Psalter, and actively encouraged by a number of his acquaintances, he never, it seems, had much of a chance. Boyd's friend, Baillie, clearly understood this when he wrote, "Our good friend, Mr. Zacharie Boyd, has put himself to a great deal of pains and charges to make a Psalter, but I ever warned him his hopes were groundless to get it received in our churches, yet the flatteries of his unadvised neighbours makes him insist in his fruitless design."[25] The Commissioners finally settled on what is generally called Rous' version, which was then amended by a committee of the General Assembly of which Boyd was a member. So, while Boyd's text was not the one chosen, he did play a role in the creation of a new Psalter. His role was significant enough to justify the special thanks of the General Assembly minuted on January 1, 1650.[26]

So it was that Gabriel Neil mounted an attempt in the nineteenth century to overcome Boyd's reputation as a poor poet.[27] To a certain extent, Neil was successful, for, in choosing to publish a selection from *Zion's Flowers*, Neil recognised that Boyd's best poetic efforts had not appeared in print. Boyd's previously published verse was for the most part rhymed doggerel justly deserving condemnation, while, by contrast, the dramatic poems of *Zion's Flowers* demonstrate Boyd's sense of dialogue and his flair for psychological realism. As well as suggesting that Boyd could write good poetry, Neil helped

Boyd's reputation by turning attention away from his poetry towards his prose, and by reminding readers that Boyd was by nature and training a preacher rather than a poet.

Of Boyd's published prose works, the one most worthy of attention is *The Last Battell of the Sovle in Death*, which, in a dialogue between a dying man and his pastor, recounts how one prepares for death. The work results from Boyd's own skirmish with death, which is documented in the preface to the reader when he writes how "in September, Anno 1626, I was like Epaphroditus, sicke nigh vnto death. For when I arose out of that Feuer, I found in my studie my winding sheete among my Bookes. This gaue mee occasion painfullie to search and describe vnto the world this *Last Battell of the Sovle*. I pray God to make it profitable for thine vse."[28] In *The Last Battell*, Boyd draws on the well established and wide spread tradition of the *ars moriendi*, which began with the anonymous *Tractatus artis bene moriendi* (c. 1414–1418), translated into English thirty years later as *The Book of the Craft of Dying*; and the shorter work commonly called the *Ars Moriendi*, which is a derivative of the *Tractatus* and significant for its eleven woodcut representations of deathbed temptation.[29] While Boyd uses the dialogue form in *The Last Battell* for obvious pedagogic reasons, he goes beyond writing Christian instruction to capture in the pastor's entreaties and the dying man's lamentations the spiritual crisis to which the deathbed brings all persons. Thus he aims to reveal what the reader can expect in the agony of death, how he must act during his final days of life, and what he must do on his deathbed to nurture the spiritual assurance he is of God's elect.

With the exception of *A Cleare Forme of Catechising* (1639), which reveals Boyd's very practical devotionalism, and *Four Letters of Comforts, for the Deaths of the Earle of Hadingtoun, and of the Lord Boyd* (1640), which suggests that Boyd was not without important social connections, the remainder of Boyd's published work is comprised of several sermons probably preached from his Barony parish pulpit. Of these, *A Cordiall of Comforts for a Wearied Soule* (1629) and *The Balme of Gilead Prepared for the Sicke* (1633) express many of the same sentiments as *The Last Battell*, and are likely additional results of Boyd's illness in 1626. While both sermons are written with the themes of the *memento mori* squarely in mind, dwelling as they do on how "beautie is but a folie that will faile you,"[30] their ultimate aim is consolatory, as suggested when Boyd writes, "obserue well O man what I say . . . While thou are tempted to think that the Lord hath cast thee off . . . I can assure thee that thou hast him even now, and shall haue him also for ever."[31] Boyd never forgets that man is fundamentally a sinner and that this world is inconsequential, but his focus remains on divine mercy and the hope for salvation basic to the Christian message.

Other of Boyd's published sermons also pivot on the distinction between world and spirit implicit in the *memento mori*. Included here are *A Sermon of Preparation to the Commvnion* and *A Sermon for the Day of the Sacrament*, published together as a single volume in 1629, in which Boyd stresses the need to labour in God's vineyards, despite his expressed Calvinism in spurning the notion that "any man can merit the meat which endureth to *everlasting lyfe*,"[32] and his assertion that "everlasting life is the gift of God."[33] Such "*evangelical* labour" is, not labour for worldly things, but a labour to reject them, to see them as vanity, and to "follow the LORD for nothing so much as for himself."[34] This work is completed only under the guiding hand of God, and thus in another collection of sermons, *Two Orientall Pearles, Grace and Glory* (1629), Boyd stresses the significance of Grace and divine initiative, how God "when he hath done all the good that can be done vnto vs in this lyfe, by beeing *with vs continualy*, and by *holding vs by our right hand*, and guarding vs by his counsel, all ends with this that he receives vs to glory."[35] What these sermons express is, if not an anti-world attitude, then certainly a warning against indulgence in the vanities of the world.

UNPUBLISHED WORK

While most of Boyd's prose remains unpublished, this is not to say that Boyd had no plan to publish his works. Indeed it was with this intention in mind that he repaginated an appreciable number of sermons, grouping them into several large collections and adding title pages. It is generally accepted, as well, that Boyd's bequest to Glasgow University was made on the understanding that the university would publish a selection of his works. On this the intent of Boyd's deed is quite clear:

> Lykeas, it is heirby speciallie provydit, that, out of the reddiest of the haill foirnamed soumes, thaire be desbursed be the said Principall Professors, and Mrs. and y'r successors, als much money as will suffice to print in one volume in folio, consisting nearly of four hundrethe sheets of paper, my workes, quhilk are alreddie printed in severall pieces, together with dyverse Sermons and other Treatises, quhilk I have besyde me yet unprinted, to be addit, y'rto eftir the same is revised be the persons heirefhr designed; referring to the said revisours to make choose of such of my works, either already printed or lying besyde me unprinted as they sall think fitt to be published in print. And for this effect I appoynt Doctor Johne Strang, and Mr. Robert Bailzie . . . to revise my foresaid works; and failing of them, it is hereby provydid that the Rector of the said Universitie, Deane of Facultie, with the Prin'all, Professors and Regents of the said College, and y'r other Assessors, nominate and choose one or moe able godlie, and learned man or men, to revise my said works to the effect above specified.[36]

Whatever the intent of Boyd's will, however, it seems little effort was made to publish either part or all of what Boyd himself prepared for publication. There is conjecture that a later publication was planned, dependent on whether the university realised a 6000 merks bond due by the Earl of Loudon, which was part of Boyd's original bequest. The 6000 merks were apparently never collected, and university administrators likely felt released from their commitment to publish Boyd's works.

Boyd's unpublished sermons and devotional tracts number two hundred and fifty four, and probably represent what Boyd felt were the best of his output. Consistent with Boyd's biography, which suggests that his contributions lay outside the arena of political and religious controversy, Boyd's sermons concentrate on the general spiritual life of the Church. At the same time, though, Boyd's sermons fall into a number of broad classifications, which are used in ordering the works contained in this selection of his prose.

I. On Scripture and Preaching
Few things reveal the Reformation spirit so well as how the Reformers saw and used scripture, and Boyd is no exception

to this rule. The Reformers themselves wrote much on their hermeneutical practices, although Boyd's hermeneutics must largely be ascertained from his actual use of scripture, and the same must be said for his views on the related matters of preaching and the role of the preacher. Boyd's first sermon on St. Paul is important, therefore, because it is one of the few times he directly addresses these matters, and because it so clearly fixes him in the tradition of Calvinist hermeneutics, whereby the Old and New Testaments constitute a historical continuity and a gradual revelation of divine will. Boyd in this regard accepts a system of typological correspondences that sees the Old Testament anticipating the New, and the New Testament revealing the full implications of the Old. Further, he brings the significance of events in both Old and New Testaments forward to have direct contemporary relevance in the continuous working out of divine will through history. Underpinning this is Boyd's acceptance of the literal meaning of scripture as understood through rational exegesis that parallels the notion that scriptural interpretation must never go outside scripture. Consistent with Protestant hermeneutics, as most notably articulated by Joseph Hall in *The Art of Divine Meditation* (1606), Boyd turns away from the imagination to reject the allegorical, tropological and anagogical modes of scriptural interpretation so popular in mediaeval homiletics.

Boyd's sermon begins by telling how God chooses to speak at different places in different ways, and from this Boyd draws out the sermon's several teachings. Most obvious of these is that God's different voices are an expression of divine will. As well, they reveal God's love in understanding human need; or, as Boyd himself says, "God knoweth better then we what is good for vs: his will is our will. More then Gods allowance is more hurtfull then helpfull" (5).[37] Crucial here is that one never presumes to question divine intention, although, at the same time, Boyd stresses how God never ceases to care, and in this regard adds the consolatory observation, "great is the care that God hath euer had of mans saluation. This he hath shewen by speaking vnto him whiles in one fashion & whiles vnto another. Surely the time was neuer that God did faile vnto his Church" (6). What Boyd also affirms is the notion of the preacher as God's instrument, which is implicit in the idea of calling central to Reform theology. Accepting that irresistible grace is manifested in a particular calling to serve God, Boyd sees prophet, apostle, and preacher as "Gods interpreters," who "haue neede to begge the spirit of God that wee maye teach you the true meaning of the wordes of God" (11).

It is with this in mind that Boyd rejects "humane learning" as by itself sufficient for interpreting scripture and passing on the meaning of scripture to others. The ability to interpret comes, not from man, but from God, or, as Boyd writes, "if a man had all the philosophie of Aristotle in his head, if he haue not the spirit of God in his heart, he will neuer vnderstand the right sense of scriptures" (12). This is not to say that Boyd rejects all "humane learning"; his own sermons reveal this is not the case. What is the case is that scripture takes precedence over all else, and that the individual must never presume to think he can embellish or improve upon it; as Boyd warns, "let vs not be wise in our owne conceits. God that is wisdome is more wise then we all" (15). Thus Boyd returns to his main text: even though God speaks in different ways at different times, what he reveals is always sufficient to meet humankind's needs. A final message of the sermon is that, just as the spirit is necessary if the preacher is to understand and pass on God's word, so too is the spirit needed if the listener is to comprehend what he hears. "Surely," Boyd says, "no more shall yee of the people be able to vnderstand their [the preachers'] interpretation without the same spirit" (13). Incumbent on all who come to hear God's word is to request of God, "make me to vnderstand the waye of thy precepts" (13). Important is that this capacity to hear, to understand, and to respond to God's word serves as a crucial indication of God's favour, and of one's inclusion among God's elect.

II. On Matters Theological

While Boyd was trained in theology, none of his extant works can be explicitly labelled a theological treatise. At the same time, Boyd, as a preacher, does not ignore theology, and his sermons express clearly his Calvinist orientation. Boyd's Calvinism is hardly surprising, for, despite the early influence of Luther and Zwingli in Scotland, the Church was recognisably Calvinist by the period of the National Covenant, as it really had been since Knox and the *Confession of Faith* of 1560.[38] This Calvinist orientation was affirmed in *The Westminster Confession*, which was drawn up in the 1640s, and accepted by the Scottish Church as an official statement of doctrine.[39] So, even while the Kirk was divided on the issue of church government, it remained theologically homogeneous, and never was there in the Scottish Church the Calvinist sectarianism that characterised, for example, its English counterpart.

The Scottish Church of the sixteenth and seventeenth centuries was, then, dominated by an explicit Calvinism, which stressed the immeasurable distance between God, who, according to the *Confession of Faith*, is "eternall, infinite, unmeasurable, [and] incomprehensible,"[40] and an unregenerate humankind, which in its fallen state is a slave to Satan and destined for everlasting death. Because humanity is immersed in sin, men and women are incapable by themselves of doing anything to correct their alienation from God. Everything is left to God, who determines with Himself to extend salvation to His elect. Thus the *Confession* asserts how regeneration comes from the Holy Spirit "wirking in the hart of the elect of God ane assureit faith in the promeise of God."[41] It is by faith that God's elect are justified in His eyes and are inspired to good works, although always it is made clear that, as sanctification flows from justification, there is nothing inherent in humankind that allows for free participation in the process of regeneration.

Even though humankind has no say in the working out of individual salvation, this does not remove the necessity for good works, and Calvinism therefore articulates an entire code of ethics for everyday life. The psychological impetus for righteous living comes, not from the belief that good works earn salvation, but that good works and faith are signs that one is of God's elect. Simply put, the individual is looking for assurance of his spiritual state, and to this end Calvinism is characterised by an inward turning of the individual, who looks to examine the condition of his soul. A concomitant of this concern is the notion of calling, which asserts that God calls His elect in a general way to His true Church, and in a specific way by which the individual must perform a particular vocation in life. Assurance of election, then, comes from pursuing one's calling, and from this there arises the work ethic traditionally and persistently associated with Protestantism.[42]

Although Boyd wrote over seventy years after the *Confession of Faith*, he is, in sermons such as *The Christian His Pilgrimage* and *Christ Ovr Righteousnesse*, as faithful to the *Confession* as it is to Calvin's *Institutes of the Christian Religion* (1536). In *The Christian His Pilgrimage* Boyd writes how men exist "dead in their sinnes" (36), and how there is nothing they can do to correct themselves. "No man," Boyd says, "is saued by his owne handiwork" (36) . Through obedience unto death, however, Christ has merited for man forgiveness of sin and thereby allowed man to enjoy a new life with God. Boyd affirms how forgiveness is found "onely [in] Christ who spiritually and temporally giueth eyes to the blind and eares to the deafe, a tongue to the dumb and legges to the lame" (20). Boyd does not forget, however, the rigour of the Law, as he asserts in *Christ Ovr Righteousness* that the Law reveals to man his sin and misery, and forces him to seek the help of God: "*the end of the law*, O man, is to make thee an honest man. When the law hath taught with figures and terrified a man with threatinings, he must needes runne to Christ" (28). Clear, as well, is that the Law does not operate independently: the Law is "a dead letter" (20) without "the quickining spirit of Christ" (20). Without Christ, the Law condemns and confirms the reprobate in the path of sin; with Christ, it brings the elect to God and allows for the realisation of the true Church.

As a cornerstone of Calvinist theology, justification by faith is central to Boyd's theology. Therefore he exhorts us to "striue to get faith and to increase our faith by hearing, readeing, prayeing, and meditateing, night and day in that word, which *is the power of God* to *saluation*" (33). From faith comes everything else, particularly the ability to hear and understand God's message, as Boyd suggests in his sermon on Paul discussed earlier. Boyd instructs, "if, O man, thou would have faith, thou must love sermons. Goe to them preparedly, heare them attentiuely, for *faith* is *by hearing*" (33). It is not, however, simply a matter of faith, and to be called "Gods *workemanship*" (36) is not merely to be capable of believing. It is also to do good works, even though good works are not a condition of salvation. Therefore Boyd outlines in *The Christian His*

Pilgrimage the spiritual process of the regenerate person, which, while initiated through faith, is manifested in good works which "God hath ordeined" (50).

The individual has no say in his spiritual destiny; if he is of the elect, God will move within him. Therefore the central concern is, as the dying man in *The Last Battell* declares, "how a man may know by the workinges of the Spirit *within*, whether he be a Reprobate or one of Gods chosen Ones."[43] To this end, Boyd's sermons repeatedly focus on how the desire for Grace is as much a sign of divine favour as faith and good works. Boyd makes clear, though, that God's elect are not immune to sin, and outlines sanctification as a process by which the individual repeatedly feels remorse for breaking the Law and repents for his transgressions. In other words, the wayfaring Christian will in time overcome his weaknesses, and partake more and more in God's glory; as Boyd writes in *The Christian His Pilgrimage*, "the Christians pilgrimage is from sinne to grace, & from grace to grace, till at last he come to glory . . . . As from grace to grace, there is a waye, so also is there a waye from grace to glory, yea & from glory to glory" (53).

III. On the Need for Church Reform

The National Covenant of 1638, which resulted, in part, from the liturgy introduced into Scotland by Charles I in 1637, eventually led to the condemnation of episcopacy and the laying down of presbyterian principles.[44] It signals, therefore, how matters of liturgy and church government were central in the confrontation between the Scottish Church and Charles' Laudian churchmen.[45] It also makes it surprising that Boyd, although talking at length about Church reformation, does not seem especially concerned with issues that preoccupied many other Scottish divines. While Boyd is as vehement as any Protestant reformer on the irreconcilability of "God and the masse" (81), and expresses typical anti-Catholic sentiments about the *Scottish Prayer Book*, he tends, with few exceptions, to stress Church reform as the general moral reform of individual Christians who together will produce a spiritually revitalised Church. This moral reform has, for Boyd, a long way to go, as he talks about how "the Church of this land, yea the whole body of this land, is in a feuer" (79), and warns that God's patience can be tested only so far that, as he writes, "the day is fast comeing wherein all the lamentations of Jeremie shall not be able sufficiently to expresse our calamities" (82).

While Boyd may not have stressed religious controversy, one must not presume that he was indifferent to contemporary events; rather it was that he saw a deeper spiritual significance in these events and directed his sermons accordingly. Moreover, it should be recognised that homiletic writing tends to stay away from contentious doctrinal and liturgical issues in favour of basic instruction that emphasises individual Christian devotion. A recurring feature of religious writing in the sixteenth and seventeenth centuries is that genres are clearly separated;[46] works of devotion are kept quite separate from works of theological exegesis, and each of these avoids the vituperative rhetoric of polemic, although this is not to say that preachers such as Boyd were not vituperative when they chose to be.

For Boyd, the strength of the Church comes from the strength of its members, and so he is especially critical of how men and women use the Church to further their own worldly ends. In *The Cleansing of the Temple*, the reference to Christ driving out the money-changers is a pointed one; as Boyd writes, "wee haue a great reason in these dayes to complaine that men, for the most part in the Church vnder glorious colours of godlinesse, are seekeing no thing but their owne aduancement to make vp great estats to their posteritie" (65). Whether Boyd had specific persons or events in mind is impossible to determine, especially as the sermon is undated.[47] Regardless of specifics, however, the message remains the same—there are many in the Church who abuse it in pursuing their own worldly ends—and in this very general context, Boyd's references to kings and courts comprise a persuasive allusion to the vanity of earthly glory and a warning to those consumed by it.

For many, the National Covenant affirmed the idea of the Church of Scotland as the specially called Church of God.[48] Here Boyd talks of the Church as the Israel who had forgotten God: its members are as Saul, Ahab, and Jeroboam, who "because they honoured not him that had honoured them, he scourged them from their thrones, and cast downe their crownes to the ground" (69). That the prophets had so warned is not lost on Boyd, as he too warns against rampant worldliness and against letting the Church become "a house of merchandise" (72). Like Israel, the Scottish Church will feel God's scourge, and Boyd bemoans how "many will not giue eare vnto this vntill the scourge of God either come vpon their soule, or their body, or their estate, or their children" (73).

Yet Boyd retains the belief that affliction serves a further divine purpose. In *Zions Teares*, Boyd, while dwelling on "the most lamentable miseries of Gods Church" (87), does not present God as persecuting his people but as God wishing his people to hear Him. Here Boyd himself speaks with a distinctly prophetic voice, stressing how "Gods pipes are the ministers mouthes. The piping is the preaching of the gospell" (88). Thus Boyd insists that, despite the Church's sufferings, it is time to rejoice, for in lamentation is a sign that one is saved. In *The Refvge of the Chvrch*, Boyd goes so far as to say, "let Gods children . . . learne that the correction of God is a great blessing, a thing to be sought for as a preservative from sinne, a subdueing of our pride and sinfull vanities" (114). Boyd's point is that one must look to the condition of one's soul. In the case of sin uncommitted, "the regenarat man will mourne and lament, for he perceiues the diuell busie like a shreud midwife" (95), while, "where sinne is present," there will be "open shame" (96), and the "terrible terrours of a conscience crammed with the horrours of hell" (97).

IV. The Purified Church

While Boyd stresses how affliction is a sign of God's concern for His Church, he also celebrates how God brings the Church out from under affliction. Again it is not so much that one group of sermons possesses one element and another does not; rather it is a question of emphasis. It is not coincidental, though, that sermons dwelling on the Church's liberation from episcopal "oppression" date from the late 1630s and early 1640s. Although these sermons are more closely tied than any others to the events surrounding the imposition of Charles' *Scottish Prayer Book* in 1636, they still do not clarify Boyd's allegiances. Despite Boyd's initial reluctance to sign the Covenant, he nonetheless praises the General Assembly that met in Glasgow late in 1638, writing in *The Weapons of the Chvrch* of God's "wonderfull workes in the wonderfull harmonie of the National-all Assemblie conveened in this citie" (171). In the same sermon, he associates the *Prayer Book* with "Romanish" influences,[49] and identifies the National Covenant and the General Assembly as a necessary step in ridding the Scottish Church of these influences. Thus he defends the Covenant against those who see it "as a treasonable league, which is most fals and vntrue" (169).

Although in *The Weapons of the Chvrch* Boyd's principal message is the need to pray in time of tribulation for the wellbeing of the Church, this sermon is also important for how it expresses Boyd's hope for a peaceful reconciliation between Charles and the Scottish Church, for, in Boyd's mind, the health of the Church as well as the nation depends on this reconciliation. "When matters hid in darkenesse shall be more clearly brought to light," he hopes that "our gracious and dread soueraigne . . . shall discerne his worthy and religious nobles and other faithfull professours from these merchands of Rome" (169). The "merchands of Rome" are the Laudian prelates from whom Charles took his advice. It is in talking about the king, as well, that Boyd stresses how the king has both secular and spiritual responsibilities. "If the king care not for God," Boyd insists, "God will not care for him," and "will soone persuade the subiects to deny homage to their kings" (146). If this occurs, moreover, there will be political and spiritual anarchy, and therefore Boyd entreats "God most earn-estly that God would send his good spirit betweene our king and his nobles" (146), and warns how Satan never sleeps and is "by vnsanctified braines deuising and plotting . . . to take peace and trueth from vs" (147). Boyd wishes not to fault either side, and the general tenor of the sermon is clearly conciliatory.

Although *The Weapons of the Chvrch* extolls God's people to pray for the wellbeing of the Church, *The Triumph of the Chvrch* is a celebration of how the new Israel has been delivered from "the rage of the wicked" (155). "This Church of Scotland hath many a time beene afflicted by the enemies of this gospell" (159), but now Boyd takes comfort in how the "Lord hath most wonderfully this day deliuered our Church" (167). The sermon extolls God's greatness which makes insignificant the power of those who would use the Church to further their worldly ends. This power is but "the foolish things of the world" (166) and signifies nothing in the face of divine will. If *The Trivmph of the Chvrch* is a celebration, *Scotlands Hallelviah* is even more so, written as it is on the occasion of "a publick thanksgiving to God after the settling of all our troubles both in Church and commoun wealth" (127). This sermon constitutes one of Boyd's few truly vehement statements on the *Prayer Book* matter. To be subject to an English liturgy is for Boyd a calamity not unlike "pest or famine or povertie" (130). Deliverance from the *Prayer Book* is an event as important for the Scottish Church as anything experienced by the ancient Israelites; as Boyd writes, "by deliuering vs from the hands of our enemies, from the bondage of a service booke made like a fairded whore for to allure the land to returne vnto Egypt, . . . the Lord by his blessings wonderfull . . . hath made vs merry" (127-8).

V. General Devotion

Of Boyd's sermons, the majority fall under the category of "General Devotion." Revealing in these sermons is a particularly Protestant approach to Christian instruction, although it goes without saying that this approach is characteristic of just about all Boyd's sermon writing. While the National Covenant defined a Church and a nation, it was also tied to the notion of a new covenant of Grace which fulfilled the old covenant of the Law. In this context, Boyd's sermons, in outlining the individual's obligations under the new covenant, express a distinctly Protestant form of casuistry that, in dealing with cases of conscience, supplied answers to the questions of inquiring and committed Christians.[50] Catholic and Protestant agreed with Aquinas that "we judge that something is well done or ill done, and in this sense the conscience is said to excuse, accuse, or torment."[51] Catholic and Protestant differed, however, as to the extent the conscience played in moral decision-making. While Catholic casuists provided highly detailed instruction, the Protestant casuist maintained that no moral code could deal with every circumstance, and insisted that personal judgment was a crucial factor in spiritual growth. This distinction should not come as a surprise. For the Catholic, universal Grace frees humankind from sin, thus making possible the consciously virtuous choice. By contrast, the Protestant Church saw spiritual growth as a sign of Grace; and, as something initiated by God, there was no need to map out what an awakened and aware conscience can determine for itself. Protestant devotionalism, then, centers on general Christian instruction, in large measure going little beyond what is in scripture.

While the stress in Protestant devotionalism might be on the need to be assured of election, this does not excuse the individual from being morally responsible, for, after all, the ability to repent is a crucial sign of the presence of the Holy Spirit. There is, therefore, a psychological sense of responsibility, even if there is not a theological one. Thus in *A Sermon of Repentance*, while Boyd writes, "I will not enterprise . . . to handle the controversie of mans free will" (182), he still exhorts "Gods people" to repent, indicating in very general terms that repentance signifies "cease to doe euill" and "learne to doe well" (177). He articulates, moreover, why God commands us to repent: His word must be obeyed, repentance is for our well-being, sin is to be feared, sin offends God, and sin brings sickness upon us.

Much in evidence in Boyd's sermons is how Protestant spirituality is taken up with self examination, the looking inwards to determine the condition of one's soul. This is especially the case in Boyd's considerable number of sermons connected with the Lord's Supper, which again express his staunch Calvinism. According to the *Confession*, the Lord's Supper, as well as Baptism, create a visible difference between God's elect and those at war with Him. More than this, however, the sacraments, as "the certane and infallible signes of the trew kirk," serve as a sign that "everie . . . persone joyned with sick ane cumpany, be ane elect member of Christ Jesus."[52] Boyd therefore talks of the Last Supper as a way in which the individual informs the Church of his inward faith. Because participation in the sacrament without faith confirms one even further in sin, Boyd argues how one must look inwards to determine the presence of this faith. Thus he writes, "if any man come without due preparation, without a serious examination of his life . . . he shall eate & drinke condemnation to his soule" (199). What Boyd suggests is that mere participation in the sacrament is insufficient, and he warns that the whole enterprise of looking for signs of one's election must not be construed as participation in rites that guarantee salvation.

Here one might wonder about the need for such statements. It is clear that Boyd assumes that he is speaking to the elect; after all, only the elect will hear and obey his exhortations in the first place. Consequences to the reprobate if they participate in the sacrament must therefore be seen as yet another psychological ploy used to persuade the elect to look inwardly. It is, moreover, a way of calling together the Church and an instrument of the Law. More important for Boyd, though, is the need to have confidence in God's mercy, and in *The Godly Man His Confidence*, Boyd indicates exactly what it means to have such confidence. It is to know one's deficiencies, to be assured that God will give man what he needs, to wait on God with constancy, and to keep one's eye ever on God as "the author of euery good gift & perfect donation" (236).

VI. Occasional Sermons

Like any preacher, Boyd often writes for particular circumstances. The three examples in this section are typical in this regard, although, at the same time, these sermons tend to look at the fundamental issues that preoccupy Boyd in virtually everything he wrote. In *A Sermon for a Fast*, the "plague of famine" (245) is a judgment of God, from which it must be concluded "that there be some sinnes in this land whereby God is highly offended" (245). To fast is not so much to appease God's anger as it is to force each member of the Church to ask forgiveness. "The Church this day," Boyd writes, "hath brought out her greatest canon, euen fasting and prayer, for thereby to overthrowe and cast downe all wicked *imaginations*" (246). Boyd's sermon is a reminder of the "great sinnes & fearefull abominations [that] haue beene committed in this land" (251), an exhortation to repentance, and a celebration of the mercies God extends to those asking forgiveness.

The Sick Man His Svte is written along much the same lines. Sickness is a sign of God's disfavour, as well as a directive given a disobedient child by a loving father. Boyd writes, "Gods custome is that he will not strike men without a cause. He striketh not till, with their sinnes . . . they presse downe the Lord" (261). Sickness, therefore, is a reminder to "powre out your prayers vnto God" (261), not to relieve the suffering, but to ask forgiveness of sin. From sickness comes consolation, for sickness is a "lesson of mercy" (269), although Boyd also stresses that one must not question too closely or make too many assumptions about what God does. "The lesson is this," Boyd says, "take it not for a token of loue to be without trouble, neither for a token of hatred to be in trouble . . . . *the Lord seeth not as man seeth* . . . , neither iudgeth he as man iudgeth" (265).

A Sermon Preached at the Excommunication of a Rebellious Adulterer affirms Boyd's recognition that not all persons are moved by God, although it is interesting to note that the guilty party in this sermon does make amends. Boyd again stresses that just because Grace begins with God does not excuse human responsibility. Boyd is also consistent with general Reform teaching in his insistance that excommunication is intended for correction rather than punishment, and in the way he stresses the extent of God's compassion and the preacher's responsibility to preach mercy. He also makes clear, however, that God's compassion is not without limits for those who remain rooted in sin, although he insists that the Church must never give up trying to bring the sinner into the fold, for it is only God who truly knows His intention for each person.

STRUCTURE AND STYLE

It hardly needs debating that Boyd's expression falls under the general category of the plain style. Most immediately associated with the sermon, the plain style signals a general movement in seventeenth-century prose away from the florid and witty style that produced the Euphuistic and Arcadian varieties of secular prose and that surfaced in sermon literature with elaborate and highly figurative explications of scripture, replete with learned allusions and quotations. Preoccupation with style over content in the second half of the sixteenth century is most visibly seen in such handbooks as Richard Sherry's *A Treatise of Schemes and Tropes* (1550), Richard Rainolde's *A Book called the Foundation of Rhetoricke* (1565), and Henry Peacham's *The Garden of Eloquence* (1577).[53] This preoccupation with *elocutio* is parallelled by a rigorous adherence to the conventional *dispositio* of the Ciceronian oration, as most notably propounded by Thomas Wilson in his *Arte of Rhetorique* (1553), and then directly applied to the sermon in W. Zepper's highly influential *Ars Habiendi et Audiendi Conciones Sacras* (1598). The plain style[54] is a response to this complexity of style and structure, serving, as well, as an expression of growing anti-Ciceronianism, and an indication of how Aristotelian peripatetics were being replaced by the simple dichotomies of Ramist logic that did away with elaborate argument and description considered harmful to didactic purpose.[55]

The movement away from classical models also neatly corresponded with the doctrine of *sola scriptura* and the need for clear literal interpretation of scripture espoused by the European reformers. As early as 1548, John Jewel produced his *Oratio contra Rhetoricam*, a condemnation, not of rhetoric, but of the stylistic excesses to which it had deteriorated. While still adhering to Ciceronian principles of *dispositio*, Neils Hemmingsen in *The Preacher, or Method of Preaching*, also anticipated what was to come later in insisting that the preacher must "expounde . . . in a plaine and common speache . . . to aduance the glory of God,"[56] as did Andreus Gerardus in *The Practis of Preaching* (1577) when he exhorted how a sermon ought "to consist of playne and perspicuous speache."[57] Emphasis on the plain style finds perhaps its most notable exponent, however, in William Perkins, whose Ramist influenced *Arte of Prophecying* (1595) stands as a seminal work in the Protestant sermon tradition. For Perkins, *elocutio* must be "both simple and perspicuous, fit both for the peoples vnderstanding, and to expresse the Maiestie of the spirit."[58] *Dispositio*, too, is radically simplified, as the structural divisions of the Ciceronian oration are replaced by a simple fourfold method of opening a scriptural text. Perkins writes that an effective preacher must be able

1. To read the Texte distinctly out of the Canonicall Scriptures.
2. To giue the sense and vnderstanding of it being read, by the Scripture it self.
3. To collect a few and profitable points of doctrine out of the naturall sense.
4. To apply (if he have the gift) the doctrines rightly collected, to the life and manners of men, in a simple plaine speech.[59]

While Boyd might be a Scottish preacher, he also quite clearly belongs to the English sermon tradition, and stands, despite his lapses from time to time into Greek and Latin, as a major exponent of the English plain style. Nothing could be clearer, as when the pastor in *The Last Battell* says:

> As yee must one day make a reckoning to God of that which yee heare, so must I that selfe same day give an account of that which I *teach*. My Sermons must bee read before him, that sent mee to preach, for hee will know how I have fedde his Lambes. If I build upon Christ, the fundamental Stone, the *Pearles and precious stones* of Christe's passions, I shall get a reward but if I build vpon him *Stubble, Hay,* or Wood . . . of humane words, of worldlie eloquence, I shall be saued verie handlie, only by the fire of great affliction. For this cause, knowing the great danger, I wish that all my comfortes to you and all others bee onlie of Christ, who is both our Suretie and Sauior.[60]

Boyd's sermons all follow the basic pattern of *dispositio* articulated by Perkins: the statement of text, along with a brief comment on the text; the division or *partitio*; and the amplification, which includes a statement of doctrines along with their several uses. It goes without saying that such an arrangement can degenerate into a mechanical sameness, and that Boyd's sermons from time to time show this tendency. Nonetheless it does have the advantage of clarity of argument, and in the case of Boyd there is a simple power in his words that largely offsets such structural repetitiveness.

Consistent with the literal opening of scripture, itself suggestive of the general reluctance to use sermons as a vehicle of "humane learning," and the general Protestant aversion to the imagination, Boyd stands opposed to any kind of stylistic excess. In line with Perkins' principle that "the sense and vnderstanding" of a passage should be revealed "by the Scripture it self," Boyd uses scriptural examples for corroboration and exemplification, and the margins of his sermons and devotional works are checkered with scriptural references. As well, Boyd relies on colloquial images that have a direct meaning to his audience. Perhaps the strongest single feature of Boyd's style is his use of such simple rhetorical devices as anaphora, inter

xxxiii

rogative, and parison, which he uses, as in the following, to confront his reader and force him to look within.

> Let all men consider heere whether they be created in Christ or not. Let them behold them selues whether they be like vnto Christ or not. He that is created in Christ hath the image of Christ. Behold thy selfe, O man, in the glasse of Gods word; & see whether thou be like vnto Christ or not. Is thou a proud man? Thou is not like Christ, for Christ was *meeke & lowly* [Matt 11:29]. Is thou a fals man? Thou is not like Christ, for no man euer could chalenge him of a lie. Is thou a couetous man? Thou is not like Christ. Christ cared not for *all the kingdomes of the world* while they were offered vnto him [Matt 4:8]. Is thou a reuiler? Thou is not like Christ. Christ, while he was reuiled, reuiled not againe. Tell me, O drunkard, if thou be like Christ. Can thou thinke that euer Christ looked as thou lookes or spake as thou speakes? Ye fornicators & yee adulterers who, like fedde horse, *neye after* your *neighbours wife* [Jer 5:8], whose super-scription have yee? Such sinnes committed with pleasure are the very image of the diuell. . . . He that dyeth with the diuels image, by the iustice of God must goe to the diuel. It is Gods iustice that he that serueth the diuell vnto the terme should receiue the diuel his wages. (45-6)

EDITORIAL PROCEDURES

A number of criteria figured in selecting those of Boyd's works included in this selection of his sermons. Most important was the concern that they be representative of Boyd's unpublished prose works. This is best revealed in the various headings under which the sermons are grouped. Effort was also made to include sermons that reveal Boyd's attitude about contemporary developments in the Scottish Church. It was also a concern that the works included in this selection present Boyd at his best, which is, after all, how most writers wish themselves remembered, even those, like Boyd, whose major purpose was the saving of souls. Here length was a factor because it points to a number of additional issues. While most of what Boyd writes extends to about thirty manuscript pages, he also demonstrates the penchant of the times to write very long and excessively tedious commentaries on scripture. Although important as the literary curiosities of a pious age, these works reveal little about Boyd either as a writer or a religious thinker, although they do reveal his formidable command of the Biblical text. A point to be remembered is that Boyd is at his best as a preacher. Within the limited confines of the sermon, Boyd has considerably greater control of his material, and remains for the most part immune from the excessive repetition commonplace in much sermon literature of his time. A single exception to this is *Zions Teares*, which, while running to 648 manuscript pages, contains some of Boyd's most impassioned prose. A selection from this work has therefore been included.

While Boyd's published work is extant in several British universities, his unpublished work is housed exclusively in Glasgow University Library. The Boyd manuscripts are in good condition, and suffer only infrequently from fading and bleed through. The sermons are bound in badly frayed nineteenth-century bindings.[61] Boyd intended each collection for publication, and, as previously mentioned, the sermons have been repaginated when collected together.[62] The rationale behind each collection is for the most part obvious. MS Gen. 382 and MS Gen. 389, for example, contain sermons exclusively focusing on the sacrament of the Lord's Supper while MS Gen. 390 contains sermons focusing on a specific text, namely Paul's Letters to the Hebrews. In some cases, however, a collection is little more than a grouping of miscellaneous sermons; typical is MS Gen. 386, which contains sermons of thanksgiving, sermons concerning the state of the Church, and sermons of general devotion. If not explicitly indicated in the title, the date of each sermon remains unknown. There are no apparent stylistic trends to distinguish earlier works from later ones. Whether Boyd wrote more than what is contained in his manuscripts is unknown, although one must assume this to be the case, given that he preached from the pulpit of the Barony Church for over thirty years.

Boyd wrote in a "mixed" hand combining features of italic, secretary, and round typical of the seventeenth century.[63] Boyd's hand is well formed, suggesting that he was under no urgency to complete his task, and was likely copying or revising from earlier versions or notes. This is further suggested by a lack of scribal errors, and by the odd case when a passage is repeated, suggesting that Boyd was careless in where he left off copying a particular sermon. What remains problematic is whether it was Boyd, in fact, who committed the sermons to paper and grouped them as they are found today. That there are so many sermons, and that the handwriting of the sermons and original pagination matches the handwriting of the revised pagination makes it unlikely that the writing was done by anyone other than Boyd.

The text of Boyd's sermons is produced in a form as close to the original as possible. Boyd's spelling is inconsistent, as is his use of upper case letters, although this is characteristic of the age; there is no consistent use, for example, of the final "e." Although Boyd also punctuates inconsistently, it is also clear that what punctuation he does use is determined by rhetorical issues rather than grammatical principles, and that, in rewriting his sermons for publication, he made no special allowances for the reader as opposed to the listener. The same can be said of Boyd's paragraphing, which is virtually nonexistent. Punctuation and paragraphing in the present text are therefore editorial. Boyd's major headings and subheadings are, however, retained and highlighted in the text. Boyd is fond of underlining, although his reasons for doing so are unclear. In some places, it seems to be for emphasis; in others, Boyd seems to underline scripture; and in yet others, he appears to be supplying himself with lines upon which to write. Given this inconsistency, all such underlining is left out of the present text. Latin and Greek spellings are Boyd's, except for breathers and accents in the case of Greek, which Boyd often omits. Quotations are translated in the "Notes" only when Boyd does not himself translate a passage or where he takes liberties with his own translation.

Boyd for the most part quotes from the King James Version, although he has recourse to the Geneva Bible from time to time. One suspects much of Boyd's quotation is from memory, although this is conjecture based on what was common practice for the time. That Boyd quotes from memory is affirmed by those occasions when he misquotes. Boyd's recourse to both the Authorized Version and the Geneva Bible should come as no surprise. While other versions of the Bible circulated in

Scotland, the Geneva Bible remained dominant until the issue in 1636 of the "Canons and Constitutions Ecclesiastical," which demanded that each parish have an Authorized Version.[64] Boyd's scriptural references, which are indicated in the margins of the manuscript, are included within square brackets in the text. When Boyd gives an incorrect reference, the correct one is substituted with an indication in the Notes.

THE PUBLISHED AND UNPUBLISHED WORKS OF ZACHARY BOYD

PRINTED WORKS

1. *The Balme of Gilead Prepared for the Sicke.* Edinburgh, Iohn Wreittoun, [1633].

2. *A Cleare Forme of Cathecising, before the giving of the Sacrament of the Lords Supper. To this are subjoined two compends of the Catechisme, fit for little children.* Glasgow, George Anderson, 1639.

3. *The Battell of Newbvrne: Where the Scots Armie obtained a notable victorie against the Scottish Papists, Prelats, and Arminiens, the 28 day of August, 1640.* Second edition. Glasgow, George Anderson, 1643.

4. *The Battel of Newbvrne: Where the Scots Armie obtained a notable victorie against the English Papists, Prelats, and Arminiens, the 28 day of August, 1640.* The second edition. [Glasgow: George Anderson 1643]. Edinburgh, 1853.

5. *1. Crosses, 2. Comforts, 3. Counsels. Needful to be considered, and carefully to be laid up in the Hearts of the Godly, in these boysterous broiles, and bloody times.* Glasgow, George Anderson, 1643.

6. *Four Letters of Comforts, for the Deaths of the Earle of Hadingtoun, and of the Lord Boyd, with two Epitaphs.* Glasgow, George Anderson, 1640.

7. *Four Letters of Comforts for the Deaths of the Earle of Hadingtoun and of the Lord Boyd [1640].* Edinburgh, 1878.

8. *The Garden of Zion: Where in the life and death of godly and wicked men in Scripture are to be seene, from Adam unto the last of the Kings of Judah and Israel, with the good uses of their life and death; The Second Volume of the Garden of Zion: Containing the Books of Job, Proverbs, Ecclesiastes, and Song of Songs, all in English Verse.* Glasgow, George Anderson, 1644.

9. *The Last Battell of the Sovle in Death.* Edinburgh, Heires of Andro Hart, 1629.

10. *The Last Battell of the Soule in Death.* Edited by Gabriel Neil. Glasgow, G. Richardson, 1838.

11. *Oratio Panegyrica in Academiae Glasguensis* ΧΑΡΣΤΗΡΙΟΝ *Ad Augustissimum Monarchum Carolum.* Edinburgh, R. Junius, 1633.

12. *The Psalmes of David in Meeter: With the Prose interlined.* Glasgow, George Anderson, 1648.

13. Prefatory Verses in Robert Boyd, *Epistolam Pauli Apostoli as Ephesios.* London, 1652.

14. *Rex Pater Patriae Instar Pelicani liberos suos severe debet. Ad*

Carolvm Magnae Britanniae, Franciae, & Hibern. Edinburgh, Iohn Wreittoun, 1643.

15. *Spiritual Songs or, Holy Poems. A Garden of True Delight, Containing All the Scripture Songs that are not in the Books of Psalms, together with several sweet Propheticall and Evangelicall Scriptures, meet to be composed into songs.* Edinburgh, Heir of Andrew Anderson, 1686.

16. *The Sword of the Lord and of Gideon: To this is subjoined a Prayer for an Armie going to Battell, and a thanksgiving after the Victorie.* Glasgow, George Anderson, 1643.

17. *Two Orientall Pearles, Grace and Glory; The Godly Mans Choise; A Cordiall of Comforts for a Wearied Sovle.* Edinburgh, Iohn Wreittoun, 1629.

18. *Two Orientall Pearles, Grace and Glory; The Godly Mans Choise; A Cordiall of Comforts for a Wearied Soul.* Edinburgh, John Moncur, 1718.

19. *Two Sermons for These Who are Come to the Table of the Lord; A Sermon for the Day of the Sacrament.* Edinburgh, Iohn Wreittoun, 1629.

20. *Zion's Flowers; or, Christian Poems for Spiritual Edification.* Edited by Gabriel Neil. Glasgow, George Richardson, 1855.

UNPUBLISHED WORKS (in Glasgow University Library)

MS Gen. 380
The Most Notable Places of the Bible Expounded

MS Gen. 381
Zions Teares, Wherein are contained the most Lamentable Miseries of Gods Church

MS Gen. 382
1. The Cleansing of the Soule
2. A Cleare Exposition of the Institution of the Lords Supper (11 sermons)
3. A Cleare Exposition of the Sacrament of the Passeover in all its rites and ceremonies applyed to Christian vses
4. The Communicants Examination of Him self, or A treatise whereby all faithful communicants may know how to come worthily to the table of the Lord (3 sermons)
5. Foure Sermons of Thankes after the Lords Supper

6. A Notable Prayer of King Hezekiah after the receiving of the Sacrament of the Passeover
7. A Sermon of Preparation for the Lords Supper
8. Sermons upon the Sacrament (2 sermons)

MS Gen. 383
1. Blind Zeale
2. The Chariot of Charitie (2 sermons)
3. Christ the Lamb of God
4. The Christian His Pilgrimage
5. The Godly Mans Strength
6. Five Sermons. 1. Gods delight 2. The prayer of the afflicted 3. Godly resolutions 4. The discoverie of hyprocrisie 5. The bowels of Gods mercy
7. Philip and Nathaneel
8. Ioshuas Covenant with God (3 sermons)
9. Christs Contact with Scotland, England and Ireland
10. A Compend of the Bible
11. De Profundis. A Sermon for a Fast
12. The Doctrine of Fasting. Showing a moste cleare way how wee may be delivered both from publick and private calamities, and how we may enjoy the unspeakable blessings of God
13. The Faithfull Shepheard
14. The Old Mans Prayer
15. A Manuel of Popish cheefest doubts propounded by F.A. and resolved by M Zacharie Boyd preacher of Gods word at Glasgowe
16. A Sermon for a Fast. Anno 1634
17. A Sermon of Repentance made at a publick fast during the troubles in Scotland for the Booke of Common Prayer
18. The Soules Salvation preached the seventh of August 1637 at a fast
19. To Whom Shall We Go?
20. The Water of the Well of Life
21. The Weapons of the Chvrch

MS Gen. 384
Divers Sermons fit for the Edification of Gods People
1. Gods Providence is the Godlys Inheritance
2. The Richhesse of Gods Mercy
3. God Ovr Refvge
4. The Afflictions of Israel in Babylon (4 sermons)
5. A Sermon for a Fast Anno 1635 (Lam 3:22)

6. A Sermon for a Fast Anno 1636 in time of great famine (Psal 79.8)
7. A Sermon for a Fast Anno 1636 (Psal 79:9)
8. A Sermon for the Time of Warre
9. Gods Axe at the Roote of the Trees
10. The Barren Tree Bvrnt
11. The Sinners Sute
12. The Sicke Man His Svte
13. The Marriage of Mercy with Salvation (2 sermons)
14. Ioyes Ioined with Sorrowes
15. Christs Spiritvall Boxe and Battels
16. The Penitent His Peniel Teares
17. A Sermon Preached at the Excommunication of a Rebellious Adulterer
18. The Lame Healed
19. Christ and Cesar
20. A Sermon for a Fast in Time of Warre
21. The Godly Man His Confidence
22. Christ Naked Vpon the Crosse
23. Mercy and Miserie
24. The Safetie of the Chvrch
25. Sermons Vpon the Sixt Psalme (5 sermons)
26. The Maner of the Destrvction and of the Restavration of the Towne and Temple of Iervsalem
27. Sermons Vpon the Prophesie of Zechariah (8 sermons)

MS Gen. 385
Iacobs Testament wherein are contained the bequests or legacies which he bequeathed unto his twelve sonnes on his death bed

MS Gen. 386
1. The Christians Glory (3 sermons)
2. The Christians Treasure
3. A Sermon of Thankes After Harvest
4. The Fierie Furnace of King Nebuchadnezzar (8 sermons)
5. Christes Prayer Booke (18 sermons)
6. The Light of the Gospell
7. The Trivmph of the Chvrch (2 sermons)
8. The Restoreing of Peter to His Apostleship
9. The Refvge of the Chvrch
10. A Sermon of Repentance
11. Scotlands Hallelviah
12. The Counsell of Christ

13. The Watchword of Christ
14. The Linnen Girdle
15. A Signe from Heaven
16. The Signe of Ionas
17. The Mourners Marke
18. Peters Three Denials and His Repentance

MS Gen. 387
A Treatise of a Troubled Conscience
1. The Questions of a Troubled Sovle
2. Gods Answere to the Troubled Sovle
3. S. Peters Voyage Vnto Christ Vpon the Sea
4. The Sovles Refvge
5. Christ Ovr Righteovsnesse
6. Mercy For Zion
7. A Sermon of Thankesgiuing preached the fifteene day of September after a Generall Assemblie in Edinburgh 1639
8. The Cleansing of the Temple
9. The Worlds Condemnation
10. Peters Preaching Concerning Judas
11. A Royall Precept
12. The Death of the Wicked
13. A Sermon of Thankis After Harvest Ann. 1638
14. Retvrne O Lord, How Long?

MS Gen. 388
1. Scripturae Flores. Christian Meditations upon the most Rare Places of Genesis and Exodus
2. Meditations upon the Second Booke of Moses called Exodus

MS Gen. 389
Sermons upon the Passion of Jesus Christ Preached at the receiving of the Sacrament of the Lords Supper (30 sermons)

MS Gen. 390
Sermons upon the Epistles of S. Paul to the Hebrewes (31 sermons)

MS Gen. 391
Sermons upon that most excellent Song of Moses made a little before his death (29 sermons)

MS Gen. 392
1. Holy Meditations for the Help of Gods People to receive the Sacrament worthily

2. A Manuel for the Sabbath Dayes Exercise
3. A Sermon before the Lords Supper
4. Second Sermon for the Lords Supper
5. The Wedding Garment

MS Gen. 393-394
[Zion's Flowres;] Christian Poems for Spiritual Edification

MS Gen. 400
The Four Evangels in English Verse

MS Gen. 401
The English Academie containing Precepts and Purpose for the Well
Both of Soule and Body

NOTES TO INTRODUCTION

1. Discussion here draws on A. J. Aitken, "Introduction," *The Concise Scots Dictionary* (Aberdeen: Aberdeen University Press, 1985), p. xi; and David Reid, *The Party-Coloured Mind* (Edinburgh: Scottish Academic Press, 1982), pp. 1-3.

2. Boyd's life is documented in several places, although by far the most complete is Gabriel Neil's "Introduction" and "Appendix" to *Zion's Flowers; or Christian Poems for Spiritual Edification* (Glasgow: George Richardson, 1855).

3. Saumur was a Protestant university founded immediately after the Edict of Nantes in 1599 by Philippe du Plessis-Mornay (1589-1621). It was suppressed on January 8, 1685, and an order for the destruction of the church was made on January 15, several months before the revocation of the edict. See Jacques Pannier, "Scots in Saumur in the Seventeenth Century," *Records of the Scottish Church History Society*, Vol. 5, Part 2 (1934), 140-143. While Pannier lists a number of notable Scots at Saumur, he makes no mention of Boyd.

4. John Marshall Long, *Glasgow and the Barony thereof—a review of three hundred years* (Glasgow, 1895), p. 47.

5. See *Extracts from the Records of The Burgh of Glasgow AD 1630-1662* (Glasgow: Scottish Burgh Records Society, 1881), pp. 36-37.

6. Walter Makey supplies a detailed account of the yearly stipends for ministers of various Scottish parishes; he estimates the average yearly stipend to be about £500. See *The Church of the Covenant, 1637-1651* (Edinburgh: John Donald Publishers, 1979), pp. 106-122.

7. J.D. Mackie, *The University of Glasgow, 1451-1951* (Glasgow: Glasgow University Press, 1954), p. 93.

8. *A Biographical Dictionary of Eminent Scotsmen* (Glasgow: Blackie and Son, 1875), I, 171.

9. Long, p. 51.

10. Zachary Boyd, *The Battell of Newbvrne: Where the Scots Armie obtained a notable victorie against the English Papists, Prelats, and Arminiens* (Glasgow: George Anderson, 1643), n.p.

11. See Gordon Donaldson, *Scotland: James V to James VII* (Edinburgh and London: Oliver & Boyd, 1965), pp. 324-340.

12. See James Pagan, *Sketch of the History of Glasgow* (Glasgow: Robert Stuart & Co., 1847), pp. 43-44; and James Coutts, *A History of the University of Glasgow* (Glasgow: Glasgow University Press, 1909), p. 131.

13.   Quoted in Pagan, p. 44.
14.   Robert Wodrow, *Collections Upon the Lives of the Reformers and Most Eminent Ministers of the Church of Scotland* (Glasgow, 1845), p. 130.
15.   Ibid., p. 352.
16.   Zachary Boyd, *The Balme of Gilead* (Edinburgh: Iohn Wreittoun, 1629), sig. 2r.
17.   Zachary Boyd, *The Garden of Zion* (Glasgow: George Anderson, 1644), sig. Ar.
18.   Wodrow, p. 352.
19.   Quoted in James Moffatt, *The Bible in Scots Literature* (London: Hodder and Stoughton, 1924), p. 132.
20.   "Preface to the Reader", in Zachary Boyd, *Spiritual Songs, or Holy Poems* (Edinburgh: Heirs of Andrew Anderson, 1686), n.p.
21.   Ibid., n.p.
22.   Samuel Colvil, *Mock Poem or, Whigs Supplication* (London, 1681), sig. A7r.
23.   Quoted in "Appendix" to *Zion's Flowers*, ed. Gabriel Neil, p. xxiii.
24.   John Sleazer, *Theatrum Scotiae* (1693; rpt. Edinburgh: William Paterson, 1855), p. xxiii.
25.   Quoted in *A Biographical Dictionary of Eminent Scotsmen*, I, 174.
26.   See "Appendix" to *Four Poems from Zion's Flowers*, ed. Gabriel Neil (Glasgow: George Richardson, 1855), p. xvii. The 1562 Scots Psalter, as well as Rous' Psalter, are discussed in William McMillan, *The Worship of the Scottish Reformed Church, 1550-1638* (London: James Clarke & Co., 1931), pp. 74-86.
27.   See "Introduction" to *Four Poems from Zion's Flowers*, ed. Gabriel Neil. For a recent assessment of Boyd's poetry and of his published prose, see D.W. Atkinson, "Zachary Boyd: A Reassessment," *Proceedings of the Third International Conference on Scottish Language and Literature*, ed. Roderick J. Lyall and Felicity Riddy (Glasgow: University of Glasgow, 1981), 436-456.
28.   Zachary Boyd, *The Last Battell of the Sovle in Death* (Edinburgh: Heires of Andro Hart, 1629), sig. A2v. A.G. Aldis claims the 1629 edition of *The Last Battell* is a reissue with new titles of a 1628 edition that is not extant. See *A List of Books printed in Scotland before 1700* (Edinburgh: National Library of Scotland, 1970), nos. 674, 698.
29.   See D.W. Atkinson, "Zachary Boyd and the *Ars Moriendi* Tradition," *Scottish Literary Journal*, Vol. 4, No. 1 (1977), 5-16.
30.   Zachary Boyd, *Two Orientall Pearles, Grace and Glory; The Godly Mans Choise; A Cordiall of Comforts for a Wearied Sovle* (Edinburgh: John Wreittoun, 1629), p. 109. The pervasive

influence of the *memento mori* is discussed in Johan Hwizinga, *The Waning of the Middle Ages* (1924; rpt. New York: Doubleday & Co., 1956), pp. 137-140; also see Philippe Ariès, *The Hour of Our Death*, trans. Helen Weaver (New York: Alfred A. Knopf, 1981), pp. 127, 218-219, 256-259.

31. Zachary Boyd, *Two Orientall Pearles etc.*, p. 151.

32. Zachary Boyd, *Two Sermons for Those Who Came to the Table of the Lord*; *A Sermon for the Day of the Sacrament* (Edinburgh: John Wreittoun, 1629), p. 113.

33. Ibid., p. 112.

34. Ibid., p. 45.

35. Zachary Boyd, *Two Orientall Pearles* etc., pp. 32-33.

36. "Boyd's Bursaries," *Deeds Instituting Bursaries, Scholarships, and other Foundations, in the College and University of Glasgow* (Glasgow: The Maitland Club, 1850), p. 37.

37. All page references to Boyd's unpublished works are to the text and are inserted parenthetically.

38. See Makey, p. 7.

39. The Calvinist nature of The Westminster Confession is discussed in R.T. Kendall, *Calvin and English Calvinism to 1649* (1979; rpt. Oxford: Oxford University Press, 1981), pp. 167-208; Scottish input into the *Confession* and the relationship between the Scottish Presbyterians and the English Puritans is documented in William Haller, *Liberty and Reformation in the Puritan Revolution* (1955; rpt. New York and London: Columbia University Press, 1967), pp. 100-112. A good survey of Calvinism in the Scottish Church is in Gordon Marshall, *Presbyteries and Profits: Calvinism and the development of capitalism in Scotland, 1650-1707* (Oxford: Clarendon Press, 1980), pp. 39-112.

40. *The Confessioun of Faith Professit and Belevit be the Protestants Within the Realme of Scotland*, in *The Works of John Knox*, ed. David Laing (Edinburgh: Woodrow Society, 1846-64), II, 97.

41. Ibid., II, 98.

42. The formative statement in this regard is Max Weber, *The Protestant Ethic and the Spirit of Capitalism*, trans. Talcott Parsons (London: George Allen & Unwin, 1930).

43. *The Last Battell*, p. 414.

44. See Rosalind Mitchison, *A History of Scotland* (London: Methuen & Co., 1970), pp. 190-191; and Gordon Donaldson, *Scotland: James V to James VII*, pp. 308-311.

45. Laud's impact on the Scottish Church is discussed in Hugh Watt, "William Laud and Scotland," *Records of the Scottish Church History Society*, Vol. VII (1941), 171-190.

46. This tendency is demonstrated in Helen White, *English*

Devotional Literature [Prose]: 1600–1640, University of Wisconsin Studies in Language and Literature, No. 29 (Madison: University of Wisconsin Press, 1931).

47. There are several possibilities here. As a work of the early 1640s, this sermon may be interpreted as an objection to how the nobles looked to use the General Assembly in open confrontation with the king; alternatively, Boyd's reference to those who "are so exercised in posting after fauours at kings courts that they forget God, their flock, and them selues" (65) may place the sermon later in the 1640s in pointing at those clergy who entered into negotiations with Charles against the English.

48. Donaldson, pp. 315–316.

49. By far the most thorough study of the contents of the *Scottish Prayer Book* is Gordon Donaldson, *The Making of the Scottish Prayer Book of 1637* (Edinburgh: The University Press, 1954).

50. See David W. Atkinson, "Devotional Responses to Doctrinal Dilemmas: Piety in the English Reformed Church," *Historical Magazine of the Protestant Episcopal Church*, Vol. LII (June, 1983), 167–179.

51. Thomas Aquinas, *Summa Theologica*, trans. Fathers of the Dominican Province, (New York: Benziger Brothers, 1947), I, 408.

52. *The Confessiun of Faith Professit*, II, 119.

53. The content of these rhetorics is described and analyzed in Alan Fager Herr, *The Elizabethan Sermon: A Survey and a Bibliography* (New York: Octagon Books, 1969), pp. 87–89. One of the most thorough studies of the courtly writers is George Philip Krapp, *The Rise of English Literary Prose* (1915; rpt. New York: Frederick Ungar, 1963), pp. 271–384.

54. For a discussion of the plain style, see Perry Miller, "The Plain Style," *Seventeenth Century Prose*, ed. Stanley E. Fish, (New York: Oxford University Press, 1971), pp. 147–186.

55. The earliest English edition of Ramus' *Dialecticae Libri Duo*, translated by Roland MacIlmaine, was published in 1574 as *The Logike of the moste Excellent Philosopher P. Ramus Martyr*. The impact of Ramistic logic is discussed in Perry Miller, *The New England Mind: The Seventeenth Century* (1939; rpt. Cambridge, Mass.: Harvard University Press, 1954), pp. 312–330; William S. Howell, *Logic and Rhetoric in England 1500–1700* (1956; rpt. New York: Russell & Russell, 1961), pp. 142–246; and Walter J. Ong, *Ramus: Method and the Decay of Dialogue* (Cambridge, Mass.: Harvard University Press, 1958).

56. Neils Hemmingsen, *The Preacher, or Methode of Preaching*, trans I.H. (1574; rpt. Menston, Scolar Press, 1972), p. 18.

57. Andreus Gerardus, *The Practis of Preaching*, trans. I. Ludham

(London: 1577), p. 15. Gerardus is commonly known as Hyperius of Marburg.

58. William Perkins, "The Arte of Prophecying," in *The Workes of that Famovs and Worthy Minister of Christ in the Vniuersitie of Cambridge Mr. William Perkins* ([1600]; rpt. London, 1612-13), II, 670-671.

59. Ibid., II, 674.

60. Zachary Boyd, *The Last Battell of the Sovle in Death*, p. 21.

61. The binding is that of the early nineteenth-century bookbinder J. Carss & Co., Glasgow. See Charles Ramsden, *Bookbinders of the United Kingdom (Outside London), 1780-1840*, privately printed, 1954.

62. Boyd's unpublished prose works are listed in their present groupings in Glasgow University Library's *Index to 1691 Library MS Catalogue*, which is the earliest record of manuscripts in the University's collection. Boyd's unpublished poetry is a later addition donated by John Paterson (1632-1708), who became Archbishop of Glasgow in 1687.

63. See L.C. Hector, *The Handwriting of English Documents* (1958; rpt. London: Edward Arnold, 1966), pp. 63-64.

64. Lloyd E. Berry, "Introduction" to *The Geneva Bible: A facsimile of the 1560 edition* (Madison: The University of Wisconsin Press, 1969), p. 22.

I. On Scripture and Preaching

An Exposition of the Epistle of S. Paul to the Hebrewes, Chapter 1

v 1. *God who at sundrie times, & in diuers maners spake in time past vnto the fathers by the prophets,*
v 2. *Hath in these last dayes spoken vnto vs by his Sonne, whom he hath appointed heire ouer all things, by whom also he made the world.*

S. Paul, who had heard in paradise *vnspeakeable wordes which were not lawfull for a man to vtter* [2 Cor 12:4], who had receiued abundance of reuelations, was content to spend his whole life in learning the knowledge of Christ & of his crosse. Such is the corruption of mans nature that the reuelations made in the third heauens vnto him will passe him vp, except that the Lord giue to him *a thorne in the flesh* [2 Cor 12:7]. But to knowe the thornes of Christs passion is a saueing knowledge, a humbling knowledge. Well is the man that getteth it. Christ to him shall be both in life & death aduantage [Phil 1:21].

The most part of this epistle is so imployed that they who will come with well prepaired hearts to the hearing of it shall blesse God that euer they heard it. There is no heart that can come well prepaired for to heare it except that that determination be in it in some measure, which was in the heart of him that wrote it. What was Pauls determination, will yee saye? Heare him selfe: *I determined not,* said he, *to knowe any thing among you, saue Jesus Christ & him crucified* [1 Cor 2:2].

the diuision of the chapter

In this first chapter, there be two cheefe parts to be considerred: in the first part, the law & the gospell are compaired to gether, & that in the first verse & in a part of the second verse; in the second part, the dignity of Christ is set downe, & that from the last part of the second verse vnto the end of the chapter. As for the doctrine of the law, the apostle speaketh this of it: God *at sundrie times and in diuers maners spake in time past vnto the fathers by the prophets.*

3

In these wordes wee haue fiue distinct things to consider: 1. who spake, it was God that spake; 2. how he spake, viz πολψμερῶς, *particulatim*, that is by parcels & in diuers maners; 3. at what time, in time past; 4. vnto whom, vnto the fathers; 5. by whom, by the prophets.

1. who spake

The first word of this epistle is the name of the speaker, viz God, euen God the Father, for incontinent after is subioined the name of the Sonne. This is he who is author of the Old Testament. S. Paul saith here that he spake it of old vnto the fathers by the prophets.

Heere let vs obserue the worth and excellencie of the Old Testament: it is the booke of God. God is the author thereof. When euer thou begins to read the Old Testament, remember of the beginning of this epistle that God is the author of it. There be many things there, cheefly in the booke of Leuiticus, touching ceremonies that will make a man wonder wherefore they did serue. But thou, O man of God, what euer thou reads into that booke, reade it with reuerence & saye, *the mouth of the Lord* hath said it [Isa 40:5]. All the prophets armed them selues with thus, saith the Lord.

2. how he spake

It is said heere that he spake at sundrie times & in diuers maners. πολψμερῶς is turned *multis vicibus*. The Greeke word properly signifieth many parts, as if the apostle had said that Gods word was deliuered vnto the fathers but by parts, whereas wee that are vnder the gospell haue gotten the whole booke of God. By parts indeed the fathers receiued Gods word, for more was reuealed vnto Isaac then to Abraham, & more to Jacob then to Isaac, & more to Moses then to them. In Moses dayes, there were but fiue bookes of Gods word. To them was added part after part. But in the New Testament, all the Lords pen-

4

men were men who liued in one age. The whole worke was ended into one age.

Doctrine. The lesson wee learne is of Gods great liberalitie toward vs. God in the beginning dealt more sparingly with the fathers then he hath done with vs. With some of the fathers also he dealt more liberally then with others.

The Vse. The vse is this: the more liberally that God hath dealt with vs, let vs deale the more thankfully with Him. The more talents a man receiue, he shall be the more countable. Gods talents are like siluer put to vsurie. The more be lent out, the more is looked for. Woe vnto vs if we profit not: it is not for want of meanes.

Doctrine. Another lesson I obserue heere is that the Lords word was giuen to the fathers by parts, little at the beginning, more after, & so forward by incressing till Christ him selfe came. This is the custome of God: he giueth little at the beginning to men to see how they will vse it, & after he will giue more & more. His goodnesse incresseth like the morning light. This is not after the custome of men who haue great shewes of kindnesse at the beginning, but incontinent faint & fall back. Satan is kindest at the first meeting. So are many men, but their kindnesse cooles. And, as for the loue of man, it is often like a hote sunne bleinke,[1] the forerunner of a storme. From thence is the prouerb, after hote loue cometh hasty vengence.[2]

The Vse. Let our loue to God be like his benefeits towards vs. They incresse; let our loue incresse also.

Doctrine. The third doctrine I obserue of that: that God of old did deliuer his doctrine by parts. What euer part God gaue vnto them, it was sufficient for them. In euery time, Gods children were content with that portion it pleased God to bestowe vpon them. In Moses his dayes all their Bible was but a small part of the Bible that is now, yet Israel was content with that part of scripture.

The Vse. The vse is this: let euery one of vs be content with that part & portion it shall please God to giue vnto us. God knoweth better then we what is good for vs: his will is our will. More then Gods allowance is more hurtfull then helpfull. *My grace is sufficient for thee*, said God to Paul [2 Cor 12:9]. Were our portion neuer so small, if wee get grace with it, it shall be sufficient for vs.

5

Doctrine. The fourth doctrine I obserue heere concerning scripture giuen by parts is that Gods people was content with that which it pleased God to bestowe on them.

The Vse. Despise not the gift of him whom God hath called to be thy teacher. Though his gift be little but a part of a gift, though his gift be little if he be a faithfull man, thou shall find it profitable. A little with Gods blessing is meakill[3] worth. He that made the little meale & little oyle last, & feede both Elias the widowe & her sonne sufficiently [1 Kgs 17:12], maye make that mans little, so full of foyson,[4] that it shall be able to nourish thy soule to saluation. This much concerning the wordes diuers times or diuers parts.

He addeth & in diuers maners. How was this? To one prophet he spake in one fashion, to another prophet in another fashion. This is euident by that which the Lord said to Aaron & Miriam, when he rebuked them for their pride & rebellion against Moses. *If there be a prophet among you*, said the Lord, *I the Lord will make my selfe knowen vnto him in a vision; & will speake vnto him in a dreame. My seruant Moses is not so, who is faithfull in all my house. To him will I speake mouth to mouth, euen apparently, & not in darke speaches; & the similitude of the Lord shall he behold* [Numb 12:6-8]. Behold heere what diuers maner of speakeing he vsed of old. When he spake to the prophets, he spake vnto some in a vision, to others in a dreame, in darke speaches, in a similitude more clearly, as vnto Moses mouth to mouth euen apparantly. Elihu declaires breefly his diuers maners of speaking, viz *in a dreame, in a vision of the night when deepe sleepe falleth on men in slumberings vpon the bed* [Job 33:15]. God also by Vrim and Thummim did shewe his will vnto men [Lev 8:8].

Doctrine. The doctrine I obserue heere is of the great fauour of God towards man: great is the care that God hath euer had of mans saluation. This he hath shewen by speaking vnto him whiles in one fashion & whiles vnto another. Surely the time was neuer that God did faile vnto his Church. That daye was neuer wherein the Lord might not saye truely, *what could haue beene done more to my vineyeard that I haue not done* [Isa 5:4]? There is no man that can deuise a better maner of speaking then that which God hath vsed toward man.

Vse. The vse is this: hath God beene so carefull for mans well? Let man be carefull for Gods glory. Hath God beene so

6

busy to doe all that could be done for the well of his vineyeard? Let vs beware that God haue not to complaine of vs as he did of Israel. When I looked, said he, that *it should bring forth graipes, it brought forth wilde graipes* [Isa 5:4]. Hath the Lord taken paines to speake for mans well in diuers maners? Let man in all maners he can striue to obeye Gods word, what euer haue beene the maner of speaking of it, whether by vision or by dreame, or by similitude of the Lord.

3. at what time spake

The time of his speakeing is called heere the time past. The time which is called heere the time past is all the time of the Old Testament vnto the comeing of Christ. God spake all that time vnto men by his prophets at sundrie times & in diuers maners.

Doctrine. In that God from the beginning of time did speake vnto men, wee maye learne the eternitie of God. There was no time wherevnto God spake not vnto man, and therefore it behoued him to be before all time. Daniel calleth him the *auncient of dayes* [Dan 7:9]. Though he be ancient, he waxeth not old. In this time present, he is the same he was in time past. I ame the Lord & change not. Dauid, speakeing of him selfe, saith, *my dayes are consumed like smoake* [Ps 102:3]; *my dayes are like a shadowe that declineth, and I ame withered like grasse* [Ps 102:11]. Yea, which is more, he saith, the heauens & the earth shall perish. *Yea, all of them shall waxe old as a garment. As a vesture shalt thou change them, & they shall be changed* [Ps 102:26]. Time is subiect to the disease of the fluxe. It hath continualy the fluxes thereof; it shall neuer be healed. Of this time that is now within a little space shall be said, it is past; & againe, that is past till at last God shall saye, there shall be no more time [Rev 10:6]. When yee heare that time is past, considder that there is no thing heere so precious but it will passe with the time. Of God onely may be said, *thou art the same, & the*[5] *yeeres shall haue no end* [Ps 102:27]. It was he that spake in time past before we were. He also shall speake in time to come when we shall not be.

The Vse. Let vs make this vse when euer wee heare of time.

7

Let vs remember to spend well the time, for it is a transitory thing. There be but three times, the past, present, & to come. I correct my selfe: there is no time but the present time. The time past is past & is not: the time to come is not come. This present is the market houre where in wee maye buy without money [Isa 55:1]. Now the waters of the poole are moued [John 5:4]; now it is to daye. In this thy daye, said Christ to Jerusalem [Heb 3:15], so say I to thee in this thy daye. Yesterdaye is past; it is no more thine.[6] The morrow is to come. What if it be said to thee, as was said to the foole, *this night thy soule shall be taken from thee* [Luke 12:20]? No man can tell what a daye will bring forth; and therefore to daye, if ye heare his voice, harden not your hearts [Ps 95:8].[7]

4. to whom God spake

It is said that he spake vnto the fathers, that is to all these faithfull men & weemen that were before the comeing of Christ. To these it pleased God to speake & reueale his will.

Doctrine. The doctrine is this: wee maye see the mercy & goodnesse of our God that was so good vnto our fathers as to teach them the waye of saluation. Though Christ was not come vnto them in the flesh, yet God early in the morning spake vnto them for their learning.

The Vse. The vse is that we loue God & striue to doe his will because he hath beene good to the fathers. If any man honour our father, wee thinke it done to our selfe. Dauid was kinde to Mephibosheth for his fathers sake [2 Sam 9:7]. Let vs be thankfull to God for his kindness, & kind vnto his Mephibosheths. He hath beene good to the fathers but better vnto vs as wee shall heare heerafter.

5. by whom God spake

Now followeth that wee heare by whom God spake vnto the fathers of old: it was by the prophets. In the first language, it is ἐν προφήταις, that is in the prophets. God in the prophets spake vnto the fathers; so God in the apostles spake vnto the

Christian world. *It is not yee that speake*, said Christ to his disciples. Who is it than *but the spirit of your Father in you* [Matt 10:20]. S. Peter expounds how the prophets spake, or rather how God spake by the prophets. *Prophecie*, saith he, *came not in old time by the will of man, but holy men of God spake as they were moued by the Holy Ghost* [2 Pet 1:21]. Such men were called θεόπνευστοι, *diuinitus inspirati*, men inspired of God.

The spirit of God was in the prophets, & also in all the faithfull but in a diuers maners. In the faithfull, the spirit of God is for to teach them to praye. It is he that within them worketh faith & repentance & all other good things that are within them. But in the prophets, God was in a particular maner. S. Peter saith that they were φερόμενοι, *acti a spiritu sancto*, that is borne & caried by the spirit [2 Pet 1:21]. This caryeing at some time was strange. It wrought strange effects vpon the body of the prophets, as yee see of Ayabus who foretold Pauls bonds in a strange forme, by binding him selfe with Pauls girdle [Acts 21:11]. Often, because of some gestures not vsuall, they seemed vnto naturall men to be fooles & madde men. Festus thought Paul to be madde [Acts 26:24]. That yong man, one of the children of the prophets, while he came to anoint Jehu by the commaund of Elisha, the captaines of the hoste tooke him to be a foole; & therefore, after that he was gone awaye, one of the captaines said vnto Jehu, *is all well? Wherefore came this mad fellow to thee* [2 Kgs 9:11]? While the propheticall spirit was workeing in them, their countenance & other gestures were often changed & strangely caried.[8] But they could not miscarie in the doctrine which they taught. As for vs who now teach you, wee are not this wise φερόμενοι, caried; & therefore we maye miscarie. The words which God hath spoken in them & by them are the rule & squaire of all our doctrine.

Of the forme of Gods speaking in & by the prophets, wee shall gather some doctrines whereof wee shall also obserue the vses & so goe forward.

Doctrine. First of all heere I obserue the great loue & mercy of God toward man that would daine to speak by his spirit, either by him or in him. Man after his fall was more fit to haue beene an organ vnto the diuell then vnto God. It had beene righteous with God that he who beleeued the diuells speach

9

more then Gods word should haue beene giuen ouer vnto the diuell, that he might both speake in him, & by him, as he did in & by the serpent, his deceiuing instrument [Gen 3:1]. Yet such is the mercy & loue of our God that he choiced rather to meete man in mercy then in his merits.

Vse. The vse wee should make of this is to take heede heereafter that we beleeue not the diuels speaches. Though we haue not the spirit of God in such a measure or maner as these that were inspired of God, yet in some measure euery one of the godly maye saye with S. Paul, I thinke I haue the spirit of God. Seeing then God daines to be present with men, yea in men, in prophets by inspiration, in others by operation, let vs not liue leudly in such a presence. Let vs not beleeue any more the speaches of Satan, for he is a lyar & the father of lyes [John 8:44]. He tells to the harlot that pleasure is good, to the couetous that gaine is sweete, to the ambitious that honour will doe his turne, to the drunkard that wine is health. God that spake in and by his prophets, God that is in vs, affirmes the contrary. *Let God be true* & all men lyars [Rom 3:4]. Meakill more he that is the father of lyes [John 8:44].

Doctrine. The second doctrine that I obserue heere is that the prophets, as Christ said of his apostles, spake not of them selues. It is not yee that speake, said Christ, *but the spirit of your Father* [Matt 10:20]. It is certain that men could not haue spoken such things as are in the writs of the prophets without the spirit of God in them. As they could not worke miracles by their owne force, so could they not teach such doctrine by their owne wisdome. When Paul had healed that creple of Lystra, the men of Lystra lifted vp their voice in the speach of Lycaonia, *The gods are come downe to vs in the likenesse of men* [Acts 14:11]. They perceiued not that it was the finger of God within Paul and Barnabas that wrought the worke, but they looked vnto the men, as if it had beene done by their power. But what said Paul to that? Sirs, why doe yee these things? Wee also are men of like passions with you, as if he had said, it is God that hath done this & not we.

The Vse. Let vs neuer in word or worke that seemeth great in our eyes gaze vpon the instrument. Heares thou a man make an excellent sermon whereby all the powers of thy soule are shaken, so that thou is forced to quite thy sinne? Saye not, O the preacher! O the wonderfull man! Loue the man the meanes of thy mercy. But saye not, O the man! But saye rather, God is mighty in the man. Look ouer the man & gaze vpon God; fixe thy eyes vpon him & wonder at his word. Again, if thou see any man doe a great worke, were it Shamgar with his oxe goade [Judg 3:31], or Gideon with his trumpets [Judg 7:8],[9] or Joshuah with his rammes hornes, or Samson with a iawe bone [Judg 15:15], or Ehad with his dagger [Judg 3:16], or Dauid with his sling & stones [1 Sam 17:40], looke not to the men or to their weapons, but saye the spirit of the Lord is vpon the men.

The hand of God hath wrought wonders. As thou should neither gaze on him whose word thou heares & whose worke thou sees, so neither should he that speakes the word admire him selfe, neither he that hath wrought a good worke vaunt him selfe thereof, but saye, it is the Lord & not I. Were I as powerfull a preacher as euer was S. Paul, who for his eloquence was called *Mercurius* [Acts 14:11], I must not saye, this is my eloquence. I haue said well to the matter: no not woe to me if I thinke it. But I must saye, God hath assisted me mercifully. It is God that put the wordes in my mouth. All the seasoning thereof is from his salt. Againe, if euer thou doe a good worke, kisse not thine owne hand as if it were the doer, but saye, it is God that hath ledde my hand. All the glory of the prophets doctrine is heere ascribed vnto God. Let him also haue all the glory of all our preachings & of euery good worke that is worthy of praise. It is he, saith Isaiah, that doeth all our turns [Isa 26:12]; and therefore all that is spoken or done should be vnto the praise of the glory of his grace.

Doctrine. The third doctrine I obserue heere is that, seeing it was the spirit of God that spake in the prophets & by them, it must also be the spirit of God onely that can giue the right sense & interpretation of the wordes. None can so well vnderstand a mans wordes as he that spake them him selfe.

The Vse. Seeing it is so, wee that are Gods interpreters haue neede to begge the spirit of God that wee maye teach you the true meaning of the wordes of God. Many thinke that if a man be a learned man, well vnderstood in his philosophie & in the tongues, that he is more then sufficient for to be a minister. I thought this many a time my selfe that any learned man might

11

easily be a minister. But heere is my retractations. Heere I confesse my ignorance. A good minister is a raire man: he is Gods interpreter. There be many learned men in the land, but I will assure thee that God hath not many interpreters. Elihu calleth Gods interpreter one of a thousand [Job 33:23]. If a man had all the philosophie of Aristotle in his head, if he have not the spirit of God in his heart, he will neuer vnderstand the right sense of scriptures. The doctrine of the prophets that was dyted[10] by the spirit can not be interpreted but by the assistance of the same spirit. He must be a holy man that is minded to be an interpreter; otherwise he shall euanish in his imaginations.

Wee that are already called to this great worke haue great neede to take heede wee doe no thing whereby God maye be moued to withdrawe his presence from vs. When God was awaye, Samson said that he would speke him selfe as at other times; but he was disapointed because he knewe not that the Lord had left him [Judg 16:20]. If the Lord leaue vs, there is no power in vs to speke out a word that will doe good to any miserable soule. *Our helpe is in the name of the Lord* that made the heauen & the earth [Ps 124:8]. Without me, said Christ, yee can doe nothing. Awaye man with thy interpretation, if thou want the spirit. Awaye with thy logic & the flourishes of thy rhetoric, if thou want the spirit. Thou for all thy learning is but a *sounding brasse & a tinkling cymball* [1 Cor 13:1]. Thou shall neuer winne a soule to God. Neuer shall thou say to thy God, behold heere I am & the children that God hath giuen mee. The word without the spirit is but a dead letter, he that preacheth the word without the spirit maye well saye. So fight I, as one that beateth the ayre; not as S. Paul, who had the spirit, said, so fight I, *not as one that beateth the ayre* [1 Cor 9:26]. Well is him that runs & not as vncertainely. This much for actuall ministers.

As for you that are young & are minded to be interpreters, thinke it not enough that yee proue good shollers[11] & in the meane time haue no care of holinesse. Is thy will bent to ill? Is thy mind defiled? Is thy mouth ill seasoned with vnsauory wordes & rotten speaches? Is thou accustomed to badry[12] lan- guage, to sweare, to saye aboue forsooth, aboue *yea yea & nay naye* [Matt 5:37]? It is a wonder if euer the Lord daine to make thee a minister. If he suffer thee to come to that honour, he shall not call thee as Aaron [Heb 5:4]. He maye well suffer thee to creepe in at the windowe as a theefe & robber [John 10:1], but at last thou shall fall into the justice hands. Thy end shall be shamefull. He that cometh to interpret Gods word, & finds not the pull of his spirit working holinesse in his heart, shall at last proue but a lowne[13] minister of all lownes the greatest. If so thou enter, O man, if thou edifie not with life & doctrine all the thanks thou shall get at the hinder end shall be this, *what hadst thou to doe to declare my statuts* or to *take my couenant in thy mouth* [Ps 50:16]? God will not tell his mind but vnto these that are holy. *Wee haue the mind of Christ* [1 Cor 2:16], saith the apostle. These that haue his spirit haue his mind: these that want his spirit want his mind & can not vnderstand his wordes.

Againe is this true that ministers can not vnderstand Gods word for to interpret it vnto you, except that they haue Gods spirit, the author of it? Surely no more shall yee of the people be able to vnderstand their interpretation without the same spirit; and therefore, before ye come to heare, seeke the spirit of God, that while ye heare, ye maye vnderstand. Many bring in into Gods house an ill spirit with them & they goe out with a worse. They come in with a deafe diuell that will not let them heare the preaching; & they goe out with a dumb diuell, so that they cannot tell a word of all that was preached. When the spirit of God departeth from a man, the spirit of the diuell waiteth on him. Hast thou these dayes by past banished the spirit of God from thee by drunkennesse, whooredome, blood, deceit, or lyes? From these actions is thou come in heere to heare the preaching without a broken heart, without resolution neuer to returne to such vomite? The deafe diuell hath conveyed thee to the Church to daye; & the dumb diuell shall goe back againe with thee, except that God in mercy pitie thee. Brethren, be earnest to get the spirit; seek all the spirit of God; crye vnto him with Dauid, *teach me thy statuts* [Ps 119:26]. Make me to vnderstand the waye of thy precepts. So shall I talke of thy wondrous workes.

Doctrine. The fourth doctrine to be obserued heere is the wisdome & mercy of God toward man that would not speake vnto men immediately in the glory of his maiesty but by his prophets. If God himselfe should speake vnto vs, the houre of preaching should be to vs a fearfull houre. All faces should

13

gather blacknesse. When the Lord tooke a proofe of this vpon Sinai, all the men of Israel cryed, Lord, speake thou not vnto vs but let Moses speake vnto vs [Exod 20:19]. It was not possible to them to behold the mans face that had spoken with God face to face. They were so dazeled with a glimpse of his glory [Exod 34:30]. Wee will surely dye, said Manoah, for wee haue seene God [Judg 13:22]. When Joshiah sawe Christ, the captaine of the Lords host [Josh 5:14], he fell on his face. When Elijah heard the voice of God comeing neere him, he couered his face with his mantle [1 Kgs 19:13]. Which among you for the space of an houre darre behold the face of the sunne that is but a creature, a seruant made for man? O man the master, hast thou a seruant whom thou darre not behold in the face? What thinkes thou of the face of him that made that face? Yet the light of the sunne is accessible, but God dwelleth into an inaccessible light [1 Tim 6:16], whereof the sight should be death vnto vs so long as wee dwell in sinfull flesh. For this cause, God forbade Moses to seek a sight of his face. For none, said he, shall see my face & liue. For this cause, the Lord, beeing both wise & mercifull hath made choice to speake to man by man, in and by his prophets.

The Vse. The vse is this: let vs not despise Gods ordinance. Sees thou a man like thy selfe teaching Gods word, thinke not the lesse of that word; but rather lift thy heart vnto God & giue him thanks that he hath dealt so loueingly with thee, as to make one to speake vnto thee that is subiect to like affections as thy selfe [Acts 14:15]. It maye be some of you thinke that yee would rather beleeue if God should come & speake to you him selfe or send one from the dead. If God should send from heauen the minister that was heere before me, some would thinke that his preaching now would make you all to beleeue. So thought the glutton in hell way? He desired Abraham to send some from the deade to testifie vnto his brethren, lest they also should come into that place of torment. What answered Abraham? *They haue Moses and the prophets; let them heare them* [Luke 16:29]. But heare the wisdome of hell. Nay, father Abraham, said he, but if one went vnto them from the dead, they will repent. But heare the wisdome of heauen. If they, said Abraham, *heare not Moses & the prophets, neither will they be perswaded, though one rise from the dead* [Luke 16:30]. Though your minister that is now with God should come from the dead & declaire vnto you the ioyes of heauen & the torments of hell, yee that would not beleeue him, while he did preach in the dayes of his flesh, would not be perswaded, though he should rise from the dead. Though in very person he were standing heere speakeing vnto you, let be to be perswaded to report you of your sinnes. I thinke hardly should yee be perswaded that it were he. His words should be like Rhodas report concerning Peter. While she said that Peter was at the doore, they said she was mad. But while *she constantly affirmed that it was euen so, then said they it is his angel* [Acts 12:15] or worth. If there should be such difficultie to perswade you that one come from the dead were come from the dead, how much more difficile[14] should it be to men to repent by the perswasion of one come from the dead? Truely Abraham spake wisely & truely. If they heare not Moses & the prophets, neither will they be perswaded, though one rise from the dead.

Seeing it is so, let vs blesse God for his benefeits. Let vs be content with that which he hath thought most expedient. Let vs hate vaine inuentions. It is by the foly of preaching that God will haue vs to be saued [1 Cor 1:21]. Let vs not be wise in our owne conceits. God that is wisdome is more wise then we all. He knoweth what is most needfull. He giueth to vs that which is best. A sinfull father can giue good things vnto his children [Luke 11:13], & will not giue them ill things as stones for bread, serpents for fish, scorpions for egges. How much more then will our truely good & heauenly father giue good things to his owne children? Can a mother forget her child that she haue not compassion of the fruite of her wombe [Isa 49:15]? Though she should, yet I will not forget thee, saith the Lord. What euer God doeth vnto vs, what euer he speaketh vnto vs, by whom so euer it be, it is for our will. It is he that maketh all to worke to our best [Rom 8:28]. This is the Lords doeing, for the *Lord is good. His mercy is euerlasting, and his trueth endureth to all generations, to him be glory for euer,* [Ps 100:5] Amen.

II. On Matters Theological

Christ Ovr Righteovsnesse

Rom 10:4.

Christ is the end of the law for righteousnesse to euery one that beleeueth.

In the first verse of this chapter, the apostle declareth his zeale for the well of Israel. *My hearts desire and prayer to God for Israel,* saith he, *is that they might be saued.*[1] In the second verse, he giueth them this praise: *that they* had *a zeale of God.*[2] In the third verse, he declareth their errour: that their zeale was *not according to knowledge,*[3] *for they being ignorant of Gods righteousnesse, and goeing about to establish their owne righteousnesse, haue not submitted them selues vnto the righteousnesse of God.*[4] This was their errour: they knewe not *that righteousnesse which is of faith*[5] but did goe about to make good their owne *righteousnesse, which is* by the workes *of the law.*[6] In this text, the apostle teacheth that the law leadeth men vnto Christ, who is the onely author of righteousnesse vnto all that beleeue in him.

the diuision of the text

In this text there be three parts: in the first part is declared what Christ is, *Christ is the end of the law*; in the second part is declared for what, *for righteousnesse*; thirdly, to whom, *to euery one that beleueth.*

1 Part
what Christ is

In the first part is declared what Christ is, *Christ is the end of the law.* The word τέλος, heere turned end, is interpreted after three diuers significations, which all may be orthodoxe and serue for good vses. First some interpret τέλος as if it were τελεί, ωσι, ναρσιγμα πλήρωμα, that Christ is the fulfilling or perfection of the law. This taken in a right sense is true, for the law without Christ is but a dead letter [2 Cor 3:6] that bringeth no thing to perfection. How shall a dead letter put life in a man? Vntill the bodie of a man get a soule, the man is not perfect, yea is not a man. So likewise, vntill a man get the quickining spirit of Christ, the soule of our soule, he is no more a Christian then a dogge or a horse. It is Christ that maketh the Christian. In Christ it is that the Christian hath his life, his beeing, and his moveing.

As for the law, what can a dead letter doe? What can *beggerly elements* [Gal 4:9] doe without Christ in whom our life is hidde? The law indeede will prepare vs for life, but wee shall neuer liue vntill Christ be preached vnto vs in his gospell, which *is the power of God* to *saluation* [Rom 1:16], the word of life. The preaching of the law is like Ezekiels first prophecie among the dead bones, which made *sinewes and* [. . .] *flesh* to come *vpon them* with the skinne [Ezek 37:8], but could not bring breath into them. But the preaching of Christ is like that second prophecie made among the bones, which made all these slaine men to liue and to stand *upon their feete, an exceeding great armie* [Ezek 37:10]. The law can not make a man to stand vpon his feete vntill Christ come. It is Christ that raiseth the dead. It is he that maketh creeples to goe. To him onely it belongs to cry, *Lazarus come foorth* [John 11:43]. Who but hee can say with power, *tolle grabbatum, take vp thy bed and walke* [Matt 2:9]. It is onely his [Mark 7:34] *ephphatha*[7] that is able to make the deafe eare to open. It is onely his *talitha cumi* [Mark 5:41][8] that was able to quicken the maide that was dead.

It is onely Christ who spiritually and temporally giueth eyes to the blind and eares to the deafe, a tongue to the dumb and legges to the lame. Blind Bartimeus [Mark 10:46] could neuer recouer his sight vntill he came to Christ. The lepers could neuer be cleansed vntill they found Christ [Luke 17:12], the sonne of Dauid, that, bedred at the poole of Bethesda, waited eight and threttie yeeres and could not be healed vntill he sawe Christ [John 5:5]. The physitians could take the poore womans gold [Luke 8:43]. They put a fluxe in her purse, but could not heale her of her bloody fluxe. She euer waxed worse and worse vntill she touched Christs garment. The sinnefull woman that entered into Simons house could neuer get rest to her soule vntill with teares she had washen Christs feete [Luke 7:38]. That

20

euill sorte of diuels would not depart from their possession vntill Christ came.[9] In a word, it is Christ onely that is the perfection of all things. It is only he that is τελείωσις νομον, the perfection of the law.

Indeede the law without Christ will terrifie a sinner. It will waken a sleeping sinner with most fearefull cryes of damnation. If Christ appeare not, the sinner anone will be swallowed vp of despaire. After that Judas had sold his master Christ and had put the price of his blood in his bagge, the law most fearefully cried in his conscience, traitour, thou art damned for betrayeing the innocent blood. Incontinent after that, he hastened to a gallowes where he hanged him selfe. It is said of him that he repented [Matt 27:3]. That was but the lawes repentance, μεταμέλεια, a sorrowe for sinne. But he wanted Christ, who by his gospell worketh μετάνοια, the changeing of the mind, which is the comeing of a man vnto him selfe againe. As it is said of the forlorne sonne that he came to him selfe againe [Luke 15:21], that is vnto his right wits wherefrae he had strayed, which was sauing repentance, heere yee may see that the law can bring no thing to perfection. It will worke μεταμέλεια, the beginning of repentance, which is a sorowe for sinne. But no changeing of the mind from euill to good can be wrought vntill Christ breath vpon vs his gospell, the *power of God to saluation* [Rom 1:16], the word of perfection.

Happy is that soule to whom Christ, the perfection of the law, preacheth a word of mercy. Woe to Judas whom all his sorrow heard no comfort better then this, *see thou to it, what is that to vs* [Matt 27:4]? Christ then was farre away. But happy and thrise happy was Peter, for while he was come to the highest degree of his denyells, while the oath was out of his mouth, while Satan thought him his owne, then Christ *looked vpon Peter* [Luke 22:61]. The word in the originall is ἐνέβλεψε[v], that is he looked in into Peter. Though a mans heart were covered with a breast plate of steele, the mercifull eye of God will see thorow all. This was Peters saluation, that Christ, the perfection of the law, was neere him and converted him so that he was afterward enabled to strengthen his brethren [John 21:18].[10] After that Christ had converted him, it was his glory to die for him for whom he reioiced that he was *counted worthy to suffer shame* [Acts 5:41].

21

For these and infinit more perfections, Jesus Christ our Sauiour may well be called τελείωσις νόμου, the perfection of the law. He onely is alpha and omega,[11] the perfection of all things [Rev 1:8]. Others by waye of paraphrase turne heere the word τέλος, tribut. The learned knowe that the Greeke word hath this signification. So after this interpretation, which is also orthodoxe, wee may say that Christ, the Sonne of God, is the tribute of the law [Rom 13:7]. It is a point of Gods law tribute to whom tribute custome to whom custome is due.

Behold the law of God, a most rigorous customer, not indeede like Zacheus who vsed forged cavillations [Luke 19:8]. It forbiddeth sinne but doeth no sinne. But in the rigour of iustice, it requireth all without any forgiueing to be payed. It will either haue from a man perfect obedience or the life both of his soule and body. Without the one or the other, it will not let a man goe. When Christ came into the world, he found all men taken prisoners by the law, which had fettered them in the region and shadowe of death vnder a yoke of bondage. Christ the Lord, moued with compassion, came vnto the law Gods customer, and payed for man perfect obedience; and for his bygone disobedience, he laide downe his life which was worthy the liues of ten thousand worlds [Luke 1:79].

Thus Christ Jesus payed tribut to the law that wee might goe toll free. All being finished by him [John 19:30], the law was content, and permitted all her prisoners to come out of that spirituall prisone wherein was no water, not so much as one drop of spirituall comfort. This was a great tribut as euer was payed since the world was founded. I read of a cruell taxation which Nahash, the king of the Ammonites, would haue imposed vpon the men of Jabesh Gilead for to enter into covenant with them. He appointed that the right eye of euery man should be thrust out [1 Sam 11:2]. This was a terrible tribut full of reproch. But what is it that all the eyes of the world should be thrust out in comparison of Gods blood and of the sacred life of Jesus. The God of heauen, offended by man, would not make a covenant with man againe vntill a man more worthy then all the men of the world was hanged like a theefe, and thrust downe vnto hell. It is but a small matter to haue an eye thrust out, but to be thrust vnder the infinit weight of the wrath of an angrie God is like *a wounded spirit*. Who *can* abide

22

it [Prov 18:14]? It made Christ him selfe to crie, *My God, my God why hast thou forsaken me* [Matt 27:46].

The 1 Vse. Let vs all heere learne to loue the Lord Jesus Christ. If a man had bought a man from the gallowes with his siluer, the bought man both would and should loue most dearely his buyer. Behold heere the Sonne of God hath bought vs from hell fire, not with his gold, but with his blood. Who then shall not loue him? *If* there be *any* [. . .] *that* loueth *not the Lord Jesus Christ, let him be Anathema Maran-atha, Maran-atha* [1 Cor 16:22],[12] that is *dominus moster venit*,[13] the curse of God shall be vpon him vntill the Lord come and destroye him. *Come Lord Jesus* come [Rev 22:20].

The 2 Vse. Let vs also learne heere that the pace of mans redemption is great. It is, alas, to too many but a sport to sinne against God. But, O man, thou considerest not what the life of a soule coste the Lord Jesus Christ. Alas that so many tread vnder their feete the blood of God, the vnspeakable price of our redemption. Lost creatures that wee once were, let vs now remember that if Christ had not payed our tribut, not one, either in heauen or earth, durst haue beene suretie for vs. The angels them selues, *non erant soluendo*, were not able to paye. It was not in their power to make vs toll free. None could pay that tribute but Christ him selfe, because there was no thing that could be that tribute but onely Christ him selfe. If any other thing had beene brought to pay our debts, the iustice of God had throtled vs all with these wordes of rigour, *pay me that* which *thou owest* [Matt 18:28]. But blessed be Jesus Christ for euer more, who hath taken vs out of the justice hands by the payement of so great a debt. To him be glory for euer.

This much haue I spoken vnto you concerning these two interpretations, which haue very good vses. I incline rather to followe them that turne τέλος the end, according as it is in our version, *Christ is the end of the law*. Seeing *Christ is the end of the law*, the end of the law must be good. Let vs heere consider how *Christ is* said to be *the end of the law*. For to vnderstand this, wee must knowe that there be two ends according to that distinction of philosophie, viz *finis cui et finis cuius gratia*,[14] that is an end to whom and an end for whose cause.

Christ, heere called *the end of the law*, was not the end to whom, for the law was not giuen vnto Christ, for in him was the fulnesse of the deitie, so that he neither had sinne, neither could he sinne, and so needed not a lawe. A lawe is giuen onely to these that haue neede to be directed or may faile. But the law is needelesse to him that can not transgresse. It were ridiculous to a king to make a lawe to his subiects that they should not pull downe the starres. It is as possible for a man to pull downe the sunne from the heauens as to Jesus Christ to doe any thing that is amisse.

So a law needed not to be giuen vnto him who could not transgresse. Men that are sinners are the end of the law the end to whom. But Christ is the end of the law that is *finis cuius gratia*, that is the end for whom. For the law was giuen vnto men to bring them vnto Christ. This the apostle clearely declareth: *the law was our schoolemaster* [. . .] *vnto Christ* [Gal 3:24], that is the law intended not to perfect vs as of it selfe, but became a schoolemaster to traine vs vp vnto the knowledge of Christ that by it, wee, beeing convinced of our owne vnworthinesse, might seeke for our iustification in Jesus Christ. Thus, as yee see, the law is a schoolemaster whose doctrine onely intends to bring men vnto Christ, who is heere called the end of the law.

A good schoole master, as yee knowe, must haue two things, a tongue for to teach and a rod to correct. The law, Gods schoolemaster appointed for vs, hath these two. The ceremoniall law is like a tongue for to teach vs. The morall law hath a rod for to correct vs.[15]

The cermoniall law, the great master of ceremonies by way of ceremonie, that is by types and figures, did teach men *Christ*, [. . .] *the end of the law*. This law could not let man see Christ him selfe. But, as an embassadour before the mariage of his king will cary the picture or portraiture of his prince to her whom he seeketh, for to see if she will be pleased with him, euen so, before mens spirituall marriage with Christ, the ceremoniall law brought vnto them the picture of Christ Jesus liuely shewen in types and figures, vntill he came him selfe with a bodily presence to *betroth vs vnto* him selfe *in righteousnesse*, [. . .] *in iudgement*, [. . .] *in loving kindnesse*, and in mercy [Hos 2:19].

If yee would haue that portraiture of Christ, consider in the ceremoniall law the ceremonies of the two goats whereupon Aaron did cast lots. Let vs consider them and learne what they teach of Christ. *Aaron*, said the Lord, *shall cast lots vpon the two goates, one lot for the Lord and the other* for Azazel or *scape goate* [Lev 16:8]. Both the goats were the portraiture of Christ Jesus.

As for the first goat whereon the Lords lot fell, it was offered for a sinne offering after this maner. First, it was caried without the camp vnto an vncleane place. After that, it was burnt in that vncleane place, both skinne and flesh and bones with the doung. Euen so Christ Jesus, *the end of* this *law*, on whom the Lords lot fell, was caried without the campe, without the gates of Jerusalem vnto vncleane and filthie Golgotha [Matt 27:33], where, beeing our sinne offering, he was burnt, not with a fire of coals, but with the vnspeakable heate of Gods wrath, which did burne his flesh, bones, and soule with the doung of all our iniquities.

As for the other goate, which was called the scapegoate, it was not a figure of vs who haue escaped from the wrath of God, but it was a type of Christ, *the end of* this *law*, for vpon its head Aaron did *laye* [. . .] *his hands* [. . .] *and confesse ouer him all the iniquities of the children of Israel,* [. . .] *putting them vpon the heade of the goate* [Lev 16:21]. After that, he sent the goate awaye by the hand of a fit man vnto the wildernesse, beareing vpon it the iniquities of the people. This goate was Azazel, which the Greekes called ἀποπομπαιὸν, the banished beast, the beast that was sent away as an apostle, a type of Christ Jesus, *the end of the lawe*.[16]

Heere it may be obiected and said, how could that goate be able to beare all the sinnes of the people. Sinne which hath slaine all the world might soone kill a goate. How then could a goate liue vnder the burden of all our sinnes? To this I answere, let vs learne heere Christ, *the end of the law*. Vpon the goats heade, our sinnes were laide but typically in a figure. But vpon Christ Jesus his head they were all laide really. The ceremonies of our sinnes onely were laide vpon the goate, but the Lord laide on his sonne Christ *the iniquitie of vs all* [Isa 53:6]. The goat neuer groned vnder his burden because it was but a ceremoniall loade, a shadowe of a burden, a burden of shadowes. But all the substance, all the infinit wrath of God, was laide vpon the sacred shoulders of Christ our Redeemer vntill he swate blood in his agonie [Luke 22:44] vnder the chastisement of our peace. His burden was not ceremoniall, not in a figure, but so reall that *he was bruised for our iniquities* [Isa 53:5]. All that was done vnto the goats was but a shadowe of that which was daily performed by Christ, *the end of the law*.

Heere it may be enquired wherefore were beasts as goats and lambes appointed to be types of Christ Jesus. It seemeth that men might haue beene much fitter types of Christs death then beasts. Had it not beene fitter for to haue slaine a man, and burnt him without the camp; and to haue banished another, and to haue sent him away by a fit man vnto a wildernesse? I answere that the beasts were more fit for this vse, and that, because they were innocent creatures of them selues, spotlesse and without sinne, who had neuer done any euill that had deserued death. But a man, beeing guiltie, him selfe worthy to be both banished and slaine, was not fit to be Christs figure in mater of satisfaction for sinne. That action had marred the portrature of Jesus Christ. Nay, that image had no more beene like Christ then the face of a beast is like the face of a man.

Obserue the vse of this law whereof the end was Christ. Had not Christ become our suretie? What was done to these two goates, the same and worse had beene done vnto us. The one was slaine; the other was banished. Wee all without Christ had beene for euer banished out of Gods presence. After that wee had beene put to death in hell, the most vncleane place of the world, where our skinnes, bones, and soules, with the doung of our sinnes, had beene burnt for euer. But Christ suffred all these things for vs. He was banished that wee might abide at home with our God. He was slaine that wee might liue. He suffered in an vncleane place of dead mens skulles [Matt 27:33], where he was made a burnt offering burnt with the fire of Gods wrath, which had consumed vs all. All the ceremonies doe send vs vnto him who is *the end of the lawe*.

This is the good that men should reape by the ceremoniall lawe whose lessons were all types and figures *vntill the day brake and the shadowes* did *flie awaye* [Cant 2:17].[17] And this much concerning the ceremoniall law which teacheth vs to runne to Christ, the *high priest of good things to come* [Heb 9:11]. This it did by *meats and drinks and diuers washings and* other *carnall ordinances imposed* by God *vntill the time of reformation* [Heb 9:10].

As the ceremoniall law teacheth men to goe to Christ, so the morall law scourgeth and vrgeth men to goe to Christ, *the end of the law*. The greatest scourge of the morall law is that curse against all these that are not perfectly righteous in them selues, cursed by *euery one that continueth not in all things which are writen in the booke of the lawe to doe them* [Gal 3:10]. Now what shall a man doe for to escape this most fearefull curse of God! Surely there is no other refuge but to runne to Christ, *the end of the law*.

By all this yee maye see how *Christ is the end*, both *of the* ceremoniall and morall *lawe*. The ceremoniall law pointed out Christ in types and figures. In the morall law, the voice of God, like a commoun bell, did sound for to conveene all the iudgements of God against *euery one that* continued *not in all things which* were *writen in the booke of the lawe to doe them* [Gal 3:10]. These terrible threatinings affrighted the spirits of men, and made them in all haste to runne and seeke a remedie which is onely to be found in Christ, the end of the law. Both the lawes did end in him, who is the beginning and the end of all things.

Heere it may be obiected and said how can Christ be called *the end of the law*, seeing the law *is the strength of sinne* [1 Cor 15:56]. How can Christ who is essentially good be the end of *the strength of sinne*, or can *the strength of sinne* haue a good end? I answere that the law is called *the strength of sinne*, because sinne in a naturall man neuer manifesteth so much its strength as when he is forbidden by the lawe to sinne. *Nitimur in vetitum*,[18] corrupt nature desireth most to doe that which is most forbidden. The sinnes of men are stirred vp by the lawe as the stinke of carrion is stirred vp by the sunne. It is not the sunne but the corruption of the carrion that is the cause of the stinke. Thus the law, like a sunne, bringeth a stinke out of mens soules, but all this is from the corruption which is in their carrion hearts sold vnder sinne. But, as for the law, let vs heare the apostle, *the law is holy and the commandement is holy,* [. . .] *iust, and good* [Rom 7:12-14].[19] Of such a law, Christ is the end, for the onely end wherefore either ceremoniall or morall law was giuen was to bring men vnto Christ Jesus, the onely Sauiour of this lost world. For this end, partly the ceremonies of the law did prefigure Christ, partly the morall and the iudiciall law did so convince men of their sinnes, and threaten such iudgements against them that behoued them to seeke the remission of their

27

sinnes and the fauour of God which can not be found but onely in Christ Jesus.

2 Part
for what Christ is the end of the law

In the first part of this text, wee haue heard how *Christ is the end of the law*. In the second part, the apostle declareth for what *Christ is the end of the law*, it is *for righteousnesse. Christ is the end of the law for righteousnesse to euery one that beleeueth*, that is that euery one that beleeueth in him may be made righteous that indeede is to be an honest man. *The end of the law*, O man, is to make thee an honest man. When the law hath taught with figures and terrified a man with threatinings, he must needes runne to Christ. Otherwise the lawe will pursue him vnto death. It will neuer leaue him vntill it see his soule in hell.

When the soule is come to Christ, what thinke yee be the earand for which it cometh vnto him? It goeth to him neither for siluer nor gold. It is not for the want of such things that the law pursueth it. Though Christ, O man, should giue vnto thy soule all that Satan offered vnto him, euen *all the kingdomes of the* earth *and the glory* thereof [Matt 4:8] that would neuer pacifie the law, thou must get the gift of his righteousnesse. Otherwayes there is not a letter in the law but it shall be a killing letter for the destruction of thy soule [2 Cor 3:6]. Indeede if a man had perfect righteousnesse of his owne, the law would neuer pursue him, but salute him as a friend and a worthy seruant of God, the lawgiuer. But as soone as the law seeth a man naked as *Aaron* [. . .] *made* the people *naked* [Exod 32:25], that is denuded of righteousnesse, it draweth the sword of justice to kill both his soule and his body. It neuer ceaseth from pursueing him vntill he be couered vnder the righteousnesse of Christ.

Behold in what sense *Christ* is said heere to be *the end of the law for righteousnesse*. As soone as this righteousnesse of Christ is obtained, the sword of iustice is put vp into the scabberd, the law becometh a friend because God is pleased and pacified. O righteousnesse of Christ but thou art precious. O most glorious righteousnesse, where art thou to be found?

I heare one in the booke of Job inquireing for the place of wisdome. *But where*, saith he, *shall wisdome be found? And where is the place of vnderstanding* [Job 28:12]? The answere is made: *man knoweth not the price thereof, neither is it found in the land of the liuing* [Job 28:13]. *The depth saith it is not in me*; [. . .] *the sea saith it is not with mee.*[20] If man also should enquire where is righteousnesse to be found and where is the place thereof, I will answere, man knoweth not the price thereof, neither is it found in the land of the liuing. The earth and the sea will answere for them selues that it is neither in them nor with them. In man this righteousnesse cannot be, for while he is in nature, he is like Elymas, the sorcerer, an *enemie of all righteousnesse* [Acts 13:10]. Where shall it be found then? I answere where shall light be found but in the sunne? So righteousnesse is onely to be found in *the sunne of righteousnesse* [Mal 4:2]. It is onely to be found in *the sunne of righteousnesse*. It is onely he who is that true Melchisedek, the king of righteousnesse.

As for man, if thou seeke righteousnesse in him, thou shall find a crie. What can thou find in him but that which God him selfe found in man? I, said the Lord, looked for righteousnesse. *But behold a crie* [Isa 5:7], a crie of sinne, a crie of cricing sinnes, which crie for vengeance. It is onely in Christ that saueing righteousnesse is to be found. It is onely he that brought it from the heauens vnto the world, that he might be *the end of the law for righteousnesse* for *euery one that beleeueth.* Let vs now make some vses of that which hath beene said.

The 1 Vse. Seeing it is Christ that hath the gift of righteousnesse, let vs learne what wee should cheefely seeke from Christ in our prayers. Let vs neither seeke siluer or gold but his glorious righteousnesse, which, if wee get, wee shall find both God and his law to be our friends. The Lord shall provide for vs euery thing that is necessarie. *The* [. . .] *lions* shall *lake and suffer hunger, but they that seeke the Lord* and his righteousnesse *shall not want any* [. . .] *thing that* is good [Ps 34:10]. This was Christs counsell: *seeke* [. . .] *first the kingdome of God and his righteousnesse, and all these things shall be cast vnto you* [Matt 6:33]. Many, like the dogge gapeing after the beguiling shadowe, losse the substance.[21] For what are all the best things that are cast vnto men but shadowes of good things to come whereof Christ is the high priest [Heb 9:11]? What are all the most desired things of this world but *vnrighteous mammon* [Luke 16:11]?[22] Though the world call their riches mammon, that is *firmitudo*, strength, from the word *aman*,[23] which signifieth to beleeue, as though these worldly things were yea and amen, both firme and sure, if they be without this righteousnesse of Christ, they are but abominations in Gods eyes. Of such things is truely said, *that which is highly esteemed among men is abomination in the sight of God* [Luke 16:15].

The 2 Vse. Secondly, seeing it is *Christ* who *is the end of the law for* our *righteousnesse*, let our soules cleaue fast vnto him and waite vpon his service. Many courtiers spend many of their dayes weering and weareing them selues with waiting vpon the princes of this world that goe to nought. And what for to get? A trifle which death may take from them. The very night they get it, to them may be said, as was said to that foole, this night thy soule shall be taken from thee. This is the height of mens hopes at mens courts. And of these how many are disapointed? But who did euer seeke *the kingdome of God and his righteousnesse* [Matt 6:33] but he found all other things cast vnto him? God giueth grace and glory; he couereth vs with his righteousnesse. Let vs therefore resolue to be the seruants of this righteous Lord, like that seruant that gaue his eare to be boared with an aule[24] by his master in token that he would be his seruant for euer [Exod 21:6]. Lord so boare our eares that wee may both heare this and doe it, Amen.

The 3 Vse. Seeing Christ hath brought vnto us from the heauens this precious pearle of righteousnesse, let vs highly esteeme of it. It is our treasure. Let therefore our hearts be where it is. It is the soules garment wherewith *the shame of* our *nakednesse* is covered [Rev 3:18]. Let vs keepe it cleane by a holy and spotlesse life, hateing the very *garment spotted* with *the flesh* [Jud 23].

The 4 Vse. Seeing *Christ is the end of the law for righteousnesse to euery one that beleeueth*, let vs not seeke righteousnesse in any other. There is righteousnesse in Christ sufficient for all these that beleeue. Let these that want faith to beleeue seeke righteousnesse in them selues, or in others as in the merits of deade saints: this is papistrie. Papists haue no faith to beleeue, nay they are the great enemies of faith; and therefore *Christ is* not *the end of the law for righteousnesse* to them. But, without this righteousnesse, they shall neuer be iustified. But what care they? New coined pharisees can iustifie them selues. But before whom? Before men, but not before God. As no serpent of brasse or gold but that which was by Gods direction could heale these that were hurt by the fierie serpents, so no righteousnesse but the righteousnesse of God can heale a soule bitten with that old serpent the diuell.

Let all other righteousnesse be hidde like a menstruous cloth in a secret place that it neuer be seene [Isa 64:6]. If wee lay our sinnes vpon the heade of Christ, our scape goate, he shall carie them all away vnto a wildernesse where they shall neuer be seene. But he will not beare our righteousnesse. If men laye vpon his heade the pride of their owne righteousnesse, his heauenly Azazel shall, with the hornes of his power, push them downe to the lowest hills. *Christ is the end of the law for righteousnesse*, not to men that are righteous in their owne conceit, but *to euery one that beleeueth*. The Lord be our righteousnesse that one day wee may stand before the sonne of man.

3 Part
to whom Christ is the end of the law for
righteousnesse

Wee haue heard that *Christ is the end of the law for righteousnesse*. Now it followeth that wee heare to whom. It is heere said, *to euery one that beleeueth* this is the worlds great jubile. The Jewes vnder the law had a great jubile euery fiftie yeere.[25] At that day all debts expired. Euery man that was put from his possession returned vnto it. Christs day was the worlds jubile. Vntill Christ came, it was neuer heard to euery one, as well gentiles as Jewes. Abraham, said Christ, sawe my day and *was glade* [John 8:56]. What if Japhet, with his forlorne and banished gentiles, had seene his day? O what ioye and gladenesse. O what halleluiahs had beene heard among the nations.

Behold heere a great blessing *to euery one that beleeueth*, whether Jewe or gentile, rich or poore. Before that Christ came into the world, there was a partition wall betweene the Jewes and gentiles. Then were the Jewes *a fountaine sealed* and *a garden inclosed* [Cant 4:12] Isaiah calleth a vineyard hedged in [Isa 5:5].

31

They were a people that dwelt alone and was not *reckened among the nations* [Num 23:9]. All other nations were without God in the world. They had no thing to doe with *the commoun wealth of Israel* [Eph 2:12]. All were vncircumcised and vncleane. But as soone as Christ the Lord came, he knat[26] them altogether with the Jewes, typically in that sheete which S. Peter saw come downe from heauen [Acts 10:11]. Then he made all cleane that was vncleane before. In that sheete were all maner of beasts, both cleane and vncleane, which were a type of the cleane Jewes and vncleane gentiles. But the voice from heauen declared that he had cleansed the vncleane gentiles. At the first, Peter vnderstood not this vntill he had spoken with Cornelius, the vncleane man whom Christ had cleansed. Then opened he *his mouth and said, of a trueth I perceiue that God is no respecter of persons* [Acts 10:34]. But in euery nation he that feareth him and worketh righteousnesse is accepted with him. In euery nation, said S. Peter. To euery one, saith S. Paul in my text, this is the worlds jubile. In Christs day, all the debts of the world did expire. In that day, euery man, euery nation might returne to his old possession, which had beene sold by Adam in the day he sold him selfe to transgresse his Lords commandement. Heere beganne the Catholick Church, in euery nation, to euery one.

Let vs obserue heere that he saith not absolutely to euery one, but to euery one that beleeuth. There is no righteousnesse for thee, O man, except thou beleeue. If thou want faith to beleeue, thou may say farewell to all Christs righteousnesse. If a man want faith to beleeue, it had beene better for him he had beene borne without a soule. Indeed faith is not of all, but happy is that man that beleeueth. Whether he be rich or poore, Christs righteousnesse shall be his, for Christs righteousnesse is *to euery one that beleeueth.* These wordes are wordes of great liberalitie. If a beggar beleeue in Christ, he shall be saued. If a king beleeue not, there is no thing but hell for him. Our *God is no respecter of persones* [Acts 10:34]. If it had beene said, *Christ is the end of the law for righteousnesse* for *euery* man that is wise in the world, or to euery one that is rich, or to euery one that is noble, the simple, the poore, had remained comfortlesse. But blessed be God; it is not so. God, who is no respecter of persones, hath least respect vnto these whom the world respecteth most:

not many wise [1 Cor 1:26], not many rich, *not many noble*. Some of all sortes haue the promise of saluation that none should despaire.

So heere Christs righteousnesse is *to euery one that beleeueth*. If a king will come vnto Christ with true faith, he shall be welcome vnto Christ not withstanding of all his worldly pompe and glory. Againe, if a ragged beggar come to him with faith, he shall be welcome with all his ragges of pouertie. Though a faithfull man were a Lazarus full of putrifyeing sores, the Lord Jesus shall take him in his armes and put him in his bosome. This is the priviledge of *euery one that beleeueth*.

The 1 Vse. Let vs now make some vses of that which hath beene said. I see heere that no man can be saued without faith, for Christ is righteousnesse to no man but to him that beleeueth. Seeing it is so, let euery one of vs striue to get faith and to increase our faith by hearing, readeing, prayeing, and medi-tateing, night and day in that word, which *is the power of God to saluation* [Rom 1:16]. If, O man, thou would haue faith, thou must loue sermons. Goe to them preparedly; heare them attentiuely, for *faith is by hearing, and hearing by the word of God* [Rom 10:17]. What paines should wee refuse for to get that precious thing whereby our soules are iustified [Rom 5:1] and sanctified. By faith, wee liue; by faith the righteousnesse of Christ is made ours. All that the saints euer did or suffered with honour was all by faith. Behold that long catalogue of Gods worthies: *by faith Abel*[27] etc., *by faith Abraham*[28] etc., *by faith Moses* etc., the number at last increased so that the Spirit of God came to these wordes, and *what shall I say more, for the time will faile me* [Heb 11:32]. All these worthies are much remoued for their faith. They all obtained these degrees of honour by faith? There is no thing in this world that hath obtained such a commendation as faith hath. Where is it said, yea doubled and tripled in Gods book, that by wisdome, by riches, by nobilitie, or by learning, such and such men did such and such things, all these things are within the fashion of this world that goeth awaye.

For this cause brethren build *vp your selues* vpon *your most holy faith* [Jud 20], if yee haue faith. If yee haue it not, neuer cease vntill yee get it. Say, as Dauid said touching another purpose, *surely I will not come into the tabernacle of my house, nor goe vp into my bed* [Ps 132:3]. *I will not giue sleepe* vnto my *eyes or slumber* vnto my *eye lids* [Ps 132:4] vntill I find faith in my heart to beleeue in Christ, *the end of the law for righteousnesse to euery one that beleeueth.* How darre wee goe to bed without faith? What if death take vs awaye before wee awake? These that want faith haue no share in Christ Jesus. *If I wash thee not,* said Christ to Peter, *thou has no part with me* [John 13:8]. If wee beleeue not, wee haue no part with Christ. *What part hath he that beleeueth with an infidell* [2 Cor 6:15]? Or what part can an infidel haue with Christ? If wee haue not faith, wee in the eyes of Christ are but infidels. Christ shall neuer acknowledge vs. When he shall bring forth his treasures to giue gifts vnto men, he shall say vnto all these that want faith that which Simon Peter said to Simon the sorcerer. *Thou hast neither part nor lot in this matter* [Acts 8:21].

Christs great desire is that men should beleeue for to get a part of his righteousnesse. To the end that Thomas might get faith, he guided him among all his wounds from wound to wound vntill he came to the hole of his heart. There, Thomas cried, thou art *my Lord and my God* [John 20:28]. Euen so, O man, Christ in his gospell setteth foorth all his wounds that thou *be not faithlesse but beleeuing* [John 20:27]. He will by faith haue vs Christiens indeede and altogether and not almost with King Agrippa. An almost Christian shall almost be saued; that is not saued at all [Acts 26:28].

The 2 Vse. Last of all, the end: wee may be in the number of these to whom Christ is righteousnesse. Let vs liue righteously; let our faith be seene in good workes; let vs beware of sinne, for sinne hindreth the soule to beleeue. Like Satan at Jehoshuahs right hand [Zech 3:1], it marreth the workes of faith which worketh by charitie towards men [Gal 5:6]. But most of all, it marreth that worke of faith sitting vpon Christ like a bee on a floure. It maketh it vnable to suck out of him the sacred sappe of righteousnesse, a precious nectar *sweeter* [. . .] *then the hony and* [. . .] *hony combe.*[29]

Seeing sinne is such a foe to faith, let vs *stand in awe and not sinne* [Ps 4:4]. The saints of God are described by two properties: first, *they* [. . .] *keepe the commandements of God*; secondly, they keepe *the faith of Jesus* [Rev 14:12]. These who haue not care to keepe Gods commandements will neuer keepe faith, which can not be keept but in a good conscience. It is a holy thing. S. Jude calleth it our *most holy faith* [Jud 20]. It can not liue with a corrupt life. S. Paul said a great word, *I haue keept the faith* [2 Tim 4:7]; but it was after he had said, *I haue fought a good fight.*[30] If wee fight this good fight and keepe the faith with S. Paul, then shall our conclusion be with S. Paul. *Hence foorth there is laid vp for me a crowne of righteousnesse, which the Lord, the righteous judge, shall giue me* in *that day* [2 Tim 4:8]. To him be glory for euer, Amen.

The Christian His Pilgrimage preached the ninteene day of August 1627

Eph 2:10

For wee are his workemanship, created in Christ Jesus vnto good workes, which God hath before ordeined that wee should walk in them.

The prophet Dauid, considering his deadnesse in spirituall things, made this prayer vnto God: *quicken [. . .] me according to thy* iudgements [Ps 119]. In this chapter whereout of I haue taken my texte, we are said to be dead in our sinnes. All the sonnes of Adam are naturally dead in their sinnes [Eph 2:1]. We can doe no good till the life of God be put in vs. No man is saued by his owne handiwork. All our righteousnesse is like a menstruous cloath [Isa 64:6]. Let proud pharisees come forward with their brags of thanksgiuing that they *are not* like *other men* [Luke 18:11]. But our best is to stand a farre, followe the publican in his humble confession that we are miserable sinners.

What euer good wee haue, it is not of our selues. *By grace are yee saued through faith*, saith the apostle, *and that not of your selues. It is the gift of God* [Eph 2:8], *not of workes lest any man should boast* [Eph 2:9]. Heere cleerly may be seene that it is of saluation as of promotion. It *cometh neither from the east nor from the west, nor* yet *from the south*, but from God who plucketh downe one, & setteth vp another [Ps 75:7]. As promotion is from God, so is saluation. It is by grace that wee are saued, not of our selues, not of workes. What shall we saye then of good workes? Heere is an answere: *wee are his workemanship, created in Christ Jesus vnto good workes* etc. In those wordes is contained a reason whereby the apostle proueth that we are not saued by any thing in vs, but, as for good workes, wee are *created in Christ vnto* them *that we should walke in them*.

the diuision of the texte

In the wordes we haue read, we shall considder these six things: 1. how we are called Gods *workemanship*; 2. how we are made, we are *created*; 3. in whom we are created, viz *in Christ*; 4. to what, *vnto good workes*; 5. what are these *good workes*, viz *workes which God hath before ordeined*; 6. the end of all these *good workes* is *that we should walke in them*.

1 Part
how wee are said to be Gods workemanship

Men are said heere to be Gods workemanship because of the worke of our redemption & regeneration. We are also his workemanship because He created vs. But, if we will compare our creation with our redemption, our creation was but a word & our redemption was a worke. In the creation God but spake. But in the redemption God both did & suffered. God swate not at the creation. But at our redemption he swate both blood & water [Luke 22:44]. The worke of creation was both great & glorious, but the worke of mans redemption was more glorious, like the second temple of Jerusalem. *The glory of this latter house,* said Haggai, *shall be greater then of the former* [Hag 2:9]. So is it of the worke of redemption, the second creating the glory thereof is *greater then of the former*.

Of all the creatures, God hath taken greatest paines vpon man. All other creatures haue passed but once thorow his hands, but man his workemanship hath beene twise thorow his hands. When the angels spilt his worke, the Lord would neuer laye his hand on them againe to renewe them. Vpon them he practised his precept, *let him* that is filthy *be filthy still* [Rev 22:11]. But as for man, while God found him cast out in the open field to the loathing of his person all bathed in blood, he said twise vnto him, liue [Ezek 16:6]. God tooke him vp out of his miserie & beganne a second worke vpon him, a worke more difficile then the first. As for the first, it cost God but a word; but the second cost him the life of his Sonne. Before that that worke could be wrought, the pleasure of Gods Saul did beare the dint of his wrath, yea was so ladened with stripes till he cryed, *my God, my God, why hast thou forsaken me* [Matt 27:46]?

The elect conuerted sinners, as wee see, are not in their owne, neither of their owne makeing, but are as the apostle saith heere,

Gods workemanship. The last good thought that is within vs is *his workemanship*. In a word, the whole man that is redeemed & regenerate is heere called Gods workemanship. This must be a glorious worke.

Men will gaze vpon the workes of men, as the apostles gazed vpon the temple, sayeing, *Master, see what maner of stones & what buildings are* there [Mark 13:1]. So Nebuchadnezar, wondering at his castell said, *is not this great Babylon which I haue* builded [Dan 4:30]? All such buildings are but Babels, confused heapes of stones. But O who could see the worke of a conuerted soule, which God his fingers hath wrought? Men might both look & saye, behold *what maner of stones & what buildings are* there. By the workemanship, yee might easily knowe the hand of the worker. The Church is the Lords workeing house. The instruments of the worke are heere, viz the preaching of the word & administration of the sacraments. Heere soules are renewed: this is the place ordained for our second creation. Yee haue all great neede to praye that this daye God, in his owne house, would work vpon your hearts & manifest his handyworke vpon you. The worse matter that can be wrought on is the heart of man. The potter will easily forme his claye. The smith will worke on brasse, on yron & steale. By the force of fyre, he will molten them & bring them to some forme; but no hand but the hand of God can frame or fashion in any point the heart of man. A locksmith can make keyes for opening of locks, but the locked heart none can open but he that opened the heart of Lydia [Acts 16:14].

Heere then wee maye see that all the good that is in vs is Gods workemanship. Faith, loue, repentence are things which his fingers haue wrought. This is the foly of fooles that think they shall repent when they are old, as if they might repent when they please, as if they were there owne workemanship. To daye, saith the Spirit of God, *if ye* [. . .] *heare his voice, harden not your hearts* [Ps 95:7]. When the worke is great, it should not be delayed.

If any would knowe what part of man the Lord doeth worke vpon, the words, *wee are his workemanship*, declare plainely that it is not the head of man, or the eye of man, or the tongue of man, or the hand of man, but the whole man. Man is like a house of three house height hauing an vpper chamber, one in

38

the middest, & one belowe. In the vpper chamber dwelleth the mind, in the second stage dwelleth the will, in the third belowe vpon the ground doe the affections of man dwell.[1]

All these chambers are defyled with sinne & haue neede to be sweept & garnished. As for the mind, S. Paul saith that it is darkened, that is blindfolded [Eph 4:17]. When the mind is darkened, it can not look vpon God. As pharaoh bad Moses, goe out of his sight [Exod 10:28], so the darkened mind desireth not to haue God in its sight. Christ, speakeing of these that crucified him, said that they knewe *not what they* did [Luke 23:34]. As for the will, it is also blind & is guided, hoodwinked by the blind mind. Now, if the blind guide the blind, both must *fall into the ditch* [Luke 6:39]. As for the deepest part of the dungeon where the affections dwell, God no fewe wordes declares, who dwelleth there, viz the affections, the thoughts, & imaginations of the heart, which are euill at all times [Gen 6:5].[2]

Behold these three chambers that are in man. In the best of them, there is not a place wherein Christ can lodge. All is filthy *from the sole of the foot* [. . .] *vnto the* crowne of the *head* [Isa 1:6]. It is writen that, when Jesus went to eate the passeouer, he came to a chamber which was trimmed. In vs all there is not a trimmed chamber for Christ till God prepare it. In one chamber lodgeth foolishnesse, in another riot, in another drunkenesse, in another chambering & wantonnesse, in another strife & enuie,[3] in another is scornefull Michal, in another dwelleth Festus, who esteemeth zeale to be madnesse [Acts 26:24], in another dwelleth worldly wit, which esteemeth religion to be foolishnesse [1 Cor 1:18]. So from the highest mind to the lowest affection, *there is no soundnesse in* the soule *but wounds & bruises & putrifying sores* [Isa 1:6].

2 Part
how wee are wrought

Wee haue heard that wee are Gods workemanship. Now followeth that wee heare how wee are wrought. It is said heere that wee are created.

To create in scripture is taken diuersly. Properly, it signifieth to produce a thing from no being to a being. Secondly, it signifieth to restore grace, as touching the feeling & fruit thereof. In this sense, Dauid prayed that God would *create in him a cleane heart* [Ps 51:10]. Thirdly, to creat signifieth to giue & worke grace where it is not. In this sense heere are we said to be *created in Christ Jesus vnto good workes*.

We reade in scriptures of diuers things which must be done ouer againe in a better sorte before that man can come to God. He that is borne of a woman must be borne againe, viz of the spirit. *Except that a man be borne againe*, said Christ to Nicodemus, *he can not see the kingdome of God* [John 3:3]. As it is of the birth, so is it of that which preceedeth the birth, viz of our generation. There is a first & a second: a first generation, which goeth before the first birth, this is carnall; & a second generation, viz our regeneration, which goeth before the second birth, this is spirituall. By the first generation, wee are brought vnto the world; so, by our regeneration, wee enter into heauen. As of birth & generation, so is it of creation? There is a first creation & a second creation. As for our first creation, it was by Christ; as for our second creation, it was in Christ. As for the first creation, all *things were made by* Christ [John 1:3]; as for the second, as wee see heere, it was in Christ *wee are his workemanship created in Christ Jesus*. The first creation was done with a word. All the labour was in a word, *let there be light, & there was light* [Gen 1:3], & so of all other things. But this second creation was a worke of great paine, which made God to sweate, yea the best blood in his body.

Let vs obserue heere how the spirituall worke of our regeneration is called a creation, where we may learne how voide of grace we are all by nature, for where there is a creation, it is manifest that there is no preceeding matter whereof the creature is made. We must not think that our regeneration is like the clatching vp or reparing of an old house, wherein some things are helped & made better. No not: it is a new building whereinto the dead stones of the former building maye not be laid. When a house was declared in Israel to haue lepper walles after that it had beene once scraped, it was ordained by the law of God that the house should be broken downe, & that the stones & timber & morter thereof should be caryed *forth out of the city*

[Lev 14:45]. There was nothing in that vncleane house which might be put into another building againe. As was the lepper house, so is the lepper man, the man that is borne in sinne & conceiued in iniquitie. There is no thing in his lepper nature to be laid into the temple of the Holy Gost. All that is old must be scraped & taken awaye & new things put into the place thereof.

The old heart of Adam in him must not be repaired & made better; but it must be taken awaye, & a new one put into the place thereof. *A new heart* [. . .] *will I giue you*, saith the Lord [Ezek 36:26]. The old spirit must depart & giue place to a new spirit. *A new spirit will I put within you*, saith the Lord [Ezek 36:26]. Gods workemanship is all new. These who are this workemanship must be all newe. They must *be renewed* into *the* very *spirit of* their *mind* [Eph 4:23]. They must haue new hearts with newe thoughts. They must haue new eyes to behold *as in a glasse the glory of the Lord* [2 Cor 3:18]. They must haue new eares wherewith they maye hearken what God the Lord will saye. They must haue new mouthes for prayer & for praise. They must haue new hands for workeing out the worke of their saluation. They must haue new feete for to *run the way* of Gods *commaundements* [Ps 119:32]. In a word, we must be newe without & new within. This God in his word commaundeth to be done, while he biddeth vs put *off concerning the former conuersation the old man* [Eph 4:22], & *put on* that *new man which after God is created in righteousnesse & true holinesse* [Eph 4:24].

Obserue heere how this new man is said to be created. For this cause, all the good that is in man is called the *newe creature* [Gal 6:15], where I saye that a man must haue a new spirit, a new heart, new eyes, new eares, new hands, & new feete. This creation is not to be vnderstood of the substance of the heart, hands, & feete, for the same flesh remaineth into the reformed mans heart that he had while he was wicked, as Moses his cleansed hand was of the same flesh whereof it was while *he tooke it out* of his bosome *leprous as snowe* [Exod 4:6]. When it was cleansed of its leprosie, it was not said that God tooke all the old lepper flesh off his hand & put on new flesh. No not, but that *it was turned againe as his other flesh* [Exod 4:7].

The change was made in the qualities. It is so of the creation of the workemanship heere. Wee are said of new to be created when we are turned & changed by God from ill to good. God createth our mind when he chaisseth awaye the darkenesse of errour & ignorance out of our mind, & bringeth in into it the torch of his trueth, wherewith it is inlightened. And againe God createth our will when he maketh it vnwilling to ill, & willing to good. This is also Gods creation when he cleanseth awaye the abominations of our filthy affections. This being once done man is said to be a new creature. Before this be done in some degree, man is *abominable & filthy*, drinking *iniquity like water* [Job 15:16].

In this second creation, let vs acknowledge two things: first, Gods mercy; secondly, our owne miserie. As for God his mercy, it is great in that he dained euer to touch vs for to reforme vs, who had once spilled such a glorious workemanship & that by our pride & presumption. While we sinned against God, did we not breake downe his image within vs, as who should in great indignation breake downe an idol? Did we not set vp an idoll into the place of that image, euen the *image of ielousie* [Ezek 8:5]? Yet for all this God hath looked vpon vs in mercy, & for his glory & our soules saluation hath put his hand to a new creation.

Againe, as in this creation, we see God his mercy, so also see we our owne miserie. For while we heare that we haue beene *created* [. . .] *vnto good workes*, wee maye knowe that there was no thing in vs whereof to make a good man or a good woman. No not, but, as the apostle saith, it is God *that hath wrought vs for the selfe same thing* [2 Cor 5:5], so heere is it said that wee are his workemanship created. Wee saye ordinarly ill stuffe to make it of. But alas, what can be made of ill stuffe? Shall a man build a house of lepper stones [Lev 14:45]? Let vs all considder this daye what stuffe we haue brought in heere before the Lord, for to make any good thing of the best of vs all by nature is like Ephraim as an vntamed calfe [Jer 31:18]. Considder thy mold O man. Speake in conscience. What if God had giuen thee all thy hearts desire? What if he had suffered thee to fulfill all thy lusts? What mischeef had thou left vndone? In what plight had thy poore soule beene ere now? Thou & I & all that are heere, if God should suffer vs to runne out the courses of our crooked inuentions, should ere it be long runne our selues headlongs into hell. If, in thy lifetyme, thou hast not fallen into some filthy blot, saye, not grand-mercy to flesh & bloud; but saye, as Dauid said, who blessed God for keeping him from the slaughter of Nabal [1 Sam 25:32], which he had intended. Learne heere the lesson of mercy & of miserie. What euer good is in thee, O man, knowe it is Gods creation. In that new creature, acknowledg the Creator. But againe, what euer be in thee that is not good, it is of the old man. It is thine; thinke shame of it. Strike vpon thy thigh with Ephram & saye, fye what haue I done? Beat thy breast with the publican & crye for mercy to a miserable sinner [Luke 18:13].[4] God sees thy heart within thy breast as clearly as though it were within a case of cristall.

Before I end this point, let me breefly declare vnto you where this second creation is begunne, & how it is brought to perfection. It is begunne in the heart; from thence is the reformation of the whole man. All the members of the body come vnto the heart, as the souldiers came vnto Johne [Luke 3:14]. With what shall we doe the heart among the members is like a centurion, which sayeth to one, *come & he cometh*; to another, *goe & he goeth*; & to the third, *doe this & he doeth* it [Matt 8:9]. He that can saye with Dauid, *my heart* meditateth *a good matter*, may easily sobioine, *my tongue is the pen of a ready writer* [Ps 45:1]. The eye & the eare, the tongue, foot & hand doe still waite vpone the beckening of the heart. This dead heart is reuiued by God, as the Shunamits dead child was restored to life by Elisha. It is said that the prophet went to the bed where the child laye dead, & *lay vpon the child, & put his mouth vpon his mouth, & his eyes vpon his eyes, & his hands vpon his hands, & he stretched him selfe vpon the child* till *the flesh of the child waxed warme* [2 Kgs 4:34]. After that life came in, &, for to declaire that it was so, *the child [s]neesed seuen times & [. . .] opened his eyes* [2 Kgs 4:35]. Euen so, Christ, finding vs laid vp dead vpon our deathbeds, came, &, as it were, stretched him selfe vpon vs hauing his eyes vpon our eyes & his mouth vpon our mouth, & his hands vpon our hands. While he did this, he powred out his heart vpon vs & restored vs to life & vnderstanding. These be God his owne words: *I will powre out my heart vnto you & make you vnderstand my wordes* [Prov 1:23].[5] In this is our new creation, our vnification; all other inuentions are but like the prophets staffe, which being layd vpon the face of the dead child could neither make him speake nor heare when all that man can doe is done. He must saye, as was said of the layeing on of the staffe by Gehazi, *but there was neither voice, nor hearing* [. . . .] *The child is not awaked* [2 Kgs 4:31]. It is the powring out of Gods heart vpon a man which reuiueth the soule. It is the power of his word whereby the dead soule is awaked. *Awake thou that sleepest, & arise from the dead, & Christ shall giue the light* [Eph 5:14].

Behold in these wordes our first resurrection & our second creation. He that is of the second creation is of the first resurrection. Against such, *the second death* shall not preuaile [Rev 20:6]. To end all this in a word, this resurrection is the Lords, this creation is the Lords. All the good that is within vs, it is a created workemanship whereof God is the worker & not wee. What could dust doe for the creating of it selfe?

3 Part
wherein wee are created

Now let vs see wherein wee are created. That where in wee are created is Christ. *Wee are his workemanship created in Christ Jesus.* I reade in scripture of two generations, of two births, of two deaths, of two resurrections, of two creations. The first generation is naturall & is from our earthly father. The second generation is spirituall; it is called regeneration. The first birth is out of our mothers wombe. Our second birth is *of the spirit* [John 3:6]. This is that birth whereof Christ spake to Nicodemus, who wondered how a man could be borne when he was old. The first death is that whereby sinners are dead in their sinnes [Eph 2:5]. As for the naturall death, it is but the godly mans sleepe [John 11:11]. The second death is euerlasting in hell. The first resurrection is a rysing from sinne; the second resurrection is a rysing from the graue. He that is partaker of the first resurrection the second death shall not preuaile ouer him [Rev 20:6]. As in generation, birth, death, & resurrection, there is a first & a second, so is it of creation. The first creation was by Christ the word. S. Johne saith that *all things were made by him* [John 1:3].

But in this second creation, we are created in Christ. Christ is, as it were, God his calmes[6] or mould wherein the godly are formed of whom they receiue their shape. When we come out of Adam, we beare the image of Adam. It is writen of Adam, after that he had sinned, that he *begat a sonne in his owne likenesse* [Gen 5:3] that is sinfull. So these that are created in Christ are created in his owne likenesse, which is holinesse. As the ingrauen stampe set vpon the waxe maketh in it an impression like vnto that which is ingrauen into the stampe, so Christ the ingrauen image of God [Heb 1:3], being set vpon the heart of a man, maketh in it such an impression as it is easy to knowe whose image it is. This image is holinesse. This is the shape & forme & likenesse, which the soule receiueth by this creation in Christ. As Cesars moneyes had Cesars superscription, so these that are created in Christ haue Christs image & inscription [Matt 22:20].

Let all men consider heere whether they be created in Christ or not. Let them behold them selues whether they be like vnto Christ or not. He that is created in Christ hath the image of Christ. Behold thy selfe, O man, in the glasse of Gods word; & see whether thou be like vnto Christ or not. Is thou a proud man? Thou is not like Christ, for Christ was *meeke & lowly* [Matt 11:29]. Is thou a fals man? Thou is not like Christ, for no man euer could chalenge him of a lie. Is thou a couetous man? Thou is not like Christ. Christ cared not for *all the kingdomes of the world* while they were offered vnto him [Matt 4:8]. Is thou a reuiler? Thou is not like Christ. Christ, while he was reuiled, reuiled not againe. Tell me, O drunkard, if thou be like Christ. Can thou thinke that euer Christ looked as thou lookes or spake as thou speakes? Ye fornicators & yee adulterers who, like fedde horse, *neye after* your *neighbours wife* [Jer 5:8], whose superscription haue yee? Such sinnes committed with pleasure are the very image of the diuell. As these that beheld the superscription in the moneye said that it was Cesars,[7] so they who behold the superscription of such superfluitie of wickednesse maye truely saye this superscription is the diuels. Yea I will saye vnto thee that if thou beare the diuels superscription, the diuell will chalenge thee to be his owne, & if thou amend not thy sinnes by breaking them off by vnfained repentance, Christ shall neuer take the from the diuel. As he said, giue vnto Cesar that which is Cesars [Matt 22:21], so shall he saye, giue vnto Satan that which is Satans. God, the rule of iustice, will not wrong the diuell. He that dyeth with the diuels image, by the iustice of God must goe to the diuel. It is Gods iustice that he that serueth the diuell vnto the terme should receiue the diuel his wages.

Let vs praye to God earnestly that he would make vs partakers of this second creation that is wrought in Christ, that in him we maye become newe creatures, not like the men and weemen we haue beene of before. We saye of a conuerted man who before was wicked, he is a farre changed man now. Well is the man that changeth for the better. Well is that man whose soule is in Christ like wax vnder a stamp.[8] He shall be like him, who is said to be the fairest *among ten thousand* [Cant 5:10]. This is not a fading fairenesse like the beauty of a lilly, *which to daye is, & to morrow is cast into the ouen* [Matt 6:30]. This image is like these *bags* of the gospell *which waxe not old*, like the heauenly treasures which faile not [Luke 12:33]. All other things are transitory; all things belowe, yea the heauens aboue, *waxe old as doeth a garment* [Ps 102:26]. *As a vesture shalt thou change them*, saith the psalmist; *and they shall be changed* [Ps 102:26].[9] But as for that which is of God, it is euer the same like him selfe, *thou art the same. And thy yeeres shall haue no end* [Ps 102:27]. This image of Christ is for to speake so the youth of the godly, a youth that is dayly *renewed like the eagles* [Ps 103:5]. Of all the workes of God, maye wee well saye, but particularly of the workes of the second creation, in Christ *the workes of the Lord are great* [Ps 111:2]. *His work is honourable & glorious* [Ps 111:3]; holy & reuerend is his name.

Some man maye inquire & saye how was this creation wrought in Christ? Who deuised it first? I answere that it was done by the counsell of the whole Trinitie. God at the first creation made all other creatures as it were lightly with a word. But when he came to the creating of the king of creatures, he did goe more slowely to worke, as it were with deliberation & counsell. The three personnes (if I maye speake so) were conueened. In this conuention, the Father, first in order, propounded that man should be made like them selues. *Let vs*, said

46

he, *make man* according to *our* owne *image* [Gen 1:26]. Thus man in the first creation was beautifull. All the creatures feared him because, when they sawe him, they sawe God into him. But after, by the deceit of the diuell, this image was miserably defaced, & in the place of it was set the image of the diuell. Thus man lossed all the beauty he had in his first creation, so that he had not so much as any draught of Gods pincell. The creatures that reuerenced him before would not acknowledge him any more, because they sawe no more of God in him. Thus man was gone. Yet God looketh on him, & pitieth him & againe conuocateth the counsell, [and] propoundeth the matter that man was lost.

The Father first in order begineth the speach, man whom we loued, so that we made him lik our selues, is seduced by the diuell. He hath lost our image, the beauty of his creation. What now is to be done? Thou my Sonne, the expresse image of my person, shall be the mould of a newe creation. In thee will I create him ouer againe & restore our likenesse. Goe downe, goe downe, & take his flesh vpon thee. Beare my wrath. Doe, suffer, dye, & satisfie my iustice. Shall Christ the Sonne refuse the burden? No not, my Father, would he saye, I accept the charge for man whom I loued euer. Though he hath lost our image, he hath not lost my loue. I will goe take flesh vpon me that I may blead my blood for him. And though I thinke it no robberie to be eaquall vnto thee, yet for his sake I will take *vpon* me *the* shape *of a seruant*,[10] & become subiect vnto death, yea vnto the ignominious *death of the crosse*.[11] If thou will create him againe, let the creation be made in me. Open my breast & my bowels, & powre him into my heart till he be slayen there in the likenesse of God. O the mercy of these bowels, *the desire of all nations* [Hag 2:7]. O these earning bowels of loue that would open that in them the second creation of such a vile creature might be made. What saith the Holy Ghost? I shall be busy at that worke. By my presence & my power in the word, I shall drawe the draught of that image into him. In all his distresses, I shall be his comforter. I shall guide him, & I shall guard him. I shall bring him thorow many tribulations, & shall neuer leaue him till I bring him vnto glory. Behold the counsell of the new creation, & wonder at the loue of the Trinitie, Father, Sonne, & Holy Ghost, to whom be glory for euer.

4 Part
whereunto wee are [. . .] created in Christ

Now followeth that wee see in our texte whereunto *wee are* [. . .] *created in Christ* Jesus. It is heere declaired, viz vnto good workes.

Most men thinke they be come into this world for to passe their time at cardes, & at dyce, & other games. Thus they spend their dayes in daliance. The glutton bad his soule take rest, *eat, drink, & be merry* [Luke 12:19], as though he had gotten a soule from God for no other vse but for pampering of his belly. This is the course of all gluttons: *let vs eate & drinke, [for] to morrowe wee shall dye* [1 Cor 15:32],[12] as though they did liue for to eate & not eate for to liue. This is the life of the harlot: he liues to fulfill his lusts. All such liuers are like these wanton widowes, of whom S. Paul said that they were dead while they liued [1 Tim 5:6].[13] Such persons remember not whereunto they are created.

He that is *created in Christ* is created *vnto good workes*: he must lead a good life. He that is in Christ, saith the apostle, let him be *a newe creature* [2 Cor 5:17]. This is called the new man, the spirit guided by the lawe of the mind. Foolish men, though their life be leude, thinke to be in heauen before their feete be cold. Many thinke them selues holy if they doe no ill workes. We saye commonly he is a good man, for he doeth ill to no body. But what good doeth he to any body? Christ shall condemne the world, not particularly for their ill workes, as for that they did not good workes. He shall not saye to the wicked, I was hungry, for yee tooke my meat from me, but I was hungry & *ye gaue me no meate*; not, I was thirsty for ye tooke away my drinke, but *I was thirsty & ye gaue me no drinke* [Matt 25:42]; not I was naked because ye striped me naked, but I was *naked & ye clothed me not* [Matt 25:43]; not I was in prison because ye put me into prison, but I *was in prison & ye visited me not* [Matt 25:43]. See how Christ speaketh not in his last iudgement so much of ill workes, which the wicked haue done, as of the good workes, which they haue left vndone. It is not heere said that wee are created not vnto ill workes, but we are *created in Christ* [. . .] *vnto good workes*. If thou haue no good workes, thou art not a creature of the second creation. Woe to those that worke not. Ydle drones shall neuer dwell with God.

48

In these wordes that we are *created* [. . .] *vnto good workes*, we learne two things. First, that wee must take heede of ill workes, the workes of the night, *riot & drunkennesse*, [. . .] *chambering & wantonnesse*, [. . .] *strife & enuie* [. . .] [Rom 13:13]. Secondly, that we be not ydle in this world. A Christian, as yee see heere, is a man created to worke. A Christian man therefore, as yee see heere, is not an ydle man for to doe no thing but, as we define a gentle man, to goe & his cloak about him. If a gentle man be an ydle man, he is not *created in Christ Jesus*, for who is created in him is created *vnto good workes*. If thou be a sonne of Adam, God hath ordained thee to worke & to eate thy bread *in the sweat of thy face* [Gen 3:19]. If thou be a creature in Christ, thou must also worke, not onely workes which make the body to sweate in thy lawfull calling, but thou must also worke good workes, workes worthy of amendement of life [Matt 3:8].

If any man desire to knowe whether he be a creature of God wrought by the second creation, let him consider his workes. If thy workes, O man, be not good, thou hast no thing to doe with the second creation. Thou art but a creature of the first creation. Thou art a creature of God, as a dogge is a creature. A dogge is partaker of the first creation, yea in that he is better then thou, because he hath remained still as God made him, viz a beast. But thou, being created a man according to God his image, hast not kept thy first estate, but by thy ill workes hast made thy selfe worse then a beast [Jude 10].[14] What I saye to thee I saye to all. There is no man that can doe a good work till he be created againe. Viewe the world & spye out one, if thou can, who doeth good before he hath passed thorow the calmes & mould of the second creation. It is said in the psalme that God *looked downe from heauen vpon the children of men to see if there were any that did vnderstand & seeke God* [Ps 14:2]. If there had beene any, certainely God his eye had fund him out. But what is said? *They are all gone aside; they are altogether become filthy. There is none that doeth good, no not one* [Ps 14:3].

5 Part
what are these good workes

Now it followeth that we know what be these *good workes*

49

whereunto God hath created vs. They be workes which God hath ordeined.

This is the true tryall of good workes. The workes which God hath ordeined are good workes. The workes which he hath not ordeined, were their shewe neuer so great before men, are not good before God. There be many workes in this world named good which God hath neuer ordeined, as papists workes, as scourgeing of them selues, walkeing in haire, begging in Israel. Item: *touch not, taste not, handle not* [Col 2:21], *which all are to perish with the vseing.* Those be but ordinances, *commandements, & doctrines of men* [Col 2:22]. The apostle telleth vs that such things haue a great *shewe of wisdome* [Col 3:23], but all is but wilworship.[15] Wilworship, as not worship, so will workes are not workes, that is worship which God hath ordeined. So workes are *good workes* which God hath ordeined.

Papists are foolish in their workes. Though all their workes were good & ordeined by God, they haue one worke, a barbarous worke with a barbarous name called *opus operatum*, the worke wrought, which, like a dead flie, maketh all their perfume to stinke [Eccl 10:1]. The most part of all their workes haue no ordinance from God. When they haue done them all, God maye saye of the most part, who hath required such things at your hands? Awaye foolish papist with the workes of thy owne inuention. Awaye with thy foolish imaginations. Awaye with euery worke which God hath not ordeined. Would thou know the workes which he hath ordeined? Keepe the commandements; doe that which the Lord requireth of thee. The Lord *hath* shewen to thee, *O man, what is good. And what doeth the Lord require of thee, but* that thou *doe iustly,* & that thou *loue mercy,* & that thou humble thy selfe, and *walke* [. . .] *with thy God* [Mic 6:8]. These be the *good workes* whereunto we are *created in Christ Jesus.*

6 Part
What we should doe with these good workes

In the last point of my texte, we haue to considder what we should doe with these *good workes* whereunto we are created. It is said heere that *we should walke in them.*

Heere obserue that good workes are ordeined by God that *we should walke in them*. He saith not that we should merit by them, but that *we should walke in them*. Heere maye clearly be seene that *good workes* are, as a father said well, *via regni non causa regnandi*, that is the waye to the kingdome, but not the cause of reigning. It is by the blood of Christ that we are iustified, but these who are iustified must walke in good workes. The Israelites, being ready to goe out of Egypt toward Canaan, did two things at their passeouer. First, a lamb was slaine & the blood thereof was sprinkled vpon the posts of the doore [Exod 12:7]; secondly, that done, they girded their loines, put shoes on their feete, & had a staffe in their hands [Exod 12:11], as men makeing for a iourneye. As they did, intending their iourneye from Egypt to Canaan, so must we doe in our iourneye from the house of bondage vnto Canaan which is aboue. First, the blood of Gods lamb, Christ, must be sprinkled vpon vs which is our iustification. After that, our loines must be girded with sanctification, & we must take our iourneye by the waye of *good workes*, which is *via regni*, that wee maye walke in them.

In the words of my texte, I see the vse of good workes. It is that *we should walke in them*. Heere I obserue that one good worke is not enough for a man that would come to heauen. No not, there must be good workes. We must not sit downe vpon one good worke & saye it is enough. No not, we must walke in *good workes* from one to another. When a man hath done one good turne, he must not lye downe & puffe with these lazy priests in Malachie sayeing, *behold what a wearinesse is* in *it* [Mal 1:13]. *He that is holy* must *be holy still* [Rev 22:11]. As the ending of one houre is the beginning of another, so must the ending of one worke be the entery to another. As the breath continualy cometh & goeth, as the pulse beateth continualy, as the sea is euer in motion, as the heauens are euer in a course, so must man be euer doeing good, goeing from one good worke to another. This is the Christians pilgrimage. In this pilgrimage, if man goe not forward of neede force, he shall goe backward. He is like the sea, which beginneth to ebbe whil it ceaseth to flowe. The tyde is euer comeing in or else goeing out. So is it of man, if he cease to doe good, he will beginne to doe euill. One saith very well, *nihil agendo male agere discimus*, by doeing

51

no thing, we learne to doe euill. This is a commoun answere to what are ye doeing? I ame doeing no thing, that is I am learning to doe euill. Be ware of doeing no thing, for it is the schoole of euill doeing. Beware also that, after thou hast done a good turne, thou cease from doeing farther.

Many are in their workes, as Joash was in his shots who shot *thrise & stayed* [2 Kgs 13:18] while as he should haue shot fiue or sixe times. They stand at three while as they should come to sixe. Like Lots wife [Gen 19:26], at once they looke ouer their shoulder; &, like the foolish ploweman, they *put their hand to the plow & looke backe* againe [Luke 9:62]. Such men will not come to Jerusalem. The night will fall vpon them before they come there. It will faire with them as with the Leuite. They shall be forced *to lodge in Gibeah* [Judg 19:15], a dungeon of death, a denne of darkenesse. He that thinks to lodge in heauen must walke in workes from worke to worke, from grace to grace, till he come to glory. There be many who, if they haue done any point of God his commaundements, will bragge of it, as if they had done all. If they haue stepped in into one worke, they imagine that they haue walked in *good workes* & are come so to persec[u]tion that they neede no further. So Saul thought he had done well because he had killed the leane & naughty beasts, notwithstanding that he had spaired the fattest sheepe & oxen against God his commaundement. When Samuel came to him, before that Samuel could open his mouth to reproue him, he beganne to praise him selfe sayeing, *I haue performed the commaundement of the Lord* [1 Sam 15:13]. If papistrie had beene in these dayes, Samuel might haue said, Saul, as I perceiue, thou art a papist. But what said Samuel? Hast thou *performed the commaundement of the Lord*? It is well done. But *what meaneth* the *bleating of the sheepe in mine eares & the loweing of the oxen which I heare* [1 Sam 15:14]? He had slaine the leanest & spaired the fattest.

Many doe with their sinnes, as Saul did with the Amalekites sheepe & oxen. They will kill the leane & naughty, but the fat sheepe & fedde oxen, their fattest sinnes & greatest sinnes, they keepe aliue. Their bleating & their loweing is heard in the heauens like the crye of the sinnes of Sodome. There be many Sauls in the world who will make conscience of little sinnes, & keepe aliue the greatest & the fattest, like the pharisees who did *straine* the gnat & *swallowe* the *camel* [Matt 23:24]. Many are like Herod, who came to Johne his preaching, & heard him gladely, & did many things at his desire. But the fed oxe of incest which laye loweing in a filthy stable would he not kill [Matt 14:4]. Naye, because Johne bade him kill it, he killed Johne.

Let vs learne heere our lesson: let vs not spaire our fattest sinnes, which like the Amalekites cattell, should be put to the edge of the sword. It is a good work to put out the life of sinne. It is a good worke to destroye the workes of the diuell. To doe good & to destroye ill are the good workes of the second creation. We are ordeined by God to walke in them. This is the last point of my texte, viz *that we should walke in* good workes.

In this last part wee shall briefly considder these seuen points: 1. wherefrom we should walke in this spirituall walkeing; 2. whereto; 3. what be the waye; 4. the time of our walkeing; 5. how we should walke; 6. what hinders be in the waye; 7. what helps maye be had.

1. That wherefrom we should walke is the corruption of our nature. From this, the prodigall did walke *when he come to him selfe* againe [Luke 15:17]. He that walketh toward heauen must turne his backe on Sodome, the puddle of pollution. Well is the soule that is turned from that wherein it once tooke pleasure whereof it is now ashamed. This is *terminus a quo.*

2. That whereunto *we should walke in* our good workes, it is glory in the heauens. The Christians pilgrimage is from sinne to grace, & from grace to grace, till at last he come to glory. This Dauid desired in his prayer, sayeing, *thou shalt guide me with thy counsell, & afterward* shalt *receiue me* into *glory* [Ps 73:24]. As from grace to grace, there is a waye, so is there also a waye from grace to glory, yea & from glory to glory. For by *beholding* into *a glasse the glory of the Lord,* we *are changed into the same image from glory to glory* [2 Cor 3:18]. This is *terminus ad quem quo non datur vltra.*[16] Heere end the trauels of the patriarchs. This is the Lords resting place appointed for wearied soules.

3. The waye is Christ & *good workes. I am the waye* [John 14:6], said Christ. Heere it is said *that we should walke in* good workes. *Good workes* are *via regni,* the waye to the kingdome. Christ is both *via regni et causa regnandi,* the waye & cause of

the kingdome. This waye be the prophet is called *the auncient path* [Jer 18:15]. Let this my preaching be like a voice behind you, cryeing vnto you, *this is the waye, walke ye into it, when ye turne to the right hand, & when ye turne to the left* [Isa 30:21]. The prophet Jeremie cryed vnto the people of his time, stand in the wayes; behold & aske for the old waye which is the *good waye, & walke therein, and ye shall find rest* to *your soules* [Jer 6:16]. Christ & good workes are the good old waye. In them alone is rest for the wearied soule. But the merits of workes are the papists new waye, wherein if a man walke, though he should walke to the worlds end, he shall neuer find rest to his soule. There is no man but he that walketh in Christ & good workes that truely can say, and now my soule returne vnto thy rest.

4. The time of our walkeing is the daye time. *The night is farre spent & the daye is at hand* [Rom 13:12], said S. Paul. What inferreth he vpon that? *Let vs walke* [Rom 13:13]. The daye is for workeing & walkeing; the night is for resting. God hath ordeined the night for man to rest. *The night cometh* whereinto *no man can* walke.[17] If death or darkenesse come vpon vs, be where we will, there must we stand like a tree, which must lye *where* it *falleth* [Eccl 11:3]. So long as wee haue life & gospell, we maye walke. Such a time is our daye. Our youth is our morning. Wayefairing men saye ordinarly that it is best to take the morning. Our voyage is long: it is from the earth to the heauens. The daye of our life is short, and we are slowe. Wee are loth to leaue our sinnes, our old companions, with whom we haue beene so much acquainted from the craddle. Our daye is often gone before we haue ended our adewes. We could spend Methusalems yeeres in giueing but our bonay[18] lays to our sinnes, to riot & to *drunkennesse*, to *chambering* & to *wantonnesse*, & to *strife & enuye* [Rom 13:13].[19] We growe graye headed before all our bonay layes be done. If wee were wise, we should make such hast to God that we should not take laiser[20] to turne were it to kisse our father.

Let vs beginne early. Let God get the floure[21] of our age. What should God doe with the dregges of our dayes? What shall God doe with thee? What can thou doe for God after that thou hast spent all thy force in thy sinnes? What shall God doe with thee when thou art become an old rotten, toothlesse, bleared, deafe & coughing creature, a burden to thy selfe, & a cumber[22] vnto others [Eccl 12:2]? Had wee Methusalems yeeres to liue, we would not haue too much time to repent & returne to our God. This we all knowe. Yet Lot will not goe out of Sodome till an angel pull him out by force [Gen 19:1]. We leaue all to the afternoone. We saye all that we shall be wise, & with the sluggard that we shall arise. But while we are, like a doore turning vpon our hings [Prov 26:14], for the most part we die in our foly. Oh, that we were wise.

5. It followeth now that we see how we should walke in this waye. S. Paul biddeth vs walke honestly: walke honestly as in the daye.[23] He walketh honestly who walketh without deceit or guile. Christ, seeing Nathaniel walkeing toward him, called him an honest man. The definition of his honesty was that in his heart was *no guile* [John 1:47]. Secondly, he that walketh in *good workes* must walke circumspectly. It is written of Moses that, before he slewe the Egyptian that oppressed the Israelite, he *looked this waye & that waye* [Exod 2:12]. He had neede to look well about him who would walke in *good workes*. For this cause, Christ commaundeth his simple doves to be *wise* like *serpents* [Matt 10:16]. Thirdly, as we should walke honestly & circumspectly in *good workes*, so must we walke constantly in them more swiftly at the ending then at the beginning. As the naturall motion, so is the motion of grace swiftest toward the end. The longer it hath bene absent & farrer it hath beene off, it cometh the more swiftly the neerer it be to its rest which is God him selfe. Thus shall yee know a faithfull man & an hypocrite. Ye shall knowe them by their walking. Hypocrites will runne fast at the first in mens appearance, but they runne, as did the foolish Galatians to whom S. Paul said, *yee did runne well*, as if he had said, *yee did* once *runne well* [Gal 5:7]. It would be counted but a little praise to saye to a man, yee were once a honest man. The race of the godly is other wise. It is like the race of the sunne that wearieth not into his course, but reioiceth *as a strong man to run a race* [Ps 19:5]. It is good to begin well, but onely *he that* perseuereth *to the end* [. . .] *shall be saued* [Matt 24:13]. The Christians pilgrimage is like a bell-race; he hath neede both of spurre[24] & wand.[25] Happy is the man that hath so run that he maye saye with Paul, *I haue finished my course.*[26] *Henceforth* [. . .] *is laid vp for* [*me*] that man the pryze of the race,

55

viz *a crowne of righteousnesse, which the Lord, the righteous iudge, shall giue* him *at that day.*[27] In this the Christian differs from the hypocrite. The hypocrite will make great haste at the first, but incontinent he lyeth by. But the Christian *finisheth* the *course.* He runneth that he maye obtaine [1 Cor 9:24]. The best of vs is of a lazy nature. We haue all neede to praye with the spouse, *drawe me & wee* shall *run after thee* [Cant 1:4].

6. Now breefly let vs see what hinders, rubs, & lets be whereby we are hindered in our Christian course. There be diuers, some without & some within vs: the heauy flesh & burdens of sinne within vs, Satan & the world about vs. Satan is euer like *dan,* [. . .] *a serpent* in *the waye, an adder in the path.* By his bite, he will cause a man vpon horseback *fall backward* [Gen 49:17]. A fall by the way is a hinder into our race. What are our dayly sinnes in wordes, thoughts, & workes, but the biting of that *adder in the path*? There be burdens also of worldly cares, which hinder much the soule by the waye. There is also lazinesse & want of courage. *There is a lyon in the waye,*[28] saith the sluggard. There be also in the waye *murices ferrei*, the caltraps of diuers temptations, where with the feet of the soule are wounded, except that they be well *shod with the preparation of the gospell* [Eph 6:15]. Last of all, of all hinders, ill companie is not the least. Thus the prophet was hindered in his iourneye by perswasion of that old fals prophet, & so became a praye to a lyon [1 Kgs 13:28]. Thus the Leuite, by counsell of his father in law, was detained so that he was forced to lodge in Gibeah among the sonnes of Belial [Judg 19:12], which had a ferall & fearfull euet.

7. Last of all, let vs see what helps are needfull for to further vs forward in our Christian pilgrimage toward our heauenly Canaan. When Israel made them for the iourneye for to goe out of Egypt toward Canaan, they vsed foure helps for their iourney: 1. they prepaired meete, for they caused kill the lamb of the passeouer; 2. they girded vp their loines; 3. they put shoes on their feet; 4. they had staffes in their hand. All these outward things did represent spirituall helps which we must haue in our iourneye toward heauen. 1. Our soules muste haue meet. While Eliiah was sleeping, the angel bade him arise & eat; & againe he said, *arise & eate* [1 Kgs 19:5], for *the iourneye is* [. . .] *great* [1 Kgs 19:7]. All the food that Elijah got was but

56

a cake baken vpon the coales & a drink of water. But coale baken bread will not feed the soule. The soules food is *the bread of life* that feades to life eternall [John 6:35]. 2. As the Israelites girt vp their loines, so must we *gird vp the loines of* our *mind* [1 Pet 1:13]. Our long side trailing affections must be bund vp that we may runne the waye of Gods commaundements. 3. As the Israelites were shod with shoes for feare of bruising, so must our soules be *shod with the preparation of the gospell* [Eph 6:15]. 4. With all these helps we must haue the staffe of faith, the soules third foot, wherewith we may leape ouer the ditches of all difficulties. Many other helps be required, but these be the speciall wherewith. If we be furnished, we shall walke toward God in the waye of *good workes*; & so at last shall enter into his rest, vnto which the Lord bring vs all, for Christ his Sonne his sake, to whom with the Father & Holy Ghost be honour and maiestie, power & dominion for euer, Amen.

III. On the Need for Church Reform

The Cleansing of the Temple

John 2:13

And the Jewes passeouer was at hand, and Jesus went vp to Jerusalem.
v.14. And found in the temple these that solde oxen, and sheepe, and
doues, and the changers of moneye sitting.
v.15. And when he had made a scourge of small cordes, he droue them
all out of the temple, and the sheepe and the oxen, and powred out
the changers moneye, and ouerthrewe the tables.
v.16. And said vnto them that sold doues, take these things hence;
make not my Fathers house an house of merchandise.
v.17. And his disciples remembered that it was writen, the zeale of
thine house hath eaten me vp.

In this chapter, there be three cheefe things to be considered.
In the first, the euangeliste declareth the historie of Christs first
miracle, whereby in Cana at a mariage he turned water into
wine. In the second part, he sheweth how Christ the Lord
purged the temple by driuing out the buyers and the sellers. In
the third part, the euangelist declareth how the Lord defended
this his fact. In this text, wee haue how the Lord purged the
temple by casting out the buyers and the sellers.

the diuision of the texte

In the wordes of my text, take these foure parts. In the first,
the time of the fact is declared: it was a little before the feast of
the passeouer. Secondly, wee haue the occasion of the purification of the temple: the Lord him selfe found in the temple
those that sold oxen, and sheepe, and doues, and the changers
of the moneye sitting. Thirdly, the euangelist declareth how
the Lord did purge his house: when he had made a scourge of
small cordes, he droue them all out of the temple etc. Last of
all is declared what the sight of this action wrought in the
disciples hearts: his disciples remembered that it was writen, the
zeale of thine house hath eaten me vp. This text is like an eare
of corne. *Spica hac fricanda est,*[1] let vs rubbe it that wee maye
eate it, as the apostles in their hunger did. Blessed is that soule

61

that hath appetit for to eat Gods roll, for it is that meate that feedeth to life eternall [John 6:27].

1 Part
the time

First heere is declared the time when the Lord came to purge the defiled temple of Jerusalem: it was a little before the feast of the passeouer. The Lord vnder the law had commanded his people to keepe a feast vnto him three times in the yeere [Exod 23:14].

The first was in the moneth of *Abib* [Exod 23:15] answerable to our March, by the Greek called the moneth of new fruits, the first moneth of the yeere vnto Israel, because of their comming out of Egypt therein. It was called the feast of vnleuened cakes [Exod 23:15], because, for the space of seuen dayes, the people did eate vnleuened bread, or bread of povertie, in remembrance of their great haste that night they went out of Egypt. This feast was also called the passeouer. The Hebrewe word is *Pesah*,[2] which signifieth *transilitio*, a leaping ouer. The feast was called a passeouer or leaping ouer because that night, wherein the destroyeing angel killed the first borne in euery house of the Egyptians, he did leape ouer the houses of the Isrealites whose vpper doore postes were sprinkled with the blood of the lamb. *When I see the blood*, said the Lord, *I will passe ouer you* [Exod 12:13]. This feast was appointed for a continuall remembrance of their coming out of Egypt in haste [Deut 16:3]. The word imports feare & trembling.

The second feast was called the feast of weekes [Exod 34:22] or of seuens, because it was seuen weekes after the former feast vpon the fiftieth day following [Lev 23:16]; & therefore by the Greekes was called the Pentecost, that is the feast of fiftie. It was also called the feast of haruest [Exod 23:16] because in Canaan, a hote countrey, they at this time beganne their haruest, & in signe of homage and thankefulnesse to God, it was ordained at this feast that men should bring of the first fruits, and giue vnto the Lord as he had blessed them. At the time of this feast, euen fiftie dayes after Israel came out of Egypt, the Lord gaue vnto Israel his law at Mount Sinai. At the same time of the yeere, clouen tongues as of fore appeared and sat vpon the apostles [Acts 2:3].

The third feast of the Jewes was called the feast of ingathering, which was in the end of the yeere when men had gathered in their labours out of the field [Exod 23:16]. This befell in the seuenth moneth, which wee call September, called by the Hebrewes *Ethanim*.[3] It was also called the feast of boothes and of tabernacles [Lev 23:34]. This feast was keept in remembrance of Gods fauour toward Israel in the wildernesse, where they dwelt in boothes or tabernacles made of boughes of greene trees and *willowes of the brooke* [Lev 23:40].

At these three feasts, it behoued euery male of the people to appeare before God [Exod 23:17]. According to this law, the Lord Jesus, by waye of humilitie and obedience, would not be absent from the feast of the Jewes passeouer. For our cause, he was made subiect vnto the law, not onely the morall, but also vnto the ceremoniall law vnder the elements of the world [Gal 4:3]. This was the apostles doctrine: *when the fulnesse of time was come, God sent forth his Sonne, made of a woman, made vnder the law to redeeme them that were vnder the law* [Gal 4:4-5]. For this cause was he circumcised, and, being circumcised, he became a debtour to the whole law [Gal 5:3].

The Doctrine. Obserue heere the wonderfull mercy and loue of Christ, who, for to saue vs from euerlasting bondage became a slaue vnto ceremonies, yea a subiect vnto death. There is no obedience comparable vnto his. If men obeye and serue, it is their duetie. For this cause were they borne. If angels be seruants, it is no wonder, for this end were they created to be ministring spirits [Heb 1:14]. But as for Jesus, he, beeing in the forme of God, and thinkeing it no robbery *to be equall with God* [Phil 2:6], tooke vpon him the fashion of a man and humbled him selfe, not onely to obey ceremonies, beggerly elements, for to deliuer vs from such beggarly fashions, but also *became obedient vnto death, euen the death of the crosse* [Phil 2:8] for to deliuer vs from the curse of God.

The Vse. As the apostle speakeing of this mater said, so say I: *let this mind be in you which was also in Christ Jesus* [Phil 2:5]. Take Christ for a paterne of humilitie, for, except wee followe him in his humilitie, wee shall neuer be exalted in his glory. *Learne of me*, said Christ, *for I am meeke and holy in heart* [Matt

11:29], so also humble in heart. The diuel is a teacher of pride. These who are proud haue the same mind in them which is in the diuel. One day they shall be seene comeing downe like lightining.

The 2 Vse. Let vs be thankefull to Christ who hath deliuered vs from such a burden of ceremonies. What a burden in this one thing that it behoued all the males thrise in the yeere to come to Jerusalem.

2 Part
the occasion of the purification of the temple

In the second part followeth what was the occasion of the purification of the temple. The Lord *went vp to Jerusalem and found in the temple these that solde oxen, and sheepe, and doues, and the changers of moneye sitting.* By such doeings, the house of God was fearefully defiled before the comeing of our Lord. Behold what abuse in the house of God. When Christ Jesus came vnto it, he found these foure abuses specified: first, sellers of oxen; secondly, sellers of sheepe; thirdly, sellers of doues; fourthly, changers of moneyes.

Vnto what was now Gods house like? It was not like a temple, but was rather as one saith well, *bouile, ouile, columbarium,* an oxe stall, a cowe house, a sheepe coate, or a doue house. Thus was the house of God like a stable defiled with cowes and doues doung. Neere vnto all this doung sate the changers of moneye whom S. John heere calleth κερματιστὰς, from the Greeke word, κείρειν, which signifieth *in minuta frusta concidere,* to cut into small pieces. Beza[4] heere expoundeth the Greeke word, *nummularios,* that is bankers or that make gaine by changeing of moneye. In the verse followeing, the euangelist hath κολλυβιστῶν, which signifieth *trapezita,*[5] one who for gaine giueth small moneyes for to change pieces of siluer or gold. All this was done vnder a shadowe of pietie that these who came to Jerusalem might find oxen, sheepe, and doues in all readinesse for Gods sacrifice; and also the changers of moneye in the temple would seeme to further the service of God by fur-nisheing exchange in all readinesse to these that desired to buy

64

beasts or soules for sacrifice. But their cheefe end was but worldly gaine.

The Doctrine. Obserue heere how sinne and iniquitie couereth it selfe with the garments of pietie. There is no such wickednesse committed against God in his worship, but men will find a faire cloak for the same. When Saul had receiued direction from God to destroy Amalek, he spared the best of the spoile vnder a shewe of pietie, for thereof to make sacrifices vnto the Lord [1 Sam 15:21]. When Jeroboam, fearing that if the people should goe vp to Jerusalem, their heart should returne againe vnto their Lord, deuised two calues of gold, the one to be set in Bethel, the other in Dan. Behold how he couered this euill action with a shewe of the peoples commoditie. All this, said he, is for your ease, for *it is too much for you to goe vp to Jerusalem* [1 Kgs 12:28]. So the murder of Nabeth by Ahab and Jezabel was couered by a fast [1 Kgs 21:9], so these men of my text did couer their filthie gaine with shewes of godlinesse.

The apostle speakeing of godlinesse calleth godlinesse great gaine [1 Tim 6:6], but many men esteeme gaine to be godlinesse. Where gold is mans god, there gaine is godlinesse [1 Tim 6:5]; and where gaine is godlinesse, there Gods vengeance lieth at the doore. A popish writer vpon this place hath a good obseruation vpon it. Obserue, said he, that the wrath of God and vtter extriminion was neere vnto this people of the Jewes, *cum eorum religio maxime ad auaritiam declinasset: quod si verum est, imo quia verum est, merito tremendum nobis est, nam et nostra religio plane ad quastum et auaritiam declinauit*,[6] that is the destruction of the Jewes was neere when their religion beganne to decline to couetousnesse, which if it be true, yea, because it is true, wee haue great cause to feare, because our religion is altogether set for filthie gaine. Wee haue a great reason in these dayes to complaine that men, for the most part in the Church vnder glorious colours of godlinesse, are seekeing no thing but their owne aduancement to make vp great estats to their posteritie.[7] They are so exercised in posting after fauours at kings courts that they forget God, their flock, and them selues, and so become beasts before God, asses and sheepe, so that the temple of God by their presence is turned into a cow house or sheepe house.

The Vse. Let vs beware of vaine shewes of pietie which is

65

but hypocrisie. But cheefely let vs beware of couetousnesse, the cause of all the hypocrisie of these men of my text. It is of all sinnes most dangerous and most abhorred of God; it is the root of all euill and so in sinning sinne. The apostle calleth it idolatrie [Col 3:5]. When once church men beginne to be φιλάγγυροὶ, they will sell Christ him selfe with Judas for siluer. They will bring into the temple to be preachers oxen and sheepe men that can no more preach then an asse, a cowe, or a sheepe. *His afinis obstruat ora deus,*[8] the Lord close the mouthes of such, and make a faire and a free waye to these whose lips God hath touched with a liue coale from his altar [Isa 6:6-7].[9]

3 Part
how the Lord did purge his house

In the third part of my text, the euangelist declareth how the Lord did purge his house of such corruptions. *And when he had made a scourge of small cordes, he droue them all out of the temple, and the sheepe and the oxen, and powred out the changers moneye, and ouerthrewe the tables. And said vnto them that sold doues, take these things hence, and make not my Fathers house a house of merchandise.* Here are *verba et verbera.*[10] In these wordes, the euangelist declareth foure things which the Lord did: first, he made a scourge of small cordes; secondly, he droue them all out of the temple, and the sheepe, and the oxen; thirdly, he powred out the changers moneye, and ouerthrewe the tables; fourthly, he commanded these that sold doues to take their doues awaye, and not to make his Fathers house a house of merchandise.

First, it is said that the Lord him selfe made a scourge of small cordes. In the originall, it is φραγέλλιον ἐκ σχοινίων, the scourge is heere called φραγέλλιον, which is not a proper Greeke word, but is turned from the Latin word *flagellum.* Diuers other wordes of this sorte occurre in the New Testament as κουστωδία πραιτώριον σπεκουλάτορ. The word that is inter- preted heere a scourge signifieth properly the small braunches or twigges of a tree. Of such were made scourges or whips. Heere it is said that the Lord made this scourge ἐκ σχοινίων, of small cordes. The Hebrewes call a scourge *shot*, from turning a thing a round about or from compassinge. Satan said he came without from compassing [Job 1:7].

The Doctrine. Obserue heere, when the Lord is offended by men, he will not want a scourge wherewith to correct them, *a whip for the horse*, and *a bridle for the asse, and a rod for the fooles backe* [Prov 26:3]. As the scourge of Christ heere was made of many cordes, so hath the Lord many afflictions for the sinnes of the godly, and many iudgements for the sinnes of the wicked.

The 1 Vse. Let this serue for instruction to teach vs to beware of sinne, for it is the seede of sorrowe. If wee multiplie our sinnes, God shall multiplie our sorrowes, famine, sword, pestilence, distresse of estate, troubles of mind, sicknesse of body. Diuers sortes of death are like the many cordes of Christs scourge wherewith he correcteth these that worship him not in spirit and trueth [John 4:23].

The 2 Vse. Let this serue for reproofe to these who sinne securely against the Lord, and still dreame of immunitie from Gods iudgements. Wee, say they, *haue made a covenant with death, and with hell are we at agreement; when the ouerfloweing scourge shall passe thorow, it shall not come vnto vs, for wee haue made lies our refuge* [Isa 28:15].

The Doctrine. Againe, whereas it is said that the Lord made this scourge of small cordes, I obserue that the Lord in wrath remembers mercy. He tooke not great cordes but small cordes; he tooke not a sword in his hand to cut them into pieces, as Samuel did to Agag [1 Sam 15:33]. Neither tooke he vp an yron barre for to *dash them into pieces like a potters vessell* [Ps 2:9]; but, like a father, he made a scourge of small cordes for to correct them like children.

The Vse. When God sendeth vnto vs light afflictions, gentle visitations, let vs turne vnto him from our euill wayes. The small cordes of such afflictions tell vs what wee haue done, and that our Lord is offended, and that wee doe no more foolishly. But if men continue in euill doeing, let them knowe that the Lord hath a scourge of great cordes, of great iudgements, which shall be the destruction both of their soules and bodies.

Secondly, it followeth that wee heare what the Lord did with this scourge: it is said heere first that he droue them out of the temple, and the sheepe and the oxen with them. In the originall, it is ἐξέβαλεν, *eiecit*, he cast, thrust, or flang out; and

67

though he had a scourge in his hand, it is not said that he did strike therewith, but he droue them out or cast them out by the terrour of the whip that was in his hand.

The Doctrine. Obserue heere how vnwilling the Lord is to strike his owne creatures. If the feare of his scourge seene can driue men to their duetie, his stroakes will be fewe. The Lord is wonderfull in mercy, and can not strike except that he be sore prouoked; his iudgements are called his strange worke. Strange sinnes enter into a nation, temple, citie, or familie before the Lord make a scourge for to driue men out of either nation, temple, city, or familie.

The Vse. Let vs beware to prouoke the Lord in this great light of so glorious a gospel, for, after a long forbearance, *the ouerfloweing scourge shall passe thorow* [Isa 28:15]; and the Lord shall driue vs from our countreye, and shall cast vs out of his house, and out of our owne houses where wee haue prouoked the eyes of his glory. These men were driuen out of the temple because they had offended God in the temple. So the sinnes of a people make Gods temple, their houses, or the land, to spewe out the inhabitants. Where the place where the Lord is frequently offended is at last compelled to spewe. If a king be vicious, his throne will spewe him out; if nobles be vicious, their greatest towers, sicke of their sinnes, shall spewe them out; if magistrats be bribers proude or carelesse, their places of honour, sicke of their pride, shall spewe them out; if ministers be sluggards and careless in their callings, their chires[11] shall spewe them out; if the people be given to vice, not careing for Gods word preached vnto them, the land shall spewe them out.

How is this that, of all degrees, wee see so many driuen from their station and others in their place? It is the Lord, who with his scourge hath driuen them from their thrones, towers, places, pulpits, and their habitations of ease. He who continues to prouoke the Lord to anger is worthy to smart in all the veines of his heart. He who within the temple will not serue God as he should, let him be thrust out at doores. He who within doores prouoketh still his God, let him be with these who stand without, and who at last shall without comfort cry, Lord, Lord, open vnto vs. He who without conscience walketh in his wayes, were he a lord or a king, let him looke at last to be driuen from his station. With God is no respect of persones. King Saul, King

Ahab, Jeroboam were kings, but, because they honoured not him that had honoured them, he scourged them from their thrones, and cast downe their crownes to the ground. Judas was an apostle, but, because he was a theefe, the Lord sent him vnto his owne place [Acts 1:25]. Corah, Dathan, and Abiram, with their companie, were *princes of the assembly*, and *famous in the congregation*, and *men of renowne* [Num 16:2]; but because they were princes of faction and of rebellion against the Lord, *the Lord made a new thing, the earth opened her mouth and swallowed them vp* [Num 16:30].

According to that of the Psalme with the froward [Ps 18:26], God wrestleth or speweth him selfe froward. Let vs therefore heere learne to be no more froward. If wee sinne, the Lord will make a scourge at the first bit of small cordes, but, if we continue in our sinnes, he will scourge vs with scorpions, yea break all our bones with the yron barres of his wrath [Ps 2:9]. Jerusalem was at the first scourged but with Christs small coardes, but because they would not weepe and repent, the Romane emperour[12] was sent to scourge them with swordes, to burne their temple, and make slaues of them selues.

Obserue also heere that it is said that he also droue out the sheepe and the oxen. Dauid, in another purpose, said, *but these sheepe what haue they done* [2 Sam 24:17]? All the creatures faire the worse for the sinnes of men for their cause: the Lord curseth the fruit of their land, the increase of their kine, and the flockes of their sheepe [Deut 28:18], and also the fruit trees of their land. The apostle saith that *the whole creation groaneth & trauaileth in paine together* [Rom 8:22]: behold how the whole frame of this world is said to suffer and to groane vnder the sinnes of men; behold how man hath procured to all the creatures much woe and mischeefe. Before man sinned, he liued on the fruits of the trees. After that sinne came into the world, the beasts, fishes, and foules lost their life for to nourish him; and thousands of them died by sacrificeing that in their death man might see his owne deseruings, and also might be taught by such shadowes to come vnto Jesus, that onely sacrifice which hath made peace betweene the heauens and the earth for the sinnes of men. All creatures belowe are subiect to vanitie. Againe, whereas it is said heere that the Lord droue out the sheepe and the oxen, he thereby did declare that all such beastly sacrifices were at an end. When the bodie is come, the shadowes must flie awaye. One of these wordes saith well, *tempus erat vt cessaret figura veritasque succederet*,[13] the time of types and figures was now at an end because the trueth and substance was come.

Thirdly, the euangelist heere declareth particularly what the Lord did to the changers of moneye: it is said that he powred out the changers moneye and ouerthrewe the tables. First, he cast downe their moneyes; secondly, he ouerthrewe the tables whereupon they did count the moneyes that they should not so easily continue their traficke. Doubtlesse these covetous men were in a great rage when they sawe their moneyes powred out, and their tables, the instruments of their gaine, throwen downe. Their moneyes were dearer vnto them then Micahs images of siluer, which when they were taken from him he cried, and *what haue I more* [Judg 18:24]? And what had these men more? They had lost their gaine, their god. Their little gods were powred out by the hand of Christ. The tables, the instruments of their gaine, were ouerthrowen; and what had they more?

The Doctrine. Obserue heere that these, who with the dishonour of God or preiudice of the good cause shall meddle with moneyes for their propre profit, shall at last find all their profit cast into a bottomelesse bagge. What they haue receiued from the hands of men shall be powred out by the hand of God, and they and theirs shall be ouerthrowen like these tables set in the temple by the changers of moneye.

The Vse. Let vs not labour for that which will at last be powred out and will perish. Let vs goe to the house of God to seeke aduantage, but let it be the aduantage of Christ. Our blood, our life, our soules may be powred out like the moneye of the changers; but the aduantage of Christ shall neuer be powred out, for he is aduantage both in life and death [Philip 1:21]. He who preferreth moneye vnto Christ and his glory shall, with Simon Magus, perish with his moneye [Acts 8:20].

Fourthly, it followeth that wee heare what the Lord said to the sellers of doues: he commanded them to take their doues awaye out of the temple. *Take*, said he, *these things hence*, and *make not my Fathers house a house of merchandise*. Heere are two things, a precept and a reason. The precept, take these things hence.

The Doctrine. Obserue heere that the Lord dealeth more gently with the sellers of doues then with these that sold the sheepe and oxen. As for them, he droue them out and also droue out the sheepe and oxen. But to the sellers of doues, he said, *take these things hence* etc. The sellers of doues were but of the poorer sorte. As one obserueth well, *columbo erant pauperum mercimonia*, doues were the wares of poore ones. In this they were more to be excused then the rich changers of moneye and sellers of oxen; and yet their sinne is reproued by the Lord: *take these things hence*.

The Vse. Let no man pretend any thing, whether pouerite or necessitie whatsoeuer, to an euill action were it but to gather stickes on the sabbath day [Num 15:32]. What God hath forbidden to be done, necessitie must not pleade for it. Wee can not liue except that wee sell doues in the temple might many of these poore ones haue said. But the Lord passing by all such things said vnto them, *take these things hence*: vnlawfull gaine will neuer make a man rich. It is the Lord, said Job, that giueth [Job 1:21]. Wee haue heard of the precept, *take these things hence*. The reason is subioined: Gods house must not be made a house of merchandise. *Make not my Fathers house*, said the Lord, *a house of merchandise*. While he calleth the temple, which was Gods house, his Fathers house, he did let them see by what autoritie he did these things. Seeing he was the Sonne of God, it belonged vnto him to be carefull for his Fathers house. The apostle, compareing Christ with Moses, saith that Moses was faithfull in all Gods house as a seruant [Heb 3:5], but *Christ as a sonne* [Heb 3:6]. Not as a sonne as wee are, who are but by adoption, but he was the sonne by an eternall and vnspeakable generation, and so was the Lord and master of the house.

The Vse. Let vs who are but sonnes by adoption learne of Christ, the naturall sonne, to be carefull that God our Father be not dishonoured. If naturall affection be so strong in the hearts of children for the honour of their earthly parents, how strong should our spirituall affections be for the glory of God, our heauenly Father, who honoured vs with the honour of his children, after that he had found vs cast out in the open field to the loathing of our persone polluted in our owne blood [Ezek 16:6], beasts, dogges and swine, all full of botches, boiles, and putrifyeing sores [Isa 1:6]. That which he reproueth is that

71

they had made his Fathers house οἴκον ἐμπορίου, a house of merchandise. In Mathew he reproued such merchands more sharpely, saying that they of Gods house had made *a denne of theeues* [Matt 21:13]; in effect, they are but theeues, who of Gods house make a house of merchandise. Such merchands can not be true but must be fals men, double deceiuers, for what but deceit can be in the heart of man that feareth not God? The merchand that feares not God must be a theefe, for such a man maketh no conscience to deceiue; if he can catch aduantage, he careth not how. But of all theeues, he that maketh of Gods house a house of merchandise is the greatest theefe.

The Doctrine. Obserue heere in what estate the house of God was when Christ came: it was become a house of merchandise, yea and a denne of theeues; and therefore it was high time for Christ to come with his scourge. The corruptions that are now presently in Gods house clearly declare that the Lord is not farre off. It was long since said, *omnia Roma cum pretio coelum quoque*,[14] all things are to be sold at Rome. Yea the heauens also, the forgiuenesse of sinnes, Gods free gift is sold at a rate according to the nature of the sinne. Thus haue the papists this day turned Gods house into a house of merchandise. Well to them may be said, as to the pharisees among the Jewes, *nundinatio est tota vestra pietas; templum est forum et emporium potius quam schola pietatis*, all your pietie is but a buying and a selling; your temple is rather a faire or market then a schoole of godlinesse.

The 1 Vse. Let vs in the reformed Church learne to beware of such merchandise, for if once wee beginne to buy and sell in Gods house, which should be a house of prayer, wee shall not faile to feele the scourge of God vpon vs. Christ either by one iudgement or other shall sweepe vs like dung out of his sanctuary.

The 2 Vse. Let this serue for reproofe to these disciples of Simon Magus, who enter into the service of the ministrie by bribes [Acts 8:20], some buying and some selling the gifts of God for moneye. The day shall come that such shall repent such bargaines, when Christ, the master of the house, shall in his day scourge their conscience, not with small cordes, with the greatest cordes of his wrath.

The 3 Vse. Let this also serue for reproofe to these who not

72

onely make merchandise in Gods house but also sell the house it selfe, euen them selues, as Ahab sold him selfe vnto wickednesse. *Knowe yee not*, said the apostle, *that yee are the temple of God* [1 Cor 3:16]? If any man defile the temple of God, him shall God destroye. Sinnes and iniquities as riot and drunkenesse; chambering and wantonnesse; strife and envie; malice, murder, and deceit; and other such sinnes are no thing but the selling of mens soules, a defiling of the body, the temple of God. And therefore, if without repentance wee continue to defile this temple, wee shall one day knowe the trueth of this threatning: if any defile the temple of God, him shall God destroye. Wee must not sell our selues vnto sinne, for wee are not our owne but *bought with a price* [1 Cor 6:20]. Woe to these who defile the temple of God with such merchandise. And what I say against the profaners of Gods house, that I say also against the profaners of his day. Men, who for filthy lucre spare not this day, may well be said, make not the Lords day a day of merchandise, a day of labour. Many will not giue eare vnto this vntill the scourge of God either come vpon their soule, or their body, or their estate, or their children. He, who on the Lords day will not rest from his labours in this world, shall find no rest in the world to come. Woes for euermore shall be vnto him who, after he hath toiled all his life seekeing the earth, can not say at his death, and now my soule returne vnto thy rest. He that will not rest when God commands him to rest shall find no rest when he shall desire to rest.

4 Part
what this reformation wrought in the hearts of the apostles

In the last part of the text, the euangelist declareth what effect the purgeing of the temple by Christ had in the apostles hearts. It is said, *and his disciples remembered that it was writen, the zeale of thine house hath eaten me vp*. Heere first is a commendation of the apostles memorie that they remembered that portion of scripture.

The Vse. Let vs striue to fill our memories with Gods word, that in all occasions wee thereby may be instructed and directed.

73

It is said to the euerlasting praise of Marie that she keept Gods word in her heart [Luke 2:51].

The 2 Vse. Let this serue for reproofe to these who haue no memorie for Gods word, but haue a strong memorie to remember iniuries done vnto them by men. I say they will forgiue him, but I will neuer forget. Gods words and his benefits are soone forgoten, but, alas, often our memories are filled with beastly baggage, either of mighty tastes, or of abominable sinnes.

Now let vs consider that which the apostles are said heere to haue remembered: it is said that they remembered that it was writen, *the zeale of thine house hath eaten me vp*. These wordes were first spoken by Dauid in the threescore and ninth psalme where he said, *I am become a stranger vnto my brethren, and an aliant*[15] vnto my mothers children, for the zeale of thine house hath eaten me vp [Ps 69:8-9]. As Dauid in his afflictions was deserted by his neerest and dearest friends, as if he had beene a stranger, so the Lord Jesus was forsaken by his seruants the apostles; and as Dauid had an eating zeale moueing his desire wonderfully to build a house for the Lord, so the Lord Jesus had a most feruent zeale to purge the house of God, which mercenarie men had defiled with their merchandise. For this cause, it is said that the zeale of Gods house did eate him vp.

To the end wee may vnderstand these wordes the better, wee shall first consider what zeale is. Secondly, I shall declare diuers sortes of zeale whereof mention is made in scripture. Thirdly, I shall consider the sense of these wordes, *the zeale of thine house hath eaten me vp*.

1. what zeale is

Zeale cometh of the Greeke word, ζέω, which signifieth to be feruent, hote as fire, and signifieth in scripture a most earnest and ardent desire either to doe a thing or to hinder a thing to be done.

2. the diuers sortes of zeale

As the doeing or hindering of a thing is either lawfull or vnlawfull, so the zeale that carieth men in such actions is either good or bad. As for lawfull zeale, it is either in God or man. The zeale of God is that most earnest loue which he hath for his owne glory and the well of his Church. In this sense, the prophet Isaiah, speaking what ioy shall be in the midst of afflictions by the kingdome and birth of Christ [Isa 9:6-7],[16] saith the zeale of the Lord of hostes shall performe this. As for the zeale of man which is lawfull in doeing of good, it is a holy desire either to imitate or goe beyond others in well doeing, proceeding from a sound knowledge and hearty loue of God and our neighbour. According to this, Gods people is called a people zealous of good workes [Titus 2:14]. The forewardnesse of the Corinthiens in ministering to the distressed saints is called their zeale. *Your zeale*, said the apostle, *hath provoked very many* [2 Cor 9:2].

The zeale of hindering euill things is in my text whereby the Lord, beeing vehemently inflamed, did with his scourge driue the buyers and the sellers out of the temple. As for vnlawfull zeale, it is a fierce and fiery bitternesse in a bad cause. Concerning this zeale, Paul in his ignorance persecuted the Church [Philip 3:6]. Profane men often haue great earnestnesse and affection in good things, but faile both in the maner and end. Such was the zeale of Jehu [2 Kgs 10:16], who did well in executing that which was right in Gods eyes by sheding the blood of Jezreel, for which he was rewarded with the throne vntill his fourth generation. But because he did it not with an vpright heart, the Lord said that he would *avenge the blood of Jezreel vpon the house of Jehu* [Hos 1:4]. The zeale of Christ in my text was goode both in the mater and maner and also in the end thereof, for it was all for the glory of God. It was in Christ in so great a measure that it is said to haue eaten him vp. *The zeale of thine house*, said he, *hath eaten me vp.*

3. how the zeale of Christ did eate him vp

Last of all, let vs consider how the zeale of Christ heere is said to haue eaten him vp. The word in the original is κατέφαγε, which is interpreted *deuoraunt*, hath deuoured me. The zeale of God is said to deuoure or eate vp a man, when he preferreth the glory of God vnto him self and vnto all that concerneth him. As a thing that is deuoured or eaten vp is no more in account, so he that is eaten vp by zele for the glory of God accounteth no thing of him selfe, if so be he can aduance the glory of his God. So Moses was so forward for the glory of God that his zeale in a maner did eate vp the saluation of his soule, so that before his God should be dishonoured, he choised to be bloted out of Gods booke [Exod 32:33]. The zeale of Phineas did so eate him vp that with a iavelin he thrust thorow Zimzi and Cosbi [Num 25:7-8][17] in the act of their whooredome. The zeale of Elias did eate him vp. *I*, said he, *haue bene very iealous for the Lord* [. . .] *of hostes* [1 Kgs 19:14]. The zeale of Steuen did eate him vp when he said vnto the Jewes, *yee stiffnecked and vncircumcised in heart and eares, yee doe alwayes resist the holy Ghost. As your fathers did, so doe yee* [Acts 7:51]. But as for the zeale of Christ Jesus, it was like Goliahs sword: it had none like it. It was pure and perfect, both in the matter and maner and in the end thereof. It was within him like a consumeing fire because he sawe his Fathers house dishonoured. The scripture heere saith that it did eate him vp.

The 1 Vse. Let this serue for instruction for to teach vs with Elias to be very iealous for the Lord of hostes [1 Kgs 19:14], yea and with Christ our Lord to be eaten vp. If yee would knowe who are eaten with that holy zeale, S. Augustin declares the same clearly, *Quis comeditur zelo domus Dei? Qui omnia qui forte ibi vndet perversa, satagit emendare, cupit corrigere, non quiescit; si emendare non potest tolerat, gemit.*[18] That is, who is eaten vp with the zeale of Gods house? He who endeauours to amend that which is euill, who desires to correct it, and taketh not rest, if he can not cure the same he suffers and groanes. Let our zeale be thus exercised that wee may be eaten vp thereby.

The 2 Vse. Let this serue for reproofe to these whose zeale wants teeth so that it cannot eate them. He is not worthy to eate who in some measure is not eated vp with the zeale of Gods house. If the zeale of Gods glory eate vs not vp, his wrath shall consume vs, for our God is a consumeing fire, to him be glory for euer and euer, Amen.

Mercy for Zion

Ps 102:13

Thov shalt arise and haue mercy vpon Zion, for the time to fauour her, yea the set time is come.

Times of ioye are for songs, but dayes of sorrowe should be past in prayer; the dayes wherein wee liue call vs to mourning and to sackcloth. God from the heauens this day hath said, *blow the trumpet in Zion, sanctifie a fast, call a solemne assembly, gather the people, sanctifie the congregation, assemble the elders, gather the children and these that sucke the breasts, let the bridegroome goe foorth of his chamber and the bride out of her closet, let the priests and ministers of the Lord weepe betweene the porch and the altar, and let them say, spare thy people O Lord* [Joel 2:15-17].

This is the summe of my text this day: that the Lord would spare his people. *Thou shalt arise and haue mercy vpon Zion* etc. In this psalme, the psalmist prayeth earnestly that God would haue compassion on his Church greeuously oppressed in the captivitie of Babylon.

the diuision of the text

In the wordes which I haue reade, there be two parts. In the first part, there is a prayer, *thou shalt arise and haue mercy vpon Zion*. In the second part, there is an argument whereby the Lord may be moued to deliuer his people; and that in these wordes, *for the time to fauour her, yea the set time is come*.

1 Part
the prayer

The wordes of the psalmists prayer are these, *thou shalt arise and haue mercy vpon Zion*.

Before I consider the wordes, I shall first obserue the forme of this prayer: it is full of faith which is ἐλπιζομένων ὑπόστασις πραγμάτων ἐλέγχος οὐ βλεπομένων, *the substance of things hoped for, the evidence of things not seene* [Heb 11:1]. I say this prayer is full of faith, yea, and in forme a prophecie that God will not faile to deliuer his people. *Thou shalt arise and haue mercy vpon Zion.* So in another place, *thou shalt guide me with they counsell* [Ps 73:24].

The Vse. Let vs learne heere how wee should seeke any thing from the Lord. It must not be done with a heart sicke of the palsey, trembling with doubts, or staggering like a drunkard. No not, but wee must so pray in faith that wee may say to God, thou shalt arise and graunt me my desires. This was the praise of Abraham: he staggered not at the promises of God. This was the praise of Moses when he was compassed with difficulties on all sides. He in a strong faith said to Israel, *stand still and* yee shall *see the saluation of the Lord* [Exod 14:13]. S. James counsell is good: if any of you lacke any thing, *let him aske of God* [Jas 1:5], but *let him aske in faith no thing wauering* [Jas 1:5]. If he wauer, *let not that man thinke that he shall receiue any thing of the Lord* [Jas 1:6-7]. Wee haue many things to seeke from God this day, and for this cause wee must, with Hannah, powre out our sowles before the Lord in prayer [1 Sam 1:15]. But let vs take good heede that wee stagger not, but stand still with Moses vntill wee see the saluation of the Lord.

Now let vs come to the wordes of the prayer. *Thou*, said the psalmist, *shalt arise and haue mercy vpon Zion.* Heere be two petitions: first, that the Lord would arise; secondly, that he would *haue mercy vpon Zion.* First, he saith, *thou shalt arise*: that is as one saith well, *serio te comparabis ad hoc opus,*[1] thou shalt with all diligence make thee redy for to help vs. This is a forme of speach borrowed from the fashions of men, for God properly neither setteth, nor ariseth, nor walketh. If he would sit, where is the chire he should sit in? If he would walke from what place, and to what place should he goe? Behold, said Solomon, the *heauens of heauens can not containe thee* [1 Kgs 8:27]. Seeing it is so, when God is said to arise, it is from the fashions of men, who, when they haue an earnest desire to help their friend in danger, arise from their places with all diligence. On the other part, when God seemeth to our weake faith to neglect vs and to misregard our prayers, he is said to sit or to sleepe. The psalmist, complaining that Gods children for his sake were killed all the day long, cryed and to God in his prayer, *Awake,*

78

why sleepest thou O Lord? Arise, cast vs not off for euer [Ps 44:23]. So heere Gods people in great distresse cryeth vnto God, *thou shalt arise*.

The Doctrine. The doctrine I obserue heere is this: wonderfull is the mercy of God towards man who debaseth him selfe to speake vnto man in his owne language, or to suffer man to speake vnto him wordes which can not expresse the glory of his maiesty.

The Vse. Let vs heere learne both to speake to God and of God with all reverence. Wee are full of infirmities, but as a father pitieth children, so doeth the Lord pitie these that feare him. If wee feare Him, he will be our Father. A father will be more moued with the halfe wordes of his deare child then with all the eloquence of the most famous oratours. *Thou shalt arise*, that is, O Lord arise, and prepare thy selfe to help vs. This is the petition that wee haue all to make to God this day, that he would now arise. The Church of this land, yea the whole body of this land, is in a feuer. Except the Lord arise, it shall be a sicknesse vnto death. If your father, mother, husband, wife, children were sicke of a dangerous disease, yee would with all hast runne to the physition cryeing, arise and come with speede. When Christ was sleeping in the ship sore tossed with a tempest, these that were in the ship were wonderfully afraide, for the sea was so troubled that the ship was covered with waues [Matt 8:24]. While his disciples saw the danger, they *came to him and awoke him, saying, Lord saue vs wee perish* [Matt 8:25]. It is so that wee should doe this day. Our Church is like a ship on the sea. There is a wonderfull commotion in this land: the Church, like a ship, is almost all covered with waues. Christ to many seemeth to be lying, and he seemeth to be sleeping. This great day is appointed by the Church for old and young, rich and poore to cry vnto the Lord that he would awake and arise, and haue mercy vpon Zion.

Now dearely beloued, would yee be instructed how to moue the Lord to heare your prayer to awake and arise. Obeye yee his precept, and he shall heare your prayer. His precept is this: *awake thou that sleepest, and arise from the dead, and Christ shall giue thee light* [Eph 5:14]. If wee sleepe on in sinne, He will not awake for our cryes. *If I regard iniquitie in my heart*, said the psalmist, *the Lord will not heare me*.[2] If wee lye still in the death bed of securitie and refuse to arise from the dead, the Lord of life will refuse to our help. These who set at nought Gods counsell [Prov 1:25] shall heare God laughing at their calamitie, and mocking at their feare when their destruction shall come vpon them as a whirle wind.

The second petition heere is that God would haue mercy vpon the Church and whole estate. *Thou shalt arise and haue mercy vpon Zion.* By Zion is not onely vnderstood the Church because in Davids dayes the ark was there, but also the commoun wealth, for on it was a strong hold and diuers faire houses, which Dauid there did build for which cause it was called the citie of Dauid [2 Sam 5:7]. So while the psalmist prayed God heere to haue mercy vpon Zion, he desired him to take a care both of the Church and policie, for all was decayed. This wee must know, that the Church and commoun wealth are like two twinnes which haue such a sympathie that they are both sicke and whole together, both white and rudie together, both sicke and pale together, for religion putteth life, strength, and courage into men to stand fast in the maintenance of the liberties of a kingdome.

The strength of God is with such so that all hearts faint before them and can make no resistance. *Fiue of you*, said God, *shall chase an hundred; and an hundred of you shall put ten thousand to the flight* [Lev 26:8]. But O if the palace of David be honoured on Zion, but not the arke of God. If religion growe pale and sick with the euill honours of mans inventions, then all sortes of miserie are in post hast comeing against that land. All the glory of that land shall wither and fall downe like Jonahs gourd.[3] Their riches shall decay, their siluer shall be turned into tinne, and their gold shall become coper; and the vilest shall be set vpon high places, and the worthiest shall sit at their foot stoole. Thus all shall be turned vpside downe, if while men giue vnto Cesar that which is Cesars, they neglect to giue vnto God that which is Gods. That both may goe well, the arke and the palace, the prayer heere is made that God would haue mercy vpon Zion. Heere is a salue for all the sores of Zion: that God would haue mercy vpon Zion. If the Church be wounded, heere is the balme of Gilead, that God would haue mercy vpon Zion. If the commoun wealth be sicke, heere is the onely remedie, that God would haue mercy vpon Zion.

Let us consider what the psalmist heere cheefely seeketh for Zion: it is mercy. *Thou shalt arise and haue mercy vpon Zion.* Obserue heere that he cryeth not for vengeance against the enemies of Zion, but that the Lord would haue mercy vpon Zion.

The Vse. Let vs heere learne how in these dayes of trouble wee should behaue our selues. Let our exercise be cheefely to seeke mercy from the God of heauen, as for our enemies that trouble Zion. Let vs learne of Christ what to say. As he said of his enemies [Luke 23:34], let vs say of ours, Father forgiue them, if there be any forgiueness appointed for them. But if they be Gods enemies imploieing their wits and counsells against our Zion, both Church and commoun wealth, the Lord confound the counsells of Ahitophels. If they be haters of Zion, who of our Zion would make a Babylon? *Let them all be confounded and turned back that hate Zion; let them be as the grasse vpon the house tops, which withereth afore it groweth vp* [Ps 129:5-6]. All the curses that euer were heard from Heball make all their designes with them selues to be *like the chaffe, which the wind driueth away* [Ps 1:4]. Let them goe with all the curses of God like vagabonds with Cain. Where euer they dwell, were it in kings palaces, let sinne lie at their doore [Gen 4:7].

But as for vs, our cheefest exercise this day must be to intreat God to haue mercy vpon our Zion. My reason is this: if wee had not sinned, wee should not haue seene such traitours, troubles, and confusions this day both in Church and commoun wealth. Though wicked men haue a hand in the businesse, it is our owne wickednesse that is the cheefe cause of all our evills, our riot, our drunkenesse, our chambering, our wantonnesse, our strife, our envie [Rom 13:13]. The land is defiled with idolatrie. God and the masse will no more agree together then the arke and Dagon.[4] The land is defiled with blasphemie. The name of God is abused, and cold are the advocats that pleade for him. The sabbath day is profaned, fathers and mothers and magistrats are contemned, the land is defiled with blood and blood toucheth blood. Adulterers breake out more frequently then fornications in other nations; vilest incests goe away vnpunished, fathers with their daughters, brethren with sisters, brethren in law with their sisters in law. For ceremonies, men shall be hunted and more diligently searched for then Saul searched Dauid. But such crying sinnes meete with deafe eares. Stealing and lying are in all places of this land. For such and such sinnes, and more then I can number, the Lord, who knoweth them all, hath a controversie with this land [Hos 4:1].

Except the Lord haue mercy vpon our Zion, the day is fast comeing wherein all the lamentations of Jeremie shall not be able sufficiently to expresse our calamities; and therefore it is our duetie in this day to bend all the powers of our soule, and with fasting and prayer to cast out these euill sortes of sinnes, which are like that sorte of diuels who would not remoue from their possessions in the poore man, except they were constrained by the force of fasting and prayer [Matt 17:21]. By fasting and prayer, divells are ouercome; by fasting and prayer, all sortes of sinnes are ouercome; by teares and prayers, Jacob ouercame God him selfe [Hos 12:4]. *Preces et lachryma sunt arma ecclesia*, tears and prayers are the weapons of the Church. Let vs now muster with these weapons and come vpon the Lord by violence, beeing fully resolued not to let him goe vntill he arise and haue mercy vpon our Zion.

2 Part

In the second part, the psalmist bringeth an argument to moue God to haue mercy vpon Zion.

the argument
the time to fauour her was come

The argument is in these wordes: *for the time to fauour her, yea the set time is come.* Some referre this set time to the end of the seuentie yeeres of their captivitie in Babylon. The Lord gaue his promise by Jeremie to his people that, at the end of these seventie yeeres, he would deliuer them, and make them to returne to their owne countreye. The wordes of his promise are very remarkable. *After seuentie yeeres [. . .] accomplished at Babylon*, said the Lord, *I will visit you and performe my good word towards you in causing you to returne to this place. For I knowe the thoughts that I thinke towards you*, saith the Lord, *thoughts of peace and not of euill, to giue you an expected end.* [Jer 29:10-11]. *And yee shall seeke me and find me, when yee shall search for me with all your heart* [Jer 29:13]. Behold the promise of God giuing vnto his people a set time of deliuerance. When the set time is come, they cry vnto him to arise and *haue mercy vpon Sion, for the time to fauour,* for *yea the set time is come.*

The Vse. Let vs heere learne to lay hold vpon the promises of God in the dayes of our aduersitie. When a man is fallen into a deepe water, he layeth hold on all things, branches of trees, stones, stickes, straies, weedes, or any thing whereby he may saue him selfe from an imminent danger. Heere is the safest waye to saue our selues in the greatest dangers of the Church, to lay hold vpon the promises of God which haue a set time for deliuerance of his owne children. Although the Lord say not vnto vs, as he said vnto Israel after seuentie yeeres accomplished, I will deliuer, or after a yeere, a moneth, or a weeke, or a day, I will deliuer you; yet he hath giuen vs a set time for his fauour, and that is the day of our repentance. If this day, this solemne day of our fast, this land truely be humbled before the Lord; if euery one, as the king of Niniueh commanded his people, turne from his evill waye[s], and *from the violence that is in their hands* [Jonah 3:8]; if euery one *loose the bands of wickednesse,* and *vndoe the heauy burdens, and let the oppressed goe free, and breake euery yoke* [Isa 58:6]; if euery one deale his bread to the hungry, and bring the poore that is cast out to his house; if when thou seest the naked thou couer him, and *hide not they selfe from thine owne flesh* [Isa 58:7]; if euery one rest his heart and not his garments; if euery one doe iustly loue mercy, humble him selfe, and walke with his God [Mic 6:8]; if euery one cease to doe euill [Isa 1:16], and learne to doe well; in a word, if this land this day will truely repent of all their bypast iniquities, and resolue to be better seruants to God then they haue beene; if these things be the time to fauour vs, yea the set time is come, our God shall not faile to make his promise good who hath made the time of our repentance the set time to fauour vs. At whatsoeuer time a sinner shall repent, saith the Lord, I will put his wickednesse but of my remembrance.

Thus, as yee see, the time of our repentance is a set time for our deliuerance. By our owne doeings, wee may knowe what God is minded to doe with vs. If wee fast this day *for strife and*

83

debate, and to smite with the fist of wickednesse [Isa 58:4], and thinke it enough for a day to afflict our soul; if wee bowe downe our head like a bulrush for a day; if wee fast from meate but not from sinne, let vs knowe that the time to punish vs, yea the set time is come. Gods wrath is neuer so neere vnto a people as the day he is scorned by a formall fast. When our fast day, the very salt of our dayes, is become vnsauory, the set time of vengeance is come.

The Vse. Let euery man examine him selfe and see what a time this day is vnto him: if this day thou find thy heart melt; if this day thou be ashamed of all thy bypast transgressions; if this day thou renewe thy couenant with thy God, esteeming all thy bypast pleasures how sweete so euer they haue beene to be more bitter then gall and wormeword; if this day wee can cry from the sinceritie of our hearts with Daniel, *O Lord the great and dreadefull God* [Dan 9:4]. *Wee haue sinned and committed iniquitie, and haue done wickedly, and haue rebelled, euen by depart-ing from thy precepts, and from thy iudgements. Neither haue wee hearkened vnto thy seruants the prophets which spake in thy name vnto our kings, our princes, and our fathers, and to all the people of the land. O Lord, righteousnesse belongeth vnto thee, but vnto vs confusion of faces, as at this day* [Dan 9:5-7]. If at this day wee be thus exercised, this day is a time, yea a set time, wherein the Lord hath appointed a reparation of all the breaches which Satan and wicked men haue made in this Church these many yeeres bygaine. If, at this day, wee be thus exercised and stand fast in Gods couenant, the Lord shall be vnto vs a pillar of a cloud by day to hide vs from our enemies [Exod 14:19-20],[5] and a pillar of fire by night to shewe vs the way to Canaan. If, at this day, wee fast such a fast as he requireth, he shall haue mercy vpon our Zion. Both Church and commoun wealth shall prosper. Our Church shall looke *forth as the morning*. She shall be *faire as the moone, cleere as the sunne, and terrible as an army with banners* [Cant 6:10].

All our papists with their gun powder shall hide them selues in the clifts of the rockes. The hearts of all our enemies shall tremble like aspen leaues. The craftie papists and arminiens[6] shall not be able to close so the windowes of our Church, but she shall looke out as the morning. Though they with violence cut the eares and slit the noses of her worthiest professours, she shall be in Christs eyes faire like the moone; and though they bring vp the deepths of the diuell [Rev 2:24] for to darken her light, she shall remaine cleare as the sunne. See what a set time of mercy is this day for our Church, if this day of our fast wee will repent and amend our life.

Againe, as for the other part of Zion which is the commoun wealth, and these other things that concerne the libertie of our countreye, the welfare of euery particular persone, in the things of this life, if this day wee will returne to our God, it is a time, yea a set time, for all your contentments, peace, plentie, health, wealth. The foraine enemies shall not come against you. He that made the entrells to direct Nebuchadnezars armie goe where he desired shall direct the entrells of all nations to passe by you. If yee repent and amend, the set time is come that God will no more plague you with intestine diuisions. Whereas our nobles were all in former times hunting one another with the bloody sword, yee shall see them all embraceing one another as brethren, yea as members of Jesus Christ; and this worke is now to be seene, and it is wonderfull in our eyes.

Againe, if yee repent and amend your life this day, the set time is come wherein the Lord shall multiplie his blessings vpon you. All the blessings of Guerizim[7] shall gather them selues together like a cloud and shall raine downe vpon you. *Blessed shall* yee *be in the citie, and blessed shall* yee *be in the field; blessed shall be the fruit of* your *body*, yee shall haue good and godly children; *blessed shall be the fruit of* your *ground, and the fruit of* your *cattell, the increase of* your *kine and the flockes of* your *sheepe; blessed shall be* your *basket and* your *store; blessed shall thou be when thou comest in, and blessed shall thou be when thou goest out* [Deut 28:3-6]. *The Lord shall command the blessing vpon* you *in* your *storehouses, and in all that* yee settest *thine hand vnto* [Deut 28:3-8]. O beloued in the Lord, what would yee the Lord to say more vnto you? He loues you from his heart; he desires to doe you good this day; he hath set this time for to blesse you spiritually and temporally; he hath commanded me to declare vnto you these wordes of his loue. *I knowe the thoughts that I thinke towards you, saith the Lord, thoughts of peace and not of euill, to giue you an expected end* [Jer 29:11].[8]

Seeing it is so, let vs all with one mind and one mouth this day forsake the diuell and all his workes, let vs repent and

85

amend our life, let vs cry shame on our selues and on all our sinnes, let vs seeke mercy from the God of heauen; and I will assure you that this day shall be a time, yea a set time, wherein the Lord shall arise, and haue mercy on our Zion vnto the praise of the glory of his grace, to the comfort of all good Christians, and to the confusion of Babylon and of her beast, and of all these who either with powder or policie haue beene seekeing the desolations of our Church and commoun wealth. To our God be glory for euer, Amen.

Zions Teares

Wherein are contained the most lamentable miseries of Gods Church, by M. Zachary Boyd, preacher of Gods word at Glasgow.

Isa 62:1

For Zions sake I will not hold my peace; and for Jerusalems sake I will not rest vntill the righteousnesse thereof goe foorth as brightnesse, and the saluation thereof as a lampe that burneth.

Lam 2:1

How hath the Lord darkened the daughter of Zion in his wrath? And hath cast downe from heauen vnto [. . .] earth the beautie of Israel?[1]

Teares and terrours followe after sinne as the shadowe followeth the body. This is a great miserie of man that he knoweth not his owne miserie. If wee knewe how froward a generation wee are, and how hardly moued to acknowledge the day of our visitation, it would make teares to gush out of our eyes, and drops of blood to fall downe from our hearts. But, alas, such is our stupiditie that wee can neither be moued by the curses of Ebal nor yet by the blessings of Guerizim. Wee reioice not at his promises, and wee mourne not at his threatinings for this cause: Christ Jesus, the Sonne of God, the great apostle of our profession, that doctour which came downe from heauen out of the bosome of the Father willing to set foorth the great corruption of mans nature, that can neither be moued by prosperitie nor yet by aduersitie, said, *whereunto shall I liken [. . .] this generation and what thing are they like vnto. They are like vnto little children sitting in the market place, and crying one to another and saying, wee haue piped vnto you, and yee haue not danced. Wee haue mourned vnto you, but yee haue not wept* [Luke 7:31-32].[2]

Some heere may enquire, what was this piping, and what was this dancing, and what was this mourning, and what was this lamenting? I answere, Gods pipes are the ministers mouthes. The piping is the preaching of the gospell that Jesus is come to *saue his people from their sinnes* [Matt 1:21], and that he is the golden horne of saluation [Luke 1:69] and most glorious *day-spring from on high* [Luke 1:78], which the Lord, through his tender mercies, hath sent to visite vs for to make a sure peace betweene him and vs, which should be the greatest matter of our ioye.

After that the angel had told the shepheards that the Sauiour was borne, the best tidings that euer were heard on earth, straight way a multitude of heauenly souldiers came like as many musicitians praising God and saying, *glory be to God in the high heauens, and peace in earth, and towards men good will.* [Luke 2:13-14].[3] If the angels so reioiced with springs of praise for the saluation of man that was once lost, with greater reason should wee, who haue receiued the benefit, say to the Lord with Dauid, all my springs or hearts affections shall be in thee [Ps 87:7].

Wee, Gods seruants in these publicke assemblies, like little children in the market places, haue preached the mercies of Christ vnto you. But who among you hath danced? But what is this dancing will yee say? It is nothing but the reioiceing of the heart, when, for the saluation of Christ, the hearts of Christians spring in their breasts, as John the Baptist sprang in his mothers belly at the salutation of Marie [Luke 1:41], the mother of our saluation. Let vs all trie if our hearts leape for ioye when wee heare that glory is vnto God in the high heauens, whom wee and our fathers haue so greatly dishonoured. If our hearts reioice not at the glorie of God, whom wee should loue better then our owne soules, all other ioye is no thing but matter of mourning. Who shall not reioice when he heares that there is *peace on earth and towards men good will* [Luke 2:14]?[4]

O what ioye would that poore afflicted Church of Christ in France[5] haue to heare this day, their peace proclaimed with sound of trumpet? What gladenesse of heart would they haue to be assured of the loue and fauour of their king for euer, that so they might breake their swordes into mattockes and their speares into siethes [Mic 4:3], and so sit in peace vnder their figge trees and vnder their vines?

But what should such a peace be in comparison of this peace

88

which hath beene proclaimed from heauen by the mouthes of angels, declaring that there is towards men good will, and that God will be their friend for euer? No man can esteeme of this peace nor reioice in it as he should, but onely he who by experience hath felt what it is to haue warre at home in his conscience. He who by his experience can say, it is a fearefull thing to fall into the hands of the liuing God, is onely fit for to reioice when he heares of this peace and good will.

Let vs all heere reioice before wee lament, for I, by Gods assistance, intend to speake at length of great and fearefull lamentations. This first knowe that he, who in this world could neuer reioice in God, could neuer rightly lament. The greater a mans ioye be in God when he is assured of his grace and good will, the greater shall his sorrowes be when his sinnes haue made a separation between him and his God. Now dearely beloued, what ioye should this be vnto vs to feare that an euerlasting peace is made betweene heauen and earth? Now wee all may clap hands together for ioy that wee, what euer our affliction be, haue the good will of the euerliuing God. What can our hearts wish for more then to haue Gods good will?

This is that which maketh the broken bones to reioice [Ps 51:8]. This is that which maketh the heauy heart and wounded soule to dance and leap like the creple whom Peter healed, who, as soone as he perceiued that his feete and ankle bones had receiued strength, he could not stand still in one place, so glade he was. But as the scriptures testifie, *he leaped vp*, and *stood, and walked, and entred into the temple, walking and leaping and praising God* [Acts 3:8].[6] Consider what diuersitie of actions in leaping, in standing, in walking. He entered into the temple walking, and leaping, and praising God. This is the right dance of the soule, but there be fewe that can dance so. There be few that can dance before the ark with Dauid: Gods pipes reioice them not.

But let the diuell come with his musicke and play a note of pleasure to the yong man, or of profit to the couetous man, or of preferment to the presumptuous man, and they all shall runne and leape and dance like madde men. But to praise God with the creple[7] of the Actes, they vnderstand not. Many be lumpish[8] at the preaching of Gods word, though it be for the saluation of their soules, who will easily be roused vp at the smallest tune of pleasure or profit. It is a very strange matter to be a man sleeping at Christs feete, while, with Marie, he should be seekeing the best part, which could neuer be taken from him, and thereafter be so nimble for the gaine of this world, which must either be taken from him or he from it. The daughter of Herodias and others like her may dance pleasantly, and please men so that some John the Baptist thereby shall want the head. But the diuell is such a minstrell that his wages at the dance he will not be content with heads, except that he get hearts and soules. So whosoeuer he be that danceth at the diuels piping, be it for pleasure or profit, may truely be called that which Mical falsly called Dauid when he danced before the arke, viz an vncouered foole. [2 Sam 6:20].

Let vs all heere learne when wee reioice to reioice in God, so that, when Gods messengers shall make vs heare the musicke of Gods mercie, wee may, as Dauid did, dance before the Lord [2 Sam 6:21]. Let this be sufficient concerning our ioye. Now let vs come to the matter of this time, viz lamentation, mourning, troubles, and teares. My text is a text of teares, not of Esaus teares, but of Jacobs teares, of whom it is said that he wept and made supplication. The Church heere weepeth: heere are *lachryma Zionis*,[9] Zions *teares*.

To all things, said Solomon, *there is an appointed time*: [. . .] *a time to be borne, and a time to die*; *a time to plant, and a time to plucke vp that which is planted*; *a time to slay, and a time to heale*; *a time to breake downe, and a time to build*; *a time to* laugh, *and a time to* weepe; *a time to* dance, *and a time to* mourne [Eccl 3:1-4].[10] I wish from my heart, if it were Gods pleasure and will, that this time were to Gods Church a time of laughing and dancing, for wee are all obliged to pray for the peace of Jerusalem. If that peace were, which is not, I should laugh and be glade to laugh with you. I should reioice to heare you saying with Sarah at the end of my sermons, God hath made me to reioice [Gen 21:6].

But, alas, the time of laughing is past, and now is no thing but the time of teares and of lamentations. The neckes of Gods saints are vnder the bloody sword. Our deare brethren in France,[11] Christs members, his iewels, and his darlings, are hunted from bush to bush by mightie hunters, who, like bloudhounds, thirst for no thing so much as the blood of the saints. For this cause haue I chosen this day to discourse vpon Jerimiahs lamentations, that in this time of weeping wee may be moued to mourne, while wee consider the troubles and the teare of Zion.

When the prophet Jeremiah intended to moue the people to mourne, he said, I am the man that hath seene affliction in the rod of his indignation [Jer 2:1-2]. If that can touch your hearts, I may also say, I am the man that hath seene affliction in the rod of Gods wrath, I haue heard Ephraim lamenting, I haue seene the affliction of Joseph. Where fore will yee lament if yee refuse to mourne for the affliction of Joseph? Where fore will yee weepe if yee weepe not for the troubles and teares of Zion? Yee can not deny but there be teares; in your heads, nature hath not left you destitute of a prouision of teares. Whereupon thinke yee to bestowe them if yee redenye them to the calamities of Gods secret ones? Deceiue not your selues in thinking that these waters shall remaine in your heads not to be powred out. Not not: some shall gush out for the losse of your goods; some for the losse of your good name; some for the losse of your health; some for the losse of your wealth; some for the death of your parents; some for the death of your children; some for your husbands and some for your wiues; and some for thousand idle and needelesse toiles and turmoiles, which shall drye vp that moisture which should be cheefely spent in the bewailing of sinne and in weeping for the distressed saints, who now in France suffer the bloody persecution because they hold fast the profession.

Dearely beloued, remember now that the time will come that yee shall mourne for father or mother, for husbands or wiues or children. That time will come, but now is the time present that yee must weepe for the glory of God, which should be dearer vnto vs then father or mother, sister or brother, yea then our soules saluation. Behold now the rageing enemies, who by all meanes with all their might goe about seekeing to bereaue the Church of her glory, viz of Gods word, which is a greater glory then was the arke, the glory of Israel. If wee haue a sparkle of zeale, or as much of pietie as the smoke of flaxe, we must now be moued to mourne. When old Eli heard that his two sonnes, Hophni and Phineas, were slaine, his heart was sore wounded; but when he heard that the arke of God was taken, he became like a dead man, and so fell from his seat backward, and *his necke brake, and he died* [1 Sam 4:18]. When the armie did march to the battell, he was in a great feare for Hophni and Phinehas, but *his heart trembled for the arke of God* [1 Sam 4:13]. When Phinehas wife heard that her husband was slaine, her heart was pierced with great griefe. But when she heard that the arke of God was taken, *she bowed her self and trauailed* [1 Sam 4:19]; and while she was dyeing, she cryed not where she was dyeing, she cryed not where is my heart, Phinehas. My deare husband is slaine; no not, but *the glory is departed from Israel, for the arke of God is taken* [1 Sam 4:22]. Icabod, where is the glory?

Dearely beloued, ane arke of shittim wood[12] couered with gold was not of so great importance as is the gospell, which is the onely cause wherefore our enemies persecute our brethren that make profession thereof as wee may see this day. Shall our brethrens blood be powered out for the cause of Christ? Shall their walls be battered downe and their houses spoiled? Shall they be affrighted with the horrible roaring of the enemie, and hewen downe with the weapons of warre? Shall their churches be rased? Shall they be banished from their possessions and suffer so many things, and shall not wee be touched with their calamities for to mourne with these that mourne? For this cause haue I this day chosen a text of lamentations and of mourning that I may stirre vp all your hearts for to weepe for the desolations of Gods Israel.

I knowe that there be many that be at their ease in Zion, bellie gods[13] with out God, who care little for the affliction of Joseph. If it goe well with their back and their bellie, they care for no more. They *lye vpon beddes of yuorie, and stretch them selues vpon their beddes, and eate the lambes of the flocke and the calues [. . .] of the stall. They sing to the sounde of the viole* [Amos 6:4-5].[14] They *drinke wine in bowles, and annoint them selues with the chiefe ointments* [Amos 6:6]. What followeth vpon that? They become frozen in their dregges so senselesse that not one of them is sorie for the affliction of Joseph.

Tell men that are at their ease that others are in afflictions, and hardly shall they hit vpon a good word for their comfort. They can not affoord them so much as one alas with a sigh, so cruell are the compassions of the wicked. Tell these wantons, while they are swilling and bowling at the wine, and warmeing themselues at the sunne of their pleasures; tell them that the time of mourning is come, and they shall laugh and haue you in derision, so little are they touched with the death and martydome of Gods saints. But heare yee transgressours: *woe vnto you that are at ease in Zion* [Amos 6:1] while Zion is in teares. Anoint your selues still; sing, drinke, and be merrie still. The saints of God require not of you that yee weepe for them, but, as Christ said to the daughters of Jerusalem, so say they to you, weepe not for vs but weepe for your selues, weepe for these woes that shall come vpon them that are at their ease in Zion. Let such keepe their teares for them selues till the day of *weeping and gnashing of teeth* [Matt 8:12] come. For to conclude this point, *woe* [. . .] *to you that laugh now, for yee shall mourne and weepe* [Luke 6:25].

I come now to you brethren and sisters, who not onely confesse the communion of saints, but also beleue the communion of saints, who as yee professe your selues to be their fellow members haue also a fellow feeling. I intreat euery one of you, for the Lords sake, to lament your owne sinnes. First and thereafter, let vs come and lament for the sinnes and afflictions of our brethren. It is not possible that a man that can not weepe for his owne miserie can be moued to compassion towards others. Moreouer, the Lord will laugh at your lamentations for others, if he find you sporting in your owne sinnes and turning his grace into wantonnesse. Let vs therefore first weepe for our owne sinnes; and after that let vs hang vp our harpes vpon the willowes,[15] & with our hearts lament together the desolations of our deare and worthie brethren, who in this bloodie warre are partly slaine, partly exiled, and partly yet among their enemies hands.

They are the Israel of God. Let therefore euerie one of vs seeke to haue a heart like the heart of Jeremiah that wee may sigh for them as he did for Israel. If your hearts be not of stone, yee shall powre out riuers of teares for their calamities. Behold brethren the precious blood of Christ gushing out of their wounds. Some are pining away with hunger: their flourishing churches are laide flatlings to the ground, their pleasant songs are turned into howlings. All their people sigh and are dayly

93

in heauinesse. They looke pitifully vnto their brethren of Britaine. In their mourning, they sigh and say, *heare I pray you all people and behold my sorrowe* [Lam 1:18]; behold and consider, haue yee no regard all yee that passe by this way? *Behold and see if there be any sorrowe like vnto my sorrowe, which is done vnto me, where with the Lord hath afflicted me in the day of his fierie wrath* [Lam 1:12]. *He hath made me desolate and dayly in heauinesse* [Lam 1:13].[16] Hearken yee peoples who haue bowels of compassion. Stop not your eares at their grones, and yee shall heare a noise as of a woman trauailing, euen the voice of the daughter Zion that sigheth and stretcheth out her handes [Jer 4:31].[17] Woe is me now, for my soule fainteth because of the murtherers. Alas, alas, may many truely say, *Zion stretcheth out her hands and there is none to comfort her* [Lam 1:17].[18] And therefore, as truely may she say, whiles wee waited for our vaine help, our eyes failed, for, in our waiting, wee looked *for a nation that could not saue vs* [Lam 4:17].

Afflicted, tormented, and persecuted Church of Christ, who shall haue pitie of thee? Or who shall be sorie for thee? Or who shall goe pray for thy peace? *What thing shall I take to witnesse for thee? What thing shall I compare to thee* [. . .]? *What* thing *shall I liken to thee that I may comfort thee,* [. . .] *for thy breach is great like the sea* [Lam 2:13]? O daughter Zion, wee will mourne and lament with thee and for thee; wee shall weepe continually in the night. Our teares shall without ceaseing trickle downe our cheekes. Euery godly soule among vs shall be in distresse for thee and shall say, *If I forget thee O Jerusalem, if I doe not remember thee, let my tongue cleaue* vnto the *roofe of my mouth* [Ps 137:5-6].[19]

By mourning for our sinnes and for the sinnes and afflictions of Gods people, wee shall reape this comfort, that wee shall be hid in the euill day of the Lord when these who laugh now shall begin to weepe for euer. This is euident by that which the Lord said to the *man clothed* [. . .] in *linnen, which had* [. . .] a *writers inke horne by his side* [Ezek 9:3]. Marke, said the Lord, vpon the foreheads of them that mourne, and cry for all the abominations that be done in the citie. Not one of the citie was spared except the marked mourners; not one of this world shall be saued after death, but onely these who did mourne and lament while they liued.

Let vs therefore now prepare our selues for lamentations. Let it not be grieuous vnto vs to weepe this day, for better is it to be in the house of mourning then in the house of dances. It is farre better to be at the crosse of Christ weeping with good Marie then to be dancing in King Herods hall with the daughter of that vile strumpet Herodias [Matt 14:6]. I had rather be washing the blessed feete of Jesus with my teares in Simons house with that sinnefull woman [Luke 7:38] then be sitting at Diues, his daintie dishes clothed in purple and skarlet [Luke 16:19]. I had rather be lying in the stockes with Joseph [Gen 39:20] then dancing about the golden calfe with idolaters [Exod 32:19].

3. sortes of lamentations

That wee may knowe how wee should lament wee must knowe the diuers sortes of lamentations. Lamentations are chiefely of three sortes: 1. first, godly men lament for the feare of sinne that is not yet committed; 2. secondly, men lament for sorrowe for sinne already committed; 3. last of all, men lament for the iudgements or chasticements of God, which fall vpon men after that they haue sinned.

1. lamentations for the feare of sinne that is not yet committed

Before that sinne be committed, while it is but in the conceiuing, in the concupiscence, as in a fertile wombe, the regenarat man will mourne and lament, for he perceiues the diuell busie like a shreud midwife to bring foorth sinne that death may ensue. This fearefull law that is in his members euer fighting against the law of his mind maketh him continually to lament and grone and cry, *O wretched man that I am, who shall deliuer me from the body of this death* [Rom 7:24]? The brittlenesse of mans nature, and this strong inclination that he hath to sinne, should euer make his heart to tremble. For this cause, the Lord hath giuen a precept to euery one of his seruants to worke out the worke of their saluation with feare and trembling. Where feare and trembling are present, lamentation and mourning can not be absent.

2. lamentations for sinnes already committed

Lamentations and mourning and miserie followe after sinne as the shadowe followeth the body. Where sinne is present, there shame will not be absent; where shame is, there is paine; where paine is, there is mourning. *Wee haue sinned*, said Daniel; wee *haue committed iniquitie* [Dan 9:5]. But what followed vpon that? O Lord, said he, vnto vs apperteineth open shame. If the feare of sinne not committed causeth men to lament, how much more shall shame for sinne committed make men to mourne [Dan 9:8]? But which is yet worse then shame by sinne? The soule is so darkened that in Gods light it can not see light. It is onely sinne that hideth Gods countenance from the soule. It is onely sinne that maketh a separation betweene God and the soule. From thence come these lamentations: will the Lord *absent him selfe for euer, and will he shew no more fauour; is his mercie cleane gone for euer* [Ps 77:7-9]?[20] Hath God forgotten to be mercifull? Hath he shut vp his tender mercies in displeasure?

Sinne is like a pill of aloes couered with sugar, sweete with out but bitter within, sweete in the mouth but bitter in the belly like gall or wormewood. All the painted pleasures of sinne are but like tombes hauing no thing within but rottenesse and stinke. Young man, take thy pleasure in sinne in the dayes of thy youth, but knowe that, *for all these things, God will bring thee to iudgement* [Eccl 11:9]. Sinnes in youth cost old age many a sore sigh and many a Gods mercie.

Thou shalt feele the trueth of this one day if either grace or glory be appointed for thee. Goe to these that are old, and enquire of them what profit they haue now of these things whereof they are ashamed. And they shall say to thee, O if wee haue not beene fooles! O if wee had beene wise, and had done the good which wee haue not done, and not done the euill which wee haue done! Woe is vs now because wee haue sinned [Lam 5:16].

When Peter denied his master, he thought that he had done much for himselfe in sauing his owne life. But after that Christ

96

had turned and loked vpon him, he *went out and weept bitterly* [Luke 22:62]. Behold Dauid in his palace, glauncing with his eyes toward Bathshebah, woeing her afarre off with his lookes till he obtained his desire. After that, he couered his adulterie with murther. Now, said Dauid in him selfe, I haue wisely guided the matter. Seeing her husband is killed, of my whoore she shall be my wife. See how he tasted the sweetenesse of sinne. But while this sugar was in his mouth, behold Nathan before him with his wormewood of the parable of the sheepe, which ended in this: thou art the man. Then all his ioye was turned into mourning, so that out of the bitternesse of his heart, he cryed out with a heauie lamentation, I haue sinned against the Lord.

Obserue this well yee who take pleasure in dalliance: looke first to Dauid followeing his lusts, and, after that, heare him in his lamentations; and yee shall see him fainting in his mourning, and causing his bed euery night to swimme with his teares [Ps 6:6]. Heare him in another place howling and crying, *wash me throughly from mine iniquitie, and cleanse me from my sinne* [Ps 51:2]. Who now would buy these deceitfull pleasures with such, such terrible terrours of a conscience crammed with the horrours of hell? Solomons counsell to the yong man is that he keepe him selfe from the sinnes of youth. His reason is he shall mourne at the end when he hath consumed his flesh and his body [Prov 15:11]. Let men be carelesse in sinning, but, when their sinne is ended, they shall smart for it when the dart shall strike them through the liuer [Prov 7:23]. Thy least looke to sinne is a spot which thou must washe with teares before thou die. The least taste of it shall set thy teethe on edge so sowre is that grape.

As for the wicked, though they seeme to sinne securely and to be very merrie, yet in laughing their heart is sorrowful. Their day is fast comming when all their ioyes shall end in endlesse sorrowes. When Judas kept the bagge, the stollen pennies were sweete. To Judas, thirtie pieces of siluer [Matt 27:3] for the life of his master seemed to him to be a great gaine. Now, said Judas in him self, I am rich, I haue cause to be glad seeing I haue my wages in my hand. But O as soone as the diuell, who at Christs table entered into him, beganne to ouer turne his conscience and to let him see the blood of God which he had betrayed, he cast bagge and siluer all from him and went and hanged him selfe. Where was all Judas his ioye now? The stollen waters were sweet [Prov 9:17] to her that played the harlot in adulterie; but when her husbands ielousie beganne to kindle, he brought her to the priest, who made cursed and bitter waters to enter into her bowels, which made her belly to swell and her thigh to rot [Num 5:27]. And where were all her pleasures then?

3. lamentations for the iudgements and chastisements which followe after sinne

Let vs now come to the iudgements of God that followe sinne. There be fewe that can lament for the feare of the inclination they haue vnto sinne for the law that is in their members [Rom 7:23]. Few groned because of that law. With wishes they were delyuered from the body of death. There be also few that can lament after that sinne is committed. None can doe that but onely Gods secret ones. But all men, both good & bad, will weepe & lament when the iudgements of the Lord come vpon them. The harlot & the oppressour & the couetous & the slaunderer, the proude & the idolater, will all howle and yell together, & cry vnder a iudgement, *woe vnto vs now for we are destroyed* [Jer 4:13].[21] Item: woe is vs now because of the murtherers [Jer 4:31]. But onely the godly can cry from the heart in time of trouble, *woe vnto vs* now, for *we haue sinned* [Lam 5:16]. The wicked mans woe is not for his sinne, but because of the murtherers, because he is destroyed. He howles like a dogge onely because he is beaten, & not because he hath made a fault. But the godly mans woe is, not onely because he is beaten with stripes, but chiefly because of his sinnes, which he sees in his stripes as in a mirrour. The wicked mans cry to God is ay, deliuer me from this plague. But the godly mans cry is chiefly forgiue me my sinnes, which are the cause of the plague. Pharoah did often intreat Moses to pray that the plague should be remoued, but he could neuer beseach him to pray that his sinnes might be remoued. He cared not for Gods kindnesse, so that he had beene free of the plague.

So yee see that the lamentations of the wicked are onely for the plagues of God that trouble them, as dogges howle when they are beaten with a cudgell. But the godly man laments cheefely for his sinne, which is the cause of the plague that is come vpon him. It will often befall that a child of God will laugh and loiter in sinne, while he should lament for his sinne. But when the Lord runneth vpon him like a giant, breakeing him with breach vpon breach, then will he arise from his securitie, and will weepe, lament, and confesse.

This may be cleared by examples. Let Josephs brethren be at ease after they sold their brother like a beast; & they shall laugh, [and] say what is now become of our master of dreames with his particoloured coat? *We shall see* now *what will become of his dreames* [Gen 37:20]. But tary a little till they be gripped in Egypt as spyes & as theeues, & cast inward; & then ye shall see them looke pitifully one to another & say, *we are verily guilty concerning our brother, in that we saw the anguish of his soule, when he besought vs, & we would not heare. Therefore is* all *this distresse come vpon vs* [Gen 42:21].

Let Ezechia be in health & ease, & his heart shall swell & be puffed vp with pryde. But let his body swell with a deadly boitche, boile, & the swelling of his heart shall fall, and he shall mourne like a doue & chatter like a crane or a swallow [Isa 38:14]. Let men neuer be sicke or sore & they shall become fooles. But fooles, because of their transgressions & because of their iniquities are they afflicted? Then, saith Dauid, *they cry vpon this Lord in their trouble* [Ps 107:19]. Let the sea euer be calme & free from tempests, & the merrie mariners shall daunce & play. But little shall they remember their sinnes committed vpon the shore. But let a boisterous wind come forth & make them stagger & reele to an[d] fro like drunken men, till they be at their wits end. Then shall they be sory & confesse their sinnes; then shall *they cry vnto the Lord in their trouble* [Ps 107:28].

Let Dauid be in Gods owne schoole. If ye hide the whip from him, he shall run away & play the truand. But let the Lord first scourge him, & after put the clog to his foot; & he shall become the best schooler in all the schoole. Yea, he shall passe his masters in knowledge, & teach faith & repentence vnto others.

Let Manasses liue in peace, & he shall liue in sinne. He shall plodde on from one sinne to another: from idolatrie to murther,

& from murther to witchcraft. But let him be taken by his enemies & bound in double chaines of brasse. Then ye shall see him weepe & be a very humble man before the God of his fathers.

Let Jerusalem be fedde with the sweete wordes of fals & flattering prophets [Jer 8:11], & she will licke her lippes & scorne at Jeremiah. But let the Lord feede her with wormewood, & giue her waters of gall to drinke [Jer 9:15]; & she shall lament & crye, woe is vs now *for we are distroyed* [Jer 4:13].[22] Let Jerusalem be in prosperitie, & she shall despyse the pretious word of the Lord. *I spake vnto thee when thou wast in prosperitie*, saith the Lord, *but thou saidest, I will not heare* [Jer 22:21]. But let prosperitie giue place vnto aduersitie, then shall she be glad to heare the word of the Lord. Yea, she shall trot from sea to sea for to heare it [Amos 8:12]. There is no man more peart then a theef, so long as he steales impuné[23] & is not discouered. But let the theef be found & he shall be ashamed [Jer 2:26]. Hold the iudgment of Pharoah & he shall neither care for God nor man. Yea, he shall blaspheeme & say who is the Lord? I knowe not the Lord, but let blood and boitches, lyce, frogs, & flees come vpon him & vpon his land; & the tyran[t] shall be so dasht that he shall be faine to make his prayers to the sely poore seruant of that Lord. Moses, will he say, pray for me.

Let Nebuchadnezzar speak & boast as he lists; & ye shall see him strouting in his palace with this bragge, is not this great Babel, which I haue built [Dan 4:30]? But let him be brought to eate with the oxen, & bowe downe his head to the grasse, and ye shall heare him blessing the most high & praising & honouring him that liueth for euer. Let Belshazzar without stoppe drink on still with his concubines, & he will still be vaine. But let the fingers of Gods scribe come out & wryte before him vpon the plaister of the wall [Dan 5:5], *Mene Mene Tekeel*; and his thoughts shall so trouble him that the ioynts of his loynes shall be loosed, & his knees shall smite one against another.

By those examples & dayly experience, it is more then euident that there be no man who will not lament when Gods iudgements are powred out vpon him. For this cause, the heauie iudgements of God are called lamentations, mourning, & woe [Ezek 2:10]. The lamentations of our prophet are not onely for the iudgements & plagues that came vpon this people, for so they should be no better then the howlings of a dogge. But the chief mater of this holy mans teares were the sinnes of this people, whereby they had prouoked the eyes of Gods glory. Great were their sinnes, as it may be seene by the greatnesse of their desolations: great sinnes, great iudgements; and againe great iudgements, great sinnes.

Now that we may the better vnderstand these lamentations, we must considder the beginning and proceeding of the desolations of this people Hebrewe till they were vtterly desolate. While I looke downe to the deepe pooles of the afflictions of this people, my heart trembleth; and I am constrained to cry, O Lord heere, *one deepe calleth another deepe by the noise of thy water spoutes* [Ps 42:7].[24] Like the iawes of the sea, one affliction followes vpon another till at last all Jerusalem is swallowed vp as it were into a bottomeless gulf.

The first decree of all these woes was set downe by God in the dayes of Ezekias, because of the loftinesse of his heart, which had moued him to make a vaine shew of all his armour & treasures vnto the seruants of Beredach-Baladan, son of Baladan, king of Babylon [2 Kgs 20:12]. Behold, saith the Lord, the dayes come that all that is in thy house, & that which thy fathers hath laid vp in store vnto this day shall be carried to Babylon. No thing shall be left, saith the Lord.

Behold the decree of all the lamentations of Jeremiah, wherein was included the vnseparable condition of all the threatinings of God, viz except they repent. By this, ye see that the Lord takes no pleasure to come vpon sinners vnawares: he euer threatens before he destroy. A man of warre, meeting with a ship vpon the sea, will not at the first set vpon her with all his canons for to sinke her. But to the end he may saue her & get her to him selfe for a pryse, he will first shoot a musquet; or, for to terrifie her, he will let a number of canons goe that she may yeeld & come in will. If not, he will let her see what his artaillerie can doe, & so at last will thunder vpon her & batter her till she be broken & perish.

O brethren, the Lord is a mightie warriour. Behold how he meets with Jerusalem: he shoots threatining after threatining to the end that they would yeelde by breaking off their sinnes by repentance. First, he shoots at their kings, and the first cracke is against Ezekias. Thy treasures shall be spoiled & thy sonnes shall be transported vnto Babylon & made eunuches. After Ezekias comes Manasses not afraide for all that had bene said vnto his father; & he prouokes so the Lord to wrath by his idolatrie, bloodshed, & witchcraft, that the Lord lets off another canon at Judah, but chiefly at Jerusalem, which made such a noise that whosoeuer did heare it both his eares did tingle. *I am bringing such euill vpon Jerusalem & Judah*, saith the Lord, *that whosoeuer heareth of it both [. . .] eares shall tingle* [2 Kgs 21:12] etc. *I will wipe Jerusalem as a man wipeth a dish, wiping it, & turning it vpside downe* [2 Kgs 21:13]. Because of this mans sinnes, the Lord said that he would not shew mercie vnto Jerusalem if they did not repent.

Yet for all this, Jerusalem would not yeeld & come in will. After Manasses comes Amon, his sonne, more vnkind then his father, for he walked in all the wicked wayes of Manasses, his father. Yea he surpassed him in wickednesse, in that, after he had sinned, he *humbled not himselfe before the Lord as Manasseh, his father, had humbled him selfe* [2 Chr 33:23]. But as the scriptures beare record, this Amon trespassed more & more, for all this Jerusalem would not repent. After Amon comes the good Josiah, who (while pharaoh Neco was coming against the king of the Assyrians through his land) come forth in battell array against pharoah & was slaine at Megidd; and that by his owne fault, for, before that pharaoh would come to stroakes with him, he did cry vnto him, what haue I to doe with thee, king of Judah. I came not against these this day but against mine enemie, & *God commaunded me to make haste* [2 Chr 35:21]. Now the Lord was in great wrath against the land while he suffered so good a king to be taken from them. As he giues an euill king in his anger, so takes he away a good king in his fury. So this good king being slaine, *all Judah & Jerusalem mourned for Josiah* [2 Chr 35:24], but neither Judah nor Jerusalem would mourne for their sinnes. They would not yet for all this yeeld vnto their God, & breake off their sinnes by repentance.

Now behold after this a floode of iudgements runs through the whole land, all the Lords canons come forth. Hereafter ye shall heare of no thing but of spoiling, & of bonds, & of chaines, & of fetters, & of seeges, & of slaughter, & of captiuitie till at last Jerusalem be vtterly ouerthrowne. After Josiah came

102

Jehoarhaz, who did euill in the sight of the Lord, yea so that by the direction of God, pharoah Neco put him in bonds at Riblah [2 Kgs 23:33], and brought him in chaines vnto the land of Egypt [Ezek 19:4], where he died. Moreouer, he did put the land into a tribut of an hundreth talents of siluer & of a talent of gold; and in the reigne of Jehoabaz, he made Eliakim, the son of Josiah, king, whom he called Jehoiakim. But Jehoiakim did that which was euill in the sight of the Lord. In his dayes came Nebuchadnezzar, king of Babylon, & Jehoiakim became his seruant three yeeres. But at last, haueing rebelled against him, the bands of the Caldees and the bands of the Syrians & of the Moabites came against Judah to destroye it. The king him selfe was taken & bound with chaines [2 Chr 36:6], & at last his dead body cast out like carion, not honoured with buriall according to the wordes of Jeremiah. *Thus, saith the Lord against Johoiakim, [. . . .] they shall not lament him saying, ah my brother or ah sister; neither shall they mourne for him, [. . .] ah Lord or ah his glorie. He shall be buried as an asse is buried, euen drawen & cast forth without the gates of Jerusalem.* [Jer 22:18-19]. Yea his dead body was *cast out in the day to the heat, and in the nyght to the frost* [Jer 36:30]. This was he that burnt Jeremiahs roule [Jer 36:27], so at last Judah was destroyed by the bands of the Caldees, & of the Syrians, & of the Moabites that came vp against it.

But at whos commandement came they against the land? *Surely at the commandement of the Lord came this vpon Judah, to remoue them out of his sight.* Wherefore they? *For the sinnes of Manassely,*[25] *according to all that he did.* [2 Kgs 24:3] *And also for the innocent blood that he shed, [. . . .] which the Lord would not pardon* [2 Kgs 24:4]. Yet Jerusalem would not yeeld nor breake off their sinnes by repentence. After Jehoiakim came Jehoiachin called Conias and Jechonias [Jer 37:1]. Now be hold how the desolations incressed: Jerusalem hath now the one foote in the graue; the day of her changing is at the dawning. This man reigned but a yeere [2 Chr 36:20] when Nebuchadnezzar, king of Babel, came against the citie [2 Kgs 24:11], & besieged it. But Jehoiachin, by the counsell of Jeremiah, came forth & yeelded him selfe vnto the king of Babel, who tooke & carried him away to Babel. Moreouer, he caried out thence all the treasures of the house of the Lord & the treasures of the kings

103

house, & brake all the vessels of golde. He also carried away all Jerusalem, & all the princes, & all the strong men of warre, & all the worke men, & cunning men, so that none remained except the poore people of the land. He caried also away the carpenters & lockesmithes, & all that were strong & fit for warre did the king of Babel bring to Babel captiues. Yet for all this would not Jerusalem yeeld nor breake off her sinnes by repentence.

Last of all, in comes Mattaniah, Jehoachins uncl, & he is set vpon the throne by Nebuchadnezzar, who *changed his name to Zedekiah* [2 Kgs 24:17]. But he did euill *in the sight of the Lord*: he *humbled not him selfe before Jeremiah the prophet* [2 Chr 36:12], but rebelled against Nebuchadnezzar, who had caused him to sweare by God that he should be loyall & faithfull, in token whereof he had giuen his hand to Nebuchadnezzar [Ezek 17:18]. Moreouer, he had so hardened his necke, & made his heart obstinate that he might not returne vnto the Lord God of Israel.

Now the cuppe is full & Jerusalem is come vnto her terme. And all the world had saide contraire [Ezek 22:4]: she must to the ground. The Lords patience will hold no longer. So out comes Nebuchadnezzar with a terrible & mightie armie, being in a rage both against Rabbah, a towne of the Amonites, & also against Jerusalem. Behold, as he is coming from Babel, he comes to the parting of a way [Ezek 21:21]; & there he doutes what he shall doe, whither he shall take to the left hand against Rabbah or to the right hand against Jerusalem. In the meane tyme, the men of warre are making their armour cleare & their arrowes bright. While the king was, in this doubt, resolued that, where the dirt of their stroakes should light, the markes should appeare thereafter, at last the king, for to be resolued of his doubt, consults with idole, & causes a beast to be brought & riped vp that they might looke in the liuer [Ezek 21:21], after the custome of the pagans that, by some marke seene in the liuer, he might direct his course, either to the right hand or to the left. Now the Lord, who hath both the heart & liuer of man & beast in his hand, disposes so the liuer of the beast that there was diuination at his right hand against Jerusalem [Ezek 21:22]. The Lord might haue so affected that liuer that all that armie should haue rushed against Rabbah.

But Jerusalems cuppe was full of iniquitie, euen to the brimme. The time & terme was come that he would powre out all the viols of his fierce wrath vpon that sinful citie. So all this huge great armie, in the nint yeere of Zedekiahs reigne, the tent moneth, & tent day of the moneth, came against Jerusalem, and pitched round about it & built fortes against it [2 Kgs 25:1]. After this maner, they besieged it vnto the elleuenth yeere of his reigne, till at last in the fourth moneth, the nint day of the moneth of this elleuenth yeere, the famine was so great that the citie was broken vp, & all the men of warre fled & went out of the citie by night [Jer 52:6-7]. Some did goe into thickets & some clamme vp vpon rockes [Jer 4:29]; some ran to one place & some to another for to escape the sword of the enemie. But the armie of the Caldeans pursued after the king & tooke Zedekiah into the desert of Jericho, & all the hoste was scattered from him. Then they tooke the king & caried him vp vnto the king of Babell to Riblah where he gaue iudgement vpon him. There he slewe the sonnes of Zedekiah before his eyes, & all the princes of Judah. After that Nebuchadnezzar had put out his eyes, he bound him in chaines, & carried him to Babel, & put him in prison till the day of his death.

Now what rests more to be done? Is there yet any viole of vengeance to be powred out? Behold Jerusalem stands yet: she must be brought to the ground & made desolate. And yf therefore in the fift moneth & seuent day[26] of the moneth came Neduzaradan, chiefe steward & seruaunt of the king of Babel, to Jerusalem [Jer 52:12], & *burnt the house of the Lord, & the kings house, & all the houses of Jerusalem, & all the great houses burnt he with fire. And all the armie* that *were with the chiefe steward bracke downe the walles of Jerusalem round about* [Jer 52:13-14]. Not content with all that, such was the greedinesse of the men of warre, that most barbarously they did rifle the very graues, not spairing the carkesses of their kings, of their priests, & of their prophets. The bones of all those did they cast out of their graues, & *spread them before the sunne & the moone* [Jer 8:1-2] without any care to bury them againe, so that they did lye there, *euen as the dung vpon the* open *field* & [. . .] *the handfull after the mower* [Jer 9:22].[27] Moreouer, all being so wracked, the rest of the people was caried awaye in captiuitie to Babylon.

105

Behold now at last the desolation[s] are come, which Jerusalem neuer looked for: now is the wrath accomplished.

The Refvge of the Chvrch
preached in A Sermon at a Fast
the 26 of Februar 1643

Jer 10:23

O Lord, I knowe that the waye of man is not in himselfe: it is not in man that walketh to direct his steps.

24. O Lord, correct me, but with iudgement, not in thine anger, lest thou bring me to nothing.

25. Powre out thy fury vpon the heathen that knowe thee not, and vpon the families that call not vpon thy name: for they haue eaten vp Jacob, and devoured him, and consumed him, and haue made his habitation desolate.

The servants of the Lord that preach Gods word should be very watchfull to forsee a danger and to give Gods people warning. Balaam, bragging of his virtues, called himselfe a man that had his eyes open, even while he was in a trance or sleepe [Num 24:4]. Gods watchmen have great neede to have open eyes in these dangerous dayes wherein wee live. Wee haue all neede to be seers to see and foresee [1 Sam 9:9], to see the sinnes of the land and crye against them, and also to forsee the iudgements of God comming that the people, being fore-warned of their danger, may turne vnto the Lord by repentance; and he may turne vnto them by mercy according to his owne saying, *turne [. . .] vnto me, saith the Lord of hostes, and I will turne vnto you, saith the Lord of hostes* [Zech 1:3].

The prophet Jeremiah was busy in this chapter dischargeing this dutie. Above all things, he desired Gods people to beware of idolatrie. *O house of Israel*, said he, *thus saith the Lord, learne not the wayes of the heathen, and be not dismayed at the signes of heaven* etc. *The customes of the people are vaine for one cutteth a tree out of the forrest; [. . . .] they deck it with silver and with gold; they fasten it with nailes and with hammers that it moue not* etc; *they must needs be borne because they can not goe. Be not afraide of them, for they can not doe evill; neither also is it in them to doe good* [Jer 10:1-5]. But Gods people would not obeye, but defiled Gods holy land with their abominations; and therefore the Lord threatned to throw them, as with a sling, out of their owne

107

countreye [Jer 10:18]. When a nation is sinnefull, the land speweth out the inhabitants [Lev 18:25]. The prophet Jeremiah, heere forseeing the terrible iudgements of God hard at hand, cried vnto the people, as from his watch towre, *behold the noise of the bruit is come, and a great commotion out of the north countrey to make the cities of Judah desolate and a den of dragons* [Jer 10:22]; that is, many strong and cruell enemies are in readinesse to bring a desolation vpon Gods people. The prophet, seeing the danger both to be great and neere, hath his refuge to God by prayer, the onely refuge of the Church. *O Lord*, said he, *I knowe that the waye of man is not in him self; it is not in man that walketh to direct his steps. O Lord, correct me but with iudgement, not in thine anger, lest thou bring me to no thing* etc.

the division of the text

In these wordes, I shall consider these foure parts. In the first part, the prophet maketh a description of mans weakenesse. *O Lord*, said he, in the Churchs name, *I knowe that the waye of man is not in himselfe; it is not in man that walketh to direct his steps.* In the second part, he intreateth God to deale with him in mercy: *O Lord, correct me, but with iudgement, not in thine anger, lest thou bring me to no thing.* In the third part, he intreateth the Lord to turne his wrath against the wicked: powre out thy fury vpon the heathen that knowe thee not, and vpon the families that call not vpon thy name. In the fourth and last part, he giveth a reason wherefore he did thus pray against the wicked: *for,* saith he, *they haue eaten vp Jacob, and devoured him, and consumed him; and haue made his habitation desolate.*

1 Part
a description of mans great weakenesse

In the first part of this text, wee haue a declaration of the great weakenesse of man: *O Lord, I knowe that the waye of man is not in himselfe; it is not in man that walketh to direct his steps.* In these wordes, I shall consider these two things: first, the certaintie of their trueth; secondly, the true sense of the wordes.

As for the certaintie, the prophet said, O Lord, I knowe what is said heere by Gods servant is not said by waye of doubting or by gessing, but from certaine knowledge.

The Doctrine. Obserue heere that great is the prerogatiue of Gods seruants. The Lord manifesteth his will vnto them; he openeth their hearts and maketh them to vnderstand what they speake concerning him and his wayes. They are onely the men that truely haue their eyes open [Num 24:4], the onely men of knowledge. All the learning of the world without the knowledge of God is but ignorance. To what vse served all the learning of Athenes? By all their philosophie, they could not attaine to the knowledge of the true God. In an altar of that toune of learning and knowledge was writen in great letters, *vnto the vnknowen God* [Acts 17:23].[1] Onely the faithfull darre lift vp their face to God, and say with Jeremiah, O Lord, I knowe.

The Vse. Let vs by all meanes strive to get the true knowledge of God and of ourselves. It is a beastly thing to be ignorant of Gods wayes. Many men be more ignorant than beasts. *The oxe*, saith Isaiah, *knoweth his owner, and the asse his masters crib* [Isa 1:3], but my people have no knowledge. Christ telleth vs that men by knowledge are saved. *This*, said he, *is life eternall: to knowe thee the onely true God and Jesus Christ whom thou hast sent* [John 17:3]. It is a great mercy of God that a man knoweth his owne weakenesse, as Jeremiah did heere. This was the miserie of Laodicea, that she knewe not that she was miserable [Rev 3:17]. This is Gods controversie with vs: there is no knowledge in God in the land.

Wee haue heard of the prophets knowledge [Hos 4:2]. Now let vs consider the sense of the wordes containing the matter of his knowledge. *O Lord*, said he, *I knowe that the waye of man is not in him selfe; it is not in man that walketh to direct his steps*. These wordes be diversly expounded. Some take them after this maner, as if they were spoken of Nebuchadnezzar, king of Babylon, Gods hammer and battle axe, by whom he did cut into pieces many nations. Before Nebuchadnezzar came against Gods people to make a desolation, he was in purpose to make warre against the Moabites and Ammonites. But hearing of Zedekiahs rebellion, he set his armie to goe against Jerusalem. The prophet Ezekiel declareth how the king of Babylon came with his armie, and stood at the parting of a waye at the head

109

of two wayes. There he consulted by divination and made his arrowes bright. He consulted with idoles and looked in the liver. At last, the Lord made the divination to be against Jerusalem: *to appoint captaines to open their mouth in the slaughter*, and *to lift vp their voice with shouting, to lay engines of warre against the gates, to cast a mount and to build a fortresse* [Ezek 21:22].[2] The Lord, who guides all things, made the liver of the beast, wherein the king looked, to direct his course not against Rabbah of the Ammonites, but against his owne rebellious people for to punish them for all their transgressions. Vpon this consideration of, some thinke the prophet Jeremiah heere said these wordes, *O Lord I knowe that the waye of man is not in him self; it is not in man that walketh to direct his steps*; that is, Nebuchadnezzar without thee had never come against Jerusalem.

The Doctrine. Vpon this ground, I observe that mighty princes with their armies can not march in foot against any nation, province, or citie but by the Lords direction. The captaines may beate their drummes, the generall may command the armie to march; but no thing is done but by Gods appointment. He hath the hearts of all men in his hand like rivers of waters, and turneth them what waye it pleaseth him best. *It is not in man* [. . .] *to direct his steps; the waye of man is not in him selfe*.

The 1 Vse. Let this serve for comfort to Gods Church: their most mightie enemies can not direct a step in the waye against them but as he appointeth. When they intend to goe east, he hath a bridle in his hand to turne them west or about, as a man on horsback will turne easily his beast from the waye he would be at. *I will put my hook in thy nose and my bridle in thy lips, and I will turne thee back* [Isa 37:29], said God to Senacharib. Jonas would haue sailed to Tarshis when God commanded him to goe to Ninivee, but all the rowers of the ship could not rowe against God. He commanded the winds. It is neither in him that rideth, neither in him that walketh, neither in him that saileth to direct his steps. *The waye of man is not in himselfe*.

The 2 Vse. Let this serve for instruction to teach vs to beware to provoke God and so to make him our foe, for he can direct a mighty and cruell armie, at the parting of the wayes, to come directly the waye for our destruction. Though the enemie had a mind to destroye some other part, as Nebuchadnezzar was minded to goe against Rabba, yet he can so direct men, whether by idoles or by the liver, or by a thousand other wayes to passe from their former intentions, and come with furie against our persones and places wherein wee dwell, and vtterly destroye vs and make our habitations desolate.

Others take these wordes of the text to be spoken of the weakenesse of the prophet and of all Gods people, whom the Lord had threatned with captivitie for their sinnes. Whereas the prophet heere saith, *O Lord, I knowe that the waye of man is not in him self,* he confesseth in a humble maner that they were destitute of all power and strength to resist Gods decree or to flie from his iudgements, as if he had said, I and all the faithfull servants with me, knoweing that thy iudgements are to come vpon the people of the Jewes, wee will not presume that, by any waye through our owne strength, wee can be able to escape the calamities that thou has decreed against this sinnefull and rebellious nation.

The Doctrine. Observe heere that when the Lord is provoked against a nation, a citie, or a man by their sinnes, there is no thing in them, neither wisdome nor strength, whereby they can deliver them selves. The wordes of the text are plaine: *the waye of man is not in him self; it is not in man that walketh to direct his steps.* Solomon saith that *mans goings are of the Lord* [Prov 20:24], also this preparation of his heart and answere of his tongue [Prov 16:1].

The 1 Vse. When God is angrie and threatneth a land with plagues, either of famine, pestilence, or sword, let vs not doe as though our wayes were in our self. Let vs remember that *it is not in man that walketh to direct his steps.* If famine be threatned, let not the rich mans heart walk in the waye to his barnes of corne, or to his coffers wherein is a wedge of gold, for, if God be angrie, all that will faile him. He shall find that *the waye of man is not in him self.* If the pestilence be threatned, let not the great mans heart walk in the waye of removeing from one house to another remote and farre off for to trust in that, for, if God be angrie, his faire and well aired houses will faile him.

As God made the frogs goe vp into the Egyptians bedchambers, and vpon their beds, and into their ouens and kneading troughes [Exod 8:3-4], so the Lord shall make the pestilence to followe him among the sweetest smelling flowres of his

111

garden; and he shall not escape, and he shall find by experience that *it is not in man that walketh to direct his steps*. Againe, if the sword be threatned, let not the man that is fearefull say, I shall save my self in such a castell or such a fort; or I shall goe out of the countrie, if I shall be a neutrall; or I shall ever followe these that prevaile. This is the fearefull beastly bodies waye that hath not made God his rock of refuge.

But O at last, such a one shall find that *the waye of man is not in him self*, that is, he shall find all his wisdome to be but folie, and that the way he hath chosen for his safetie hath beene a high waye to the danger. A man without God in danger is like a haire pursued with dogges: she hath so her eyes in her neck vpon the danger of the dogges behind that, not seeing the danger before, she runneth directly vpon other dogges that meete her in the teeth and devoure her.[3] Thus without Gods direction, as yee see, there is no escapeing, neither by force nor yet by wisdome. Let this in all dangers come into our memorie: *the waye of man is not in himself; it is not in man that walketh to direct his steps*.

The 2 Vse. Dearely beloued in Christ, seeing the waye of man is not in him self when difficulties and dangers are threatned, let vs have our refuge to him in whom are all the wayes of the world. In the valleye of the shadowe of death, God will find a way for these that seeke him. He made a waye through the water vnto Israel [Exod 14:21], and he made a waye through the fire vnto Shadrach [Dan 3:25], and he made a waye through the aire vnto Elijah [2 Kgs 2:11]. He, and he onely, is able to direct our steps in all dangers and difficulties whatsoeuer.

The 3 Vse. Let this serve for refutation against these doctors of pride who preach so much that naturall strength that wee haue to worke and walk. Alas, what worke can a dead man worke, in what waye can a dead man walk [Col 2:13]? Wee are all naturaly dead in our sinnes and our trespasses [Eph 2:1]. In any good waye of ether speakeing or doeing good, wee may well say in the wordes of this text, *the waye of man is not in him selfe; it is not in man that walketh to direct his steps*. After that Solomon had said, *mans goings are of the Lords*, he immediately subioined, *how can a man [. . .] vnderstand his owne waies* [Prov 20:24]? That is, it is not in the power of man to knowe what

112

will betide him. It is the Lord that weigheth the spirits [Prov 16:2] and giueth direction.

The 4 Vse. Let this serve for reproof to many who attribute things that befall them to fortune or chanse. If a man goeing such a way be killed or spoiled by robbers, O will they say, if he had gone another waye or had taried in such a place, he had beene safe. But such was his fortune. If our sonne or brother be drowned in the sea, incontinent our sayings are it was his misfortune to goe in such a ship. O if he had taried at home at that voyage. But what it was his fortune to goe. All these wordes are profane. At all such occasions of crosses befalling vs, let vs learne of Jeremiah heere to say, *O Lord, I knowe that the waye of man is not in him selfe; it is not in man that walketh to direct his steps*.

The Vse. Let this serve a reproof to those who speake of fortune or chance as guiders of mens wayes.

2 Part
the prophet intreateth God to deale with him and the people in mercy

In the first part, wee haue heard a description of mans great weakenesse. *O Lord*, said the prophet, *I knowe that the waye of man is not in him selfe; it is not in man that walketh to direct his steps*. In the second part, he maketh a supplication to deale with him in mercy and not in rigour. *O Lord*, saith he, *correct me, but with iudgement, not in thine anger, lest thou bring me to nothing*. In these wordes of his prayer, consider these two things: first, the preface, *O Lord*; secondly, the prayer it self, *correct me, but with iudgement, not in thine anger, lest thou bring me to nothing*.

The Doctrine. In this preface, O Lord, I observe the wisdome and true pietie of the prophet, who in distresse hath his refuge vnto the Lord. The apostles, in a worthy answere to one of Christs questions, if they would goe to any other, answered well, Lord, to whom shall wee goe? The Lord hath two things in him most comfortable for an afflicted man: he is both most willing and able for his reliefe.

The Vse. Let vs learne on whom to depend in dayes of trouble. Some trust in horses, said the psalmist, and some trust in charets. *But wee will remember the name of the Lord* [Ps 20:7]. The Booke of God is full of his power and of his kindnesse. *This poore man cried*, said David, *and the Lord heard him*, and deliuered him from *all his troubles* [Ps 34:6]. To goe to him is a doctrine of wisdome. All other things without him are but idoles, which may be called, as Jeremiah calleth *the stock, a doctrine of vanities* [Jer 10:8].

Now let vs consider the prayer, *correct me but with iudgement, not in thine anger, lest thou bring me to nothing*. In this prayer take these four things: first, what the prophet heere desireth the Lord to doe, it is that the Lord would correct him, *correct me*; secondly, he sheweth how he desireth to be corrected, it is *with iudgement* or in mercy; thirdly, he declareth how he desireth not to be corrected, *not in thine anger*; fourthly, of this he giveth a reason, *lest thou bring me to no thing*.

The Doctrine. First, whereas it is heere said that the prophet desireth the Lord to correct him, I observe that the wayes of the godly to carnall men are but wayes of foolishnesse. The naturall man, saith the apostle, vnderstandeth *not the things of the spirit of God, for they are foolishnesse vnto him* [1 Cor 2:14]. The children of God often find their corruptions so headstrong that they will, yea must, crye to God, correct me Lord. Let either one affliction or other come vpon me whereby my corruptions may be subdued, and I preserved from the fearefull wrath of God and from scandalizeing the godly. There be fewe of Gods children but they have beene vpon such considerations forced to crye to God, *O Lord correct me*, as a man, to save his life in a gangrene, will cry for a chirurgien to cut off a leg or an arme.

The Vse. Let Gods children heere learne that the correction of God is a great blessing, a thing to be sought for as a pre-servative from sinne, a subdueing of our pride and sinnefull vanities, a hedging vp of our waye with thornes that wee breake not out [Hos 2:6]. Seeing correction serves for so many vses, wee should seeke it; and, when wee are corrected, let vs give God thankes for it, professing vnto his glory with David, that before wee were afflicted wee went astray, but that now wee learne his statuts. If the rod of corrections were not whiles vpon our backs, our hearts should be crammed with a thousand folies. See how folie is bound in the heart of a child. The onely remedie is the rod of correction, which driveth vs farre awaye [Prov 22:15]. Wee would all become fooles if wee were not corrected at all. Before I was afflicted, said David, I went astraye. Nations and cities and men and women of all rankes, if Gods rod were never on them, would incontinent runne riot into most fearefull sinnes and trespasses. If the daughters of Zion were not whiles smitten with a scab on their crowns [Isa 3:17], they would make idoles of their bodies, having their minde onely vpon chaines and bracelets and mufflers, and bonnets and headbands and tablets, and earerings and rings and nose iewels, and mantles and wimples and crisping pinnes, and glasses and hoodes and vailes, and a thousand such other vanities.[4] As women, so men also, without correction would forget God, and live in this world, as though there were not a world to come.

Learne heere for preventing and for subdueing of sinnes to cry to God for correction, as men cry for a surgeon to let blood for to prevent a fever. Better it is to go with one eye, one foot, one hand to heauen, then with two to hell. Againe, consider heere whom he desireth to correct him: it is the Lord. *O Lord*, said he, *correct me*. The prophet wisely went to the right hand, when the prophet Gad was sent from God to David to give him his choise of three plagues, seuen yeeres of famine, or three moneths flieing before his enemies, or three dayes pestilence. David said, *I am in a great straite* [2 Sam 24:14], but at last be resolved to fall vnder Gods correction. Let vs fall nowe into the hand of the Lord.

The Vse. Strive so to knowe God that yee may make his corrections welcome, yea that yee may seeke them as men seeke a bitter potion, either for to prevent or cure a disease. The potion is vnpleasant to the taste, but profitable for health. So Gods correction as affliction is not pleasant for the present, but afterward, it bringeth foorth the quiet fruit of righteousnesse to these that are exercised thereby [Heb 12:11]. Secondly, it followeth that I shewe to you how the prophet desireth the Lord to correct him. *O Lord*, said he, *correct me but with iudgement*. The French version[5] hath by measure, that is in mercy or in a gracious moderation, so that, by Gods assistance, it may be patiently borne.

The Doctrine. Observe heere what sorte of affliction is a

115

benefit to a nation, a city, a familie, or private persone. It is such an affliction, that is with moderation, an affliction which a man by God is enabled patiently to beare. So God, speakeing to his owne people whom he loved, said, *I will correct thee in measure, and will not leave thee altogether vnpunished* [Jer 30:11]. The Lord, makeing a distinction betweene his iudgements on the wicked and his gentle corrections vpon his owne children, speaketh after this maner, *O Jacob, my servant,* [. . .] *I will make a full end of all the nations*; [. . .] *but I will not make a full end of thee, but correct thee in measure* [Jer 46:28], that is sparingly with a fatherly moderation.

The Vse. Let vs learne heere how to pray in our affliction or before affliction come. Let this be our sute: not that God would leave vs altogether vnpunished [Jer 30:11], but that he would correct vs in measure, in mercy [Jer 46:28], so that wee may perceive his love in the rod according to that saying of his, *whom I love, I chasten* [Heb 12:6]. The apostle saith that such corrections are *for our profit that wee* may *be partakers of his holinesse* [Heb 12:10]. These whom God passeth by and will not correct are base borne. *If yee be without chastisements,* [. . . .] *then are yee bastards and not sonnes* [Heb 12:8]. Yee see bastards for the most part to be great villaines. One of the reasons is this: there is little care taken of their education. They are not corrected when they runne from one sinne to another, vntill they fall into a mischeefe; and at last into the burrios[6] hand, putting a cord about their neck for to hang them, or bringing downe the axe or sword for to cut off their head, so as they sinned without measure. Gods hand striketh them not as his owne children whom he ever correcteth in measure [Jer 46:28].

Thirdly, it followeth that I declare how the prophet requireth not to be corrected in these wordes, *not in thine anger*. He refused not to be corrected. O Lord, said he, *correct me, but with iudgement*, that is in measure and mercy. But that which he cheefely shunneth is the anger of God: *correct me,* [. . .] *not in thine anger*.

The Doctrine. Observe heere that the anger of God is most terrible. The dearest servants of God are afraide for it; and, no wonder, for it burneth to the bottome of hell [Deut 32:22]. It is of such force that no man can either conceive or expresse it. Moses did speake of Gods wrath by waye of interrogation,

116

saying who knoweth the power of thy wrath [Ps 90:11]? S. Paul, speakeing of God in anger, saith that he is a consuming fire [Heb 12:29].

The Vse. Let vs beware to provoke God by our sinnes whereby his anger may be kindled. Let our prayer be alwayes with Dauids prayer, that God would not rebuke vs in his anger, nor chasten vs in his hote displeasure [Ps 6:1]. This petition was so necessary that he doubled it in another psalme, *O Lord, rebuke me not in thy wrath; neither chasten me in thy hote displeasure* [Ps 38:1]. Men may thinke it but a light matter to sinne against God. Many will say of their sinne, as Lot said, Belah, *is it not a little one* [Gen 19:20]? But tary vntill the wrath of God waken them out of their carelesse securitie. Then would they *give* their *first borne for* their *transgression* and *the fruit of* the wombe *for the sinne of* their *soule* [Mic 6:7]. These who haue once felt the terrours of the Lords anger will easily be perswaded [2 Cor 5:11], with all care and diligence, to flie both from Gods present anger and from the wrath that is to come [Matt 3:7].

Fourthly and last, the prophet, having intreated God not to correct him in anger, incontinent, subioineth a reason of this his petition in these wordes, *lest thou bring me to nothing*. In the originall, it is lest thou diminish me.[7] This diminution is such that if Gods wrath continue, it bringeth a man to no thing. So God, speaking of his iudgements against the house of Eli, said, *when I beginne, I will also make an end* [1 Sam 3:12]. The psalmist saith that, through affliction, men are *minished and brought lowe* [Ps 107:39].

The Doctrine. Observe heere that the wrath of the creator is the destruction of the creature. Nations and cities and commoun wealths are diminished and at last destroyed when God is provoked to wrath against them. See how he did with the foure great empires. He made a little stone to fall vpon them and bruise them all to powder, so that the golden head of Babylon, and the silver breast of Persia, and the brasen belly and thighs of Grecia, and the yron legs of the Roman Empire[8] were all *broken to pieces together, and became like the chaff of the summer threshing floores* which *the wind caried* [. . .] *away* [Dan 2:35]. By Gods anger, all these were diminished, and at last brought to no thing.

The Vse. Let vs all learne that the onely waye to haue any

117

thing for our comfort to remaine with vs, whether life, or honour, or credit, or contentment, it is to be in the fauour of God. He is called Iehovah because he giueth being vnto things. By him, wee haue our beeing and our moveing, and all our comforts and contentments.[9] But if wee provoke him, he will bring all these things to nothing. He grinds empires into pouder; he destroyes cities and faire buildings; and leaues not a stone vpon a stone, as he did to the temple of Jerusalem when *he remembered not his footstoole in the day of his anger* [Lam 2:1]. When his servants sinne, he maketh their soules bowe downe to the dust and their belly to cleaue vnto the earth [Ps 44:25].

The Doctrine. Againe, whereas the prophet maketh this a reason or argument not to correct him in anger, that by so doeing he will be diminished and at last brought to nothing, I obserue that God taketh no pleasure to destroye. *As I liue, saith the Lord,* [. . .] *I haue no pleasure in the death* of a sinner [Ezek 33:11]. The Lord Jesus weept when he looked vpon Jerusalem [Luke 19:41] because he sawe that, by their sinnes, they would provoke God to bring them to no thing.

The Vse. Let this move vs to love the Lord, who is so averse from our destruction, that he can not willingly see vs brought to nothing. Let vs make vse of this argument in these dayes of great danger, when wee praye to God to command his angel to put vp his bloudy sword, or to take away this great dearth and wrath by great sicknesse in the land, lest these wordes not be forgot lest thou bring vs to no thing.

3 Part
he intreateth God to turne his wrath against the wicked

In the first part, wee haue heard a description of mans weake-enesse, that it is not in him self *to direct his steps*. In the second part, the prophet required of God that he would deal with him and the people in mercy. *Correct me*, said he, *but with iudgement, not in thine anger, lest thou bring me to nothing*. In the third part, there is a most fearefull imprecation wherein he intreateth the Lord to turne his wrath against the wicked. *Powre out thy fury vpon the heathen that knowe thee not, and vpon the families that call*

118

not vpon thy name. The prophet hath this prayer from the psalmist, who, complaining of the desolations of Gods Church, said to God, *powre out thy wrath vpon the heathen that haue not knowen thee, and vpon the kingdomes that haue not called vpon thy name* [Ps 79:6].

The Doctrine. Obserue heere that great is the danger of these that serue not God. The heathen or gentiles called Goim[10] that knowe not God, and the families and kingdomes that call not vpon Gods name, are the obiect of Gods fearefull wrath. The Lord will not faile to heare this prayer of his seruants. He will powre out his wrath like fire and brimstone vpon all these that knowe him not, and vpon the families and kingdomes that are not giuen to prayer. Woe vnto them, for the Lord will powre out vpon them plagues of all sortes in his fierce wrath, so the Hebrewe word here importeth.

The Vse. If wee would flie from that wrath, let vs be carefull to knowe God [Matt 3:2], and see that our families call vpon his name. If men knew the trueth of this, there would not be so many ignorant of God. If men belieued this, there is not a familie in the land that durst neglect familie exercise. Heare this, O yee families who haue no prayers, yee are the families that call not vpon God. Behold heere a vengeance for you: *powre out thy furie vpon* these *that knowe* them *not, and vpon the families that call not vpon thy name*. Not to knowe God, not to pray and call vpon Gods name is, as yee see, a marke of these that are hated of God.

The Doctrine. Againe, whereas the prophet heere saith, powre out thy furie or hot wrath, so the Hebrewe word importeth.[11] I obserue that troubles, great plagues, as famine, sword, and pestilence, or any distresses that come vpon kingdomes, cities, or particular men come not by fortune or chance but from the Lord. He hath his vials or pots whereout of he powreth such things vpon his children of men. He hath vials full of wrath and vials of mercy. Out of his vials of mercy, he powreth vpon his children many benefits among which are also his corrections; but, out of the vials of wrath, he powreth destructions full of *furie vpon* these *that knowe* him *not and vpon the families that call not* on his *name*. There is no evill in the city which the Lord hath not done; there is also no evill in kingdomes or in any private families which the Lord hath not done. All the

119

plagues mentioned in the Revelation are all said to haue beene powred out of Gods vials: sometimes vpon the earth, as when that *noisome and greevous sores* fell *vpon the men which had the marke of the beast* [Rev 16:2]; sometimes his vialls were powred out vpon the sea so that *it became as the blood of a dead man* [Rev 16:3]; sometimes they were powred out vpon the floods and fountaines so that *they became blood* [Rev 16:4]; sometimes they were powred out vpon the sunne [Rev 16:8], so that *men were scorched with great heate* so that they did blaspheme *the name of God* [Rev 16:9]; sometimes they were powred out *vpon the seate of the beast,* so that *his kingdome was full of darkenesse, and they gnawed their tongues for paine* [Rev 16:10]; sometimes they were powred out vpon the aire [Rev 16:17], *and there fell vpon men a great haile out of heauen, every stone about the weight of a talent.*[12] All the iudgements come vpon this land came out of the Lord, vials which he did powre on vs. All these plagues are from the Lord, who hath an absolute power in heauen, on earth, in the sea, and aire.

The Vse. Seeing the Lord hath so many vials full of iudgements, let men stand in awe to offend him. Whether shall a man flie from his presence or from his plagues? Behold the earth can not save him, for the earth hath vials fulle of grievous sores. The sea can not save him. Behold how at his rebuke these greenish cleare waters become as the blood of a dead man. The sunne can not save him, though the sunne be a most comfortable creature to the world. If the Lords vial of wrath be powred vpon him, he will so scorch men with his heate that they will blaspheme the name of God. He hath his canonballs in the aire & stones of a talent weight to fell downe his rebellious enemies, who *stretch out* their *hands to a strange god* [Ps 44:20].

The 2 Vse. Let this serve for comfort vnto vs that God is so well armed against the enemies of his Church. Let them goe by sea or by land, or get wings and flie in the aire aloft. They shall not be able to escape the vialls of his wrath. Let vs have patience but a little space, and wee shall see the Lord powre fearefull things vpon them, the soules of them that were slaine. For the word God cried from vnder the altar with a lowd voice that God would avenge their blood on the wicked on the earth [Rev 6:10]. It was answered *that they should rest* [. . .] *for a little season* [Rev 6:11]. After that little season is past, the Lord shall powre out his wrath vpon these evill men [Rev 6:11]; and so will he doe at last vpon all the enemies of his Church whom he shall bind hand and foot, and after shall cast them into vtter darkenesse, where there is nothing but *weeping and gnashing of teeth* [Luke 13:28].

an obiection

Heere it may be obiected and said, how is this that the prophet could make such a fearefull imprecation against his enemies, as that God would powre out his furie vpon them? Christ hath said, *love your enemies, blesse them that curse you, doe good to them that hate you, and pray for them* that *despitefully vse you, and persecute you* [Matt 5:44].

the answere

In so farre as concerneth our owne particular wrongs, wee should be ready to forgive and to praye for these that persecute vs. But if wee knowe them to be the enemies of God, men fighting against God, and persecuteing his trueth, then may wee lawfully crye to God that he would powre out the vialls of his fury vpon them. In this sense, Jeremiah prayed; and, in this sense, David hath whole psalmes full of imprecations. *Let their table become a snare before them and that which should haue beene for their welfare, let it become a trap. Let their eyes be darkened that they see not, and make their loines continually to shake. Powre out thine indignation vpon them, and let thy wrathfull anger take hold of them* [Ps 69:22-24]. Like wise in another psalme, *set thou a wicked man over him, and let Satan stand at his right hand. When he shall be iudged, let him be condemned and let his prayer become sin* [Ps 109:6-7].

In that psalme are contained a heape of imprecations. Hardly can wee make the like against any particular men, and that because wee are not inspired of God with such a measure of knowledge as the pen men of Gods word were, who had the spirit for to discerne some men that were reprobates. To many of vs makeing imprecations may be said that which Christ said to James and John, desireing fire to come downe vpon these Samaritaines that would not receive their master, *yee knowe not what maner spirit yee are of* [Luke 9:55]. Too many, like Jehu, seeme to be zealous for the Lord [2 Kgs 10:16] against Gods enemies, while, as the maine wheele that turneth, all is but either an irregulare passion or some carnall respect more for them selves then for God.

4 Part
the reason of the prophets imprecation

In the third part of this text, wee haue heard of the prophets imprecation that God would powre out fearefull plagues vpon the heathen, and vpon the families that called not vpon his name. Now in the fourth and last part of this text, he giveth a reason of this his imprecation. It is contained in these wordes, *for they haue eaten vp Jacob, and devoured him, and consumed him, and haue made his habitation desolate.* By Jacob heere, I vnderstand Gods Church in a poore distressed estate, for Jacob was the base name of that holy man, so called from Esaus heele [Gen 25:26], a name which did signifie basenesse, distresse, contempt. In this consideration, God, speakeing by his prophet vnto his people, said vnto them, *feare not thou worme Jacob* [Isa 41:14], that is be not dismaied O ye my despised people of the Jewes. So when Amos stood in the gap to move God, he spare this people. He called them not Israel, but Jacob, Jacob [Amos 7:2-5].

The evills which their enemies are said heere to haue done to them are foure in number: first, that they had eaten them vp; secondly, that they had devoured them; thirdly, that they had consumed them; fourthly, that they had made their habitations desolate from such a doeing. The Romane armie was called *the abomination of desolation* [Matt 24:15]. The first three evills are similitudes taken from a hungry man or beast, who first eate a thing, and after devoure it, and at last digest it, and consume it in their stomack. Joshuah, speaking of Gods enemies when they were to destroye, said, *they are bread for vs* [Num 14:9].

The last evill by men of warre is a rifling and ransacking of houses and lands whereby men should maintaine their life.

122

When the enemie is cruell, he is not content onely to kill men and women and children, and spoile their riches; but also he will rage against their houses, either by burning or demolishing vntill the habitation be desolate. That this hath beene done in England,[13] but cheefely in Ireland these yeeres by past,[14] wee dayly both heare and see. The distresse may well be called an *abomination of desolation* [Matt 24:15].

Observe heere, first, that for the sinnes of his people God will give a large permission vnto the enemie, first, to eate them; secondly, to devoure them; thirdly, to consume them; fourthly, to make their habitations desolate. This God did vnto his owne people Jacob because they had provoked him to wrath by their sinnes.

The 1 Vse. Let these of Gods people who are in such troubles the day not despaire, as if such calamities were a powring out of his fury vpon them. Wee see that God in old times hath so corrected his people that was very deare to him.

The 2 Vse. Seeing wee heare that God, for the sinnes of his people Israel, hath so dealt with them as to make their enemies to eate them vp, to devoure them, and consume them, yea and to make their houses and habitations desolate, yee, seeing hard at our doores the enemies of God, haue done the like in England and Ireland. Let vs all be sorie for our sinnes. Let vs all repent and amend our lives. Let vs according to the direction of Zephaniah gather our selves together [Zeph 2:1]. Let vs fast and pray before the decree bring foorth, before the day passe as the chaffe, before the fierce anger of the Lord come vpon vs, before the day of the Lords anger come vpon us. Let vs now in this our day seeke the Lord; let vs seeke righteousness and meekenesse. It may be, said that prophet, that wee shall be hid in the day of the Lords anger. When he shall push downe our enemies, he shall hide vs vnder the shadowe of his wings.

The 3 Vse. If ever it shall please God to permit the enemies of his Church to come and eate vs vp, to deuour and consume vs, let vs crye to God for mercy and for his help and assistance; and let this be one of our arguments that wee are treade vnderfoot by the enemies of his glory, that wee are eaten vp, devoured and consumed, and our habitations made desolate. The Lord can not heare his people mourning in the midst of many wrongs, but he will be moved to compassion. A loving mother can not abide to heare the cryes and squeelings of her child; her bowels of mercy will be moved. God is more loving; his bowels are straiter rouled together with compassion then any mothers, for though a mother should forget her child, God can not forget his children, for he hath printed them vpon the palmes of his hands [Isa 49:16]. When children are beaten by any, their ordinary speech is I shall tell my father. Jeremiah doth so heere: he telleth the Lord, the Churches Father, what euilles her enemies had done her. *They*, said he, *hauen eaten vp Jacob and devoured him, and consumed him, and haue made his habitation desolate*, so let vs this day of our fast, for an argument to move the Lord to mercy, make a large rehearsall in the presence of God our Father of the many wrongs the enemies of God haue done to his Church, first in Scotland, and after in England and in Ireland.

Lord, thou knowest how the prelats were thrusted in vpon the Church by violence against the nationall covenant;[15] and how they vsurped Lordship ouer thy servants, and troubled the land, first with five miserable articles of faith,[16] and after with a service booke containing an English masse.[17] Lord, thou knowest how deare that booke was to this poore land, and how wee were compassed by sea and land, and how our enemies in the strong holds did make the bowels of many poore ones gush out at their sides. As for Ireland, inke of blood is fittest to write these vnheard of cruelties. Men, women, sucklings, all murdered by thousands by popish butchers; and England may tell how many thousands, heapes vpon heapes, fell aboue other in a bloody valleye.[18]

As Hezekiah speake the blasphemous letter of Rabshake [2 Kgs 19:4][19] before the Lord in the Lords house, so this day all the preachers of Scotland tell the Lord how his enemies *haue eaten vp* [. . .] *and devoured* [. . .] *and* consumed his Jacob *and haue made his habitation desolate*. The Lord looke vpon the blasphemous lettres writen against our Church, and vpon the blood of his seruants shed in the three kingdomes, Scotland, England, and Ireland; and as the prophet Zechariah, being stoned with stones at the commandement of the king, said at his death, *the Lord looke vpon it, and require it* [2 Chr 24:22], yea and requite it, Amen, Amen.

IV. The Purified Church

Scotlands Hallelviah
or

A sermon for a publick thanksgiving to God after the settling of all our troubles both in Church and commoun wealth appointed to be through the whole land the 9 of Januar, 1642.[1]

Ps 66:11

Thov broughtest vs into the net; thou laidst afflictions vpon our loines. *12. Thou hast caused men to ride over our heads; wee went through fire and through water; but thou broughtest vs out into a wealthy place.*

To every thing, said Solomon, *there is a season, and a time to every purpose vnder the heaven, a time to be borne and a time to die* etc [Ecc 3:1-2], *a time to weepe and a time to laugh* [Ecc 3:4]. Our time by past these three or foure yeeres haue beene dayes of distresse, of weeping, of fasting and prayer. The Lord hath made a mercifull change. He, as Sarah said of her self, hath made vs to laugh [Gen 21:6]. There be two sortes of exercises appointed for all Christians, and that is either to pray or to praise according to the season. *Is any among you afflicted?* saith S. James. *Let him pray. Is any merry? Let him sing psalmes* [Jas 5:13]. The great Eternall, infinit in maiestie and mercy, hath changed our dayes of affliction into dayes of gladenesse; he hath made vs all merry.

And therefore, as wee prayed vnto him in affliction, now while he hath made vs merry, let vs sing psalmes and reioice, cheefely now in this day, a most solemne day appointed to be vniuersally through this whole kingdome imployed for to give most hearty thankes vnto the Lord for all the mercies that he hath shewen both to our Church and commoun wealth. By deliuering vs from the hands of our enemies, from the bondage of a service booke[2] made like a fairded[3] whore for to allure the land to returne vnto Egypt, that Babel of Rome with whom the kings of the earth haue committed fornication [Rev 18:3],

127

the Lord by his blessings wonderfull, both spirituall and temporall of all sortes, hath made vs merry. And therefore wee resolve to sing with the psalmist heere, who said vnto God in the name of the whole Church, *thou broughtest vs into the net; thou laidst afflictions vpon our loins. Thou hast caused men [to] ride over our heads; wee went through fire and through water, but thou broughtest vs [. . .] into a wealthy place.*

This psalme is a psalme of praise for some most excellent deliverance graunted vnto his Church, and also vnto the psalmist him self, which seemeth to haue beene David delivered from a great danger, for which he voweth religious service to God, and by waye of thankefulnesse declareth Gods speciall goodnesse towards him selfe. This psalme, as yee see, is a psalme of thankesgiving, both for a generall deliverance graunted vnto his Church, and also for a particular deliverance graunted vnto David. So this psalme is most fitting for the time of this generall thankes ordained through the whole land, for this is the maine duetie of this land, that every one should bring with them thankes vnto the Lord in generall for the safetie of the Church. And who is the particular, from the generall of our armie vnto the basest souldier, from the highest vnto the lowest of all sortes, whether noble or ignoble, pastour or people, that hath not reason with the psalmist heere for their particular deliverance to vowe religious service to God and to declare Gods special goodnesse towards him selfe? And this is the substance of this whole psalme, which was writen by the pen of God to teach the posteritie how to praise the Lord, when he hath sent a deliverance, both generall and particular, as God hath done to this land, as all men whose eyes God hath opened, may most clearely see this day, and that with admiration.

And may not Scotland truely now say with the Church of God in Dauids dayes, *thou broughtest vs into the net; thou laidest afflictions vpon our loines; thou hast caused men to ride ouer our heads; wee went through fire and through water, but thou broughtest vs out into a wealthy place.* This is the text which Gods providence hath brought vnto my hands for this day set apart for a generall thankes giving most solemnely ordained to be observed through the whole kingdome, wherein wee heare the Church of God heere declareing her calamities, and also acknowledgeing thankefully that God had deliuered her from many miseries; and not onely that but also had enriched her wonderfully by bringing her vnto a wealthy place. This is the substance of the wordes.

the division of the text

This text may clearly be divided into two parts. In the first part, wee haue the great distresses of Gods Church. *Thou broughtest vs into the net; thou laidst affliction vpon our loines; thou hast caused men to ride ouer our heads; wee went through fire and through water.* In the second part is contained a mercifull deliverance, *but thou broughtest vs [. . .] into a wealthy place.*

1 Part
the great distresses of Gods Church

In the first part of this text, wee haue the great distresses of Gods Church. *Thou,* saith the psalmist, *broughtest vs into the net; thou laidst affliction vpon our loines; thou hast caused men to ride over our heads; wee went through fire and through water.* In these wordes, the psalmist, by foure metaphoricall speaches, describeth the great afflictions of Gods Church before the Lord delivered them. The first is in these wordes, *thou broughtest vs into the net.* The second is in these wordes, *thou laidst affliction vpon our loines.* The third is in these wordes, *thou hast caused men to ride over our heads.* The fourth is in these wordes, *wee went through fire and through water.*

1. Thou broughtest vs into the net

In the first forme of speach, *Thou broughtest vs into the net,* there is a similitude taken either from fishers or hunters, who set their nets round about fishes or wild beasts for to take them and for to kill them. This God is said to doe when the enemies of the Church doe such things by his sufferance or ordination.
The Doctrine. Observe heere that all the evills of affliction that come vpon the children of God, who ever be the instru-

129

ments, were it the divel him self, they can doe nothing but either as it pleaseth God to permit or ordaine. In all the troubles contained in this text, the psalmist maketh God the doer. Behold how he heere hath thrise thou, thou, thou, as three witnesses for confirmation that it is so.

The 1 Vse. Let this serve for instruction to teach vs on whom to looke in any sorte of trouble, whether it be warre or pest or famine or povertie or shame and disgrace or death or danger. In all these and in all sortes of calamities, wee must cheefely looke to the Lord, and consider his hand as the cheefe agent. This was Jobs practise, after the Sabeans had taken away his oxen and his asses and had slaine these servants, and after that the Caldeans had caried away his camels and slaine these servants; and that a great wind had throwen down the house where his children were and killed them all. Job looked over all the instruments of these afflictions and called them the Lords doeings, saying, *The Lord gave and the Lord taketh away; blessed be the name of the Lord* [Job 1:21].[4]

The 2 Vse. Let this serve for reproofe to many who in their affliction fixe their eyes onely vpon the instruments, and irreconcilably fret against men and women who are their enemies, who are nothing but a rod in Gods hand. They, not perceiving this, are like the foolish dogge that biteth the staffe not considering the hand wherein it is.[5] They will not beleeve God though he most clearely say that there is no evill in the citie [Amos 3:6], which he hath not done that is no trouble or affliction whereof he is not the author.

The 3 Vse. Let this serve for comfort to all Gods children: what ever calamitie, publick or private, come vpon the whole land, or vpon their particular families, or vpon their proper persone, it comes all out of Gods hand, which, whether he comfort or correct, may in Nehemiahs language well be called the good hand of the Lord. Whose hand, I pray you, will doe vs good if Gods hand doe it not [Neh 2:8]? Is it not his, said Moses, *thy Father that hath bought thee? Hath he not made thee and established thee* [Deut 32:6]? The Lord Jesus, to make vs sensible of Gods love and more then fatherly care, reasoned thus, *what* father *is there of you, whom, if his sonne aske bread, will he give him a stone? Or if he aske* him *a fish, will he give him a serpent* [Matt 7:9-10]? Vnto this the vse is subioined: *if yee then being* *evill knowe how to give good gifts vnto your children, how much more shall your father which is in heaven give good things to them that aske him* [Matt 7:11]? Seeing it is the good hand of our father [Neh 2:8] in heaven that is the cheefe agent in all the troubles and afflictions that come vpon vs, wee may be assured that, come what can come, it shall worke to our best. The apostle in this is plaine; his wordes are certaine knowledge. *Wee,* said he, *knowe that all things worke together for good to them that love God* [Rom 8:28].

Now let vs consider what God heere first is said to doe. *Thou,* saith the psalmist, *broughtest vs into the net.* The word in the Hebrewe hath two significations. Some derive it from a word that signifieth a tower, castle, or fortresse.[6] In the second of Samuel, wee haue this word of my text where it is said that *David tooke the strong hold of Zion* [2 Sam 5:7]; likewise, the psalmist makeing vse of this word where he saith, *the Lord is my rock and my fortresse* [Ps 18:2]. So likewise is the third verse of the thirtie one psalme: *Thou art my rock and my fortresse* [Ps 31:3]. So God, speakeing of the eagle, hath this word saying, *she dwelleth and abideth on the rock, vpon the cragge of the rock, and the strong place* [Job 39:28]. That cave in Adullam vnto which David had his refuge [1 Sam 22:1] is also so called.

If wee take the word for a fortresse, tower, or cave heere, David declareth that he was in such a distresse as these are in who are beseeged by a mighty and potent enemie, a distresse which is very terrible. Beseeged persons are often brought to very great extremities, as wee haue seene Gods hand very heauy vpon the bodies of his Churches enemies in this land. Who will ever forget the sight of the dead faces of these who east and west were beseeiged in our cheefest strong holds.[7] Though they were most miserable, it was no wonder because God was against them. But even the case of Gods servants beseeged hath beene very fearefull. Sanserres, a strong hold in France,[8] was so hardly beseeged that a father and a mother of our profession there were constrained to eate their owne child. The Rochel[9] twise was redacted to great extremitie.

The word of the text, while it signifieth a net, is driven from a word that signifieth to hunt. Of this word, Isaac made vse when he said, *where is he that hath taken* or hunted *venison* [Gen 27:33]? Hence cometh the word of this text which signifieth a net. The prophet Ezekiel, foretelling the captivitie of Zedekiah in Babylon, said, I will spread my net vpon him and *he shall be taken in my snare* [Ezek 12:13]. This saying of the psalmist heere, *thou hast broughtest vs into the net*, is a forme of speach borrowed from hunters or fishers, who compasse the beasts or fishes with their nets and so take them before they be aware.

The Doctrine. Observe heere that the children of God are subiect to very great afflictions vntill the Lord in mercy deliver them. Wee may know by the text that Gods hand is aboue all. But the wicked, who are the instruments of their calamities, are most fierce against them like hunters seekeing by all meanes the life of a beast. It is written of Nimrod that *he was a mighty hunter before the Lord* [Gen 10:9], that is he with great power hunted men by oppression, persecution and tyrannie, by craft and policie. This is not the least ill of wicked mens hunting. They circumven the simple and hide their doeings, knoweing well that of Solomon, *in vaine* is *the net spread in the sight of any bird* [Prov 1:17]. The prophet Jeremie, lamenting his sorrowes, said, *mine enemies chased me sore like a bird without cause* [Lam 3:52]; and a little after, *they hunt our steps that wee can not goe in our streets* [Lam 4:18]. As the hunters or fowlers or fishers are glade when they haue taken a beast, a foule or a fish in their net, and incontinent, runne and kill, even so the wicked haue ever their minds on their nets that by them they may catch and kill the servants of the Lord. It is their sport, yea and their meat, to doe wickednesse.

The Vse. Let vs beware to sinne against God, for, if wee proudly provoke him, he will not faile to send such fishers and hunters with their nets for to circumveene vs. The Lord, threatining his people for their idolatry, said, *behold, I will send for many fishers [. . .] and they shall fish them; and after will I send for many hunters, and they shall hunt them from every mountaine, and from every hill, and out of the holes of the rockes* [Jer 16:16]. When God is angry with a nation, a citie, a familie, or a man, there is no secret corner that will hide him. Fishes may break the nets or swimme by them and disapoint the fisher; wild beasts may breake the nets or leape over them, or may hide them selues in the clifts of the rocks; but if the Lord be provoked, where shall men hide them selves where he will not find them? See yee not how glade the dogges are to goe to the

132

hunting. So are the wicked most bent to be imployed in the destruction of Gods servants.

2. Thou laidst affliction[10] vpon our loines

The second distresse that came vpon Gods people heere is contained in these wordes, *thou laidst afflictions vpon our loines*, the Hebrewe word heere turned affliction according to the Greeke.[11] All interpretation is very well turned by some strait-nesse, such as men feele when they are thrust into a narrow place, so that they knowe not to what hand to turne them, being beset on all sides with difficulties. The word wherefra[12] this word cometh signifieth to presse downe with an exceeding great weight. Of this word, the Lord him self made vse to declare his afflictions procured by his people. *Behold*, said he, *I am pressed vnder you, as a cart is pressed that is full of sheaves* [Amos 2:13]. By this, it clearly appeareth that in this place heauy burdens are spoken of which were laide vpon the loines of Gods people, wherewith they were pressed as a *cart is pressed that is full of sheaves*.

The Doctrine. Observe heere that the people of God by Gods permission will be in great straits, and for a time be like beasts vnder burdens. As for straitnesse, David knewe it, for, when it was ordained by God that for his sinne of numbering of the people, he should either suffer seven yeeres famine, or three moneth fleeing before the sword, or three dayes pestilence, he answered, *I am in a great strait* [2 Sam 24:14]; that is, hardly knowe I to what hand to turne me. Such was the strait of Gods people heere. There were such burdens laide vpon their loines, as if they had beene beasts draweing carts, or like Issachar *crouching* [. . .] *betweene two burdens* [Gen 49:14]. And such were our afflictions in this land. Wee were in a great strait; wee were on all sides compassed about with our enemies.[13] Great ships, towres by sea, threatned vs. The strong holds in the land were possessed by our enemies, who made their thundring canons to roare against our cities and killed divers of our people. Armies on all sides did menace and threaten vs. Wee were a people inclosed round about. It seemed vnto all our neighbours

133

that wee were a people vtterly vndone, so it pleased the Lord to lay such afflictions vpon our loines.

The Vse. Let vs not forget our bygone straits, but let vs punctualy remember the burdens that our enemies had laid vpon our loines that wee may be the more stirred vp vnto thankefulnesse. For this cause, the Lord, to stirre vp his people to remember his mercies towards them in Egypt, ordained a sacrament the ceremonies whereof put them in memorie of that great hast they were in that night they went out of Egypt. For this cause, while they did eate the passeouer, they were ordained to stand haueing their shooes on their feet, their loines girded, and their staues in their hand [Exod 12:11]. Likewise, it was ordained that he that brought to God the basket of first fruits should make this humble confession before the Lord saying, *a Syrian ready to perish was my father, and he went downe into Egypt and sojourned there with a few* [Deut 26:5]. There is nothing more powerfull to make our hearts to love the Lord in our prosperitie then to remember the great straits wee haue beene in in dayes of adversitie. By this meanes, wee shall be stirred vp, both thankefully to praise God and also mercifully to pitie others in distresse. This consideration of bygaine troubles moved that pagan woman to haue compassion on the distressed Troians,[14] who said vnto them, by mine owne experience in suffering, I learne to pitie others in distresse. Yea, Christ him self, *though he was a sonne, yet learned he obedience by the things which he suffered* [Heb 5:8]. Yea, by his sufferings, he learned to pitie others in distresse, *for in that hee him self hath suffered being tempted, hee is able to succour them that are tempted* [Heb 2:18].

3. Thou hast caused men to ride over our heads

The third distresse that came vpon Gods people is contained in these wordes, *Thou hast caused men to ride over our heads*. In the Hebrewe, it is in the singular number, thou hast caused man;[15] and that either for to designe the cheefe man that did persecute Gods Church, or to declare the great virtue combination of the wicked together, who were welled together in wickednesse even in a cluster, as if they had beene but one man.

According to this, it is writen in the booke of Judges that when the Israelites arose in an armie to revenge the villainie comitted by the Beniamites at Gibeah, it is said that *all the men of Israel were gathered against the city knit together as one man* [Judg 20:11].

The Doctrine. Observe heere how wicked men will runne together in plots to doe a mischeefe, though, in other things among them selves, they haue their owne quarrels and iealousies. Yet when it comes to doe a mischeefe to Gods Church, they will stick together like burres, and passe by their particular quarrels. Men may see that there is little peace among the kings of the earth, for they all almost are most iealous one of anothers grandeur. If they can spye an opportunitie to incroach one vpon anothers kingdome, they will not be slowe. Many iarres may be seene among them, but if a time come wherein they may doe an ill turne to Christs Church, many of them will band together. Dauid sawe this in his time, and said, *the kings of the earth set them selves, and the rulers take counsell together against the Lord, and against his anointed* [Ps 2:2]. They in that case are knit together as one man. Herode was a king and Pilate was a ruler, not one of them loued another. But how were they made friends? Pilate sent Christ vnto Herod who mocked him and set him at nought, and he againe sent him back vnto Pilate. *And the same day*, saith S. Luke, *Pilate and Herode were made friends together, for before they were at enmitie betweene them selves* [Luke 23:12]. Now behold them knit together as one man at the mocking of Christ Jesus.

The 1 Vse. Let vs learne heere not to depend vpon the divisions of wicked men, as though thereby the Church of God should haue a constant peace. I knowe that sometimes the Lord will set the wicked one against another, and make them to destroye one another, as he made the Midianites lying along in the valleye like grashoppers for multitude. There it is said that *the Lord set every mans sword against his fellowe, even through out all the host* [Judg 7:22]. This was extraordinarie. But for the most part the wicked, like Herode and Pilate, will pack vp their privat quarrels that they may beare downe the godly with all sortes of calamities. The divell doth with wicked men, as Baalzebub doth with other divels, as he will not fight with them, neither cast them out, lest his kingdome be divided

135

and weakened so [Matt 12:25]. For the maintenance of his kingdome, his desire is that all the enemies of the Church may be one, as he and the rest of the divels are one.

The 2 Vse. Let this serve for reproofe to many of this land, who, though they haue most deepely and solemnly sworne and subscribed that covenant wherein all divisive motions are abiured, yet haue falsified their faith and haue broken the holy vnion by their divisive motions. The wordes of the covenant are these worthy to be considered by them to move them to repent, and also worthy to be considered by vs that wee never fall into the like, which may make vs tremble at the houre of our death, and so plunge vs in the deepths of despair where hardly shall wee find an outgate.[16] Consider the wordes, wee shall neither directlie nor indirectlie suffer our selves to be divided or withdrawen by whatsoever suggestion, combination, allurement, or terrour from this blessed and loyall coniunction; nor shall cast in any let or impediment that may stay or hinder any such resolution, as by commoun consent shall be found to conduce for so good deeds, but on the contrarie shall, by all lawfull meanes, labour to further and promove the same;[17] and if any such dangerous and divisive motion be made to vs by word or writ, wee and every one of vs shall either suppresse it, or, if neede be, shall incontinent make the same knowne, that it may be timeously obviated etc. And for this, wee call the living God the searcher of our hearts to witnes who knoweth this to be our sincere desire and vnfained resolution, as wee shall answere to Iesvs Christ in the great day, and vnder the paine of Gods everlasting wrath, and of infamie, and of the losse of all honour and respect in this world.

See heere what a fearefull thing it is either to make, allowe, or followe after any divisive motions for breakeing of our holy vnion, whereby wee should be, as it was said of the men of Israel, *knit together as one man* [Judg 20:11]. Wee haue heard of the vnion of Gods peoples enemies *knit together as one man*. Now let vs see what was the distresse that Gods people did suffer by them. It is heere said that they did ride over their heads. The psalmist saith, *Thou hast caused men* [. . .] *ride over our heads.* Some turne these wordes to sit and ride vpon their heads and necks. And so the people of God heere, as Piscator[18] observeth, is compaered vnto a camel vpon whose neck men are caried.

136

Doubtlesse the office is not so vile or base or paineful; but the wicked, when they get the vpper hand, will lay it vpon Gods servants head and neck. Heauy were these burdens of brick which the Egyptians laid vpon the backs and shoulders of the distressed Israelites [Exod 1:14]. Little were they moved with their groanings [Exod 2:24]. All this is most certaine that wicked men, whose compassions are cruell when they haue power, vse Gods servants as beasts.

The wordes doe meane a great slauerie and servile subiection. But I rather follow the English version,[19] with the most part of all the interpreters, who turne the wordes, *Thou hast caused men* [. . .] *ride over our heads*, that is tread vs downe in the dirt. Of this sorte of doeing, wee haue in Isaiah. The enemies of Gods people there, said I to Gods servants, *bow downe that wee may goe over.* To this the prophet subioineth, saying to Gods people, *thou hast layd thy body as the ground, and as the street to them that went over* [Isa 51:23].

The Doctrine. Observe heere the great pride of wicked men, who esteeme so basely of Gods people that they in a maner make stepping stones of them in vilest mires. Bowe downe, say they, that wee may goe over. Such doeings haue beene among our selves. The Lords Church in this land these yeeres bypast hath beene farre bowed downe. Men high in power, as on horseback, did ride over the heads of many deare seruants of God. A booke of bondage was ordained for all our shoulders, a service booke indeede, a booke from Babel for to bring vs againe into the antichristian bondage. For to bring in all this bagage, the Popes prelats[20] were all on horsebacke, rideing over our heads with tyrannie and oppression. A fewe yeeres agoe, well might the Church of Scotland haue said to the Lord, *Thou hast caused men* [. . .] *ride over our heads.*

The Vse. Let vs learne heere not to despaire when most wicked men are high exalted like men on horseback rideing over the heads of men. It is no new thing. Heare how the Church of old said to God, *Thou hast caused men* [. . .] *ride over our heads.* If Gods servants can have patience, they will see such riders become foot men, like Haman, who came down from all his grandeur to become a foot man for to leade the horse whereon sat good Mordicai [Est 6:11], the rider in my text, though he be called a man hath his name from infirmitie and mortalitie which bringeth all men lowe.

4. Wee went through fire and through water

The fourth distresse of Gods people heere mentioned is contained in these wordes, *wee went through fire and through water*, that is through exceeding great dangers of all sortes. These two particulars of fire and water are put for all sortes of miseries and dangers. For to passe thorow a burning fire, it is fearefull; so also to passe through deepe waters is very terrible. These two elements, fire and water, are mercilesse masters; from thence great troubles in scripture are whiles compared to fire and whiles to water. Concerning fire, the apostle, speakeing of the vnskilfull builders of Gods Church who keepe the fundation Christ, but build vpon him for precious stones no thing but haye, stubble, wood, their owne inventions, such a builder saith, the apostle, *shall be saved yet so as by fire* [1 Cor 3:15], that is he shall vndergoe most painefull afflictions. So also David, speakeing of drowning afflictions, calleth them *the floods of great waters* [Ps 32:6]. In another psalme, he cried to God, *save me O God, for the waters are come in vnto my soule* [Ps 69:1]. Heere it is said, *wee went through fire and through water*.

The Doctrine. Observe heere that *many are the troubles of the righteous* [Ps 34:19].[21] When they haue passed through the fire, then they must also passe through the water. The ending of one crosse is but the beginning of another. This made Jacob to say to pharaoh, enquireing of his age, my dayes haue beene few and ill [Gen 47:9].

The Vse. Let Gods Church heere learne that, when one trouble is past, not to be secure. If they haue passed through the fire, they must also passe through the water. Wee haue these yeeres bypast past through many troubles. Well may wee say, *wee went through fire and through water*. Yet though times be changed, wee must not dreame to be heere in a triumphing Church, where all teares shall be wiped from our eyes and all troubles from our heart. He is but a foolish pylot, who, because one storme is past and the daye is now faire, will therefore

138

reason that the winds will blowe no more and that the surges will no more be seene like mountaines, to make them *reele to and fro, and stagger like* drunken men [Ps 107:27].

The Doctrine. Againe, whereas it is said heere of Gods servants that they *went through fire and through water* also, I observe the stabilitie of the Church, the stabilitie in that they doe abide both the fire and water. Eleazar, speakeing to the men of warre & giving them a law how to purifie the spoile that they had taken from the enemie, ordained such things as silver, gold that might abide the fire to goe through the fire and also to be purified with water [Num 31:23]. But, as for that which could not abide the fire, yee, said he, shall make it *goe thorow the water*. As for the godly heere, yee see that they went both through fire and water. They abide all sortes of trialls for the Lord vpholdeth them.

Observe heere that the Church pressed with great numbers of afflictions, yet passeth thorow them all. But the wicked perish by the way, whether in fire or water. King Pharao and his armie sank downe like lead in the water [Exod 15:10], but Israel passed through. Nebuchadnezzars burrios[22] that cast Gods servants into the fierie furnace were consumed by the flame of fire comeing from the furnace [Dan 3:22]. But Shadrach and his fellowes went through. The wicked passe not through. If they escape one fire, they are consumed with another. *They*, said the Lord by Ezekiel, *shall goe out from one fire, and another fire shall devore them* [Ezek 15:7].

The Vse. Let this serve for comfort to Gods children in greatest calamities: the Lord shall give them a passe. Either he shall make iudgements passe over them, as he made his destroyeing angel to passe over the Israelites houses marked with blood [Exod 12:23]; or he shall make his servants to passe through the danger, as heere his children did who say, *wee went through fire and* [. . .] *water*. Onely Gods children come out of their troubles. In the Revelation S. John sawe a number all clothed in white robes. While he looked, one of the elders said to John, *what are these* [Rev 7:13]? John could not tell. Then the elder said, *these are they which came out of great tribulation* [Rev 7:14]. Behold how they came out and *went through fire and through water*. The end of the righteous is ever peace [Ps 37:37], for he at last passeth through.

2 Part
a mercifull deliverance

In the first part of this text, wee have heard of the great distresses of Gods Church amply declared in foure formes of speaches: first, that God had brought them into the net; secondly, that he had laid affliction vpon their loines; thirdly, that he had *caused men* [. . .] *ride over their heads*; fourthly, that *they went through fire and through water.*

Now it followeth that wee consider the second part of the text which is contained in these wordes, but *thou broughtest vs out into a wealthy place*, wordes which containe a most thankefull acknowledgment of Gods most mercifull deliverance. The word heere is turned a wealthy place or wealthy land. The Hebrewe[23] word is an adiective, the alone, but land or place is vnder stood to be ioined vnto it. It cometh from an Hebrewe word which signifieth to be made drunke by reason of abundance, also to water or overflowe. David, speakeing of his well filled cup declareing his plentie, made vse of this word saying, *my cup runneth over* [Ps 23:5]. Whereas the psalmist heere saith to the Lord, *thou hast brought vs* [. . .] *vnto a wealthy place*, it is as much as if he had said, after many troubles and calamities, thou hast at last most sweetely refreshed vs with all sortes of comforts, and that in great abundance both spiritually and temporaly. When the Lord maketh a land spiritualy rich, whateuer other temporall things be cast vnto them, that land indeede may be called a wealthy place.

The Doctrine. Observe heere that the Lord hath places of wealth for his servants, and that both in this life and in the life to come. That which maketh and in the life to come, that which maketh many turne their back vpon Christ, is the opinion they haue that there is nothing but miserie and want at his service. This made that young man in the gospell to goe away sorrowfull from Christ. S. Mathew saith that *he had great possessions* [Matt 19:22]. The gore of greedinesse had so closed his eyes that he could not imagine that Christ could, as it is in my text, bring him to a wealthy place.

I will heere boldly affirme that there is no wealthy place but where the Lord is in mercy. Wealth is no wealth where Gods love is away. Bagges of silver and gold without his grace are

140

but burdens of dirt, which bowe downe the backs of carnall drudges. But what euer the righteous man hath with Gods blessing, it is wealth; and his dwelling shall at last be found to be a wealthy place. The Lord shall make his cup to run over. *The Lord is my shepheard*, said David, *I shall not want* [Ps 23:1]. That which seemeth little in a worldlings eyes is made wealthy to a godly man because his little hath a blessing. This made Solomon to say, *better is a dinner of herbes where love is, then a stalled oxe and hatred therewith* [Prov 15:17]. And in another place, *better is a dry morsell and quietnesse therewith then a house full of sacrifices with strife* [Prov 17:1].

The Vse. Let this serve for to encourage all good men to continue in Gods service, for though they meete with many losses and crosses, the Lord who is God all sufficient will still provide for them. Such at last shall sing heere with the psalmist, *wee went through fire and through water, but thou broughtest vs into a wealthy place.*

The Doctrine. Againe, whereas it is said heere, *wee went through fire and [through] water, but thou broughtest vs [. . .] into a wealthy place*, I observe that the first things of Gods seruants are troubles and calamities. They ordinarily haue hard beginnings, but at last get a peaceable conclusion. The parts of their life are like Isaacs three wells. The first was called Esek, that is strife, because the men of that place strove with him [Gen 26:20]. The second was called Sitnah, that is hatred because the men of the place did continue to strive with him [Gen 26:21]. The third was called Rehoboth, that is roome. *Now*, said he, *the Lord hath made roome for vs, and wee shall be fruitfull in the land* [Gen 26:22] that was to come to a wealthy place.

The Vse. Let this serve to teach vs not to be displeased when wee meet with hard beginnings at Gods service. Wee must drinke of the well of Esek and Sitnah before wee looke for roome at Rehoboth. If this be true, *many are the troubles of the righteous* [Ps 34:19]. This is as certaine: *the Lord delivereth him out of them all* [Ps 34:17]. If it be the lot of Gods children to weepe in the euening, God will send a comfort vnto them at the dawning of the day. Weeping, saith the psalmist, may come in the evening, *but ioye commeth in the morning* [Ps 30:5]. To this Isaiah said well at eventide, loe *there is trouble, but afore the morning it is gone* [Isa 17:14]. Through fire and through water,

141

Gods children at last come to their wealthy place. If any get not this heere, all their losses shall be made vp in the heauens, which to speake properly is the onely place of wealth, a place where no thing is wanting, either for soule or body. This shall be done *when the time of refreshing shall come from the* Lords prayer [Acts 3:19].

The Doctrine. Last of all, whereas the psalmist heere saith to God, but *thou broughtest* [. . .] *vs into a wealthy place*, I obserue that he acknowledgeth most thankefully God to be the author of all their peace, plentie, and prosperitie, whether spirituall or temporall. The wordes are very spirituall. *Thou*, said he, *broughtest vs* [. . .] *into a wealthy place*. The psalmist said not our swordes and our bowes and our speares and other excellent armour preuailed. Neither, said he, our men were men of a braue courage. Our captaines were valiant men, as Saul said of Goliah, trained vp in warre from their youth [1 Sam 17:33]. Neither, said he, our souldiers were like Saul and Jonathan, *swifter then eagles* and *stronger then lions* [2 Sam 1:23], no not. At the psalmists giuing of thankes to God for the excellent victorie, all these second meanes stood aside to giue place to the Lords glory. They all went out of sight in the presence of his brightnesse.

The Vse. Wee may see very great things done in this land, and both Church and commounwealth brought into a wealthy place. Many a godly greeued heart hath beene comforted. But see that wee ascribe all the glory to God, saying *the Lord hath done great things for* vs [Ps 126:2]. Hee, and he onely, hath brought *vs* [. . .] *into a wealthy place*. Let all mens doeings giue place to his workes. As all the most glittering starres goe out of sight when the sunne ariseth, so all mens doeings, whatsoeuer in this our great deliuerance, must seeme nought in their owne eyes, that the Lord may haue all the praise. After that the apostle S. Paul had said, *I laboured more abundantly then they all*, he incontinent corrected him self saying, *yet not I, but the grace of God which was with me* [1 Cor 15:10]. It is so that, in all this great admirable worke done in this land, every man should say, if our most worthy, valiant and faithfull general should say I haue laboured much, if our nobles should say wee haue beene very vigilant, if the colonels, captaines, and souldiers should say wee haue shewen our courage, if ministers should say wee

142

haue powerfully preached in season and out of season, if all the nation should say wee have fasted and prayed and payed great taxations, let all be incontinent corrected with *yet not* wee *but the grace of God*, even the arme and sword of God that was with vs, hath brought *vs* [. . .] *into a wealthy place*.

Let all Scotland now say to God in this day of our publick thankes, *wee went through fire and through water, but thou hast brought vs into a wealthy place*, for which let vs all say from our hearts in these wordes of S. Pauls thanksgiving, *Now vnto the King eternall, immortall, invisible, the onelie wise God, be honour and glory for ever and ever* [1 Tim 1:17], Amen.

The Weapons of the Chvrch: A Sermon At a Fast during the troubles for the Booke of Common Prayer, Anno, 1638, the third of June afternoone

Ps 122:6

Pray for the peace of Jerusalem: they shall prosper that loue thee.

This psalme, as the most learned esteeme, was writen by Dauid when he brought the arke of the Lord from the house of Obed Edom with great ioye into the citie of David [2 Sam 6:12].

the division of the psalme

In this psalme, there be two principall parts. In the first vnto the sixt verse, wee haue Davids ioye for the prosperitie of the Church. In the second part, wee haue his singular care of the well of the Church; and that from the sixt verse vnto the end, *pray for the peace of Jerusalem; they shall prosper that loue thee.*

the diuision of the text

In these wordes, there be two parts: first, a precept, after a promise. The precept is in these wordes, *pray for the peace of Jerusalem.* The promise is in these wordes, *they shall prosper that loue thee.*

1 Part
an exhortation to pray for the Church

In this exhortation, wee haue to consider these three things: first, who exhorteth, it is King Dauid; secondly, to what, to pray; thirdly, for what, for the peace of Jerusalem: *pray for the peace of Jerusalem.*

1. who exhorteth

He who exhorteth heere to godlinesse is a king.

The Vse. As kings are first among men, so should they be the first men at the service of God. God hath called them gods [Ps 82:6], and therefore they should goe before others at the service of God. From these to whom much is giuen, much shall be required. Kings are not made kings for to glut them selues with pleasures and to doe what they please, but they are made kings to be seruants vnto God and to be among men like the master bees, directers of all the rest in the workes that are for the glory of God and the well of their subiects, either for soule or body in the Church or commoun wealth.[1] Seeing kings reigne by God [Prov 8:15], it is reason that kings reigne for God. All their honour that is from him must by waye of homage returne vnto him.

2. to what the king heere exhorteth his subiects

That which the king heere exhorteth his subiects to doe, it is to pray. The Hebrewe word is *shaal*,[2] to seeke earnestly and often. From this word cometh *Sheol*, the graue, so called from seekeing.

The Doctrine. From the doctrine I obserue heere, godly men haue godly exhortations, godly kings haue godly directions; earthly minded princes can neither pray nor exhort their people to pray. They haue no thing in their mind but tributes and taxations. If their fathers haue made the peoples yoke heauy, they will with Rehoboam adde to that yoke. If their fathers haue chastised them with whips, they will chastise them with scorpions [1 Kgs 12:14]. From this cometh that often people turne their backe vpon their princes, saying with Israel, *what portion haue wee in Dauid* [. . .] *to your tents, O Israel* [1 Kgs 12:16]?

The Vse. Let all kings heere learne of King Dauid to stirre vp their people to serue God well. Prayers and praises are two tributes which all nations must pay to God, the owner of the earth. Let kings and rulers be most carefull that this God be not

145

depriued of this due. If so they doe, they shall find it the onely waye to a *lengthening* of their *tranquillitie* [Dan 4:27].

O happy is that nation who hath a king whose cheefest precepts are precepts of prayer, that is whose cheefest care is that God in all his dominions may be worshipped in spirit and trueth [John 4:23]. If such a king say to his people pray, God shall say to his people obey. If such a king say to his people, doe all dutie to God, God shall say to that people, doe all dutie to your king. But if the king care not for God, God will not care for him. If the king denye service and homage to his king, the Lord will soone persuade the subiects to deny homage to their kings. Because King Abimelech was not thankefull to God for his kingdome and neglected to instruct his people in the right way of Gods service, *God sent an euill spirit betweene* him and his subiects [Judg 9:23]. The Lord made a fire to come out of the roots of that bramble which deuoured his greatest nobles whom Jotham in his parable called the Cedars of Lebanon [Judg 9:15]. After that, the king him selfe was killed at Thebez. Then God rendered the wickednesse of that king, and also he rendered all the euill of his wicked subiects vpon their heads. These were the fruits of that euill spirit which God for their sinnes sent betweene them.

Let vs all this day intreat God most earnestly that God would send his good spirit betweene our king and his nobles, the cedars of the land. Let vs all pray for him that in him may be the sweetnesse of the figge tree [Judg 9:11], the fatnesse of the oliue, and the virtues of the vine, whereby he may honour and reioice both God and man, that both God and man being pleased with him, peace and trueth may remaine in our land [2 Kgs 20:19].

3. for what he exhorteth to pray

That which the king heere exhorteth his people to pray for is the peace of Jerusalem. *Pray for the peace of Jerusalem*, that is for the prosperitie of the Church.

The Doctrine. Heere obserue first that the tranquillitie and peace of a nation depends, not vpon men, but vpon God. The

146

king heere knoweing this exhorted his people to pray for it. *Pray for the peace of Jerusalem.*

The Vse. Wee these many yeeres bypast haue had a wonderfull peace of more then threescore yeeres with the gospel of peace. Let vs be thankefull to God for it. Well may wee say, *Deus nobis huc otia fecit*, God hath giuen vs all this ease, to him be glory for euer. In what nation was it euer heard that the gospel remained so long with peace? My exhortation now is that yee praise God for the peace of our Jerusalem. But seeing Satan, who neuer sleeps, is night and day by vnsanctified braines deuising and plotting both to take peace and trueth from vs, let vs all runne to gether like *a threefold coard* which *is not easily broken* [Eccl 4:12], and by teares and prayers wrestle with the Lord that he would command peace and trueth to tary still in our Jerusalem.

Take courage brethren in this worke. Let vs most earnestly this day *pray for the peace of* our *Jerusalem*. I will not say with the king of Niniveh, *who can tell if God will turne* [Jonah 3:9]? I can right well tell that, if wee will turne vnto him by repentance, he will turne vnto vs with mercy. God him self hath said it by his prophet Zacharie. *Turne* [. . .] *vnto me, saith the Lord of hostes; and I will turne vnto you, saith the Lord of hostes* [Zech 1:3]. God hath sworne that he taketh no pleasure in our death. *If thou seeke him*, said David to Solomon, *he will be found of thee, but, if thou forsake him, he will cast the off for euer* [1 Chr 28:9].

I exhorte you one and all in praying this day for the peace of our Jerusalem to pray in faith, in assurance that God is a mercifull God, who will be ready to turne vnto vs. S. James teacheth vs when wee aske of God any thing to *aske in faith nothing* wauering [Jas 1:6]. Wherefore should wee wauer? Is he not our Father? Though a mother should forget her child [Isa 49:15], he will not forget these that seeke him. Hath he not said, aske and yee shall receiue, *seeke and yee shall find* [Matt 7:7]? Hath he not sworne by his life that he taketh no delight in the death of sinners [Ezek 33:11]? He afflicteth neuer willingly the children of men. To doe them good is his pleasure, but to trouble them is his strange worke. When he hath set downe his candlestick in a land, a fewe faults will not moue him to take it awaye. He will often threaten before he doe it. He will giue many tokens of his goeing away before he depart.

147

Before his glory departed from Jerusalem, it gaue them diuers warnings [Ezek 9:3]. First, it went from the Church to the threshold of the house. There is made a pause waiting vntill some godly persones should by prayer intreat it to returne. Heere first he shewe them that he meant to remoue away from them. But not all at once, but by degrees; and therefore he remoued first only to the threshold of the temple. After that the glory of God departed from the threshold of the temple and stood aboue the east gate of the Lords house [Ezek 10:19]. There it paused, attending the prayers of repenting sinners, that being desired it might returne to the mercy seat. After that it remoued to the middest of the city, but no prayers beeing made for the peace of Jerusalem. *The glory of the Lord went vp from the midest of the citie and stood vpon the mountaine* [Ezek 11:23], and after that departed, because, after so many pauses, there were no prayers directed vnto him with requeasts to returne.

Before the remoueing of their peace, yea before the first remoueing of his glory to the threshold, he set before their eyes fearefull types of his wrath to tell them that, if they prayed not for the peace of Jerusalem, all their peace and prosperitie would depart. He warned them with types of wrath for to saue them from the substance of wrath. The one was by a tyle; the other was by haire. As for the tile, the Lord said vnto his prophet, *take thee a tile, and lay it before thee, and pourtray vpon it the citie, euen Jerusalem* [Ezek 4:1]; *and lay siege against it, and build a fort against it, and cast a mountain against it; set the campe also against it; and set battering rammes against it round about* [Ezek 4:2]. As if he had said, make thee vpon a tile, a modell, or draught of the citie of Jerusalem; after that, make the modell of a siege laid against that so portrayed citie. There Ezekiel, the type of an armie besieging the modell of Jerusalem vpon a tile, was a signe from God warning all men to pray for the peace of Jerusalem. After that, the Lord commanded the prophet to take a barbours rasour, and cause it to passe vpon his head and his beard, and to divide the haire. *Thou*, said the Lord, *shall burne with fire a third part* of the haire *in the midst of the citie,* [. . .] *and thou shalt take a third part and smite about with a knife, and a third part thou shalt scatter in the wind* [Ezek 5:2]. By this, he declared that he would cut off his rebellious people by seuerall waies of destruction.

See how, by the modell of a siege vpon a tile, and by types of cutted haire, the Lord did forewarne his people to repent in time, and to pray for the peace of Jerusalem. Wee of this land haue receiued more substantiall warning, and that both by fire and water, for both wayes our enemies haue sought to bereaue vs of our peace. First by water in the eighty eight the Lord permitted our enemies to come out against vs, not with Ezekiels battering rammes against a tile, but with an armado of ships like towers filled with canons and expert men of warre.[3] When this warning was giuen, our people fell all downe before God praying for the prince of Jerusalem.[4] The Lord heard vs, and helped vs, and made his glory to runne thorow sea and land by drowning the pride of that Spanish pharaoh.[5]

After that, by water our enemies could not preuaile. They would, like Balaam goeing from hill to hill [Num 23:7][6] seeking to curse Gods people [Num 23:14], try what they could doe by fire. With six and thirtie barrells of powder were all ordained to speake treason with one sound, and to spew king, queene, prince, and all the nobles vp into the aire.[7] While wee knewe not our danger, the Lord maintained our peace. The Lord deliuered vs before wee prayed. It was a great mercy when God said to Daniel that he heard him at the beginning of his supplication [Dan 9:23].

But our mercy was greater in that he deliuered vs before wee knew our danger. The peace of our Jerusalem was established before wee knewe of that popish powder puffe. If the Lord preserued our peace before wee beganne any supplication against that danger, how much more will he now deliuer vs from these seene dangers, if in true repentance, with broken and contrite hearts, wee this daye ioine our prayers together for the peace of Jerusalem: *pax optima rerum*; *pax via triumphis*; *innumeris petier.*[8]

2 Part
they shall prosper that loue thee

In the second part of the text, wee haue a promise of prosperitie to all the friends of the Church. The promise is in these wordes: *they shall prosper that loue thee.* The Hebrewe word

Shalab[9] signifieth *tranquillum esse guiescere*, to haue tranquillitie, rest, and prosperitie. From this word, the most learned in the Hebrewe tongue esteeme that Christ by Jacob was called *Shiloh* [Gen 49:10],[10] that is *tranquillus et aeternae tranquillitatis auther*, that is calme, quiet, peaceable, and the auther of all peace and prosperitie. Heere then, as one saith well, *est Luculenta promissio*, is a faire and large promise made to all these who are friends to the Church of God? *They*, saith Dauid, *shall prosper that loue thee.*

The Doctrine. The doctrine I obserue heere is this: it is a great blessing of God to be a friend to the saints of God. Such shall not faile to prosper. Tranquillitie, peace, and prosperitie are heere promised vnto them. *They shall prosper that loue thee.* All the blessings of Guerizim shall come on thee and ouertake them. *Blessed* shall they *be in the citie, and blessed* shall they *be in the field. Blessed shall be the fruit of* their *body, and the fruit of* their *ground, and the fruit of* their *cattell, the increase of* their *kine and the flockes of* their *sheepe. Blessed shall be* their *basket and* their *store. Blessed* shall they *be when* they *come in*, and when they *goe out* [Deut 28:3-6]. *The Lord shall cause* their *enemies that rise vp against* them *to be smitten before* their *face. They shall come out against* them *one way, and shall flee before* them *seuen wayes.* Thus shall be done to these that loue Gods Jerusalem. *Whatsoeuer* they *doe shall prosper* [Ps 1:3]; they shall be happy heere and happy heereafter.

The Vse. Let this stirre all men vp to be friends and louers of Gods Church. If Dauid had reason to say, shall I not hate these that hate thee, I haue hated them with a perfect hatred, and they haue beene mine enemie, with as good reason should euery Christian say, shall I not loue these that loue thee?[11] I haue loued them with a perfect loue, and I esteeme all such to be my dearest friends.

There be many reasons to moue vs to this duetie. Fire to mourne with the saints in their sorrowe and to reioice with them in their ioye, which are the effects of loue, are a token that wee are members of one body with them. When one member of the body is afflicted, all the rest sympathize. If yee hurt your foot in its dashing against a stone, your head will not laugh at it and scorne it. Euery member in the body, according to its power, will concurre to its comfort. The eare will heare the surgions counsell for the wound, the eye will behold it with pitie, the hand will bind it vp, the mouth will tell its paine and lament it. Shall members of flesh be so sensible, and shall the spirituall members of Christs body not be touched with any sympathie?[12] Well then, seeing it is so, I will say to the Church, as Dauid said to Jerusalem, they shall prosper that loue thee. They shall haue euer this comfort in their bosome that they are of the number of these who are appointed for life eternall.

Againe, that all such may be encouraged to loue the well of Gods children, they in all their affaires shall not faile to prosper. What euer businesse they meddle with, the Lord shall be with them as he was with Joseph. It is said of Joseph, *the Lord was with* him, *and he was a prosperous man* [Gen 39:2]. There is none of you but yee desire to prosper, whether it be by sea or by land, at home or in the fields. Heere is the right way, an easy way. If yee loue the children of God and the well of Gods Church, yee shall not faile to prosper. God hath said it heere: *they shall prosper that loue thee.*

If these shall prosper that loue the Church, what shall become of these that care not for the Church in her troubles? Let such heare what Deborah said of Meros. It is writen for them: *Curse yee Meros* [. . .] *because they came not* out *to* [. . .] *help* [. . .] *the Lord, to* [. . .] *help* [. . .] *the Lord against the mighty* [Judg 5:23].[13] To such I will say that which Mordecai said to Ester, *thinke not with thy selfe that thou shalt escape in the kings house* [Est 4:13]. *For if thou altogether holdest thy peace at this time, then shall there enlargement and deliverance arise to* Gods people *from another place, but thou and thy fathers house shall be destroyed* [Est 4:14]. If such iudgements be threatned against these who hold their peace, and are not greeued for the affliction of Joseph, what shall be done to these who spend their wits and strength, some by wiles, some by force, to ouerthrowe the liberties of Gods Church? If Meros was cursed because they came not out to help the Lord [Judg 5:23], how many curses shall come vpon them who come out to hurt the Lord? If Esther was threatned with the perishing both of her self and of her fathers house, if in such time of trouble she should altogether hold her peace [Est 4:14], what shall be done to these who are either hidde or professed enemies of the Church?

I see in the psalme a great number of euills prepared for

them, even a long catalogue of miseries. What the psalmist there seeketh shall not faile to come vpon such.

1. A wicked man shall be set ouer him [Ps 109:6].
2. Satan shall *stand at his right hand* for to ouercome him [Ps 109:6].
3. *When he shall be iudged*, he shall be condemned [Ps 109:7].
4. *His prayer* shall *become sinne* [Ps 109:7]; God shall abhorre it.
5. *His dayes* shall *be few* [Ps 109:8]; God in wrath shall remoue him from the earth.
6. *Another* shall *take his office*, as Mathias tooke the office of Judas.
7. *His children* shall *be fatherles* [Ps 109:9]; he shall not liue for to be a help vnto his posteritie.
8. His wife shall be a widowe wanting protection [Ps 109:9].
9. His children shall be vagabonds continualy and beg [Ps 109:10]. Where Gods blessing is not, what can prosper?
10. The extortioners shall *catch all that he hath* [Ps 109:11]; as he oppressed others, so others shall oppresse him.
11. *The strangers* shall *spoile his labour* [Ps 109:11] that is his goods purchased by his labour; none of his owne shall be his heires.
12. None shall *extend mercie vnto him* [Ps 109:12]; as he had mercie on none, so none shall extend mercie vnto him.
13. None shall *fauour his fatherlesse children* [Ps 109:12]; they shall get no good for his sake.
14. *His posteritie* shall *be cut off* [Ps 109:13]; the name of the wicked shall rot.
15. *The iniquitie of his father* shall *be remembered*, and *the sinne of his mother* shall not be blowed out [Ps 109:14]; he shall not onely be punished for his owne faults, but God shall visite the sinnes of his father and mother vpon him vnto the third generation. Their sinnes shall *be before the Lord continualy*.[14]
16. *As he loued cursing*, so it shall come to him [Ps 109:17]; the ill he desired to Gods children shall come vpon him selfe.
17. He delighted not in blessing, and blessing shall be farre from him; God hath appointed no blessings for the wicked.
18. Because when the godly came to him, he *clothed himself with cursings* [. . .], as with a garment. The Lord shall fill his bowels

152

and his body with a curse. *It shall come into his bowels like water, and, like oyle, it shall enter into his bones* [Ps 109:18].

This shall be the reward of all Gods aduersaries from the Lord, and of all these that hate and persecute his Church. The cheefest enemies of the Church are either magistrats with Julian,[15] or counsellers with Ahitophel, or Church men with Judas. What God did to these, let all such looke for the like. The magistrate died in blood, blaspheming the Church men, and the counseller[s] hanged them selues. These who are against God shall neuer prosper; they and all their designes shall be at last *like the chaff which the wind driveth away* [Ps 1:4].

Seeing it is so, let vs be busie with God in prayer to stirre vp our hearts to the loue of the Church, that wee, not onely exhort others with Dauid in this verse to *pray for the peace of Jerusalem*, but also may with Dauid ioine our prayers with theirs saying, *peace be within thy walles and prosperitie within thy palaces. For our brethren and companions sake,*[16] wee must pray for the peace of the Church. But most of all because of the house of the Lord our God, wee must resolue all the dayes of our life for to seeke for good. If this wee doe, God, on the other part, shall resolue to blesse vs both spiritualy and temporaly. *Caro et cor*, our flesh and our heart may faile vs; but this promise of God concerning the friends of his Church shall neuer be fals. *They shall prosper that loue thee*; they shall get grace and glory heereafter in the heauens, which the Lord in mercy bring vs all his appointed time for Christ his Sonnes sake, Amen.

The Trivmph of the Chvrch
First Sermon preached the last sabbath of the yeere 1638

Ps 129:1

Many a time haue they afflicted me from my youth, may Israel now say.
v.2. Many a time haue they afflicted me from my youth, yet they haue not prevailed against me.
v.3. The plowers plowed vpon my back: they made long their furrowes.
v.4. The Lord is righteous: he hath cut asunder the coards of the wicked.

The whole substance of this psalme may well be contained in this one verse: *many are the troubles of the righteous, but the Lord deliuereth them out of them all* [Ps 34:19]. In all appearance, this psalme hath beene writen in a *day of small things* [Zech 4:10], a time wherein the Church of God hath beene vexed with the furie of wicked men. The psalmist, heere desireous to encourage the trembling hearts of many, declareth that the afflictions which the godly did suffer were both great and many, but that the Lord both had deliuered them in times past, and also would deliuer them in times to come by bringing a fearefull destruction vpon their enemies.

the diuision of the psalme

In this psalme, there be three principall parts. In the first part, the psalmist declareth the many afflictions of Gods Church: *many a time haue they afflicted me* etc, vntill the fourth verse. In the second part, wee haue the deliuerance of the Church, and that in the fourth verse: *the Lord is righteous; he hath cut asunder the cordes of the wicked*. In the third part, from the fift verse vntil the end, there is a prophecie of the destruction of all the enemies of the Children of God: they shall be ashamed, and turned back all that hate Zion etc.

154

This text may be diuided into two parts. In the first part, the psalmist declareth the many adversities and calamities of the Church. *Many a time haue they afflicted me from my youth, may Israel now say. The plowers haue plowed vpon my back; they* haue drawen *long their furrowes.* In the second part, wee haue Gods preseruation of the godly from the rage of the wicked, and also a more ample deliuerance. His preseruation is in these wordes: *yet they haue not preuailed against me.* His more ample deliuerance is in these wordes: *the Lord is righteous; he hath cut asunder the coards of the wicked.*

1 Part
the many aduersities of the godly

In the first part, the psalmist, by waye of lamentation, declareth the many miseries of Gods Church heere belowe: *many a time haue they afflicted me from my youth, may Israel now say; many a time haue they afflicted me from my youth* etc. Heere be two things, the complainer and the complaint. The complainer is Israel. The complaint is in these wordes: *many a time haue they afflicted me* etc.

the complainer

The complainer is the Church heere called Israel. *May Israel now say* the Church heere is called Israel, from Jacob, who, for his prevailing wrestling with God by teares and prayers [Hos 12:4], was by God called Israel, for, *as a prince*, had he *power with God and with men*, and so *prevailed* [Gen 32:28]. From him all the people of God were called the Israelites, that is princes who prevail with God and men.

The Doctrine. Obserue heere first that great is the dignitie of the Church. All the faithfull in Gods eyes are princes. The poorest Lazarus that hath Gods feare in his heart is an Israelite, a prince, yea a prince of the blood, not of the rotten blood of man, but of the blood of God, the royall blood of that great

King, who hath writen vpon his thigh the *King of Kings and Lord of Lords* [Rev 19:16].

The Vse. Let all men wrestle for this honour. This prince-dom at the first was purchased by paines. Iacob, before his wrestling, was but Iacob so called from Esaus heele [Gen 25:26]. He was but one that came behind at the heeles, but, O, by his wrestling with God, he became a prince, yea a prince of God. There be great wrestlings in this world for the vanities thereof, pleasure, profit, preferment. He to be first and he to be next. S. Paul, speakeing of the great paines of men for worldly honour, saith now, *they doe it to obtaine a corruptible crowne* [1 Cor 9:25]. O then, what should wee doe for to be Israelites, princes with God, Gods *peculiar treasure* [Ps 135:4], the greatest dignitie that mortall men can haue vpon this earth? Againe, let vs heere consider that, though the Church be Israel, great in Gods eyes, she hath not all contentments in this life. Behold her, heere a complainer in a most heauy complaint powreing out her soule with Hannah in grones and lamentations [1 Sam 1:15] by reason of many troubles, wherewith her enemies did afflict her.

The Vse. Let vs learne heere that the best beloued of God, his dearest princes of the blood, escape not the miseries of this life. The godly are not sent vnto this earth to passe their dayes in continuall songs of ioye. The perpetuall springs of Gods harpes are for the heauens [Rev 14:2]. This earth is a Babel, a strange land. How, said the Church, *shall wee sing the Lords song in a strange land?* [Ps 137:4] *Many a time haue they afflicted me from my youth. May Israel* heere *say*, the wicked haue exercised their vtmost spight vpon me.

the complaint

Wee haue heard of the complainer: it is the Church, Israel, these whose exercise is to weepe and pray [Hos 12:4]. Now it followeth that wee consider the Churches complaint. It is in these wordes: *many a time haue they afflicted me from my youth.* Heere is *oratio guerulosa*, the Churches lamentation, wherein I shall orderly consider these six things: 1. who they were that were the cause of her sorrow in the word, *they*; 2. what they

156

did to her, they haue *afflicted me*; 3. the frequencie of her afflictions, in the wordes *many a time*; 4. the long continuance of her afflictions, *from my youth*; 5. the vehemencie of her afflictions is declared by the repetition of the same wordes, *many a time haue they afflicted me from my youth* and againe *many a time haue they afflicted me from my youth*; 6. in a similitude from plowers of the ground, the psalmist demonstrats the crueltie of the enemies, the *plowers* haue *plowed vpon my backe*; *they made long their furrowes*.

1. they

First, let vs consider heere who they were who thus afflicted the Church. In the fourth verse, they are called *the wicked*. It is the wickeds taske to trouble God[s] saints whiles by force and whiles by fraude. *Come on*, said the Egyptiens, *let vs deale wisely with them, lest they multiplie* [Exod 1:10]. It is not one enemie heere that afflicteth Gods people but a multitude. It is not, said he or she, but they; *many a time haue they afflicted me*.

The Doctrine. Obserue heere breefely that the godly on earth are subiect to many calamities because their enemies are both wicked and many.

The Vse. Let all these who belong to God looke for many afflictions because there be many aduersaries. *All that will liue godly in Christ Jesus shall suffer persecution* [2 Tim 3:12]. When the diuels spake out of the man, they said to Christ, our *name is legion, for wee are many* [Mark 5:9]. The few chosen are but like a singular number in comparison of the many called [Matt 20:16]. If wee consider the wicked, wee shall find a pluralitie, whereas the godly are but one out of a city and two out of a tribe, a little flocke [Luke 12:32].

2. haue afflicted me

Now let vs see what the wicked haue done to the Church. *They*, said she, *haue* often *afflicted me*. In the Hebrewe, it is *tseraroum*. The word *tsour*,[1] from which the word of my text cometh, signifieth *obsidere, arctare, hostiliter premere, ligare,* to beseege, to put in a great strait, to presse like an enemie, or to bind. The psalmist vseth this word for to expresse the fearefull beseegeings of Gods wrath. *Thou*, said he, *hast beset me behind and before* [Ps 139:5].

The Doctrine. Obserue heere that the exercise of the wicked is to beset the godly behind and before. *They*, said the psalmist, *compassed me about like bees* [Ps 118:12]. When bees, once pro-voked, begin to flie vpon a man, they with great despight will beset him on all sides. They, by their stings, will wound him, except he be well fenced against them. In angrie bees see the image of wicked men, who *compasse about the righteous* [Hab 1:4].

The Vse. As long as wee are in this life, let vs prepare our selues for many assaults, both behind and before. As long as Baalzebub, the prince of flies, hath swarmes of euill spirits, and, if wicked men, they shall *compasse* vs *about like bees*, whiles before our face openly, whiles behind our backes secretly, whiles at the right hand in the dayes of prosperitie, and whiles at the left hand in troublous times. It is the lot of Gods children heere belowe to be beseeged round about with calamities, as the people of Israel in Babylon were compassed round about with rivers of teares [Ps 137:1]. Let vs not therefore thinke it strange when wee find our selues beset and beseeged on all sides both with ill tongues and ill hands. *Many a time*, saith the Church heere, *haue they afflicted me from my youth*; and, in another place, *our soule is exceedingly filled with the scorning of* these *that are at ease* [Ps 123:4].

3. many a time

Thirdly, the psalmist declareth the frequencie of the afflic-tions of the Church. The Church saith not heere once, twise, thrise the wicked haue troubled me, but *many a time haue they afflicted me*. Heere is *crebritas afflictionum*,[2] sorrowe vpon sorrowe, calamitie after calamitie, as line after line [Isa 28:13].

The Doctrine. Obserue heere that the wicked can not rest from euill doeing. One, two, or three iniuries will not satisfie their cruell hearts. They are more inhumane then Nahash, the king of the Ammonites, who was content of one eye of an

158

Israelite [1 Sam 11:2]. *Hanuns coats are too side to their crueltie.* He but cutted mens garments to their buttocks [2 Sam 10:4]. But if to day the wicked haue cut off to the buttocks, they will to morrowe striue to cut off to the shoulders. If with Nahash they get the right eye to day, they will intend to haue also the left eye to morrowe. If the wicked afflict the godly, they must afflict them many a time. They are afflicted when they afflict not, for, as Solomon saith, *they sleepe not except they haue done mischeefe* [Prov 4:16], and that by their *mighty sinnes* [Amos 5:12].

The Vse. Let not the godly be discouraged when afflictions come vpon them, haile shot in great number. It is not strange thing to see the same. It is more strange to see a godly man in peace with men but a day then to see them many a time borne downe with calamities. This Church of Scotland hath many a time beene afflicted by the enemies of this gospell; but these latter dayes, with a more then antichristian tyrannie, they would haue taken from her the vse of her two golden pipes, the Old and New Testaments, two sonnes of oyle, which *emptie golden oyle out of themselves* [Zech 4:12] to satisfie the soules of hungrie Christians; and for this golden oyle of Gods word would haue giuen vnto vs the stinkeing foole oyle of mouldie neate feete and of the rotten hearing guts[3] of many inventions. For such and such things may our Church say this day, *many a time haue they afflicted me.*

4. from my youth

After that the Church hath declared her many afflictions, she also sheweth the long continuance, euen *from her youth. Many a time haue they afflicted me from my youth* or rather from mine infancie. The Hebrewe word *nagnar*[4] signifieth *puer adhuc infans,* a child that is but an infant [Exod 2:6]. So was Moses called *nagnar.* When he was but three monethes old, he was sent away vnto the river and put in an arke of bulrushes [Heb 11:23]. From his infancie, he beganne to be persecuted. So Gods Church from her first infancie in Abel [Gen 4:5], as also from her first constitution in Egypt, beganne to be afflicted.

The Doctrine. Obserue heere that great is the malice of the

159

diuell and of the wicked against the saints. As soone as the godly beginne to haue a beeing, they persecute them. S. John in his Revelations saith that *there appeared a great wonder in heauen, a woman clothed with the sunne, and the moone vnder her feete, and vpon her head* had *a crowne of twelue starres. And she, being with childe, cried trauailing in birth and pained to be deliuered. And there appeared another wonder in heauen, and be hold a great red dragon* [Rev 12:1-3]. *And the dragon stoode before the woman, which was ready to be deliuered, for to deuoure her child as soone as it was borne.*[5] Behold heere how the primitiue Church is described bringing foorth children vnto God; and the diuel, like a dragon, waiteing for to deuoure them as soone as they are borne. See how from their youth the children of God are afflicted. Christ him selfe was no sooner borne but King Herede, like a foxe, sought to worry him [Matt 2:16]. This is the lot of the most part of Gods saints: to suffer persecution from their youth. The Church of God was young in Egypt; from her youth there many a time was she afflicted. The Church of God in all places from her youth hath beene afflicted. As soone as a Church is ready to be deliuered of any child, that red dragon, cruell and bloody, standeth before her *for to deuoure her child as soone as it* is *borne.*

The Vse. Let vs not expect for any mercy at the wickeds hands. No sooner doe holy professours appeare like dewe from *the wombe of the morning* [Ps 110:3], but the wicked intend their destruction. All that will liue godly shall find the wicked to be their enemies from their youth. So Israel beganne to scorne Isaac from his youth [Gen 21:9]. Jacob and Esau struggled so in the very belly of their mother that she, wondering said, *if it be so, why am I thus* [Gen 25:22]? Behold how these two little children bruised them selues by struggling. Such is the contrarietie betweene the children of God and the men of this world, who like mightie hunters, hunt after the life of Gods most excellent ones. Seeing it is so, let vs all from our youth prepare our selues to suffer what euills the wicked shall be able to inflict. Behold, as in a glasse, the sufferings of these that haue beene before vs. Some had triall of *cruell mockings and scourgings,* [. . .] *of bonds and imprisonement. They were stoned; they were sawen asunder; they were tempted* and *slaine with the sword; they wandered about in sheepeskinnes and goatskinnes, being destitute,*

160

afflicted, tormented [Heb 11:36-37]. Thus were they afflicted from their youth.

Let vs not deceiue our selues. Wee must be afflicted from our youth on earth, before wee be crowned in heauen. All men must suffer a hell either heere or heereafter. If wee will not suffer for Christ, wee shall neuer reign with Christ. Too many would liue like lapwings and swallowes, who euer goe awaye timeously before the winter stormes. But this wee must knowe: none shall sing in heauen but these that haue weept on earth, and mourningly haue said, *many a time haue they afflicted me from my youth*.

5. the vehemencie of the afflictions of the Church

In the forme of speach heere, wee may clearely perceiue the greatnesse of the afflictions of the Church. The words, as yee see, are doubled. After that, the psalmist hath made the Church to say, once *many a time haue they afflicted me from my youth*. He ingeminats the speach in the same wordes: *many a time haue they afflicted me from my youth*. The wordes are doubled, as pharaohs dreame of the kine and eares of corne was doubled. *For that the dreame was doubled vnto pharaoh twise, it is because the thing is established by God* [Gen 41:32]. The Greeke hath the word is true. Heere God teacheth the reason wherefore things are sundry times repeated in the scriptures. Thus, as yee see, repetitions in Gods word are not vaine tautologies like the superfluities of foolish mens wordes, which are always vpon one note like the cuckoes tune, when God speaketh and speaketh againe. It is for to let our doubting hearts of little faith knowe that what he saith is true. For this cause, the Lord Jesus, not content with one, verily doubled the wordes, *verily, verily I say vnto you* [John 13:21]. So, likewise, the doubling of the Churches word heere, like the doubling of pharaohs dreame, telleth vs as much, viz that the word is true.

The Doctrine. Obserue heere that it is an vndoubted trueth that the Church of God suffereth many afflictions. As it hath beene true in times past, so shall it be true vntil the worlds end. As the Church many a time hath beene afflicted from her youth, so shall she be afflicted vntill her old age. Can a Church be without Christ? Neither can it be without the crosse. As Christs naturall bodie was crucified, so must his mysticall bodie. The afflictions of the Church are her conformities with Christ her head. What way the head is past toward heauen, that waye the members also must followe. *O fooles*, said Christ, *ought not Christ to haue suffered these things and to enter into his glory* [Luke 24:25-26].[6] They, in Christs language, are but fooles, who think to come to glory without sufferings. All the faithfull must once be *in hoc choro eiulantrum*, in the company of these mourners, who once and againe, by waye of lamentation, say, *many a time haue they afflicted me from my youth*; and againe *many a time haue they afflicted me from my youth*.

The Vse. Seeing there is a necessitie of afflictions prepared for vs, let vs when wee are in *turbida caligine*,[7] compassed with crosses, resolue to suffer patiently. If the wordes of our afflictions be doubled, let us double our resolutions. Let vs double our prayers that wee may be so farre from feare in persecution, either by fire or sword, that wee may reioice that God shall thinke vs worthy to suffer any thing for the glory of his name. A man that hath receiued a wound at the service of his prince in the front of a battell needeth not to be ashamed of that wound when he cometh into the presence of his prince. Nay, it is his glory; it is a marke of his courage and of his loyaltie. *From henceforth*, said the apostle, *let no man trouble me, for I beare in my body* στίγματα, *mustas notas*, shamefull markes of burning [Gal 6:17] for the honour of the Lord Jesus Christ. This he accounted his glory. *God forbid*, said he, *that I should glory saue in the crosse of our Lord Jesus Christ* [Gal 6:14]. This *ambassadour in bonds* [Eph 6:20] did glory in his chaine of yron, as if it had beene of gold. It is, said he, *for the hope of Israel* that *I am bound with this chaine* [Act 28:20].

6. the plowers plowed vpon my back etc.

Sixtly, the psalmist heere, by a similitude taken from the plowers of the ground, declareth how the Church lamenteth her sorrowes: *the plowers* haue *plowed vpon my backe, they made long their furrowes*, that is *diumultumgue me afflixerunt*; they afflicted me both sore and long. Long furrowes are long afflictions and continued calamities.

In this similitude declareing the great afflictions of the Church, wee shall consider these foure things: 1. the plowers, 2. the ploughs, 3. the ploweing, 4. the ground plowed. The plowers are the wicked πονήροι, Satans seruants *more fierce then the euening wolues* [Hab 1:8], whose taske is to trouble the seruants of God. The plough[s] are their instruments of crueltie of diuers sortes, wherewith they afflict Gods seruants. The ploweing are the wicked in action, fining, depriveing, horning, and warding, like oxen draweing long their furrowes.

The ground is the backs of the saints riven vp by the culters of their cruelty. As the ground is treade vnder the feete of horse and oxen, and riven vp by the culter of the plough, so the godly are often treade vnder the feete of the wicked, who, like horse and oxen, *protrahant sulcas suos*, drawe long their furrowes vpon their backs by wounding them with all sortes of calamities. Satan, him selfe is in this plough like a bootes,[8] of him may be said, *sequitur sua plaustra*[9] bootes. The diuell followeth this plough like a dung cart. He, by his instruments *arat*, ploweth, *prarat*, ploweth ouer and ouer; *subarat*, ploweth vnder; *et rehulcat*, and ploweth againe and againe. He hath his plough wrights in readinesse to devise the plough and to help that which is broken. He hath the cordes of counsell, the culter of crueltie and the goad of gaine or ambition to prick the oxen when they beginne to be lazy or to pull away the shoulder. He hath his musick for to encourage them among the mires. As men whistle at the plough that the worke may goe on without wearieing, so hath Satan a musick at his plough. The organs sound, the quiristers[10] sing that his horse and oxen may drawe stoutly. *Lucrum cantat in aure*, fat benefices whistle so sweetely vnto them, and encourage them so to drawe this plough of iniquitie, that hardly can either rope, corde, or tugge abide the brunt of their vehemencie. This is the exercise of the wicked heere belowe, who *haue corrupted the covenant of Levi* [Mal 2:8]. They in a furious, holy, and foolish furie are plowers for Satan, draweing long their furrowes vpon the backs of the godly. Such men like plowemen, *animalia prona*,[11] haue euer their face towards the earth. They mind not the things that are aboue [Col 3:1].

The Doctrine. Obserue heere the great folie of the wicked who turne their back vpon God for to serue the divell, who, in steede of honouring them, maketh base drudges of their plowghmen to rive vp the backs of the godly. It is more honourable, both before God and good men, to be a base ploweman suffering many winter stormes among the dirtie furrowes of the earth. Yea, it is more honourable to be an hang man then to be yoked in Satans plough, to drawe long furrowes of afflictions vpon the backs of Gods children. The burrios office is to doe iustice, but theirs is to worke iniquitie.

The Vse. Let these who are entered in this plough repent and come away from such a vile service. *Service Deo regnare est*, a Seruant of God is a king, but he who, at the service of Satan, helps foreward the affliction of the saints [Zech 1:15] is but a slaue, yea an oxe in Satans plough, whose last day shall be the day of his slaughter.

The Doctrine. Againe, let vs obserue that it is said heere that the wicked plowe vpon the backs of the godly. I heare of their ploweing, but I heare no thing of their soweing. They plowe but the Lord soweth the seede. Behold heere how Satan and all his oxen, while they intend the destruction of Gods children by wounding their backs, are, in effect, according to the language of the spirit, but slaues and drudges prepareing the ground for to receiue the good seede of his word, which, being sowne, bringeth forth in some thirtie, in some sixtie, in some a hundredth fold. If the ground were not eared and plowed in vaine, should men sowe their seede, so likewise, if Gods children were not plowed with afflictions, the seede of Gods word would not take rot in their soules.

One saith very well, *doctrina euangely rectius intelligitur et promissiones ac consolationes avidius arripiustar in crure*,[12] that is the doctrine of the gospel is better vnderstood, the promises and comforts thereof are more earnestly apprehended by men while they are vnder a crosse. To this may well be subioined, *cor subactum arumnis prostantissimos sert fructus patientia invocatinis gratiarum actionis*, that is a heart is plowed with greefe and trouble bringeth forth the most excellent fruits of patience, prayer, and thankesgiuing. The earth must be plowed or digged; otherwise it will not bring forth fruits. If the fallowe ground of the heart be not riuen vp, nothing will be seene but

164

the burning nettles of wickednesse and pricking thornes of iniquitie.

The Vse. While wee are afflicted by the wicked, let vs reioice in tribulation. There is not a wound wee receiue, but it may be a comfort vnto vs, for the very wound is like prepared and well manured ground ready to receiue the good seede, which shall bring forth *the quiet fruit of righteousnesse* [Heb 12:11].[13] If a *shimei*[14] raile vpon vs and wound vs with euill wordes, the seede of Gods word sowen vpon that wound will make vs to say with Dauid, *so let him curse, because the Lord hath said vnto him, curse Dauid* [2 Sam 16:10]. This was the fruit of patience. *In their affliction they will seeke me earely* [Hos 5:15]. This is the fruit of prayer. After the Sabeans and Caldeans had spoiled Job of all his riches, he blessed God saying, *the Lord hath giuen and the Lord hath taken*, and *blessed be the name of the Lord* [Job 1:21].[15] This is the fruit of praise. Behold how the wounds of the faithfull are fruitfull.

Seeing it is so when afflictions befall vnto vs, let vs account them as furrowes prepared for soweing time. And, therefore, as a man, when he hath tilled his ground, seeketh with all diligence good seede to sowe vpon the same in hope of a plentifull haruest, so when wee feele our selues wounded and, as it were, tilled with the plough of great afflictions, let vs with all diligence goe to Church, and there seeke to haue the word of God sowen in our wounds as in furrowes, that so wee may reape a plentifull haruest of righteousnesse [Heb 12:11]. If no furrowes of afflictions be drawne vpon our backes, it is a token that wee are a ground not worthy the labouring. *Woe to* these *that are at their ease in Zion* [Amos 6:1] whom God thinks not worthy the ploweing. Hearts, hard like rocks or dirtie like mosses and mires, are neither fit to be plowed or sowen.

2 Part
Gods preseruation and deliuerance of the godly in and from their afflictions

In the second part of the text, wee haue two things. First, the preseruation of the Church in time off [sic] affliction: *yet they haue not preuailed against me*. Secondly, there is a glorious

165

deliuerance: the *Lord is righteous; he hath cut asunder the coardes of the wicked*. Heere is ἐπινίκιον, a song of victorie, the trivmph of the Chvrch.

1. yet they haue not prevailed against me

First, let vs heare of Gods preseruation. It is in these wordes: *yet they haue not prevailed against me*. *Though*, said the Lord to his Church, *I haue afflicted thee, I will afflict thee no more* [Nah 1:12]. *Behold* heere *vpon the mountaines* of the scriptures *the feete of him that bringeth good tidings. Yet they haue not prevailed against me*, though God, for a space, suffer the wicked to thrust their cruell culters into the backs of his people, He at last will let the most ignorant knowe that he hath in the great bibliotecke of his providence *a booke of rememberance* [. . .] *writen before him for* all *them that* feare him and thinke *vpon his name* [Mal 3:16]. While the wicked imagine that God hath forgot the godly, while, like furrowes, they are treade vnderfoot, behold how the Lord protects them so that they sing, and say in the words of my text, *they haue not prevailed against me*. In the Hebrewe, it is *gam loiochlou li*,[16] that is *nec tamen potuerunt contra* me, they had no power against me, *a brand plucket out of the fire* [Zech 3:2].

The Doctrine. Obserue heere the wonderfull mercy of God towards his Church. It is a companie where of the most part are neither noble nor rich nor wise nor mighty [1 Cor 1:26]. The penne of Gods Spirit calleth them the foolish things of the world, and the weake things of the world, and things that are despised, yea things which are not [I Cor 1:27-28]. Their enemies are the rich, the nobles, and the wise for the most part. *The kings of the earth set them selues, and the rulers take counsell together* [Ps 2:2]. But heere is the mercy of God. Though their charets *rage in the streets* and *iustle one against another in the broad wayes*, and *seeme like torches* and *runne like lightnings* [Nah 2:4], that is though their charets whirle with such furie that the fire sparkle out of their wheeles, and the earth shake with their noise. Though they multiplie so their forces that they driue the children of God vnto *dennes and caues* [Heb 11:38], the Church, at

166

last in Gods appointed time, shall come out with this song of holy scorne.

Yet they have not prevailed against me. This day this scripture is fulfilled: *many a time haue they afflicted me from my youth.* May this Church of Scotland now say, behold a day of grace wherein she may say out the rest of the verse, *yet they haue not prevailed against me.* No thankes to wicked men of whom she may say, *bellarunt sed non delellarunt,* they haue made warre but haue not ouercome. *Oppugnauerunt sed non expagnauerunt,* they haue assaulted me but haue not ouerthrowen me. *Voluruni sed non valuerunt,* they would but they could not, *yet they haue not prevailed against me.*

The 1 Vse. Heere is comfort for dayes of distresse for the children of God. God will not suffer their enemies to prevaile. Let Belshazzars, who are out of Gods fauour, tremble like aspen leaues when they see any finger of a iudgement writing against them [Dan 5:5]. But as for these that trust in God, when they see their enemies in number, like the sand as was the hoste of Senacherib, let not their hearts be troubled. If they will *stand still and see the saluation of the Lord* [Exod 14:13], the Lord shall one day put this song in their mouth, *yet they haue not prevailed against me.*

The 2 Vse. Let these who heare of such mercies of God towards his Church be thankefull to God for his fauour and protection. But much more, let vs who so recently haue found the Lords mighty deliuerance *praise the Lord for his goodnesse* [Ps 107:8]. When God had deliuered Israel, and had drowned their enemies in the Red Sea, Moses did sing with the men, and Miriam did sing with the women, *the Lord is a man of warre* etc. [Exod 15:3]; *He hath triumphed gloriously. The horse and his rider hath He throwen into the sea* [Exod 15:1]. The Lord hath most wonderfully this day deliuered our Church. The beginning of the worke was so small that hardly can any tell how it beganne. Our enemies were many and mighty, yet, saith our Church in her song, they haue not prevailed against me. No not, *the gates of hell shall not prevaile againste* Christs Church [Matt 16:18], for these that touch her *touch the apple of* Gods eye [Zech 2:8]. The wicked may trouble the saints but can not prevaile.

After that Gods people had suffered many miseries in Babylon, the Lord at last promised that old *men and old women* should *dwell in the streetes of Jerusalem, and euery man, with his staffe in his hand for very age* [Zech 8:4]; and that *the streetes of the citie* should *be full of boyes and girles playing* therein [Zech 8:5].

2. the Lord is righteous; he hath cut asunder the coards of the wicked

Wee haue heard of the preseruation of the Church in these wordes: *yet they haue not prevailed against me*. Now it followeth that I declare vnto you Gods glorious deliuerance. It is in these wordes, the righteous Lord, *the hope of his people* [Joel 3:16], *hath cut asunder the coards of the wicked*. The coards heere in the Hebrewe are called *gnavoth*,[17] which signifie *densos funes et tortiles*, that is strong coards plated together. According to this, the French version hath *cordages entortilles*. By the strong coards heere are vnderstood the counsells and enterprises wherewith the wicked drawe their plough of iniquitie. The Lord who is righteous in all his iudgements, when he beginneth, as Zacharie saith, to shake his hand [Zech 2:9] and to deliuer his owne, he, by his infinit power and wisdome, cutteth and confoundeth the counsels of the wisest Achitophels, *so that their hands can not performe their enterprise* [Job 5:12]. When he, in his furie, beginneth to shewe him selfe a righteous Lord, all the counsels of the wicked and their strongest cordes shall be before him like the threede of a spiders web, which is easily broken with a blast of breath.

The Doctrine. Great is both the mercy and might of God, who, for the safetie of his owne, most easily cutteth asunder the coardes and cartropes of the most wicked counsels of the most mighty and wise. Solomon, speakeing of *a three fold coarde*, saith it *is not easily broken* [Eccl 4:12]. That which is hard to men is easy to God. I confesse that sometimes the wicked haue coards and cartropes which men can not cut, but who could euer make my text fals. *The Lord is righteous; he hath cut asunder the coardes of the wicked*. What is impossible to him who saith, *I will shake the heauens and the earth, and the sea and the drie land* [Hag 2:6]? *This is the Lords doeing*; the righteous Lord hath done this and it is wonderfull in our eyes.[18] It is easy to him to cut

168

the coardes of wicked counsels, though they were strong like coardes of wire. As Samson brake Delilahs withs,[19] as *a threede of towe is broken when it toucheth fire* [Judg 16:9], so doeth the Lord most easily cut asunder all the coards of the counsels and devices of wicked men, wherewith they drawe the plough of their iniquitie vpon the backs of godly men.

The 1 Vse. Let this serue for comfort to the godly while they behold the wicked prepareing a plough for their backs. Though the coardes of their counsels be not onely threefold [Eccl 4:12] but threttie fold, platted and wreathed one with another, the righteous Lord, when the houre of his iustice is come, shall cut them all asunder. Then shall plough coardes and oxen, by the blast of his wrath, be driuen away from before him as chaffe before the wind [Ps 1:4]. He to this corner and he to that, to hide them selues with Zedekiah in inner chambers [1 Kgs 22:25]; this the righteous Lord shall doe by his owne power. If rich drinkers of wine, seekeing their ease, refuse to help the Lord, as cursed Meros did [Judg 5:23], the Lord shall ouerthrowe the wicked by lappers of water, as he did in Gideons dayes [Judg 7:7].

There be diuers sortes of men in this land. Some abhorre our covenant as a treasonable league, which is most fals and vntrue, and shall be seene so. When matters hid in darkenesse shall be more clearely brought to light, when these men of sinne shall be made yet more manifest, wee hope that our gracious and dread soueraigne, abused by their plots, shall discerne his worthy and religious nobles and other faithfull professours from these merchands of Rome, with all their adherents.[20] Others in sinceritie of heart haue subscribed *with* their *hand vnto the Lord* [Isa 44:5].

Others haue subscribed with their hand, but not with their heart, and lye indifferent betweene the two, beeing partly Jew, partly Ashdedren. They haue a saile for all winds. They neither approue all that is done by the one side or by the other, but hold a grip of both, so that what side shall prevaile, they shall be there blameing still that which they blamed in the partie ouer throwen. They haue for both sides something which they approue that they may stand with one. They also haue for both sides some thing they reproue, that what side shall fall may be found vnwise and wilfull in refuseing to doe that which they

169

required, as if the counsells of their private braine were to be preferred to all the wisdome of a generall assemblie.

But heere is our comfort: the righteous Lord hath no neede of such lukewarme Laodiceans.[21] Though man touch them not, the Lord hath a mouth and a foot of iudgement to spewe them out and trample them downe except they repent.[22] The fewer and weaker that Gods instruments be in the safetie of the Church, the better shall it be knowne that the righteous Lord by his owne power hath cut asunder the coards of the wicked. When this shall be seene, then many shall cry as in that great day of Elijah, *the Lord* [. . .] *is thee* [*sic*] *God, the Lord* [. . .] *is the God* [1 Kgs 18:39].

The 2 Vse. Seeing at last the righteous Lord cutteth asunder the coards of the wicked, let this serue for to restraine wicked men from takeing such paines in makeing coards and ploughs for to drawe furrowes vpon the backs of God[s] saints. Let such consider heere that both their paines and expences will be all in vaine. For while they are in the very heate and height of their labour, *the Lord*, who *is a* mighty *man of warre* [Exod 15:3], will in great furie drawe out his sword and will cut asunder all their coards; and, with the thunder of his wrath will so affright the oxen that they shall all runne and hide them selues in the corners of the land. This was the theologie of Eliphaz. *As I haue seene, they that plowe iniquitie and sow wickednesse reape the same. By the blast of God they perish and, by the breath of his nostrils are they consumed* [Job 4:8-9].

Seeing it is so, why should wicked men thus rage and these that are in power imagine a vaine thing? *He that sitteth in the heauens shall laugh. The Lord shall haue them in derision* [Ps 2:4]. He *shall speake vnto them in his wrath, and* shall *vexe them in his* hote displeasure [Ps 2:5]. Then shall the wicked oxen knowe that woe is *vnto them that drawe iniquitie with coards of vanitie and sinne as it were with a cartrope*. Though God suffer for a time, yet, because he is a righteous Lord, he will at last *iudge his people*, and *will repent him selfe concerning his seruants* [Ps 135:14].

The 3 Vse. Let all this which hath beene said stirre vp all good mens hearts to loue and laud the Lord for the fatherly care he hath of his Church heere in Kedar and Meshech, the places of her troubles. This is the end of all Gods workes, that God may be praised for his goodnesse. After many deliuerances from prison, from sickenesse, from shipwracke, the psalmist euer subioined, only that men would *praise the Lord for his goodnesse.*[23] And seeing this day hath beene appointed for to stirre vp your hearts, not to *burne incense* to your owne *dragge* [Hab 1:16], but to praise the goodnesse of God and his wonderfull workes in the wonderfull harmonie of the Nationall Assemblie conveened in this citie,[24] let vs all with one mind and one mouth breath out the *calves of our lips* [Hos 14:2] wordes of thankes to his euerlasting praise in the language of his owne spirit. *Now vnto the King eternall, immortall, invisible, the onely wise God, be honour and glory for euer and euer, Amen* [1 Tim 1:17].

V. General Devotion

A Sermon Of Repentance made at a publick fast during the troubles in Scotland for the Booke of Common Prayer, Anno, 1638, the third of June, before noone

Ezek 18:31

Cast away from you all your transgressions, whereby yee haue transgressed, and make you a new heart and a new spirit: for why will yee die O house of Israel? v.32. For I haue no pleasure in the death of him that dieth, saith the Lord God; wherefore turne your selues and liue ye.

Dearly beloued in the Lord, *I will,* with Dauid this day, *sing of mercy and iudgement* [Ps 101:1]. If men walke stubbornly with God, he will walke stubbornly with them but in his iustice. But, if men will turne from their euill wayes and repent, the Lord, as he did to the Ninivites, will repent *of the euill that he had said that he would doe vnto them* [Jonah 3:10], and will not doe it. *Turne* [. . .] *vnto me, saith the Lord of hostes; and I will turne vnto you, saith the Lord of hostes* [Zech 1:3]. These be the wordes of his mercy.

In the preceeding wordes of this chapter, the Lord hath defended his righteousnesse against the calamnies of his owne people, who contended that he did punish them for their fathers faults. *Behold,* said the Lord, *all soules are mine; as the soule of the father, so also the soule of the sonne is mine: the soule that sinneth, it shall die* [Ezek 18:4], as if the Lord had said vnto them, why doe yee thus reason as though I were either partiall or rigorous? For are not all soules the workes of my hand, one as well as another? And hath not euery work man a will to wish well to his owne handiwork? If men doe so, how much more I? Were it not therefore for sinne all soules should liue, and therefore heere I declare vnto you the workes of my iustice. *The soule that sinneth it shall die: the sonne shall not beare* [. . .] *iniquitie of the father* [Ezek 18:20]. That is, no sinner shall be condemned for any sinne but his owne.

It is true that that vniuersall leprosie of our first parents sinne hath spread it selfe ouer all the soules of the sonnes of Adam, the stock and root of mankind. By our proprietie therein, wee are all made liable to death. But in our personall derivation

175

from our followeing parents, if the children followe not their fathers sinnes, there can not be any guilt of death to any of them. None shall suffer for anothers fault, but he that doth righteously shall speede well with God. If any wicked man will turne from all his sinnes that he hath committed and proue truely penitent, living holily and conscionably in this present euill world, he shall surely liue and not die. But againe, when the righteous man, that is he who hath lived vnreprouably among men seeming to be righteous, shall begin to be weary of his holy courses, and so turne aside all his formerly professed shewes of righteousnesse, shall be forgotten; and he shall be dealt with according to these ill actions wherein the iustice of God shall find him exercised. Vpon these preceeding grounds the prophet heere buildeth a most notable exhortation to repentance: *cast away from you all your transgressions whereby yee haue transgressed; and make you a new heart and a new spirit, for why will yee die O house of Israel?*

the division of the text

In these wordes, there be two principall parts. In the first part, there is an exhortation to repentance, *cast away from you all your transgressions whereby yee haue transgressed, and make you a new heart and a new spirit*. In the second part, he bringeth three arguments to moue them to obeye his exhortation. The first is from their danger in these wordes, *why will yee die O house of Israel*. The second is from his mercy in these wordes, *for I haue no pleasure in the death of him that dieth, saith the Lord God*. The third argument is taken from their owne propre goods that they may live in these wordes, *wherefore turne your selues and liue yee*. Of all these, I shall speake in order as the God of heauen shall furnish me with his holy spirit and as time shall permit.

1 Part
an exhortation to repentance

The exhortation to repentance is contained in these wordes, *cast away from you all your transgressions whereby yee haue trans-*

gressed, and make you a new heart and a new spirit. Perfect repentance is heere enioined to Gods people, and to you particularly this day, which is a day of a solemne humiliation for this whole land before the Lord. This message is from God to you this day: *cast away from you all your transgressions, whereby yee haue transgressed, and make you a new heart and a new spirit,* that is in a word repent.

True repentance hath two principall parts. First, wee must cease to doe euill. Secondly, wee must learne to doe well [Isa 5:16–17]. There be two sortes of sinnes: the sinnes of commission when wee doe the euill wee should not doe, and the sinnes of omission when wee doe not the good wee should doe. Repentance is the onely remedie of both these sinnes. For the sinnes of commission, this is the onely remedie: to cease to doe euill. *Cast away from you all your transgressions whereby yee haue transgressed.* For the sinnes of omission, this is the onely remedie: to doe well; *make you a new heart and a new spirit.*

First heere wee haue cease to doe euill. *Cast away from you all your transgressions whereby yee haue transgressed.* In the Hebrewe, it is *Hashlichou*,[1] that is *proijcite,* cast away with contempt, with great force, with all your might. In the French version, it is *iettez arrière de vous,* cast behind you, that is so cast your sinnes away that yee abhorre to looke vpon them for to loue them. From the word of my text, one of the gates of Jerusalem was called *Shallecheth*[2] [I Chr 26:16], that is the dirt or dung gate, because they did cast out at this gate the excrements of the city. According to this, *cast away from you all your transgressions,* that is, cast all your sinnes away from you like dung.

There be many reasons wherefore wee should cast away our transgressions. First, God heere hath commanded vs so to doe. It is his word and therefore must be obeyed. Solomon, speaking of a king, saith, *where the word of a king is, there is power; and who may say vnto him, what doest thou* [Eccl 8:4]? If men may not say vnto a king, what doest thou, lesse may men say to God, what sayest thou? If the centurion had such power and authoritie ouer his men that they obeyed him, [Matt 8:9], whether he desired them to come or to goe, shall Gods word be contemned where mans word is obeyed?

Secondly, what God commands vs to doe heere it is for our

well. *Cast away from you all your transgressions.* If he had said, cast away from you all your riches and your honours, and come to me, who should haue had reason to disobeye? When Peter was in the ship and heard of John that the man that stood on the shore was the Lord, he did cast away the nets and fish from him, *and did cast him selfe into the sea* [John 21:7]. If Peter cast him selfe into the sea that he might come to Christ, with greater reason should wee *cast away from vs all* our *transgressions* that wee may come to him.

Thirdly, when the rod that was in Moses his hand *became a serpent, Moses fled from before it* [Ex 4:3]. When the viper in Malta came out of the fire, and fastened on Pauls hand, *hee shooke off the beast into the fire and felt no harme* [Acts 28:5]. If wee would feele no harme by our transgressions, wee must cast them away as Moses fled from before the serpent. Wee must shake them off our hearts, as Paul shooke the viper off his hand. If wee let the vipers of our transgressions hang still vpon our hearts, vengeance shall not suffer vs to liue. If the venome of vipers was able to make men to swell and to fall *downe dead suddenly* [Acts 28:6], what shall the deadly venome of sinne be able to doe? What could all the venome of all the vipers of Malta doe but make a mans body first to swell and then to die? They could not hurt the soule. Christ said, *feare not that which can but kill the body* [Matt 10:28]. But sinne is a fearefull thing indeed; it is a viper which with its poison maketh soules to die eternally. Let vs therefore cast it away as Paul cast the beast from him.

Fourthly, wee must cast away that which offends God. Because Hagar and her sonne were mater of anger vnto Sarah, Abraham sent them awaye [Gen 21:14]. How much more should wee cast away our sinnes, which onely moue God to be angrie? Though they were deare vnto vs as our right eye or hand, wee must pull them out, and cut them off [Matt 5:29]. He that loueth his eyes or his hands better then God is not worthy to be called a creature of God. Happy and thrise happy are these to whom the spirit of Jesus may say, as the apostle said to the Galatians, *I beare you record, that if it had beene possible, yee would haue plucked out your owne eyes and haue giuen them to me* [Gal 4:15]. Let vs all this day pluck out our sinnes, though deare vnto vs as our owne eyes; and let vs giue them vnto

178

Christ, as Jacobs houshold *gaue vnto Jacob all the strange gods which were in their hand, and all their eare rings which were in their eares* [Gen 35:4]. As Jacob hid all these things vnder an oake, so the Lord will hid all our transgressions. He will so burie these carions of our sinnes that they shall neuer be seene againe.

Fiftly, there is no man but he will willingly cast away that which will bring shame vpon him. If wee cast not away our sinnes, they will bring shame vpon vs. How many before sinne revealed haue beene in great estimation among men? When they heard God crying in this text, *cast away from you all your transgressions*, they would not obeye while their sinne was secret. And there fore the Lord brought their workes of darkenesse vnto light. And seeing they did boldly sinne before God because their sinnes were hidde from men, the Lord revealed their sinnes vnto men, and made them to hid them selues for shame all the dayes of their life, like a woman hidde during the space of seuen dayes after that her father hath *spit in her face* [Num 12:14].

Sixtly, if wee cast not away our transgressions, God will cast away our comforts. He will cast away our peace, and for peace send warre. He will cast away our health, and for health send sickenesse. Fooles, because of their transgressions and of their iniquities, are afflicted.

If wee cast not away our transgressions, he shall cast away our appetit. Soules of sinners *abhorre all maner of meat* [Ps 107:18]. If wee cast not away our transgressions, he will cast away our ioye. Wherefore is the liuing man sorrowfull [Lam 3:39]? Man suffreth for his sinnes. If wee cast not away our transgressions, they shall be vnto our hearts like rust in yron, like mothes in cloth. They shall eate vs and consume vs away; they shall at last be our death. I speak of the godly. *For this cause*, said the apostle, *many are* [. . .] *sicke among you*, and also *many sleepe* [1 Cor 11:30]. As for the wicked who are but cast awaye, let them keepe their sinnes like sweete morsells in their mouth. *Let him that is filthie be filthie still* [Rev 22:11]. But, as for vs, Gods children and heires, who in the wombe deserued as much as they to be reprobats and cast awayes, let vs *cast away* [. . .] *all* our *transgressions whereby* wee *haue transgressed.*[3]

The Doctrine. Againe, let vs obserue heere that the Lord saith not vnto you, cast away your transgressions, but *cast away all your transgressions*. The Lord will not haue vs to halt betweene

179

God and Baal [1 Kgs 18:21]. The Lord, with that fained and fals mother of the child, will not be content that his children be divided [1 Kgs 3:26]. God slew S. Ananias for his division.[4] It is a diuision to abhorre one sinne and loue another. The pharisee, if all that he said was true, was neither an extortioner nor vniust nor an adulterer [Luke 18:11]. Yea, he did which many of our best men doe not: he fasted *twice in the weeke* and *gaue tithes of all that* he *possessed* [Luke 18:12]. But because he cast not away all his transgressions, the Lord refused to iustifie him. As Moses would not leave a hoofe vnto pharaoh [Exod 10:26], so wee must not serue the diuell in one transgression. What Gideon *could not doe* [. . .] *by day,* [. . .] *he did it by night* [Judg 6:27]. So if wee can not cast away all our transgressions by waye of action, let vs cast them all away by waye of affection. If some of them be so fastened vnto the shoulders of our soule, like a dead body bund[5] vpon a living mans backe, if wee can not cast them altogether from vs, let vs grone vnder the burden, and by prayer cry, with the apostle, miserable *man that I am, who shall deliuer me from* this *body of* [. . .] *death* [Rom 7:24].

The Vse. Let now euery man examine him selfe. There will come a day, a great examination day, wherein the thoughts of all hearts shall be disclosed. Then shall God say to all these that would not cast away all their transgressions, *I will reproue thee and set* all thy sinnes *in order before thee* [Ps 50:21]. Obey therefore in time and be saued [Zeph 2:1]. Search your selues, iudge and condemne your selues this day. If so yee doe, the Lord, both in his iustice and mercy, shall be for you, *for if wee* [. . .] *iudge our selues, wee* shall *not be iudged* [1 Cor 11:31]; if wee condemne ourselues, wee shall not be condemned; if wee cast away all our transgressions, the Lord will cast away all his anger. He will cast away the decree so that it shall neuer bring forth either vengeance in this world or condemnation in the world to come [Zeph 2:2]. Wee haue heard of the first part of repentance which is to cease to doe euill: *cast away from you all your transgressions.*

Now followeth that wee heare of the second part of repentance, which is to learne to doe well. It is in these wordes, *make you a new heart and a new spirit.* That is, be new creatures, *be renewed in the spirit of your mind* [Eph 4:23]; not onely abstaine from euill, but also doe good. According to that of the psalme, *depart from euill and doe good* [Ps 34:14]. But because a man, except he haue *new heart and a new spirit*, can not doe *bona bene*, good well, the Lord commands his people to make them selues *a new heart and a new spirit*. An hypocrite, who hath an old rotten heart and an old rotten spirit, may doe good as to giue almes to the poore, but he can not doe good well. All his best actions are but *splendida peccata*, beautifull, gorgeous, and eloquent sinnes, which preach vnto men the praise of an hypocrite but are all abominations before God, like painted tombes full within *of dead men[s] bones* [Matt 23:27]. He that will please God with his out ward actions must make himself *a new heart and a new spirit*; that is, he must *be renewed in the spirit of* his *mind* [Eph 4:23]. His heart and spirit must be [a] newe day wherein the thoughts of all hearts shall be described. Then shall God say that is his affections and actions must be renewed.

The Doctrine. The doctrine I obserue heere is this: out ward shewes and great appearances of godlinesse are not the cheefe things wherein the Lord delighteth. His eye hath not made choice of shewes for the obiect of his delight. His eyes are not like mans eyes. He said vnto Samuel, feeding his eyes with the outward shewes of Eliab, *the Lord seeth not as man seeth, for man looketh on the outward appearance, but the Lord looketh on the heart* [1 Sam 16:7]. For this cause, the Lord heere said vnto his people which is said to you this day, *make you a new heart and a new spirit*.

The Vse. Let this serue for instruction vnto vs all, that from this day forth wee beginne a new course of life, for God will haue *a new heart and a new spirit*. This old heart of ours is naughty, this old spirit is rotten. Gods spirit will not dwell with in such an old heart; neither will he abide with our old spirit. *If any man be in Christ, he is a new creature* [2 Cor 5:17]. Without this renovation, no man can challenge to haue any right in Jesus or any station in his spirituall kingdome; and therefore wee all must be carefull to earnestly intreat him at all times to renew vs by the grace of his spirit.

It is no more time to abide yet still filthie and foolish, in riot and drunkenesse, chambering and wantonnesse, strife and envie [Rom 13:13], the workes of the old man. Hath not the apostle said more then a thousand yeeres since, *old things are past away* [2 Cor 5:17]? What are these old things? Euen the out worne conditions of our sinfull nature. Wee would be ashamed to put on an out worne hat, cloak or coat. Let vs be more ashamed to put on out worne corruptions. *A new heart and a new spirit* is required the day. He who hath made all this world hath this day commanded you all to make you *a new heart and a new spirit*. The Athenians were greatly set to vnderstand and tell newes, but the Christians cheefest newes should be *a new heart & a new spirit*.

obiection

Heere it may be obiected and said that, by this passage, it would seeme that man hath in his owne power to make him selfe *a new heart and a new spirit*.

the answere

I will not enterprise heere to handle the controversie of mans free will, which papists acknowledge to be greatly weakened by the fall of Adam, but that yet notwithstanding that fall, there remaineth such a power in man that he, beeing assisted and helped by grace, may properly fulfill the law of God, that is doe all that God commandeth him to doe, and so may make him self a *new heart and a new spirit*. If it be altogether impossible to vs to make vs *a new heart and a new spirit*, wherefore would the Lord require this of vs? To this I answere that a man may seeke from a man that which is impossible for him to doe.

A man hath borrowed from his neighbour a thousand crownes which he hath wasted among whores, dice, and drink. Shall he, who hath lent his moneyes, haue no right to seeke them againe from the borrower because he is *non sol vendo*,[6] become a bankrupt? Doeth not the law of iustice permit *to cast him into prison*[7] whereout of he shall not come vntill he hath payed all vnto the least farthin?[8] It will not saue such a man to say, wherefore seeke yee from me that which I am not able to pay? To him may be answered, who made you vnable? When God sendeth his commandements, which men are not able to

182

performe? He directeth them either to the wicked or to the godly.

As for the wicked, he commandeth them to doe as he commanded pharoah, to let his people goe. As he would not heare, neither will they obeye, though he send vnto them line after line, precept after precept [Isa 28:13], yea and plague after plague. By this, they are made without all excuse that God may *be iustified when* he *speaketh, and be cleare when* he *iudgeth* [Ps 51:4]. As for the godly before their regeneration, they are *dead in* their *trespasses and sinnes* [Eph 2:1]. In another place, God saith that they are *dead in* their *sinnes and the vncircumcision of their flesh* [Col 2:13].

What can these men doe when they are commanded to make them selues new hearts and new spirits? If, because God commandeth men to make them selues new hearts, wee should thinke that men haue in them selues a power to performe. Many absurdities should followe vpon the same. When *the hand of the Lord was vpon* Ezekiel, he *caried* him *out in the spirit of the Lord, and set* him *downe in the middest of a valley, which was full of bones* [Ezek 37:1] which were very dry, a token they had beene long dead. After that, the Lord said vnto his prophet, *prophecie vpon these bones and say vnto them, O yee dry bones, heare the word of the Lord* [Ezek 37:4]. Were these bones of them selues able to heare? They were as able to heare as man of him selfe is able to obey this precept. *Make you a new heart and a new spirit*. When Lazarus was stinking in his graue, the Lord came vnto him and commanded him to *come forth* [John 11:43]. Because Christ commanded him to come forth, shall wee say that he of him selfe had power to come foorth? No more haue wee of our selues to *make vs a new heart and a new spirit*.

How then is this done, will yee say? I answere, when God commandeth his owne children, *dat quod inbet*, he giueth that which he commandeth, as when he commanded Peter to come vnto him vpon the sea. His commandement made him to come. S. Peter knew this, and therefore said vnto him, *if it be thou command me to come vnto thee* [Matt 14:28], so when he commandeth vs to make our selues new hearts, it is as vnpossible for vs as for a man to walke vpon the sea. But he that commandeth is he that made the dead bones to liue, and Lazarus to come out of his graue. He and he onely is able to make our old hearts and old spirits to become newe. *I*, said the Lord, *will put a new spirit within you; and I will take the stonie heart out of* your *flesh, and* I *will giue* you *a heart of flesh* [Ezek 11:19]. Behold yet more clearely: I, said the Lord, will giue you a new heart, and a new spirit will I put in you; and *I will take away the stony heart out of your flesh, and I will giue you an heart of flesh* [Ezek 36:26]. *And I will put my spirit within you, and cause you to walke in my statuts* [Ezek 36:27]. That is very notable which the Lord said to Jeremiah concerning his people, *I will put my feare in their hearts that they shall not depart from me* [Jer 32:40]. Thus, as yee see, the new heart and the new spirit are the gifts of God. S. Paul saith that *it is God* that *worketh in you, both to will and to doe of his good pleasure* [Phil 2:13]. Whereof or wherewith can a man make a newe heart?

The Vse. Seeing it is so when God commands vs for our good to doe that which wee should doe, and are not able to doe, let vs in all humilitie fall downe at his feete and seeke mercy. If so wee doe, he will doe to vs as that Lord in the gospell did to his master seruant, which ought[9] him ten thousand talents. As soone as that seruant humbly fell downe before him, his Lord *was moued with compassion, and loosed him and forgaue him the debt* [Matt 18:27]. The Lord this day in this text hath begunne to reckon with you, and to seeke that which yee owe, euen new hearts and new spirits; and because yee are no more able to pay these things then that euill seruant was able to pay the ten thousand talents, the Lord most iustly may with that master, command vs to be sold, our wiues and our children, and all that wee haue vntill full paiment be made. Let vs therefore all together fall downe with teares and prayers before him, intreating him most earnestly to *put a new spirit within* vs [Ezek 11:19] and to creat a cleane heart within vs. If wee aske, wee shall receiue; if wee seeke, wee shall find; if wee knock, it shall be opened vnto vs. Christ who neuer lied hath said a great word vnto vs, whatsoeuer yee shall aske the Father in my name, I will giue it vnto you. Let vs all this day aske the Father in his name new hearts and new spirits. *Let vs aske in faith, nothing wauering* [Jas 1:6]. If this wee doe, he shall put his spirit within vs and shall cause vs to walke in his statuts [Ezek 36:27]. Behold how he shall not onely counsell and command vs, but shall also cavse vs to walke in his statuts [Ezek 36:27].

184

2 Part
arguments of repentance

In the second part, the Lord giueth three arguments to moue his people to returne vnto him by repentance. The first is taken from their danger in these wordes: *why will yee die, O house of Israel?* The second argument is taken from his mercy: *I haue no pleasure in the death of him that dieth, saith the Lord God.* The third argument is taken from their owne good: if they obey God and repent they shall liue. *Wherefore turne your selues and liue yee.* What God said to the house of Israel in time past, that he saith this day vnto the whole Church of Scotland solemnly humbled, *cast away* [. . .] *all your transgressions wherewith yee haue transgressed, and make you a new heart, and a new spirit.* It is now high time to repent and to amend your life. If yee will not, yee shall surely die; and why wilt thou die, O Church of Scotland?

The Vse. Let every man depart from his euill wayes. That which is said in generall to our whole Church, it is said to euery one in particular. Cast away your transgressions; away with them, away with all that hath offended our good God; away with our old hearts; and away with our old spirits; away with our old conversation, riot, drunkenesse, chambering, wantonnesse, strife, pride, envie. If wee put them not away, death will take vs away. Death is our danger. Wee are forewarned in the wordes that God hath giuen vnto your watchman this day, *why will yee die, O house of Israel?* As truely as God said to Adam, If thou eate of the tree of good and euill, *thou shalt surely die* [Gen 2:17], as truely shall thou die O Church of Scotland, except thou repent and returne vnto him from whom, in such a glorious a light by thy workes of darkenesse, thou hast made a fearefull apostasie. And therefore to day, *if yee* [. . .] *heare his voice, harden not your hearts* [Heb 3:15], but cast away your transgressions and *make you a new heart and a new spirit, for why will yee die, O house of Israel?* If yee feare death, feare more to offend God. If yee desire not to die, returne all to God with new hearts and new spirits. And this much for the Lords first argument in these wordes, and *why will yee die, O house of Israel?*

The second argument for repentance is heere taken from the

185

mercy of God. *I haue no pleasure in the death of him that dieth, saith the Lord God.* There be many who, after they haue sinned and sinned many times, at last thinke that they can not alter so many wrongs, haue a face to seeke Gods mercy; and so they die in despaire with Judas, Saul, Ahitophel. But O behold heere a mouth speakeing all mercie to him that will repent, *I haue no pleasure in the death of him that dieth, saith the Lord.*

The Doctrine. The doctrine I obserue is this: our God is wonderfull in mercy. After that, he hath receiued many thousands of wrongs of all sortes against the first table and against the second table of his law, for which he might come against this whole nation with wordes of excommunication. Depart sinners from this land, which yee haue defiled with riot, drunkennesse, chambering, wantonnesse, strife, and envie [Rom 13:13]. Depart from this my land, which yee haue defiled with oathes, with lies, with blood, with contempt of my sabbaths. Depart from my land, which yee haue polluted with fornications and adulteries, incests, robberies. Yee, after that peti[10] excommunication, he might come vpon vs with that last thunder, both of his eternall excommunication. Depart from me with the diuel and his angels [Matt 25:41]. This wee haue all deserued to heare from the mouth of his iustice. But O behold, heare and wonder what the mouth of his mercy crieth vnto you all this day, *cast away from you all your transgressions.* [. . .] *Why will yee die, O house of Israel? For I haue no pleasure in the death of him that dieth.*

The Vse. Let vs all returne from our ill wayes. Behold heere the mercy of God inviting vs to repentance. If God should come vnto vs as he came vnto Adam with that terrible interrogation, *Adam where art thou* [Gen 3:9], what wonder if wee should all affrighted seeke some shadowes or shelters for to hide vs? But hearken heere, dearely beloued, and heare mercy crying vnto you all, *I haue no pleasure in the death of sinners that die.* If he hath no pleasure in our death, let vs haue no pleasure to offend him. Let our greatest displeasure this day be because wee haue dispossessed him in provoking him by our sinnes vnto such a wrath, which hath made a commotion like an earthquake in the whole nation. If wee truely repent and returne to our God, he who can bring light out of darkenesse shall make this commotion like the motion of the angel in the poole [John

5:4], a meanes for the health and welfare of our Church, for, as the angel said to Marie with God, *no thing shall be vnpossible* [Luke 1:37].

The third argument whereby the Lord heere will moue his people to repentance is taken from their owne good. If they will repent, they shall liue. *Where fore*, saith the prophet, *turne yourselues and liue yee*, as if he had said, if the feare of death will not moue you, if the mercies of God can not moue you, let the loue of your life moue you to turne vnto God; as if he had said, all that a man hath he will giue it for his life. Wherefore let the loue of your life moue you to turne from your euill wayes.

The Doctrine. The doctrine I obserue heere is this: the diuels seruice is a dangerous seruice; it is an enemie to our life. But Gods service is a cordiall; his sayings *are life vnto those that find them, and health to all their flesh* [Prov 4:22]. Repentance is a salue for all sores of sinnes, which are the onely sores of our soules.

The Vse. Seeing God hath this day vsed so many arguments to moue vs to repentance, let euery one of vs turne from our euill wayes. The death of the body, if God be not present as a friend, is the most fearefull thing in the world. After it will come a second death, more fearefull. If wee repent not, if the feare of this death worke not sufficiently vpon you, let the tender mercies of God who hath no pleasure in your destruction rouse you vp to this dutie. *I haue no pleasure in the death of him that dieth, saith the Lord God*. Why, then, let vs all this day doe the Lord a pleasure. Let vs cast away all our transgressions which are not worthy the keeping. Let vs cast them away; let vs all turne vnto the Lord our God and wee shall liue. Our life shall be a life indeed; our land shall be a land of life; our gospell shall be a gospell of life; our King *the breath of our nostrils* [Lam 4:20] shall be life vnto vs; our peace and our prosperitie shall liue. All shall goe well for peace, and trueth shall be in our dayes [2 Kgs 20:19]. The Lord God of Israel make this the conclusion of all, Amen.

The Worlds Condemnation

John 3:19

And this is the condemnation, that light is come into the world, and men loued darkenesse rather then light, because their deeds were euill.
v.20. *For euery one that doeth euill hateth the light, neither commeth to the light, lest his deeds should be reprooued.*
v.21. *But he that doeth trueth commeth to the light, that his deedes may be made manifest, that they are wrought of God.*

In this chapter, the euangelist S. John handleth these fiue things: first, he declareth how Christ Jesus did teach Doctour Nicodemus the necessity of regeneration, that vntill the four-teenth verse; secondly, by the similitude of the brasen serpent, he teacheth that all men that are saued must haue faith in Christ lifted vp and dead vpon the crosse, of this vntill the sixteenth verse; thirdly, he declareth the great loue of God towards the world, and that vntill the eighteenth verse; fourthly, he teacheth that the condemnation of men is cheefely from the want of loue of Jesus, of that vntill the twentie and third verse; in the last part is set downe the baptisme, witnesse, and doctrine of John concerning Christ. In this text, wee haue declared by S. John that the condemnation of men is cheefely for their vnbeleefe. *This is the condemnation, that light is come into the world, and men loued darkenesse* better *then light, because their deedes were euill etc.*

the diuision of the text

In these wordes, there be three parts. In the first part, he declareth that the cause of the condemnation of the world is because men loue not the Lord Jesus, the light of the world; and *this is the condemnation: that light is come into the world, and men loued darkenesse rather then light.* In the second part, a reason is set downe wherefore men loue not Christ the light. It is in these wordes, *because their deedes were euill.* And this is amplified largely in the wordes followeing, *for euery one that doeth euill, hateth the light,* [. . .] *lest his deedes should be reproued.* In the third

188

part is contained a description of a good Christian, *but he that doeth trueth cometh to the light that his deedes may be made manifest, that they are wrought* of God.

1 Part
the condemnation of the world

This is the condemnation: that light is come into the world, and men loued darkenesse better then light. In the verse preceeding, S. John said, *hee that beleeueth on him is not condemned; but he that beleeueth not is condemned already because he hath not beleeued in the name of the onely begotten Sonne of God* [John 3:18]. That is, whosoeuer beleeueth in Christ Jesus, how great and greeuous soeuer his sinnes haue beene, shall not come into condemnation. But as for him that beleeuth not, he is in a certaine way of euerlasting miserie, and is deserted and left without all remedie in a state of eternall death.

After that, the apostle pointeth out clearely the cause of mens condemnation. *This is the condemnation*, that is, this is the cause of condemnation, *light is come into the world, and men loued darkenesse* better *then light.* That is, whereas Christ Jesus, the Sonne of Righteousnesse, hath clearely shined vnto men by the glorious beames of his gospell for to shewe vnto them the waye to heauen, they, remaining so wedded vnto their owne corruption, preferre the darkenesse of their ignorance vnto the bright shining knowledge of Christ, the Sauiour, which is the condemnation of their miserable soules.

First, let vs consider what is condemnation. After that, wee shall discusse the cause thereof. The word in the originall is κρίσις. It signifieth iudgement and also condemnation. S. Peter, speaking of the angels that fell from God, calleth them ἐις κρίσιν τετηρημένους, *damnationi seruatoes, reserued vnto damnation* [2 Pet 2:4].[1] Damnation or condemnation properly is the sentence of a judge adiugeing a malefactor to some fearefull punishment vpon the conviction of a fault. Heere it is taken for that eternall punishment in hell appointed for all sinners that are not in Jesus Christ. All sortes of miseries are included in this one word, condemnation, for it is both easelesse and endlesse, and that vpon both soule and body as farre as they are

189

able to endure without annihilation. These that suffer other torments, while they haue a sicke or sore body, haue often a ioyefull soule to comfort their wounded body. These that haue a troubled spirit in a whole body are in a greater distresse, but often such haue hope that God at last will succour them. But, as for condemnation, it loadeth both soule and body eternally with sorrowes, which the tongue of angels can not expresse. The scriptures declare all these things most powerfully that wee may beware of it, as of a most dangerous rocke whereupon the wicked make shipwracke both of soule and body. Woe to that soule for euer more whose portion shall be condemnation. *It were good for that man that he had neuer beene borne.*[2]

Now let vs see what is the cause of this condemnation. *This is the condemnation; that light is come into the world, and men loued darkenesse better then light.* In the cause of mans condemnation, I see two things: first, the bountie of God towards man; secondly, mans contempt of Gods mercie. The bountie of God is in that he made his light to come to the world. The vnthankefulnesse of man was in that they *loued darkenesse* better *then light. Light is come* to the *world*: behold Gods mercy. But *men loue darkenesse rather then light*: behold mans wickednesse.

Let vs first speake of this light what it was; secondly, how it is said to come into the world; thirdly, I shall consider the wickednesse of men *who loued darkenesse* better *then light.*

There be two sortes of light: a temporall light and a spirituall. As for the temporall, it was the first creature that God made: *and God said let there be light* [Gen 1:3]. One calleth it the first ornament of the world; the sunne, moone, and starres were made to be the vessels of this light. As for the spirituall light, it is either God him selfe or the beames of his graces which proceede from him vnto vs.

God is called light [John 1:4] because he is like light for two reasons: first, for the vnspeakable brightnesse of his maiestie; secondly, for his most pure and single nature, being of perfect knowledge and holinesse without any darkenesse of ignorance or sinne. S. John calleth Christ the Sonne of God, that light which *lighteneth euery man that commeth into the world* [John 1:9]. He enlighteneth euery man with reason and vnderstanding, and he enlighteneth the faithfull with spirituall graces. His *word is a lanterne* to our *feete, and a light vnto* our *path*s [Ps 119:105].

By this word, workeing by his spirit, he maketh our con-uersation to *shine before men* [Matt 5:16].

By the light of my text is vnderstood Jesus Christ, that sunne of righteousnesse, shining in his gospel. Of him is said heere, *that light is come into the world*. God, from the beginning, hath not ceased to send light among men, for first, he gaue vnto him reason like a lanterne of light to direct him that he should not goe like a beast. After this light, he sent his word, his law, and many worthy prophets, who were burning and shining lights in this world [John 5:35], preaching shame against the workes of darkenesse. After all came Christ Jesus, the Sonne of God, whom one well calleth *substantia lucis*, the substance of light, the fountaine of all light who *lighteneth euery man that cometh into* this *world* [John 1:9].

Obserue heere that it is said of this light that it came into the world. It is not said that wee sought it or that wee brought it from the heauens. But it came, as one saith, *spoute et gratia*,³ by grace and fauour.

The Doctrine. The doctrine I obserue heere is that great is the mercie of God that cometh vnto man before he be desired to come. If the Lord should not first come vnto vs, wee would neuer invite him to come. When the spouse was lyeing in her bed, the Lord Jesus vndesired came vnto her doore. So farre was she from desireing him to come that, when he was come, hardly could she be moued to open her doore to let him in [Cant 5:2].⁴

The Vse. Let vs learne heere to loue the Lord Jesus, the light and life of our soules. Wee are bound to loue these, who, being desired to help vs, refuse not. But he that doeth vs good before he be desired deserueth double thankes.

Let vs more particularly consider how Christ this light came into the world. He first came by his promise that he, the seede of the woman, should treade downe the head of the serpent [Gen 3:15]. Secondly, he came by his spirit, by which *he went and preached vnto the spirits in prison* [1 Pet 3:19], that is to wicked men in Noahs dayes whose soules are now in hell. Thirdly, he came into the world by his incarnation [1 Tim 3:16], God manifested in the flesh as light in the sunne, the life of the world. And this light did appeare vnto the world by the preaching of the gospell, first, for to let men see that all their owne doeings

191

were but darkenesse and sinne; secondly, for to let them knowe where life and righteousnesse were to be found. In a word, this light came into the world for to let men see to walke in the waye vnto eternall life, their onely happinesse; and so was this light for the well of their soules and bodies, both in this world and in the world to come.

Behold heere and consider what a care the Lord from the beginning hath taken of man. At the first, he made the world for him; after that, he made him according to his owne image. After that he had lost that light and life, the Lord sent into the world a new light to let men see to come out of the darknesse of sinne. Heere first wee may learne that man, if he perish, can not pretend ignorance, seeing the light is come. If there be any ignorance, it is a wilfull ignorance. Againe wee may heere learne that, if men be debarred from the heauens, they can not accuse God of seueritie, seeing he came into the world, not a seuere judge to condemne soules, but a light for to saue the soules that were lost.

Now let vs heare how the world made welcome this light sent for to saue them. It is heere said that *men loued darkenesse rather then light*. Behold heere what vnthankefulnesse, yea what rage. Whereas men should haue reioiced in this light, they abhorred it and *loued darkenesse better then light*. By darkenesse, cheefely heere I vnderstand the ignorance of God, blindnesse of mind, and after that, all sortes of sinnes which are called darkenesse, first, because they are *the workes of darkenesse* [Rom 13:12]; secondly, because they are opposite to the word of God, which is a light to our steps; thirdly, because they so darken the wits of a man that he becometh rather like a beast then a man; fourthly, sinnes are called darkenesse because they leade men vnto outer darkenesse. By darkenesse, heere also are vnderstood all these things which this world esteeme most, as wisdome, strength, honour, riches, etc. Though these things in carnall eyes oriently shine and glaunce, yet if yee conferre them with the spirituall graces of God, they are but darkenesse.

Now consider what is heere said of the men of this world. They have *loued darkenesse* better *then light*. That is, first of all, they haue not desired to be instructed. While they had the faire occasion of Christ, a sunne shining [Mal 4:2], they contemned the light and would not knowe. They cared more for their

192

pleasures then for Christ. *This is the condemnation* of the world: *that light is come into the world, and men* haue *loued darkenesse* better *then light*. Such can not be saued, for *he that beleeueth not the Sonne shall not see life* [John 3:36].

The Doctrine. Obserue heere that ignorance in the dayes of knowledge is a most dangerous sinne. God, who is light, will not suffer the light of his word to be loathed. Because the pagans contemned that little knowledge of God which is by the workes of nature, the Lord gaue them ouer to become more filthy then beasts. *Euen as they did not like to retaine God in their knowledge, God gaue them ouer to a reprobate mind, to doe these things which are not convenient* [Rom 1:28]. If the Lord so punished these men for contemning of the light of nature, how greeuous plagues will he bring vpon these who shall contemne the light of his glorious gospell, loving the darkenesse of ignorance better then light.

The 1 Vse. Let this serue for instruction to teach vs to loue the light of knowledge. And, seeing it is by Gods word, as by a light, that wee are guided in the waye towards heauen, let vs loue this light. Let vs take delight in it. The birds, as soone as day beginnes to breake and that they see the light, they beginne to sing and reioice in that light. So let our soules sing and reioice when wee haue any good occasion of this light. These whose hearts are sanctified find an vnspeakable ioye in this light [Ps 4:7]. It is the light of Gods countenance, which putteth more ioye in their hearts *then in the time that* [. . .] *corne and* [. . .] *wine increase* [Ps 4:7]. And, if this be the condemnation that *men loue darkenesse rather then light*, this certainly shall be the saluation, if wee loue light rather then darkenesse. And seeing now wee haue the glorious day of a bright gospell, *let vs walke honestly as in the day* [Rom 13:13]. εὐσχημόνως περιπατήσωμεν, *composite ambulemus*, let vs walke orderly. He that is in darkenesse can not walke orderly, but staggereth to and fro like a drunken man. Let vs therefore loue light better then darkenesse. What is in darknesse worthy to be loued? Is not a darke house vnpleasant to dwell in? Is not a darke night vnpleasant to walke in? The diuel is called the prince of darkenesse. Sinnes which are worse then the diuel are *workes of darkenesse* [Rom 13:12], and hell is a house of darkenesse prepared for these that *loue darkenesse* better *then light*.

The 2 Vse. Let this serue for reproofe to these who are night creatures delighting onely in darkenesse. The theefe and the adulterers day is the night. Job, speakeing of murderers, theeues, and adulterers, saith, *they are of* these *that rebell against the light* [Job 24:13] etc. *The eye* [. . .] *of the adulterer waiteth for the twilight saying, no eye shall see me; and disguiseth his face* [Job 24:15]. He and the theefe knowe not the light, *for the morning is to them euen as the shadowe of death* [Job 24:17]. Thus doe they *loue darkenesse rather then light*. All these that doe so are the companions of theeues and adulterers, who, like night foules or wild beasts, goe abroad in the night. *The sunne ariseth; they gather them selues together, and lay them downe in their dennes* [Ps 104:22].

2 Part
a reason wherefore euill men loue darkenesse better then light

Now, in the second part, wee haue to consider the apostles reason wherefore wicked *men loue darkenesse rather then light*. The reason is in these wordes: *because their deedes are euill*. And this is largely amplified in the wordes followeing: *for euery one that doeth euill hateth the light, neither commeth to the light, lest his deedes should be reproued*.

Behold heere the reason wherefore a wicked man *hateth the light*: it is because his *deedes are euill*, and, *because his deedes are euill*, he will not come to the light, *lest his deedes should be reproued*. Naturaly a wicked man hateth the light because it is light, a good thing in it selfe. But the maine reason wherefore he hateth the light, it is ἵνα μὴ ἐλεγχθῇ τὰ ἔργα αὐτοῦ, lest his euill *workes should be reproued*. This ἔλεγχος, powerfull reproofe, troubleth him so that he can not enioye his sinnes with pleasure; and therefore he hateth that which marreth his mirth, as Ahab hated Micaiah because he prophecied not good things vnto him [1 Kgs 22:8]. The conscience of a wicked man hath no will to be wakened. As a man that desireth to sleepe can not abide any stirring about him because he is seekeing rest, so the conscience of a wicked man can not abide a reproofe, because he in his pleasures is seekeing rest. The reproofe is like a flie vpon his

194

scab, like light to a sore eye, or like a candle to a theefe in darknesse.

The Doctrine. Obserue heere the nature of the wicked: they can no more abide the word of God then a theefe can abide the day. The light of the word reproueth his workes of darkenesse, and cryeth hell hell in his conscience, and will not suffer him to sinne without a checke. And therefore, while a man lyeing in sinne cometh to a soule pierceing sermon, he is like a man sitting vpon thornes or netles. He is so pricked and burnt that he had rather be in any place then where God is. As long as the sermon is vpon the sore of his sinne, his hatred within rageth both against the preaching and the preacher. As *Ahab said to Elijah, hast thou found me mine* [. . .] *enemie?*[5] so he accounteth God and his word to be his enemie because they find him in his wickednesse.

This is the effect of euill deedes or of an euill conscience, a heart full of hatred against that which reproueth their sinnes. For this, wicked men carefully seeke, *vt peccent citra dolorena aliguen, et cum voluptate,*[6] that they may sinne without sorrowe. And therefore, when wee heare of men sleeping in their beds in time of sermon, or goeing to their pleasures and pastimes, it is a token that these men haue an euill conscience and that they doe in darkenesse some things that are not honest. A neglecter or contemner of sermons, be who he will be, can not be an honest man. He can not haue a good conscience, for, if his conscience were sound, the word would be to him sweeter then the hony combe, reproofs would be to him a balme.

The 1 Vse. Seeing euill deedes trouble the conscience when they are reproued by Gods word, as wee would desire to haue pleasure, comfort, and contentment in hearing of sermons, let vs beware of them. If wee haue beene astraye, let vs repent and abhorre these euill wayes. If this wee doe, at sermon wee shall get a good help to reproue the sinnes whereat wee are offended. What is the cheefe exercise of a repenting man? It is to reproue him selfe for this bypast euill deeds. When such a man cometh to sermon of light, he loues that light because it helps him to reproue the sinnes which from his heart he abhorreth.

The 2 Vse. Seeing the word of God is so powerfull to reproue sinne, which is the well of our soules, let vs esteeme highly of it. Let the wicked contemne it as they please, because it will not let them sinne with pleasure. To all that haue a desire to feare God, *it is the power of God* to *saluation* [Rom 1:16]. This is a happy thing for man, when he meeteth with that which will not suffer him to sinne with delight. Thus the poore vnlearned man when he commeth to the sermon, if he hath any grace, he findeth him self so convinced, and *the secrets of his heart made* so *manifest* that he falleth *downe on his face* and *reporteth that God is in you of a trueth* [1 Cor 14:25]. Happy are these [that] feare God now. These filthy dreamers shall one day waken in a feare and cry rocks and mountaines fall vpon vs.

3 Part
a description of a good Christian

In the last wordes of my text, wee haue the description of a good Christian, *he that doeth trueth commeth to the light, that his deedes may be made manifest, that they are wrought* of God, this is the life of him that liueth well. He [. . .] *commeth to the light* willing that his actions be seene because *they are wrought* of God.

The Doctrine. Obserue heere first the description of a godly man. He is one *that doeth trueth*. He saith not that heareth trueth or that speaketh of trueth. No not, the diuell heareth trueth, and hypocrites will prattle much of religion. But heere is the true marke of a godly man: he doeth trueth, that is he doeth that which Gods word commandeth him to doe and that sincere truely.

The 1 Vse. Let vs all goe to the schoole of doeing. If wee tary still in the classe of hearers or of speakers, we shall neuer enter into heauens glory. In scripture, it is not said, well heard or well spoken, but *well done* [. . .] *faithfull seruant*; enter into thy masters ioye [Matt 25:21]. He doeth well that doeth trueth, that is doeth *bona bene et sincere*, good workes well in sinceritie without hypocrisie from any honest heart for a good end.

The 2 Vse. Let this serue for reproofe to the most part of men who neither vnderstand to speake trueth nor yet to doe trueth. Lying was the second pointe of Gods controuersie against Israel. *By sweareing and lying* etc. [Hos 4:2], many are so farre from either speakeing or doeing trueth, that, with Pilate, they knowe not what trueth is [John 18:38]. Of him *that doeth* *trueth* is said heere, that he *commeth to the light that his deedes may be made manifest.* As euill deeds make a man to runne and hide him selfe like Adam after that he had sinned, so a good life bringeth a man forward with all boldnesse before the face of God. His good workes tell him that, though they be not perfect, yet the Lord will be pleased with them as being the fruits of his faith.

The Doctrine. The doctrine I obserue heere: the godly man is onely a happy man. He is onely the man that darre compeare before God. While adulterers, theeues, and drunkards tremble to heare of a manifestation of their life, *he that doeth trueth commeth* foreward like an honest man, a worke man, not ashamed of his workes.

The Vse. Let this serue to encourage vs to doe well. *If thou doe well,* said God to Cain, *shalt thou not be accepted* [Gen 4:7]? If wee doe well, wee shall be accepted. If wee doe well, while the wicked, like stonechackers,[7] shall be seekeing holes vnder rocks to hide them from the face of the great judge of the world, wee who feare the Lord shall sing and reioice to come *to the light that* our *deedes may be made manifest.*

The Doctrine. Againe obserue heere that all things will one day be made manifest. There is nothing done so secretly but the Lord shall bring it to the light, which shall inlighten the greatest darkenesse.

The Vse. Let vs beware to doe before the eyes of God that wee would be ashamed to doe before the eyes of a child, for all our workes, whether good or badde, shall one day be made manifest before these eyes of fire, which see to the bottome of hell. Rockes and mountaines shall not hide sinners in that day. In the last wordes of my text, it is said that his deedes may be made manifest that they are wrought of God. In the Greeke, it is ἐυ θεῷ, which some interpret *cum Deo*, with God, *Deo veluti duce praeunte,*[8] God beeing the cheefe doer. Others interpret *secundum Deum*, that is according to Gods direction. Others interpret *per Deum*, that is, by God, because God worketh in vs both to will and to doe. In a word, the cheefe reason wherefore *he that doeth trueth commeth to the light that his deeds may be made manifest* is because the good workes which he hath done are *wrought* of *God*, and so haue him the cheefe author and doer.

The Doctrine. Obserue heere what maketh a faithfull man so bold as to come to the light with his workes. It is Gods hand in the worke that giueth him such courage. What is good in the worke is giuen, and what is imperfect is forgiuen; and therefore man, workeing by faith, cometh foorth with his workes with ioye and courage as beeing the fruits of his faith, the gift of God. If Gods hand were not at the worke, mans best workes should be but *splendida peccata*, glistering sinnes, faire without to the eyes of men, but within like a menstruous cloath or like a graue full of stinke and corruption of dead mens flesh and bones. If the most glorious virtues of pagans should come before the light of the gospell, they should all, like owles, flie awaye from that light because such deeds were not *wrought* of *God*, for neither were they wrought by faith, nor yet for the glory of God, but for their owne glory; and therefore could neuer abide the light of the gospell, which condemneth all to be sinne that is without faith. So popish merits and pharisees workes flie awaye from before this light like these that brought vnto Christ the *woman taken in adulterie*,[9] for in all such things the worke of God is not to be seene, but onely the worke of [a] vaine man seekeing his owne glory.

The Vse. When euer wee put our hand to any workes that wee would haue to make vs bold and not like cowards before the light, let vs be carefull that Gods hand be at the workes that so they may be *wrought* of *God*. If this wee find, the light of God shall be our delight. It shall be our ioye to bring these workes vnto the light that they may be seene both by God and man, by God that he may reward his owne gifts according to his promise, by men that they, seeing our good workes, may praise and glorifie our heauenly Father.[10] To him with the Sonne and Spirit of all comforts, be glory for euer, Amen.

The Danger of Carelesse Examination

1 Cor 11:30

For this cause many are weake & sickly among you & many sleepe.

The sacrament of the lords supper is a daintie, a delicate, but a dangerous meat. It is more daintie then mannah. O the sweetenesse that a well prepared soule findeth therein. *Wafers made with hony* [Exod 16:31] are no thing to that which the soule receiveth in the sacrament, for in it the soule *tastes* & *sees* how good is the Lord [Ps 34:8].

As this meat is a daintie meat, so is it a dangerous meat. It is a dangerous thing to come to the sacrament with an vnprepared heart which can discerne *the Lords body* [1 Cor 11:29]. He that comes to the table of the Lord must be a discreete man; and his discretion must cheefely be in this: that while he taketh the outward elements of bread & wine, he rightly discerne *the Lords body* & blood, that is that he receive with a religious heart the bread & wine of the sacrament as the seales of Christs body & blood, the mysteries of the most precious things of the world. To eate & drinke after this maner is to eate & drink worthily, & wisely to discerne *the Lords body*. It is a daintie meat for such, for they eate & drinke their owne saluation because they rightly discerne *the Lords body*.

But by the contrarie, if any man come without due prep-aration, without a serious examination of his life, if he be a reprobate, he shall eate & drinke condemnation to his soule. By the abuse of Gods seales,[1] he shall seale vp his euerlasting ouerthrowe. But if he be one of Christs & yet neglect the preparation & examination of his heart, & so come to *eate & drinke vnworthily*, he shall eate & drinke iudgements to him selfe because he hath not discerned *the Lords body*. That is because he hath eaten & drunke the bread & wine of the sacrament, the seales of Christs body & blood, as if they had been commoun meat & drinke appointed onely for the nourishing of our bodies. If yee would heare with what iudgements the Lord vsually plagueth his owne children, who partake vnworthily of this sacrament of the Lords supper, they are set downe in these

199

wordes of my text, *For this cause many are weake & sickly among you & many sleepe.* In the wordes preceeding, the apostle declared in generall what befalleth to them that eate this sacrament vnworthily. He said that they did eate κρίμα, fearefull affliction or iudgement. In the wordes I haue read, he particularizes the iudgements where with God vseth to chastise his owne for the carelesse receiving of the sacrament. *For this cause, many* among you *are weake & sickly* [. . .] *& many sleepe.*

the division of the text

In these wordes wee shall consider these three things: 1. what was the cause of all these iudgements that came vpon the Corinthiens; 2. what was the number of these that suffered these iudgements, they were many, many; 3. the iudgements them selues are specified, viz 1. weakenesse, 2. sicknesse, 3. death. Vnder the name of these three are included all other chastisements wherewith God afflicteth his owne children for their folies & faults, cheefely in the negligent receiving of the sacrament, the seale of our life & of his loue.

1 Part
the cause wherefore God scourged many of the Corinthiens in the apostle his dayes

The cause of their corrections was the negligent & vnworthy receiving of the sacrament. While many of them came to the sacrament to partake thereof, they discerned not *the Lords body.* That is they did eate the feast of God, the sacrament appointed for the feeding of the soule, as if they had beene eating a commoun feast appointed onely for the nourishing of the body. For this cause, saith the apostle heere, *many* among you *are weake & sickly* etc.

The Doctrine. Heere obserue how the apostle, as a learned physitian, points out the demonstratiue cause of the Corinthiens sicknesse. *For this cause, many* among you *are weake* etc. If all the physitians of the world had come to these Corinthiens weake & sick & dyeing, they could neuer haue dreamed of this cause, & so the diseases had beene vncurable to them. For if yee remoue not the cause of a disease, the disease will continue. Many many among our selues take neuer well vp the causes of many diseases. Wee are more carnall then the magiciens of Egypt, who, while the plague of lyce came, cried out, *this is the finger of God* [Exod 8:19]. Wee, who are Christians trained vp in the schoole of Christ, haue for the most part not so much grace as rightly to vnderstand in our afflictions who is the cheefe doer. Let be to take vp the cause wherefore the affliction is come vpon vs. An ill eye, a blast of ill wind, fortune, chaunce, enchauntments, Satan hath done this say many. They take him to be the doer, & this indeede is Satans doeing, that he, beeing esteemed to be the doer, may be sought vnto for to be the helper.

The Vse. When euer any affliction comes vpon vs, let vs not fret at the affliction, as the dogge that biteth the stone;[2] but let vs seeke vp to the cause wherefore & wherefraie such an evill is come vpon vs. The prophet Jeremie propoundeth the question, *wherefore* [. . .] *is the living man sorowfull?* It is answered *man suffereth for his sinnes* [Lam 3:39].[3] But it is not enough to knowe that our sinnes haue beene the cause of our sorrowe. But wee also must trye out the particular sinne which hath caused that ill that wee may say with the apostle heere for this cause. When Saul perceived God to be angrie by his silence in not makeing answere to him, he was not content to say, some haue sinned against the Lord & haue made him angrie; but he neuer tooke rest till he had found out the particular sinne & the sinner. *Draw yee neere hither*, said he, *& knowe & see wherein this sinne hath beene this day* [1 Sam 14:38]. Thus he neuer ceased till he had found out by lot, both the particular sinner & the particular sinne that had moved God to be angrie. According to this, Joshuah did after that Israel had shamefully fled before the men of Ai. So soone as God had told him the cause, viz *Israel hath sinned* [Josh 7:11], Joshuah neuer rested till he had found out the sinner. After that he had found him, he first caused *stone him with stones*, & thereafter *burne him with fire* [Josh 7:25].

It is so that wee should doe while wee find any weakenesse in our bodies, my sicknesse or any appearance of death which make *the liuing man sorowfull* [Lam 3:39]. Wee must neuer take

201

rest till wee find out the sinne that hath made God angrie at vs. Let vs carefully examine ourselues; let vs seeke thorow all the commandements of the law & search diligently for the sinne that hath angered God, & take it awaye. Then shall God blesse the remedies. Then the potions & the plasters will play their part, & by Gods blessing will bring health to the patient. After that God had forgiuen Hezekiah his sinne while he was lyeing sicke of his boile, the plaister of figues was applyed & became effectuall. The prophet proceeded orderly in his cure. First, he spake with the king concerning his sinne whereof he made him sensible. Thereafter, he directed the plaister as a physitian [Isa 38:21].

Wee, for the most part, begin at the wrong end. When any disease ouertakes vs, wee [are] incontinent & first of all send for the physitian and, when he hath giuen vs over & is at the end of his skill, then then & not till then, O fy, make hast, send for the minister. No. First, *is any sick among you let him call for* the *seruant of God etc.* [Jas 5:14], *and the prayer of faith shall saue the sicke* [Jas 5:15]. Let the man of God come first & laye his sinnes in order before him; & instruct him to seek out the particular sinne which hath angered God, and moued him to laye on that stroake. Let him teach him in all humilitie to cry for the forgivenesse of that sinne. That done, let the physitian come with his plaisters & his potions. Except that the cause of the maladie be taken away, the sicknesse will no more acknowledge the remedies then that euill spirit would acknowledge the sonnes of Sceua to whom he said, *but who are yee* [Acts 19:15]?

In my iudgement, a great number of our diseases proceede from the carelesse receiving of the sacrament. Satan knowes this, &, therefore, a good space before the communion, he will goe out of a man for to seeke other seven worse then himselfe,[4] that at the feast, at the very receiving of the sacrament, he with his companie may enter into him as he entered into Judas, with the sop, which at the table of the sacrament he had received out of Christs owne hand [John 13:26]. At such times, these that haue any drop of grace will sensiblie feele Satan armed with stronger temptations then at any other time, that thereby he may make vs communicate vnworthilie & so prouoke God, if not to destroye our soules, at least to plague our bodies with fearefull diseases & diuers sortes of death. When Satan can not get our soules, he striues by all meanes to haue our bodies plagued as he did with that child in the gospell, of whom the father said, *wheresoeuer he taketh him, he teareth him, & he fometh & gnasheth with his teeth & pineth away* [Mark 9:18]. He is a murderer, & his delight is to torment the bodies of the saints whereby he may make them vnable in the discharge of their callings wherein they might be profitable to many.

But this knowe: that Satan hardly can atchieve any thing against vs to our hurt, except that first wee haue offended God by some sinne, but particularly by vnworthy receiving of the sacrament, at which time many, while they forebeare the action of sinne, keepe still the ill intention. It is not in his power to doe vs harme if wee can keepe our hearts & hands cleane of sinne.

This Balaam made cleare, while beeing brought by King Balak with promises of great rewardes for to curse Israel, the people of God. He did what he could to winne these wayes of iniquitie. He spared no paines in goeing from hill to hill, from altar to altar, for to bring a curse vpon Israel. But he could not, nay, by the contrarie, where he intended to curse, he was forced to blesse. *Behold*, said he, *I haue receiued commandement to blesse; & he hath blessed, & I can not reverse it* etc. [Num 23:20]. *Surely there is no enchantment against Jacob, neither is there any divination against Israel* [Num 23:23].

Now what was the cause of this, that Balaam, neither by his enchantments, nor yet by his divinations, could prevaile against Israel? Balaam told the cause him selfe. God, saith he, *hath not beheld iniquitie in Jacob, neither hath he seene perversenesse in Israel* [Num 23:21]. That was the cordiall that preserued Israel from the poison of Balaams enchantments. But oh that which he could not doe by enchantments, he did by his wicked counsell. Hearken vnto me, would he say, thou Balaak, the sonne of Zippor. I shall teach thee a waye how to bring miserie on Israel. Let Israel by some policie be induced to sinne against their God. Let God once behold iniquitie in Jacob, & let him once see perversenesse in Israel, & yee shall soone see fearefull plagues come vpon them. But how shall that be done, O Balaam, might Balaak say. Take my counsell, said Balaam, choise out the fairest ladies of Moab, fard them, & attire them richly, & let them goe & allure Israel to folie; & then yee shall see what God shall doe to Israel. As he counselled, so Balaak did; & so it came to passe that Gods Israel committed folie with his daughters of Moab, for which cause the Lord, in wrath, killed of Israel foure & twentie thousand [Num 25:9].

Satan, with all his power & policie, could neuer be able to thrust Adam out of paradise till he had snared him in a sinne. Satan is busie at all times, but cheefely in the time of the holy sacrament to defile vs with one sinne or other, because he knowes that God will not faile to punish severely such an abuse. For this cause, at these times, he sends out against vs his strongest Anakins, his greatest Goliahs, his most fearefull gyants temp-tations, for to drawe vs and drive vs awaye from our God. And therefore at these times, it shall be our wisdome to double our watch, to fast & pray, lest wee be led into temptation. There be temptations like some kinds of divels which *goe not out but by prayer & fasting* [Matt 17:21].

2 Part
what was the number of these that suffered iudgements for vnworthy communicateing?

As for the number of these whom God afflicted for eating & drinkeing vnworthily at the sacrament, they are heere said to be many. *Many are weake & sickly among you & many sleepe*, that is die. In the originall language these who are said to be *weake & sickly* are πολλοί, many, but as for these who are said to die are ἱκανοί, *satis multi*, that is a good number between few & many.

The Doctrine. Heere first obserue the great mercy of God who corrects vs here while wee sinne against him, for to make vs in times to come to take better head to our wayes. It may well be said of God while he corrects vs *dum pungit vngit, by his stripes wee* haue health [Isa 53:5]. After that Ephraim was chas-tised [Jer 31:18], he turned; & *after that* he *was turned*, he *repented*; & *after that* he repented, he *was instructed*; & after that he was instructed, he *smote vpon* his *thigh & was ashamed*, [. . .] *euen confounded* [Jer 31:19].

The Vse. The vse when euer wee are chastened by the hand of God, be we fewe, be wee many in number, let vs take it in

204

good part. There be neuer so many afflicted as deserue to be afflicted; and, when wee are afflicted, wee are oblished to God for that benefite of correction, which wonderfully *yeeldeth the peaceable fruit of righteousnesse vnto them which are exercised thereby* [Heb 12:11].

The Doctrine. The main doctrine of the mercy of God heere is grounded vpon this: that his gentle corrections as weaknesse & sicklinesse he layeth on many, but, as for the sorest which is death, he striketh not so many with the same. Obserue heere the great great mercie of God, though grieuously offended by these prophane Corinthiens, who came to his table drunk & polluted with many other vices, yet inclines to correct the most part of them rather with weaknesse & sicknesse, then with death. Fewe he chastised with the death of the body, but the most part were corrected with more gentle afflictions, not withstanding that all these had deserued to die, both the first & second death for euer in the hells.

The Vse. Seeing God is so gracious as to deale so gently with vs after so great offences, let vs feare him for his mercy. The diuell & his crue feare him for his iustice: the diuell beleeues & he trembles [Jas 2:19]. All that trembling feuer is but a feare for the iustice of God. But our feare to offend God should not be so much for his stripes as for his loue, mercy, & goodwill towards vs. Mercy is with him, not that he should be contemned, but that he should be feared [Ps 130:4]. Seruants feare most the stripes of the good man of the house, but the godly spouse & children feare most his displeasure.

When wee consider how often wee haue come to this holy sacrament vnworthily, & how God hath so gently corrected vs with his calmest corrections, as weaknesse of body & other little light touches of his finger [Exod 8:19]; and againe, while wee consider how for our faults he hath afflicted some of vs with sore sicknesse but hath spared our life, whereof he hath bereft many better then wee that we might get time to repent, this should make vs both to loue him, & also feare to offend him by comeing againe to his table for to partake vnworthily. Pardons that are past, mercifull spareing with bypast gentle corrections, crye vnto vs, *sinne no more lest a worse thing befall you* [John 5:14].

Againe heere obserue that he saith for this cause, many *many are weake & sickly* [. . .] *& many sleepe.* Where yee may obserue that they were not two or three in that Church of Corinth that came to the sacrament vnworthily, but many many, the apostle heere saith, not *for this cause* some of you are *weake & sickly,* but many of you are sickly.

The Doctrine. The doctrine I obserue heere is that man is an infectious creature & easy to be infected. The pest of sinne passeth quickly from one to more, from more to many. It was well said by a pagan, *morbida namque pecus totum corrumpit ovile,* one sickly sheepe will infect the whole flock.[5] Thus, as yee see, it is no good argument, many doe so & why may not I doe the like? To this speedily it may be replied, and many shall goe to hell & why may not yee doe the like. It is no wonder to see many doe ill & runne one course in wickednesse. But it is a miracle to find one good among many. I say that it is a miracle & a greater miracle then when Christ turned water into wine [John 2:11]. It is a thousand times more easy to turne water into wine then to turne vs from our ill ways. By our owne strength, wee can no more walk in the wayes of God then a dead man can be able to goe in a iourneye. Thus to bring vs from the ill wayes, the wayes of many, it is a miracle greater than that which Christ wrought on Lazarus while he quickened him at the graue [John 11:43]. This I will constantly affirme: that it is a greater worke to put life into a dead soule & so to make it partaker of *the first resurrection* [Rev 20:5], then to raise from the dead all the bodies that in many thousands are burned in that church yeard & heere also vnder your feete.

The Vse. Let vs not aime to direct the course of our life by the example of many. Scripture is plaine that *many* are *called but fewe chosen* [Matt 20:16]. It is true that the godly are also many. The children of Abraham are many in a multitude like the starres [Heb 11:12]; and like wise *many shall come from the east* & from the *west, & shall* in heauen *sit downe* at his table [Matt 8:11]. But if yee consider the wicked & their companies, all the followers of Christ will seeme to be but a little flocke [Luke 12:32]. The wicked are like the divels who said, our *name is legion, for wee are many* [Mark 5:9]. This the Lord him selfe maketh good, saying *wide is the gate, & broad is the way that leadeth to destruction, & many there be which goe in thereat* [Matt 7:13]. Thus as yee see, though the most part of men runne away from their God in an ill course, it should not be our part to followe them. Gods precept is plaine, *thou shalt not followe a multitude to doe euill, neither shalt thou speake in a cause to decline after many* [Exod 23:2].

Behold heere in my text many weake & many sickly. If yee would not desire to be sickly with many, beware to sinne with many. If yee would not goe to hell with many, beware to followe the ill example of many, for if yee walke still in their waye, yee shall at last come to their end. It is but a foolish comfort of miserables to be miserable with many. These be the comforts of hell: many many tormented together without either ease or end. It were infinitly better to be in heauen with God alone then to dwell in hell with legions of diuells & damned spirits. The resolution of Joshuah was excellent that he would not followe the multitude to doe euill. *If,* said he to all Israel, *it seeme euill* to *you to serue the Lord,* serue whom you will, but, *as for me & my house, wee will serue the Lord* [Josh 24:15]. Againe, whereas it is said heere that many among the Corinthiens were weake & sickly for vnworthy communicateing, one of two behoued to be either this, their vnworthy communicateing had continued long among them because they were many blotted with this sinne; or else this sinne, like Davids pest, had wonderfully infected many in a short time [2 Sam 24:15].

If it had lasted long, learne the patience of God who had not rooted out this Church for such a vile abuse, for wherein can a man offend God more then in the abuse of these sacred seales to come with a dogges heart, with a swines heart; & to lay hold vpon these *tremenda mysteria,* mysteries the sight whereof should make both our hearts & hands to tremble. But if this corruption came suddenly vpon so many, consider the watchfulnesse of Gods eye ouer his Church, who, lest the whole Church should haue beene defiled by timeous corrections, did cut the course of such corruptions. This I breefely obserue vnto *the praise of the glory of his grace.*[6]

3 Part
the particular iudgements wherewith God punisheth
these that communicat unworthily

Wee haue heard of the cause of Gods iudgements powred out vpon the Corinthiens, viz their vnworthy receiving of the sacrament in *not discerning the Lords body* [1 Cor 11:29]. Secondly, wee haue heard that the number of vnworthy communicants among them were many. Now let vs heare what particular chastisements were these wherewith the Lord did correct them for such a sinne. *For this cause*, saith the apostle, *many are weake & sickly among you & many sleepe.*

The corrections or iudgements be three in number heere specified: 1. many are ἀσθενεῖς, that is *invalidi, imbecillies, fracti viribus, sine rebore*,[7] weake & without strength; 2. many are ἄρρωστοι, that is *invalidi et languide*,[8] as our new version[9] hath well sickly; 3. many κοιμῶνται, that is sleepe in Christs language, in the commoun language many die.

Heere first of all obserue that sorrowe followeth after sinne. The pleasures of sinne as yet neuer made so glade a heart, but plagues for sinne haue made a farre sorer heart. It is a sore sicknesse to many, yea a death for to speake so, to take paines for the tryeing out of the blots of their conscience & to search the hidde hyprocrites & leauen that lurke within the bowels of their bosome. They can haue no leasure from their worldly businesse, from their farmes, from the tryeing of their oxen [Luke 14:18-19],[10] from the pleasures of their mariage [Luke 14:20],[11] & from the ioyes of old companiourie, yea & of many other toyes & trifles to attend on this great businesse of iudgeing them selues. But behold heere what followeth vpon such a negligence, euen great weakenesse of body, sore & languishing diseases, & divers sortes of death.

The Vse. Now while it is time, let vs all buckle our selues diligently to this businesse of an earnest preparation of our soules, lest that, after wee haue eaten the sacrament, wee find in the stomacks of our hearts such a bitternesse that wee be forced to cry as the sonnes of the prophets cried after they had tasted the wild gourdes shred in the potage, *death is in the pot* [2 Kgs 4:40], so wee, death is in the sacrament. As Solomon speaketh of another sorte of meate, so much more may I say of this meate abused. *The morsell which thou hast eaten shalt thou vomite vp and loose thy sweete wordes* [Prov 23:8]. All the faire wordes thou can speake to God to day vnder a faire shewe of godlinesse shall be lost; and the meat that thou hast received, though thou hast found it sweete in thy mouth, it shall be as bitter as death in the bowels of thy belly.

I am fully perswaded that the sacrament to the wicked, while he receives it with a prophane heart, is to him most like vnto that sop that Christ gaue to Judas,[12] euen *Satana vehiculum a coihe*, for to carie Satan downe from his mouth vnto his soule. Likewise, I am perswaded that the sacrament, carelesly, negligently, & so vnworthily received by the elect & faithfull, is very noyesome to their soules, & very pestilent & vnwholesome to their bodies. God for such negligence ordinarily pulles away mens strength from them, deprives them of their health, so precious a thing; and, from some, he takes away the life which a man would be content to redeeme with his dearest skinne, yea & with all that he hath: if *skinne for skinne* & [. . .] *all that a man hath will he give* it *for his life* [Job 2:4]. Why, then, with less paines let him learne heere how to preserue it. Let him please God by a worthy receiving of the sacrament, & he shall find his strength to growe, his health to be confirmed, & his dayes to be prolonged by him who made a long day to Joshuah.[13]

If so it be that by negligent preparation in times bypast he hath angered God & thereby hath moved God to take his strength & his health & other contentments from him, let such a man make amends. Let him, with repenting Nebuchadnezar [Dan 4:34], lift vp his eyes to heauen, & all these contentments like Nebuchadnezars lords & counsellers shall seeke vnto him. And as Nebuchadnezar, after his repentance, *was established in* his *kingdome*, yea *& more excellent maiestie was added vnto* him [Dan 4:36], so shall the man who for vnworthy communicateing hath beene afflicted. If he repent, he shall be established in all his former good things. The Lord shall make them sure to him: his strength shall be confirmed, his diseases shall be cured, his life shall be preserued, yea with Hezekiah his dayes shall be prolonged [2 Kgs 20:6]. Yea more as to Nebuchadnezar: excellent maiestie was added to that which he had before. So God shall not onely restore to him that which he had before, but he shall also adde vnto these things some good measure of excellencie [Dan 4:36].

Let me yet say more. If for times to come, he perseuere in well doeing, in takeing care to communicate worthily, to come all trembling with faith, loue, & repentance to these *tremenda mysteria*, fearefull mysteries, the Lord shall make his blessings dayly to increase & to multiplie like the fiue loaues & two fishes wherewith the Lord did feede so many thousands [Luke 9:13]. All these comforts & contentments so farre as shall be expedient shall continue with him to the end, so that his estate shall be like the estate of Job, of whom it is writen that *the Lord blessed his latter end* [. . .] *more then his beginning* [Job 42:12].

Againe let vs obserue heere divers degrees in the Lords chastisements for vnworthy communicateing. Some the Lord weakens & maketh feeble. On others, he layeth sore sicknesse, *infirmes et languidos reddit*, he maketh them both *weake & sickly*. Others he striketh with death.

Heere some may say what could be the cause wherefore the Lord did so deale with these negligent communicants, strikeing some with death & others but with diseases. I answere that it is certaine that their sinnes were the cause of their plagues. But as concerning the degrees of the iudgements, it is very probable that the greatest sinnes met with greatest iudgements. But I darre not define; I darre not boldly say that these who died after the negligent receiving of the sacrament were greater sinners then these who were but weake & sickly. I leaue that secret to the Lord him selfe, who, according to his owne good will & pleasure in vnspeakable wisdome, layes his hand heavier on some then on others. It belongs not to man to set downe in the chire of iudgement, & there determine & say this man is the greatest sinner because he is most afflicted. No not, the matter goes not euer so. Christ the Lord in this is plaine. These, said he, on whom the tower of Siloam fell, were not the greatest sinners [Luke 13:4]. These whose blood Pilate mingled with the blood of the sacrifices were not the greatest sinners. But the Lord, by his both most free, most iust dispensation, takes some negligent communicants, & he weakens them for to move them to repent. Others he will make sickly for to moue to repent. Others of his owne children he will euen strike with death after their repentance, to the end they should not see the ill to come, nor fall into the like inconvenient againe. Others who haue also eaten vnworthily, he will not touch at all but in great clemencie. By his terrours executed on others, he will affright them so that without any farther they will come home to God & repent & amend. Now happy are they who learne wisdome by the dangers of others.

The Doctrine. Heere obserue that, while wee sinne, wee haue to doe with a terrible God. He hath many plagues at his commandement ready to come out against vs, euery one readier then another, cryeing with that ill spirit, send me [1 Kgs 22:21]. His ordinarie iudgements for vnworthie communicateing are these three messengers, weakenesse, sicknes, & death, which in name of all the rest are sent for to scourge the negligence of Gods children in the examination of them selues. Neither while the apostle specifies these three doeth he exclude other calamities & losses and warres; famine; pestilence; losse of good husbands; losse of good wiues; losse of good children; losse of good masters; losse of good seruants; losse of lands, of cornes, & of cattell; losse of riches, by sea & by land; of all other things whatsoeuer vnder the sunne which either be profitable, pleasant or comfortable vnto vs. All these good things after that wee haue offended God by vnworthy communicateing will goe awaye from vs & leave us desolate, & their contraries will succeede & come into their place for to let vs knowe the treuth of these wordes of threatning. *Thine owne wickednesse shall correct thee, & thy backslidings shall reproue thee. Knowe therefore & see that it is an euill thing & bitter that thou hast forsaken the Lord thy God, & that his feare is not in thee* [Jer 2:19].

The Vse. Let vs stand in awe & not sinne at any time, but cheefely at the time of the holy sacrament. Then must wee goe to our secret chambers, & mourne apart [Zech 12:10], & powre out teares in secret where the praising & applauding eyes of men will not perceiue vs. It was well said, *ille dolet vere qui sine teste dolet,*[14] that is his groans are good whose greatest greefe for sin without witnes striks at his heart within. Many mens & many weemens greefe striks but outwardly at their eyes & at their countenance. They haue the bull–rushes head [Isa 58:5], which they hang downe for a day, but their heart is not broken, their spirit is not contrite. They want the sacrifice which God will neuer despise [Ps 51:17]. O let vs now seeke for that broken heart, for these that shall come to this feast of God with the sorest heart shall goe awaye with the soundest comfort.

O therefore now, now in this day, in this our day, let vs double our devotion, not that heereafter wee should slack our dutie for to become prophane againe, but rather in this sacred day let our devotion be doubled that heereafter wee may be the better enabled to performe our dutie, as Elyas was commanded to eate, & to eate againe that, in the strength of that double dinner, he might the better walke without wearieing to his iourneyes end. Eate, eate, said the angel, & eate againe *because the iourneye is too great for thee* [1 Kgs 19:7]. His iourneye was but from Beersheba to Hereb, but our iourneye is greater, euen from the earth to the heavens, & where now eate, eate, & eate againe.

Now for to conclude this sermon. Is it so that for carelesse preparation God striks many with many diseases & diuers sortes of death. What thinke yee will he doe to vs if wee carefully examine our selues by rightly *discerning the Lords body*, & doe other duties required for the worthy receiving of the sacrament? Surely he shall turne our weakenesse into strength & our sicknesse into health. He will make *all* our *bed in* our *sicknesse* [Ps 41:3]. If wee please him, he will *make* our life pleasant vnto vs. He also will prolong it, for, as Moses said to Israel, it is he that *is thy life & the* lengthening of *the dayes* [Deut 30:20].

The reason of this my affection is peremptorie, for, if the abuse of the sacrament is able to bring vnto our bodies weakenesse, sicknesse, & divers sortes of death, much more shall the right vse thereof be able to maintaine our strength, health, & life. Shall it be said that the abuse of Gods blessings shall be more powerfull to crosse vs then the right vse thereof be steadable to comfort vs? Truely not, for God in the workes of mercy is ordinarily more rich & plentifull then in the workes of iustice. If in justice, he visite the sinnes of ill *fathers vpon the children vnto the third and fourth generation* [Exod 20:5], he shewes mercie to thousands of these that loue him & keepe his commandements.

Now the Lord God of gods, by a secret & sacred irradiation of his spirit, teach vs & direct vs so in this great worke of receiving worthily the sacrament, the great seale of salvation, that wee may be assured that now wee haue in our bosome the surest euidence of heauen without any flaw. To his Maiestie be glory for euer, Amen.

The Safetie of the Chvrch
preached Ann. 1638, July 15

Ps 51:17

The sacrifices of God are a broken spirit: a broken and a contrite heart; O God, thou wilt not despise.

v. 18. *Doe good in thy good pleasure vnto Zion: build thou the walls of Jerusalem.*

The Lord Jesus hath commanded vs to be *wise* like *serpents* [Matt 10:16]. It is wisdome when a man intendeth any thing among men to vse the best meanes; it is greater wisdome to vse the best meanes, when wee would obtain any thing from God. If a man would in his prayers prevaile with God, he must appeare before him empty. That troubled man in Micah knewe this; and, therefore, in the beginning of his sute, cried, *wherewith shall I come before the Lord* [Mic 6:6]? He would not goe to God without a present. So Dauid heere, before he did pray for Zion, brought vnto God a presente of *a broken spirit and* of *a broken and* [. . .] *contrite heart*, a present at all times most acceptable vnto the Lord.

the diuision

In the wordes of this text, there be two principall parts: in the first part is a present which God accepteth euer, viz the sacrifice of a *broken spirit* and of *a broken and contrite heart*; in the second part is a prayer for the Church, *Doe good in thy good pleasure vnto Zion* etc.

1 Part
a present for God

Though God be the author of euery good gift [Jas 1:17], yet he will not despise the gifts of his seruants. Heere is the gift that will please him best, *the sacrifices of God are a broken spirit* and of *a broken and contrite heart*. The Hebrewes call a sacrifice *Zevach*, from *Zavach*,[1] which signifieth, to kill. So a sacrifice is a killed creature, a creature whose life is put out. Sinne hath caused many a creature to loose its life. It crieth for no thing but for the life of the sinner. It is Satans slaughter weapon; it is the greatest enemie of man and beast. It is writen of God that he saueth both the man and the beast, but sinne destroyeth both. The wages of sinne is death. To the end that God might saue man from death, he appointed that man should kill sacrifices and offer them vnto him to the end that thereby they might testifie that they them selues deserued to be killed. As Dauid said when God killed his people with the pestilence, but what haue these sheepe done [2 Sam 24:17], so these who offered sacrifices of slaine beasts or foules might say, but what haue these poore creatures done? So the sacrifices killed were for to remember men that their sinnes deserued death; and also were types and figures of that great sacrifice of Jesus Christ, who offered vp him self in a sacrifice vnto God, his Father vpon the Crosse.

This is the difference betweene a sacrifice and a sacrament: a sacrifice is mans gift vnto God, a sacrament is Gods gift vnto man. When God is angry, man must prepare a sacrifice, a gift, for *a gift* [. . .] *pacifieth anger and* [. . .] *strong wrath* [Prov 21:14]. The men of Tyre and of Sidon, hearing that Herode was offended, *made Blastus, the kings chamberlane, their friend* [Acts 12:20]. This doubtlesse was done by a gift. So Jacob when he sent Beniamin vnto Egypt, he sent him with a present that thereby he might find fauour in the gouernours eyes. *If it must be so now*, said he, *take of the best fruits of the land,* [. . .] *and cary downe the man a present,* [. . .] *balme,* [. . .] *hony, spices,* [. . .] *myrrhe, nuts, and almonds.*[2] Vnto the present, he ioined a prayer, *and God almighty giue you mercy before the man.*[3]

If to get mercy before man a present must be sent, O what should be done for to get mercy before God! A troubled sinner would be content to giue *thousands of rammes*, yea *ten thousand rivers of oyle*, yea his *first borne for* his *transgression* and *the fruit of* his *wombe for the sinne of* his *soule* [Mic 6:7]. But these things the Lord desireth not. *Thou*, said Dauid, *desirest not sacrifice, else would I giue it. Thou delightest not in burnt offering* [Ps 51:16]. In Dauids dayes they were commanded by God, but Gods cheefe

215

desire and delight was not in that outward legall service and sacrifice.

Heere in my text are the sacrifices of Gods delight, *the sacrifices of God are a broken spirit, a broken and a contrite heart. O God thou wilt* neuer *despise.* Behold heere how the psalmist calleth the broken heart sacrifices in the plurall number, for to teach vs that it, like the loue of God, is better *then all whole burnt offerings and sacrifices* [Mark 12:33]. Let any man, had he beene as wicked as Manasses, bring a broken heart vnto God: *et sine thure litabit,*[4] and God shall haue respect vnto him and to his offerings as he had vnto Abel [Gen 4:4].

Many in their troubles take much paines to get comfort; but, like one wandered out of the right way, the more swiftly they walke, they goe the farrer astraye, like these who, for to get Gods fauour, sacrificed in Tophet their children vnto divels. Heere in my text is that one thing which shall neuer faile to pacifie the Lord in his greatest wrath, viz *a broken spirit, a broken and contrite heart.*

Wee haue great neede at all times, but cheefely now in these dayes of so fearefull commotions to search out diligently that which will please the Lord our God, whom wee haue so highly prouoked. Heere in this text it is clearly told vs, *a broken spirit* or *a broken and a contrite heart; O God thou wilt not despise.* All heere must be broken as yee see. The spirit must be broken, and the heart must be broken. The breaking of the heart and spirit is repentance. The vaine men of the world dreame that repentance consists all in a few wordes, *God be mercifull to me a sinner;* and that these wordes, like an *opus operatum,*[5] will doe all most easily, so that sinners may goe laughing vnto heauen. But such men deceiue them selues, for indeede the most part of men goe laughing vnto hell. But vnto heauen there is no waye but thorow many afflictions in this valeye of teares.

O fooles, said Christ, *ought not Christ to haue suffered these things, and to enter into his glory* [Luke 24:25-26]? There is no other way to glory then that waye wherein the Lord him selfe went, viz the waye of sufferings. Neuer a man yet entered into heauen but with a sore and broken heart. A broken spirit and a broken heart are more painefull then if there were not a whole bone in our skinne. *The spirit of a* couragious *man will* beare *his infirmitie, but a wounded spirit, who can beare it* [Prov 18:14]?[6] By

216

the broken spirit and heart, heere are vnderstood the great greefe and sorrowe which the godly haue for offending their good and gracious God. By this sorrowe, they are so vexed that they can get no rest vntill they find the mercy of God makeing this intimation vnto their soules: sonne, daughter, be of good comfort; all your sinnes are forgiuen you.

Wee offend God, not onely with our tongue and hand, but also with our heart. All our sinnes beginne there, and therefore our repentance must beginne there. It is not a rent coat, nor dust on the head, nor tree shoes on the feete, nor a knottie cord for a girdle that will please God. King Ahab covered him selfe with *sackcloth and went softly* [1 Kgs 21:27], and yet was an hypocrite. Neither the coat, nor the dust, nor the cord, nor the sandales, haue sinned. It is the heart that hath sinned, and therefore wee must rent our hearts and not the garments. The maine spring of true repentance is the broken heart which is contrition, a bruising with sore paine and sorrowe. The apostle in this is plaine. *Godly sorrowe*, saith he, *worketh repentance* [. . .] *not to be repented of, but the sorrowe of the world worketh death.*[7] Both the godly and the wicked, as yee see, haue their sorrowes and their broken hearts. But in this they differ, the sorrowe of the one is but the sorrowe of a slaue, the sorrowe of the other is the sorrowe of a child. The sorrowe of the one is onely from a slavish feare of paine, but the sorrowe of the other is cheefely from loue.

Againe, as for the sorrowes of the wicked, there is no salue for them; there is no comfort for their feares. Cain in his feare heard no comfort [Gen 4:13]; Saul in his feare got no answere [1 Sam 28:15]; Judas in his feare, *falling headlong*, [. . .] *burst asunder in the mids, and all his bowels gushed out* [Acts 1:18]. But, as for the godly, they get balme from God while they are wounded; and he *deliuereth* them *from all* their *feares* [Ps 34:4]. When Zacharias saw the angel, he was afraide; but, anone, God comforted him saying, *feare not Zacharias* [Luke 1:13]. So Marie, when she sawe the angel Gabriel was afraide[8] but incontinent, She heard these wordes of comfort, *feare not Marie* [Luke 1:30]. When the disciples sawe Christ walkeing on the sea, they were all terrified, thinkeing he *had beene a spirit.*[9] But incontinent the Lord established their hearts, saying, feare not, *it is I.*[10] When Christ, after he was dead, arose out of the graue and entered

217

among his apostles, they were *terrified and affrighted*, supposing *that they had seene a spirit* [Luke 24:37]. But anone, he most lovingly comforted them saying, *why are yee troubled, and why doe thoughts arise in your hearts* [Luke 24:38]; *Behold my hands and my feete* etc. [Luke 24:39].

That wee may the better vnderstand what *a broken spirit* and *a contrite heart* are, wee shall consider them in their effects as they are declared by the apostle to the number of seuen: first, where there is a broken heart, there is σπουδή, a *carefulnesse* to shunne euill and to doe well; secondly, ἀπολογία, a *clearing* of our selues, in that wherein wee are innocent for to giue contentment vnto these who haue heard ill reports of vs; thirdly, ἀγανάςτησις, *indignation*, that is a great hatred of any sinne committed by vs; fourthly, φόβος, a *feare* for the iudgements of God preceeding from his wrath; fifthly, ἐπιπόθησις, a *vehement desire* that God may be pleased with all our actions; sixtly, ζῆλος, zeale, a most feruent earnestnesse to goe beyond others in well doing; seuenthly, ἐκδίκησις, *revenge*, a most earnest desire to punish and afflict our selues for our rebellions against God [2 Cor 7:11].

He whose spirit and heart are broken and contrite for sinne will perceiue all these effects in some measure within him selfe. Such a man at all times is most welcome vnto God. This the prophet heere telleth vs: the *broken spirit*, the *broken and contrite heart, O God, thou wilt* neuer *despise*, that is, thou wilt most highly esteeme, yea and will blesse with blessings, both spirituall and temporall.

Doctrine. The doctrine I obserue heere is this: happy is the man not who hath neuer sinned, for that man among all the sonnes of Adam is not to be found. But happy is the man whose spirit is broken and whose heart is broken and contrite, because he hath sinned against God. The Lords eye of fauour is euer vpon that soule. Christ came into this world onely for such. *The spirit of the Lord God is vpon me*, said he, *because the Lord hath anoynted me to preach good tidings vnto the meeke* [. . .], *to bind vp the broken hearted* [Isa 61:1].

The 1 Vse. Let this serue for comfort vnto these poore cast downe soules who, in the pangs of their horrour and feare, would *giue* their *first borne for* their *transgression* [Mic 6:7]. Let such knowe that Christ Jesus was sent *to bind vp the broken* *hearted* [Isa 61:1]. Let such consider these wordes of comfort in my text, *the broken spirit and contrite heart. O God thou wilt* neuer *despise*. These are *the sacrifices of God*.

The 2 Vse. Let this serue for reproofe to these who with Eli take the mournings and prayers from a broken heart to be a fit of drunkennesse [1 Sam 1:14]. Let this also serue for reproofe cheefely to these mockers who scorne the broken heart, as the children of Bethel scorned the bald head of Elishah [2 Kgs 2:23]. Such scorne, the sacrifices of God, they contemne that which God will neuer despise. Therefore such shall be contemned.

The 3 Vse. Let this also serue for reproofe to these who *offend against the generation* of Gods children [Ps 73:15], esteeming that such terrours of mind are infallible tokens that such be defiled with some extraordinarie sinnes aboue others. As if a man should reason after this maner. Behold a number of children all fighting together, a certaine man passing by singleth out one from among all the rest and correcteth him, letting all the rest alone. Therefore he is the childs enemie. Nay, by the contrarie, it would rather seeme that he were either that childs father or a friend.

It is so of the troubles of conscience. The godly and the wicked are often sporting together in their sinnes like euill lads. But behold God the Father, passing by the wicked when he acknowledgeth not to be his, cometh directly vnto his owne children and so chastiseth whiles their bodys, whiles their spirits, whiles both that a carnall eye would iudge the Lord to be their enemie. But he that hath studied in *the sanctuary of God* [Ps 73:17] will easyly vnderstand that spareing of the rod is no loue token in Gods schoole,[11] who maketh intimation vnto all his schollers, that whom he loueth he chasteneth [Prov 3:12]. The dearest of Gods children haue all broken spirits, broken and contrite hearts, before they goe to that place of *pleasures for euermore* [Ps 16:11].

2 Part
a prayer for the Church and commoun wealth

In the second part of the text, wee haue a prayer for the Church and commoun wealth in these wordes, *Doe good in thy good pleasure vnto Zion; build thou the walls of Jerusalem.* In these wordes, there be two petitions: the first is for the Church in these wordes, *Doe good in thy good pleasure vnto Zion;* the second is for the commoun wealth in these wordes, *build thou the walls of Jerusalem.*

1. petition

The first petition is for the Church, *doe good in thy good pleasure vnto Zion.* By Zion heere, I vnderstand the Church, because in Dauids dayes the arke of God was there before Solomon had builded the temple vpon Mount Moriah. In the wordes, there be three things: first, Dauid intreateth God to *doe good;* secondly, wee haue to whom, doe good *vnto Zion;* thirdly, for what cause, for his owne cause *in* this *good pleasure.*

1. Doe good

First, let vs consider what the king desireth the Lord to doe: *Hetivah,*[12] *doe good,* deale bounteously. The word comprehendeth all things needefull for profit or pleasure. When Balaam in his prophecie would declare both the profit and pleasure of the Church, he said in the word of my text, *Mahtov,*[13] that is *how goodly are thy tents, O Jacob* [Num 24:5]. When the spouse did declare the pleasure he had in his spouse, he said vnto her, *how faire is thy loue, my sister, my spouse. How much better is thy loue then wine* [Cant 4:10].

This was the goodnesse of pleasure. The originall word signifieth also merrinesse, when one is reioiced by any thing. Of Ahasuerus, it is writen that *his heart* [. . .] *was merrie with wine* [Est 1:10]. The Hebrewe is *tov lev.*[14] All these things Dauid requires heere in these wordes, *doe good.* Gods good things onely haue profit, pleasure, and merrinesse. The worlds cry is *who will shew vs any good* [Ps 4:6]? But all these good things that come not from Gods blessings are like a flowre with a worme in the heart. They incontinent wither away like the gourd of Jonah, a pleasure of short continuance. If they haue any appearance of profit, they are full of cares, which hinder the heart to be merrie like the poore man that found the purse, merrie before he got it but full of melancholy after that he was rich. Such good things are often like a rich marchands bagge while he is goeing thorow a forrest wherein are many theeues. While he beareth the bagge of ioye, his heart trembleth for feare, like an aspen leafe,[15] whereas the poore man, wanting such feare, goeth forward with chearefull songs, *cantabit vacuus coram latrone viator*.[16]

Dauid heere goeth to God to seeke his good things. To whom should he goe? God is onely good. Wherefore *callest thou me good* [Matt 19:17]? Said Christ to that man that called him good master, God is onely good. Indeede God is onely good that is good of him selfe and the author of euery good gift [Jas 1:17]. He onely is essentialy good. His delight is to *doe good* vnto his creatures, not like the rich glutton who enioyed his good things him self but had no thing for poore Lazarus. In this case his dogges did more good then he. He would not send him a crumbe from his table but *the dogs came and licked his sores* [Luke 16:21].

It is not so of God in his goodnesse, as he is *Shadai*,[17] God all sufficient who hath abundance of good things [Exod 6:3]. He is also *Iehovah*, who doeth good vnto all in makeing his sunne to shine and his raine to fall both vpon the godly and vngodly [Matt 5:45]. He is goodnesse it self, and therefore can not but doe good. He hath continualy both his hands full of good things for all these that desire to receiue. The blessings of his right hand are onely for Zion. This is Gods exercise night and day: to *doe good* vnto the children of men.

The Vse. Christ said, *learne of me*. Let vs learne of God euer to be doeing good [Matt 11:29]. If wee would haue God to *doe good* vnto vs, let vs be carefull to doe good vnto others. To such onely shall be said in the last day, *well done* [. . .] *faithfull seruants*.[18]

The 2 Vse. Let this serue for reproofe to many who can say well but care not for doeing good. If wee said, faithfull seruant could saue men, many should be saued. The pharisees said but did not, and therefore all Christs preachings vnto them were full of woes. S. James counsell is good: *be yee doers of the word* [Jas 1:22]. Many in his dayes, but more in our dayes like Naphtali, *giue goodly wordes* [Gen 49:21] but doe no good.

221

When they see a brother naked and *destitute of dayly food*, they say *vnto them, depart in peace. Be* you *warmed and filled*, but *giue them not* the *things which are needefull to the body* [Jas 2:16]. Such haue not learned that of God whose exercise is to *doe good*. **The 3 Vse.** Let this serue also for reproofe to these who not onely doe not good vnto others, but doe much euill. They are like the diuell, who, for the euill he doeth, is called that euill one. Night and day his exercise is to doe euill, *seekeing whom he may deuore* [1 Pet 5:8]. So the wicked: *they sleepe not except they haue done mischeefe; and their sleepe is taken away vnlesse they cause some to fall* [Prov 4:16].

2. Doe good vnto Zion

Secondly, let vs heere consider to whom Dauid desireth God to doe good: it is vnto Zion. *Doe good vnto Zion*, that is vnto the Church of God. The Church was called Zion because, in Dauids dayes, the arke of God, the testimonie of Gods presence, was there before the temple was builded vpon Mount Moriah by Solomon.

This Zion, as scriptures declare, was a high mountaine in Jerusalem. On the top thereof the Jebusites had builded a fort which they keept by force vntill Dauid was made king. Joshuah telleth that in his dayes *the children of Judah could not driue them out* [Josh 15:63]. In Dauids dayes, it was so strong that the Jebusites declared that *the blind and the lame* were able to defend it against all his forces [2 Sam 5:6]. But David at last tooke it from the Jebusites and fortified it, and called it *the citie of Dauid*. [1 Chron 11:4–5] After that, he brought *vp the arke of the* Lord *from the house of Obed Edom into the citie of Dauid* [2 Sam 6:12], which was builded vpon Mount Zion. Because of the arke, it became the cheefe place of Gods worship. From this, Zion was named the Lords holy mountaine [Joel 3:17]. The psalmist calleth it the mountaine [Ps 78:68] of Gods loue. Isaiah said, *out of Zion shall goe foorth the law* [Isa 2:3]. These wordes in the psalme be very considerable. *The Lord hath chosen Zion; he hath desired it for his habitation. This is my rest, for euer; heere will I dwell, for I haue desired it* [Ps 132:13–14].

For these considerations, the mountaine of Zion was a figure of Christs Church, called by Isaiah, *the Zion of the holy one of Israel* [Isa 60:14]. The word Zion is an Hebrewe word,[19] and signifieth drienesse. And what is the Church of God in the eyes of carnall men but like a drye hill whereof there is little vse. Christ him selfe, the head of the Church, is compared to a root groweing out of a drie ground [Isa 53:2].

The fatnesse of the earth and [. . .] *the dew* is the portion of the wicked. It was promised to profane Esau [Gen 27:39]. The wicked, no more then that divell in the gospell, can not find rest in drye places [Matt 12:43]. The diuells can not abide in the drye places of Zion. Babylon, with her rivers round about [Ps 137:1], is a more fitting resting place for Jim and Zijim. There the diuels, like satyrs, *cry* euery one *to his fellowe* [Isa 34:14]. The night monster or skrich owle rest there; the fairies leape there; and one diuell daunceth vnto another. But, as for Zion, the drie places of Gods spirit, the diuells can find no rest there. They may *velitari*. Come and trouble Zion with a skirmish, but because God, according to his promise, dwelleth there for euer [Ps 132:14], they are compelled to retire. Though they, by the scandales of great men and good men both, doe many euills vnto Zion, as heere may be seene by the adulterie and murther of Dauid, yet there is a God in the heauens, a God that heareth prayers, a God who neuer closed his eare to barre out this prayer, *Doe good in thy good pleasure vnto Zion.*

Obserue heere how Dauid prayeth for the good of the Church. By his fearefull scandales, he had done much euill vnto Zion. He had provoked God; he had scandalized the godly; he had made an open waye, both to crueltie and vncleanesse. By his euill example, he had opened the mouthes of Gods enemies, and had made them to blaspheme. He had beheld him heere making amends. After he had repented and cryed for mercy to him selfe, he besought God most earnestly *to doe good* [. . .] *vnto Zion.*

The 1 Vse. Let all men, but cheefely great men, beware to sinne against God, for, by their sinnes, they doe much euill vnto Zion. If they haue sinned, let them repent, and first pray for them selues. After their peace is made, then let them cry with Dauid, *doe good* [. . .] *vnto Zion.* What I say of great men that I say of men of all sortes; by our sinnes wee haue provoked God and procured many euills vnto Zion. As one Achan, by his sinne troubled all Israel [Josh 7:25], let vs therefore this day with Dauid, hauing broken spirits and contrit hearts, cry for mercy; and, when God hath giuen vs a signe of his fauour, let vs not forget to intreat the Lord *to doe good in* his *good pleasure vnto Zion*. If Dauid said, well shall I not hate these *that hate thee*,[20] wee may say as well, shall I not loue these that loue thee? These were wordes of great loue: *if I forget thee, O Jerusalem, let my right hand forget her cunning*; *if I doe not remember thee, let my tongue cleaue* vnto *the roofe of my mouth, if I preferre not Jerusalem aboue my cheefe ioy* [Ps 137:5-6]. Happy is the man that is so affected towards Gods Church. He hath a faire promise which shall neuer faile: *they shall prosper that loue* her [Ps 122:6].

The 2 Vse. Let this serue for reproof to many who care not for the well of Gods Church. If they find a place of peace and ease, such are these who lie in beds of yvory and chaunt to the sound of the viole, but *are not grieued for the affliction of Joseph* [Amos 6:6]. Many yet doe worse who not onely are not grieued, but reioice to heare of euills done vnto Zion. Others are Doegs dogs, who persecute and rent the Church. Such haue not learned of God to doe so many euils vnto the spouse of Christ.

The godly had great neede to intreat God to *doe good* [. . .] *vnto Zion*, for Zion may say of the wicked, as S. Paul said of *Alexander, the copper smith*, they haue done *me much euill* [2 Tim 4:14]. *Many a time haue they afflicted me from my youth, may Israel now say* [Ps 129:1]. Where is that Church this day that may not say this? What needes me goe ouer sea to see the euills done vnto Gods Zion in France by diuers massacres, but cheefly that *lamiena Parisiensis boutcherie* of Paris,[21] where most treacherously the children of God, vnder colour of friendship, were like poore sheepe brought vnto the shambles?

This Church of Scotland, with Israel, may now say, *many a time haue they afflicted me from my youth. The plowers plowed vpon my back; they made long their furrowes*. But God, who euer hath done good vnto our Zion, hath cut asunder the cords of the wicked; he hath confounded and hath made all these that hate Zion to turne back. He shall make like the grasse vpon the house tops which withereth afore it groweth vp, which doeth good neither to man nor beast. He that doeth euill vnto Zion is like a bee that hath lost its sting; it can doe no more good but becometh an idle drone.

224

3. in thy good pleasure

Wee haue heard first what Dauid desired the Lord to doe, it was to *doe good*. Secondly, to whom, *vnto Zion*. Now it followeth for what cause he desired him to *doe good* vnto the Church.

The prophets cheefe argument is Gods *good pleasure* [. . .]: *doe good in thy good pleasure vnto Zion*. In the originall, it is *Biretsonecha*,[22] that is *pro bona voluntate tua*, for thy good wills sake, or for *thy good pleasures* sake. Heere is the very root of all the benefits of God both spirituall and temporall, εὐδοκία, *his good pleasure* and will [Eph 1:9]. From this is our election, predestination, vocation, iustification, sanctification, and glorification. The *good pleasure* of God is the fountaine of all the mercies wee receiue from God, who hath said, *I will haue mercy on whom I will haue mercy*.

What can he find in vs that may moue him to doe vs good? Is not our best righteousnesse a menstruous cloth [Isa 64:6]? Let that bloody child lyeing by the way side with his navill uncut [Ezek 16:4] tell to the world what moued the Lord to loue him while no eye did pitie him. Away with our worthinesse; away with Romane merits,[23] the very dung of pride; away with our righteousnesse in matter of merit.

Let vs all forsake our selues and begge at Gods gates for no sake but for his mercy and his pleasures sake. This is the right well which men by their owne wisdome will no more be able to find them. Hagar was of her self able to find the well of water which saued the life of her sonne [Gen 21:19]. Heere is the well of life. If yee find not the good will and pleasure of God, *yee shall all die in your sinnes*.[24] The Church receiueth no benefit but for this good will and pleasure sake. And therefore now, when she hath great neede of your help, cry vnto God for her that God would *doe good in* his *good pleasure vnto Zion*. If yee help her not with your prayers, the curse of God shall not faile to come vpon you. *Curse yee Meros*, said Deborah, *because they came not* out to [. . .] *help* [. . .] *the Lord, to* [. . .] *help* [. . .] *the Lord against the mighty* [Judg 5:23].

Let vs all therefore this day wrestle with the *good pleasure* of God, as Jacob did with God [Gen 32:24]. The most sweete armes full that euer wee gote is to embrace God in his *good pleasure.* Let vs hold him fast, though he say to vs, as he said to Jacob, *let me goe* [Gen 32:26]. Let vs answere with Jacob, wee *will not let thee goe* [Gen 32:26] vntill thou *doe good in thy good pleasure vnto Zion.*[25] Take courage in the worke, lay hands vpon God, powre out your hearts in prayer before him. He will not refuse you, yea he can not.

Abraham first fainted in seeking for Sodom before God failed in giuing [Gen 18:32]. God could not abide the cryes of Moses heart growing in his prayers [Exod 14:15]. The Lord had said and had commanded to preach *fourtie dayes and Niniveh shall be* destroyed [Jon 3:4]. King and people all cryed and fasted; and the Lord revoked his sentence of iustice, and in his mercy saued these whom he had threatned to destroy. Did God this vnto Niniveh, a pagan citie; and will he not doe good [. . .] vnto Zion, his deare Church, where so many thousands are all hanging vpon him like Jacobs wrestling for to get a blessing? His *good pleasure* will not runne away from so many teares, from so many grones. His *good pleasure* will not hide it selfe from so many eyes filled with the waters of Marah, the most bitter waters of repentance. His *good pleasure* will not close his eares at the cryes of so many thousands. No not: but this *good pleasure* at last shall come out with two hands full of almes. Peace shall be in the one hand and trueth in the other.

All other benefits shall followe after these two great princes. Yee shall not be destroyed with famine; your children shall not, with the little children of Israel, cry vnto their mothers dyeing for hunger, where is bread [Lam 4:4]? No not: the Lord shall *heare the heauens. And they shall heare the earth; and the earth shall heare the corne; and the wine and the oyle;* and they shall heare Gods people [Hos 2:21-22]. The goodnesse of God from his good will and pleasure shall fill our eyes and our eares, our mouthes, our hearts, and our hands, with such aboundance that, though wee should cast downe our old barnes, and build others of greater capacitie, all shall be filled. And, therefore, let vs all take courage in our prayers most assuredly, beleeuing that God at this time shall *doe good in* his *good pleasure vnto Zion.* The Lord shall watch ouer his Church, like an eagle fluttering *ouer her yong.* He shall spread abroad his wings [Deut 32:11] ouer Zion for to doe her good; and these that touch her shall *touch the apple of his eye* [Zech 2:8]. They all shall be *confounded and turned backe that hate Zion* [Ps 129:5]. Heere is the safetie of the Church.

4. petition

Wee haue heard of Dauids petition for the Church in these wordes, *Doe good in thy good pleasure vnto Zion.* The second petition is for the commounwealth in these wordes, *build vp the walls of Jerusalem.* This was the metropolitane citie of the kingdome, the mother citie, the beautie of the whole earth.

This citie was first called Salem, that is peace. In it Melchisedek was king and was called *king of Salem* [Gen 14:18]. It was also called Jebus from Jubusi, a sonne of Canaan [Gen 10:16]. It was possessed by his posteritie, the Jebusites, vntill Dauid wonne from them the fort of Zion. After that it was called Jerusalem, that is the vision of peace. King Dauid, hauing taken this citie from the Jebusites, build a wall *round about from Millo and inward* [2 Sam 5:9], and so had made it a great strength; but because, by his sinnes of murder and adulterie, he had made a great breach whereby the enemies might haue entered and destroyed all, he intreated heere the Lord to build vp the walls which he had by his folies throwen downe.

Heere obserue two things. First, it is onely sinne whereby the walls of a kingdome or citie are broken downe. Sinne is the cause of all our weakenesse. By sinne, breaches are made in the strongest holds. It was the sinne of Samson more then the shauing of his locks which made his strength to goe from him [Judg 16:19]. Dauid, by his sinne, made a fearefull breach in the walls of Jerusalem.

The Vse. Let vs stand in awe and not sinne. If wee would haue our houses, our children, our estats, to stand, if wee would in the great day at the Lord stand before the sonne of man, let vs beware of sinnes, for they will make breaches in our walls. Our soules, our bodies, our children, our friends, and our estate, our health, our wealth, shall suffer extreame decayes, if, by our sinnes, wee prouoke the eyes of Gods glory.

Secondly, obserue heere when sinne hath made a breach in the walls of a city or church. God onely is he who is able to build vp the walls. He is *architectus*, the master builder. No man,

227

except he be directed by God, can lay a stone in this spirituall or civill wall. This is not a wall of dead stones but of *liuely stones* [1 Pet 2:5]. Gods protection is the wall that goeth about both the Church and commounwealth. This is that *wall of fire* [Zech 2:5] and of brasse whereof the prophet speaketh. When God is pleased with a people, he in a maner buildeth a wall for protection to defend both Church and commoun wealth.

But, when a people offends and contemneth him, they make a breach in the walls, and expose them selues to great dangers, like a city whose walls are in diuers parts fallen downe to the ground, where the enemie may get an easy entrance. But when a people repenteth and returneth to the Lord, then the Lord beginneth to build vp the wall againe, and then the people dwell in surety, as in a city fenced throughly. These who are compassed with this wall may scorne their enemies, and with good reason say vnto them, as the Jebusites said to the seruants of Dauid while they were within their stronghold, *except* yee *take away the blind and the lame*, yee shall *not come in hither*, that is yee *can not come in hither* [2 Sam 5:6].

The Vse. When wee perceiue either Church or commounwealth to suffer breaches, let vs runne to God by prayer, interesting him most earnestly to build vp the wall. *Except the Lord build the house, they labour in vaine that build it. Except the Lord keepe the city, the watch man waketh but in vaine* [Ps 127:1]. All as yee see is in vaine without God. The pagans who had but the light of nature were forced to acknowledge this. I will giue you two notable testimonies. One said, *deiope et auxilio multo magis Republicam Romanam quam ratione hominum et consilio gabernari*,[26] that is the commounwealth of Rome is more gouerned by the help and assistance of God then by any wisdome of men. Another said, *vbi non Deus, sed mortalis aliquis praest, ibi malorum nullum est effugium.*[27]

Where mortall men beare rule without God, it is not possible to escape a mischeefe. Seeing it is so, let this be your dayly prayer for Church and commounwealth, O God, *Doe good in thy good pleasure vnto Zion, build* [. . .] *the walls of Jerusalem.* As Eli said to Hannah, so say I now to you all while yee make this prayer, *the* Lord *God of Israel graunt* you your *petition* [1 Sam 1:17]. Amen, Amen.

The Godly Man His Confidence

Psal 62: 1

Trvely my soule waiteth vpon God, from him cometh my saluation.
The cheef desire of teachers and hearers should be to haue the *trueth* of *the inward parts* [Ps 51:6], which is the cheefe obiect of Gods loue toward the sonnes of men. The outward seruice of the body without the affection of the soule profiteth little, nay it is an abomination before God. The pharisees were very busy in doeing things that men might see for to gaine mans applause. They made *cleane the outside of the cup and of the platter, but within* were *full of extortion an[d] excesse* [Matt 23:25]. They cared not for other mens soules and forgot their owne; they misregarded their saluation. Blessed is the soule that waiteth still vpon God: this is the exercise of a sanctified soule. It is heere to be seene in the wordes of my text, *Truely my soule waiteth vpon God* etc. In these wordes, Dauid, in dangers among his enemies, professeth his confidence in God.

the diuision of the text

In the wordes, there be two parts: in the first part, he declareth that his soule depends vpon God in these wordes, *my soule waiteth vpon God*; in the second part, he giueth a reason of his waiting vpon God in these wordes, *from him cometh my saluation.* The meaning of the whole text is that Dauid in all his dangers and distresse did onely rely vpon God.

1 Part
Truely my soule waiteth vpon God

In these few wordes, I shall consider two things: first, a preface; secondly, the matter.
The preface is in the word *truely*. It is short, for it is but a word *truely*. It is good for what is better then trueth?

The Doctrine. The thing I heere brefely obserue is this: trueth in mans wordes is the honestie of his speach. Whereas the tongue of trueth may be called a mans glory, *awake* [. . .] *my glory*,[1] said the psalmist to his tongue, a fals tongue in the mouth is a mouth full of shame, the enemie of glory.

The Vse. Seeing it is so, let vs beware to shame our glory. While wee speake, let truely goe before, as of a messenger to prepare a waye for our wordes. There is none that can knocke at the doore of the sanctified eare that shall be so welcome as trueth. While it cometh before in a preface, wee should thinke of it as Dauid said of Ahimaaz running post, *he is a good man and commeth with good tidings* [2 Sam 18:27]. There is no good that can followe after fals houde. Let Ananias and Saphirah tell what vantage they got by their lies [Acts 5:10]. All men should abhorre a lye for its fathers cause, the diuell, for, as trueth it selfe hath said, *he is a lyar and the father* thereof [John 8:44].

Dauid, speakeing of Gods desires, made mention of this cheefe one, *behold thou desirest trueth in the inward parts* [Ps 51:6]. He that would speake truely with his tongue, let him first seeke trueth within the inward parts, for it is out of *the abundance of the heart* that *the mouth speaketh* [Matt 12:34]. When Jesu said to Jonadab, *is thy heart* [upright] *toward me as my heart is toward thee* [2 Kgs 10:15],[2] Jonadab answered, *it is*, it is [2 Kgs 10:15].[3] Let vs striue in sinceritie & trueth to haue such a heart toward God, as he hath toward vs, euen a true heart haueing *trueth* into *the inward parts*.[4] The wicked knowe not what trueth is. *Pilate said vnto* Christ, *what is trueth* [John 18:38]? But he cared not for an answere because he was but a fals man himselfe.

In my iudgement, trueth in a man is a conformitie in good betweene tongue, heart, & hand. When all the three concurre in a good matter, then are they true. But if, while the tongue saith truely, the heart is fals, or the hand doeth ill, that truely on the tongue is but a lye couered with a coat of trueth. *Burning lips, & a wicked heart are like a potsheard couered with siluer drosse* [Prov 26:23]. Let therefore all men, while they speake, speake the good that they thinke, & doe the good which they speake, & thinke. Let men speake with their tongue what they please. Their hearts before God & their hands before men are dummies that can not lye.

my soule waiteth vpon God

Heere Dauid declareth that his soule dependeth on his God. Heere wee shall considder two things: first, who it is that *waiteth vpon God*; secondly, what it is to waite *vpon God*.

who waiteth

He that *waiteth vpon God* heere is not a poore man of no reputation. It is the soule of a king.

The Doctrine. The doctrine is this: the king of heauen must be a great king, seeing all earthly kings are but his dependers or waiters. For what king Dauid saith heere, that must all kings saye truely, *my soule waiteth vpon God*. Otherwayes it were better for them they were dogges then men. Great then I say must this king be who is waited vpon by the greatest vpon earth.

The Vse. Let all flesh stoupe before him vpon whom all the soules of kings must waite vpon. This is a royall vse that kings be humble before him who hath that great prerogatif printed vpon his thigh, the *King of Kings & Lord of Lords* [Rev 19:16]. O how great must he be who is so great that all the glory of kings can not reach aboue his thigh. Christ Jesus, this King of Kings, hath a glory of three house height vpon his browe. He hath a plate of gold wherein is ingrauen his high & loftie style, *holinesse* vnto *the Lord* [Exod 39:30]. In the second stage, he hath vpon his breast the breast plate full of precious stones with Vrim & Thummin, light & perfection [Lev 8:8]. In the third stage, vnder his girdle vpon his thigh, he hath his basest style, the *King of Kings & Lord of Lords* [Rev 19:16]. Let King Dauid teach kings if kings will not heare pastours, *be wise* [. . .], *O yee kings, be instructed yee iudges of the earth. Serue the Lord with feare & reioice with trembling: kisse the sonne lest he be angry* [Ps 2:10-12].

The Doctrine. Againe heere obserue that he saith that his soule waiteth vpon God. This is sinceritie; this answereth to his first word truely. Outward seruice, without the inward inward affection, is but a lye. One that draweth neere to God with his mouth, while the soule is not well set, is but a deceiuing

231

hypocrite. The lippes without the heart, the body without the soule, are but sacrifices of fooles.

The Vse. When euer we doe any thing at God his seruice, let vs see that our soule be at the worke. All bodily exercises perish with the vseing. Art thou prayeing? See that thy soule praye. Art thou praising? See that thy soule praise. God vnderstandeth not popish, barbarous theologie of *opus operatum*.[5] If their prayers be said vpon their gadees,[6] they thinke that all is well. *Quasi re bene gesta*,[7] after they haue mumbled their matins not knoweing what they haue said to God, they will looke for a reward for their ydle wordes of ignorance. Verily, verily, *they haue their reward*.[8] *In the Church*, said the apostle, *I had rather speake fiue wordes with my vnderstanding, that by my voice I might teach others also, then ten thousands words in an vnknowen tongue* [1 Cor 14:19]. If man should teach others with wordes of vnderstanding, he should not be a barbarian to him selfe. It is no soule seruice when the mouth babbleth without vnderstanding. Such a man can not say heere with Dauid, *truely my soule waiteth vpon God*.

The Doctrine. Thirdly, obserue heere that he saith not his *soule waiteth vpon God*, but *my soule waiteth*. He is not so curious what other[s] doe as carefull for that which he should doe himselfe.

The Vse. Let euery man striue to serue God well him selfe, that, by his good example, others may learne to be godly. This was Peters great fault: he was more curious what Johne should doe then carefull to considder what Christ had bidden him selfe doe [John 21:21]. It was his part at Christ his direction to followe, that Johne, seeing his obedience, might learne without questions to followe Christ his will. This counsell wee haue from Christ: *let your light so shine before men, that they may see your good workes, & glorifie your father which is in heauen* [Matt 5:16]. If men would teach mens soules to doe well, let their light to shine that men *may see* their *good workes* [Matt 5:16]. If men would allure mens soules to waite vpon God, let men see them practising their owne precepts, sayeing with Dauid, heere *truely my soule waiteth vpon God*.

This is no such forcible argument for the practise of pietie as to doe that which wee saye. If he that taketh vp the psalme sing well him selfe, he will allure others to followe & to sing with him. But, if he that goeth before marre all the musicke, though he should crye on others to sing well, hardly shall any be able to keepe a right tune. The most part will sit dumb when he that should guide goeth a straying.

What it is to waite vpon God

It followeth now that wee see what it is to waite *vpon God*: to waite *vpon God* properly is to abide with patience & hope of helpe from God. This waiting is in the godly with a vehement & continuall lookeing for assistance from God, for to be deliuered, either from the ill present which they feele, or from the ill to come which they feare. That wee maye the better vnderstand what it is to waite *vpon God*, wee shall considder the properties of those that waite vpon any thing: 1. a wise on waiter must considder well that that where upon he waiteth be worthy the waiting on; 2. he must loue that whereon he waiteth; 3. he must haue a sense of some want in him selfe; 4. he must haue hope to find it in him vpon whom he waiteth; 5. he must be constant in waiting on; 6. he that waiteth well vpon any must haue euer an eye vpon him vpon whome he waiteth.

1.

A wise on waiter must considder well that that wherevpon he waiteth be worthy the waiting on. Wise then is that soule that waiteth vpon God, who is not onely worthy, but worthinesse it selfe. When all things faile man, God will not faile him. *My flesh & my heart faileth*, said the psalmiste, but the Lord *is the strength of my heart & my portion for euer* [Ps 73:26]. This is he who, if we waite vpon him, shall first guide vs by his counsell & afterward shall bring vs vnto glory.

2.

There must be loue in the heart of him that *waiteth vpon God*. Except that a man loue God, he can not waite vpon God [1

233

John 4:8]. A man can not liue where he loueth not. *God is loue* [1 John 4:8], not onely because he loueth vs more then we can loue him, but because he is most worthy to be loued of vs. Well is the man who, fainting in his spirit with such a strong loue, can say with the spouse, *stay me with flaggons, comfort me with apples, for I am sicke of loue* [Cant 2:5]. Moses so loued him that, for his glory, he desired to be scraiped *out of* the *booke* of life [Exod 32:32]. S. Paul much was inflammed with such a loue to Christ that, if any loued him not, his wish was that he should be *anathema maranath* [1 Cor 16:22].[9] If a man loue not God cheefly for him selfe, he will not waite *vpon God.*

Many waited vpon Christ because he gaue them loaues [John 6:26], as a dogge will waite vpon a stranger that hath a bone into his hand, not for him selfe, but for the bone. Many waite *vpon God* his benefits, but fewe waite vpon himselfe. *There be many that say who will shewe vs any good* [Ps 4:6]? But how fewe are these that seeke God for him selfe, sayeing with the psalmiste, *Lord lift* thou *vp* the light of thy *countenance vpon vs* [Num 6:26]. If many with the dogge get once the bone of some benefite out of God his hand, they knowe him no more then if he were a stranger but nowe come into the world. There is no waiting on where there is no loue. Man is wearied to waite vpon that which he loueth not.

The most part of vs may easily knowe that we loue not God, & that by our waiting. How drowsie are wee to waite *vpon God* vntill he hath spoken but an houre vnto vs? How wearied are wee to speake to God in prayer but a quarter. We can waite vpon worldly bissinesse the whole day, & discourse with men from the morning vntill euen. But who can waite on so long, either for to heare God speakeing by preaching vnto vs, or for to speake in prayer vnto him? It is soone said, as yee heare, *my soule waiteth vpon God.* But how fewe can say, *Truely my soule waiteth vpon God*?

3.

Thirdly, who waiteth truely on God he must haue a sense of his owne wants. A laodicean soule filled with selfe conceit can not waite vpon the Lord [Rev 3:14-17].[10] So long as a man

234

singeth this requiem to his soule, that he hath neede of no thing, he waiteth vpon him selfe [Rev 3:17]. But so soone as, by the vertue of God his ego salue, he hath seene his owne blindnesse, miserie, & nakednesse, he is fit for waiting *vpon God*. A man must first renounce him selfe & all that is within him before that he can be able to cleaue vnto his God.[11]

4.

Who *waiteth* on *God* truely must be assured to find in God that which he wanteth: this is faith. *To whom shall we goe*, said Peter vnto Christ, for thou hast the wordes of eternall life [John 6:68]. S. Peter would waite onely vpon Christ because that he sawe that he had wordes such as no man had the like. If men could taste & see how good is the Lord [Ps 34:8], though he should desire them to goe from him, as Nahomi desired Ruth & Orpaly to returne to their countree, they would cleaue vnto him, as Ruth did to Nahomi whom scripture calleth *stedfastly minded* [Ruth 1:18].

5.

In waiting *vpon God*, there must be constancie & continuance. God will not [be] serued by fits & starts. He that perseuereth vnto the end shall be saued. The wicked, with these deceitfull Israelites, for a space will seeme to be bowed like a bowe for to receiue the string of the Lords law into the nocke of their heart. But incontinent they bend back from such a bensell.[12] They *turned backe*, said the prophet, *& dealt unfaithfully like their fathers: they were turned aside like a deceitfull bowe* [Ps 78:57]. These who turne back & aside can not be said to waite *vpon God*. Courtiers will waite constantly vpon kings for that which is not worth the on waiting. But fewe men will waite *vpon God*. If God incontinent make not answere to King Saul by Vrim or Thimmin, he must runne to the witch of Endor [1 Sam 28:7]. Nature despighteth grace: they are contrarily disposed.

Grace is willing to waite *vpon God*, but nature maketh hast.

235

As prophane Saul could not waite till Samuel came, but as he said *forced him selfe & offered a burnt offering* [1 Sam 13:12], euen so the wicked man can not waite vpon the Lord his leisure. In a sore pinch he will say, *flecteresi negueo supros achronta mouebo*, that is, if God will not, the diuell will. No rather, if God will not, the diuell darre not. He that will not waite *vpon God* but runneth to the diuell for helpe shall receiue Saul his comfort, a comfortlesse comfort. *Wherefore [. . .] doest thou aske of me*, said Satan, *seeing the Lord is departed from thee* [1 Sam 28:16] or rather seeing thou is departed from the Lord? *Is it not because there is not a God in Israel* that men haue recourse to witches & charmers [2 Kgs 1:3]? Woe vnto such, woe vnto their soules, for such can not say with Dauid, heere *truely my soule waiteth vpon God*.

6.

Last of all, the propertie of a good on waiter is euer to haue an eye vpon him vpon whom he waiteth. *Behold*, said the psalmiste, *as the eyes of seruants looke vnto the hands of their masters, & as the eyes of a maden vnto the hand of her mistresse, so our eyes waite vpon the Lord our God vntill he haue mercy vpon vs* [Ps 123:2]. After that, Dauid had said, *I will lift vp mine eyes vnto the hilles, from whence cometh my helpe* [Ps 121:1], that is to the force of men who dwelt into the hillie contree of Caanan. Incontinent he correcteth him selfe, sayeing, *my helpe cometh from the Lord which made heauen & earth* [Ps 121:2]. I will waite *vpon God*, would he say, my eyes shall no more be lifted vnto the hilles, but vnto him *which made* the *heauen & the earth*. By this that hath bene said may yee well vnderstand now the prophet his mind when he said, *truely my soule waiteth vpon God*.

The Doctrine. The cheefe doctrine I touch heere is this: that our God is a God well worthy to be waited vpon. He is the author of euery good gift & perfect donation [Jas 1:17]. He giueth both grace & glory, grace for this world & glory for the world to come. He is not onely *Shadai*,[13] God all Sufficient, one who hath enough for all his creatures, but also *Jehouah*, one who giueth liberaly of that which he hath [Exod 6:3]. That which he promiseth to man, he maketh it in his owne time to haue a being by a reall performance.

The Vse. Seeing our God is both rich & powerfull & willing to helpe vs, let vs in all our distresses waite truely vpon him: 1. he is well worthy to be waited vpon; 2. let vs loue him; 3. let vs considder our manifold wants & what neede wee haue of him; 4. let vs be assured to find in him all that whereof wee haue neede; 5. let vs not waite vpon him for a day like these fained fasters who like a bulrush drouped downe for a day [Isa 58:5]; 6. last of all, let vs turne our eyes from the high hilles of humane helpes, waiting till our *helpe come from the Lord which made* the *heauen & the earth*. Happy shall wee be if we can say heere with Dauid, *Truely my soule waiteth vpon God*.

It is greatly to be feared that fewe truely can be said to waite *vpon God*. If we would carefully trye our selues, wee should find that we are more wearie to waite *vpon God* then vpon any thing. Wee knowe not his worth, & therefore wee thinke him not worthy the waiting on. Where is our loue toward God? Wee are keye cold in our zeale. Wee speake not of God; wee speake not to God. We haue a sorte of sadnesse so soone as wee begin to thinke of him. Wee haue many faire shewes. But O but God is a matter of melancholie to our vnsanctified minds. Where is our loue toward him? It is over mastered with selfe loue. Where is our constancie at his seruice? Wee are not fixed & stable in waiting vpon him. Our thoughts concerning him are like feathers fleeing in the wind.[14] The thoughts of our hearts can not be stable because our hearts are double. *A double minded man is vnstable in all his wayes* [Jas 1:8].

And what shall I say more if our soules did waite *vpon God*. Our eyes would not be lifted vp vnto the hilles,[15] but would waite vpon the Lord. But alas, our eyes tell plainely that our hearts wait not vpon God. As Peter was knowne by his speach, so may wee be knowen by our lookes. *The eyes of the foole are in the ends of the earth* [Prov 17:24]. Such eyes can not waite *vpon God*. No man can directly behold the heauens & the earth together; no man can waite vpon heauen & earth together *no more then a man can* be able to *serue two masters* [Matt 6:24]. To bid a earthly minded man waite vpon God is as who should desire an Ephramitie to pronounce Shibboleth [Judg 12:6].

This much concerning the first part of my texte, which is in

237

these wordes, *truely my soule waiteth vpon God*. Others interpret these wordes after this maner, *anima silet* or *anima tacita est*,[16] that is my soule keepeth silence, as if he had said, notwithstanding that I am sore troubled & perplexed, yet because God taketh my part, I will suffer patiently; or as Job said, I *will lay* my *hand vpon my mouth* [Job 40:4].

The Doctrine. The doctrine is this: there is no thing that can still a cryeing soule but God his fauour. The wicked are euer cryeing, *who will shewe vs any good* [Ps 4:6]. But, because they get but shewes of good & not God the substantiall goodnesse, they are neuer content. Their soules can neuer be silent, but continually crye with the greedy graue, bring, bring [Prov 30:15]. Neither can their soules be silent in aduersitie, for, seeing they call not vpon God but crye vnto the creatures which no more then Baal can make answere, they crye without comfort & so can neuer say with our prophet, *anima mea silet ad deum*, my soule is silent to God. There is no silence nor resting place for the soule till it come to God [1 Kgs 18:29]. Before God came to Elijah, three restlesse posts ranne before, viz *a great & strong wind*, after which came a earthquake, after which came a fire, after all God came in the calme [1 Kgs 19:11-12].[17] There was no silence vntill God came.

The Vse. Let all these that would liue a quiet & contented life seeke their God till they find him. Without God can be no contentment. Marie seekeing Christ in the graue is the figure of a troubled soule. There is no rest till Christ be found. But so soone as he maketh his voice to be heard behind, it will swiftly turne it selfe about with a rabboni master [John 20:16]. Then it findeth rest and contentment.

2 Part
the reason of the prophet his waiting *vpon God* the reason

Now let vs come to the reason which moued Dauid truely to waite *vpon God*. The reason is in those wordes, *from him cometh my saluation*. This reason is of great weight. In it I shall considder two things: 1. what is it that the soule getteth heere, it is saluation; 2. from whom it is, viz from him euen from God.

saluation

That which the soule is said to receiue heere is saluation. I will saye a great word of saluation: it is the most deare donation that *cometh downe from the Father of lights* [Jas 1:17]. As for faith, hope, loue, repentance, they all are send downe from the Father of lights to be but seruants & instruments for the getting of saluation. If a man should winne *the whole world*, what will it availe if he get not saluation. There is no greater folie then for a man to winne *the whole world* with the losse of his *owne soule*. Great then must this reason be, *from him cometh my saluation*. Saluation is a thing which all men desire but fewe take the paines for to get it. The poore sluggard will wish to be rich but he can not take paines. The naked sluggard would gladly be clothed, but he neglecteth the meanes. The hungrie sluggard is as ready for to dine as he that hath bene woorkeing in the fields.

All the wicked would as faine be in heauen after death as the godly. As brutish Balaam could say, so can they, *let me die the death of the rightenes & let my* [. . .] *end be like* vnto theirs [Num 23:10]. The word saluation is sweete, the thing it selfe is sweeter; but the worke is soure because it must be wrought with *feare & trembling* [Phil 2:12]. Such is the stupiditie of the wicked, or rather let me say, the wicked are so bewitched that for saluation they can take no paines. For their saluation they would not be content to be bund[18] euery day to pray but an houre. The prison of prayer is more painefull to flesh then the feare of the wrath to come. Satan hath lulled most mens soules in a slumber wherein, as in a raueing dreame, they imagine that God is so mercifull that all shall be saued. But it shall faire with them as with those who goe to bed hungrie without their supper. Such may dreame to be at a feast, but, while they shall awake, their dishes shall flie awaye with their dreames & they shall be found emptie.

from whom salvation cometh

Now let vs see from whom cometh this saluation. It is heere said *from Him cometh*: that is from God. Christ, that *day spring from on high*, is the very spring of man his saluation [Luke 1:78]. Out of the breast of this pelican came the blood which brought saluation to the world.[19]

The Doctrine. The doctrine we haue to learne heere is that God, who is the author of *euery good gift*, is the author of our saluation. What Dauid saith heere, that must every saued soule say. *From him cometh my saluation*, yea & from him alone. There is no name in heauen or earth whereby wee can be saued, but onely by the name of Jesus who is the fountaine of life, the liuely spring of saluation. The musicke of heauen is saluation is from the Lord & from the lamb [Rev 7:10].

The Vse. Seeing the soules saluation is from God, let all those that would be saued seeke their saluation from God, in whom onely it is to be found. Men may *compasse sea & land* for to seeke it, as the pharisees sought proselites. But except that they seeke it from God, from whom alone it cometh, the longer they seeke it, the more shall they proue the children of hell [Matt 23:15]. Fye vpon papists, the enemies of their owne saluation. They goe about to buy that which they should begge. They wander from place to place, & wearie them selues with pilgrimages. They spend their moneyes in vaine vpon their fat monkes, who laugh in their sleeue at their ignorance. S. Peter hath well prophecied of such deceivers, sayeing, while *they promise them libertie, they themselues are the seruants of corruption* [2 Pet 2:19].

Come out of Babylon O yee people of God; come away from those *welles without water*; gaze not vpon those *cloudes that are carried with a tempest* [2 Pet 2:17]. *If any man thirst*, said Christ, *let him come vnto me & drinke* [John 7:37]. God, his *HO* in Isaiah, should make the sellers of saluation ashamed. Ly on you also yee beastly buyers. Will yee not heare God his *HO*? *HO euery one that thirsteth*, said God, *come ye to the waters*; & *he that hath no money, come ye buy & eate, yea come buy wine & milke without moneye, & with out price. Wherefore doe ye spend money for that which is not bread & your labour for that which satisfieth not* [Isa 55:1-2]? They are but fooles who thinke to find saluation elsewhere but in God. From whom it cometh, all creatures must say of saluation, as the depth & the sea said of wisdome. The depth saith, *it is not in me*, [. . .] *the sea saith, it is not with me* [Job 28:14].

The Doctrine. The second doctrine I obserue heere is that, seeing saluation cometh from God as a gift from aboue, it must be of great worth. The propines[20] that come from heauen must be precious. From aboue no little things come downe. God, who is both wealth & liberalitie, can not send down little presents from his palace. Will he send from so farre things that are not worthy the carrieing? What man of wealth would not be ashamed to send to his spouse from a farre countrie a premme[21] for a propine or a triffle for a loue token? Our saluation is God his loue token sent vnto vs from the highest. *God so loued the world that he hath giuen his onely begotten sonne* [John 3:16].[22] Againe this sonne hath so loued the world that he hath laide downe his life for the saluation of vs, who by nature are His enemies children of wrath.

The Vse. Seeing our saluation is a propine sent vnto vs from God, bought with the blood of God of so great price, let vs highly esteeme of it. Shall I cast my saluation from me? Shall I despise my Lord his propine? Shall I cast awaye my husband his gift which he hath sent to me a gift bought with his blood? Shall I exchange it with any worldly pleasure, profit, or preferment? Shall I giue from me the mariage or wedding ring to a ruffian? Shall I despise so great a saluation? *How shall wee escape if we neglect so great a saluation* [Heb 2:3]? He is but a swine that trampleth vpon this pearle [Matt 7:6]. The Lord saue vs from this sinne, & that for Christ his sonne his sake, to whom with the Father & Spirit of grace be all glory for now & euer.

VI. Occasional Sermons

A Sermon for a Fast
Anno 1636
in time of great famine[1]

Ps 79:8

O remember not against vs our *former iniquities; let thy tender mercies speedily prevent vs, for wee are brought very low.*

The life of man is like a ship in a rageing sea tossed with wind and waue.[2] The most part of Gods children are like the psalmists mariners. They reele to and fro and stagger like drunken men. But when all their cunning is gone, *then they crye vnto the Lord in their trouble* [Ps 107:28]. The Lord is mans last refuge; God is a friend indeede in time of neede. He is a friend that neuer faileth. *My flesh and my heart faileth*, said Dauid, but God faileth me neuer. He *is the strength of my heart and my portion for euer* [Ps 73:26]. When all things faile the mariners vpon the sea, *then they crye vnto the Lord in their trouble* [Ps 107:28]. So when all things faile the labourers on the land, what shall they doe but *crye vnto the Lord in their trouble*? As it was said of the mariners that all their cunning was gone, so may it now be said of the labourers that all their cunning is gone. It followeth by a necessarie configuence[3] that all that would haue bread must *cry vnto the Lord in* this *time* of *trouble*.

The cheefe iudgement of God that hath moued the Church this day to sound the alarum of a fast is the plague of famine. The most cunning labourers among you have essayed all the meanes yee can, and yet all your cunning is gone. What shall wee doe, but *crye vnto the Lord in* our *trouble*? Seeing this sea of iudgement is so furious, wee must conclude that there be some sinnes in this land whereby God is highly offended.

When these pagan mariners perceiued the sea to rage so furiously, they *were afraid and cried euery man vnto his god* [Jon 1:5]. When they did see that that prevailed not, they imagined that there behoued to some vnhappy body to be in the ship; and therefore they deuised a way to find him, and by casting of lots. [Jon 1:7]. When they had found the man at whom God was angrie, they threwe him out of the ship & cast him into the middest of the sea. Then God was pleased, and then the winds and the waues stouped and were still.

245

Doubtlesse there be some great and fearefull reigning sinnes in this land as yet not repented of. Doubtlesse the maiestie aboue is prouoked by some iniquities of a high eleuation. The tokens of his wrath are more then euident. For this cause, the Church this day hath brought out her greatest canon, euen fasting and prayer, for thereby to ouerthrowe and cast downe all wicked *imaginations, and euery high thing that exalteth it selfe against the knowledge of God, and bringing into captiuitie euery thought to the obedience of Christ* [2 Cor 10:5]. In this great day, wee must haue *in a readinesse to reuenge all disobedience* [2 Cor 10:6]. There be some sinnes like that sorte of diuels which could *not* be driuen *out but* by *fasting and prayer* [Matt 17:21].[4]

This text is a text fit for that purpos. It is a text wherein is a most humble begging of the remission of sinnes and of deliuerance from troubles. If yee would haue a text for time of warre, goe to that part of Gods booke where yee may learne of Hezekias, who had recourse to God while Senacherib was comeing against him with an armie in number like the sand of the sea [2 Chron 32]. If the pestilence rage, goe to another part of Gods booke where yee shall see Dauid humbled before the Lord and cryeing that he would spare these poore sheepe [2 Sam 24]. If the famine molest vs, let vs goe and hear the prophet Joel cryeing, *blow the trumpet in Zion, sanctifie a fast, call a solemne assemblie, gather the people, [. . .] assemble the elders, gather the children and* these *that sucke the breasts* [Joel 2:16].[5] *Let the bridegrome goe foorth of his chamber, and the bride out of her closet. Let the priests, the ministers of the Lord, weepe betweene the porch and the altar* [Joel 2:15-17]. *Then will the Lord be jealous for his land and pitie his people* [Joel 2:18].

As for this land, there is not one iudgement onely wherewith wee are afflicted but there be many, some comeing, some already come. The famine is begunne; the pestilence is makeing post-hast from Flanders for to inuade vs.[6] Wee are also threatned with diuers sortes of diseases. The worse plague of all is the plague of securitie. Wee are not so afraide for God as wee should; wee are not so touched for our sinnes as it becommeth vs to be.

The text whereof I haue made choise is not a text for one plague, but it is a text for all plagues. It takes away the root of all sortes of sorowe. The root of all the plagues of God vpon

246

man are the sinnes of men. Wherefore is the liuing man sorowfull [Lam 3:39]? Man suffereth for his sinnes. Seeing it is so, let
all these that are in sorrowe vnder the correcting hand of God,
as wee are all this day, learne what to doe in the wordes of my
text. Let them take vnto them wordes with the psalmist, and
say whether the calamitie be publicke or private. O *remember
not against vs* our *former iniquities* etc.

the diuison of the text

In these wordes, there be three parts. In the first part, there
is a petition in these wordes, *O remember not against vs* our *former
iniquities*. In the second part, there is another petition in these
wordes, *let thy tender mercies speedily prevent vs*. In the third part,
there is a reason of these his petitions in these wordes, *for wee
are brought very lowe*.

1 Part
first petition

The first petition is in these wordes, *O remember not against
vs* our *former iniquities*. The psalmist heere toucheth the maine
thing that a people in time of iudgement should require of
God, *O remember not against vs* our *former iniquities*. In these
wordes, wherein is the first sute of our fast, I shall consider
these three things: first, he intreats God not to *remember*; second,
by what? viz *iniquities*; thirdly, what sorte of iniquities, our
former iniquities.

1. Remember not

Concerning Gods remembrance in scripture, I see two sortes
of sutes: the one is for to remember, the other is not to remember.
When the children of God desire him to remember, it is
concerning some good things they haue done for his glory. So
good Nehemiah, after that he had told what good things he

247

had done for the glory of his God and the well of his people, said to God, *thinke vpon me, my God, for good, according to all that I haue done for this people* [Neh 5:19]. Likewise after that he had repressed these who profaned the sabbath day, he said, *remember me, O my God, concerning this also; and spare me according to the greatnesse of thy mercie* [Neh 13:22].

To make some vse of this sense, let all men studie and endeuoure that, what they doe, they may say of it to God, remember me O Lord concerning this. Let euery one of vs consider well our thoughts, wordes, and workes, if they be worthy to be seene in the booke of Gods rememberance. While wee thinke, speake, or worke, let vs reason with our selues, if such things be worthy to be put into Gods register.

Wee haue not heere a desire that God remember, but wee haue a prayer that God would not remember: O Lord *remember not*. This petition is for this day: wee haue not brought any thing hither whereof wee can or darre say remember. No not, but wee are come hither this day before God for most humbly to intreat him to put some thing out of his memorie. The best way to make God forget the ill wee haue done is to remember it well ourselues with a sore heart. *If wee [. . .] iudge our selues, wee* shall *not be iudged* [1 Cor 11:31]. If wee remember our sinnes, God shall forget them. If wee forget them, God shall writ them with a pen of iron [Jer 17:1].

2. what

Now it followeth that wee heare what the psalmist heere desireth God not to remember. O, said he, *remember not against vs our [. . .] iniquities*. That which he desired God not to remember were his iniquities. God had afflicted his people. Afflictions make them to remember their iniquities, and this moued them most earnestly to intreat God not to remember their iniquities.

The Doctrine. Obserue heere that affliction is very necessarie for vs in this life. It remembers vs of our iniquities and spurres vs to be earnest with God to take away our iniquities, the cause of all our afflictions. So long as Josephs brethren were at home in wealth with their father, I heare no thing of their

248

repentance concerning Joseph. I heare not one of them say with the butler of Pharoah, *I doe remember my faults* [Gen 41:9]. But tary till they all be put in ward as beeing spies come to trye the weakenesse of the land, then did they remember their faults. *Wee*, said they, *are verily guiltie concerning our brother, in that wee sawe the anguish of his soule, when he besought vs, and wee would not heare. Therefore is this distresse come vpon vs* [Gen 42:21]. So long as Jonas was in the ship in the calme, he past his time in merinesse with the mariners. Jonah then forgote his fault. But the tempest after his sleepe told to him and all the rest that he was a rebell fugitiue from the face of his God [Jon 1:10]. Dauid sleepes in his sinnes of adulterie and blood the space of nine moneth. He then had forgot all. But God first remembred him by his word and after by *the sword*, which *neuer departed from* his *house* [2 Sam 12:10].

The Vse. When God sends vnto vs any iudgment or afflic-tion vpon our body, mind, children, or estate, let vs then incontinent remember our faults. There is not a crosse but it is a messenger from the Lord to remember vs of some trans-gressions. What are all these plagues of God, both come and comming against our land? What are they but messengers from God for to waken vs and to call vs to mind how grieuously wee haue offended him?

Consider heere what iniquities these are which the prophet desires God not to remember. He calleth them our iniquities. *Remember not against vs* our [. . .] *iniquities*, the prophet saith, not remember not mine iniquities forgetting the will of Gods people. Neither desireth he God to forget the iniquities of the people not making mention of his owne, as if he had beene a man holy without sinne. No not, his prayer is heere, *remember not against vs* our *iniquities*.

First, whereas the psalmist desires the Lord to doe to the people as to himselfe, I obserue a lesson both for pastours and peoples. As for the pastour, he must dearely loue his flocke and pray to God earnestly for them and wish to them all the good he seekes for him selfe. He must be glade of their prosperitie and sorie for their sorrowes. Likewise, the people must studie to entertaine loue and to pray for their preachers. The apostle, a great man in spirituall gifts, desired the people to pray for him. If he had neede of the prayers of the Thessalonians [2

Thess 3:1], who can say that he hath not neede of the prayers of the saints?

Againe, whereas he saith, *remember not* our *iniquities*, observe how he, a man inspired of God, acknowledgeth himself to be a sinner with the rest of Gods saints. This world wonders if they see a seruant of God fall into sinne. If such a man fall, they thinke that they may doe what they please, as if his scandala[7] should be a sufficient buckler betweene them and the con-sumeing fire of Gods wrath [Heb 12:29]. But, alas, where is that seruant of God? Where is the man that is not stained with faults? Wee all, saith S. James, faile in many things. Noah was a herauld of righteousnesse and yet ouertaken with the sinne of drunkennes.[8] So was Lot. Abraham, Isaac, and Jacob wanted not their owne faults. So Dauid and Daniel, and all these whose names are writen in the booke of life [Rev 3:5], so long as they are heere clothed with mortalitie, must say with Daniel, *wee haue sinned and haue committed iniquitie, and haue done wickedly and haue rebelled* [Dan 9:5].

Let vs all heere learne after that most humbly wee haue confessed our owne particular sinnes to craue mercy for the sinnes of the whole land. *O remember not against vs our* [. . .] *iniquities.*

3. what sorte of iniquities

It followeth that wee now consider what sorte of iniquities the psalmist heere desireth the Lord not to remember. *O*, saith he, *remember not against vs our former iniquities.* By these *former iniquities*, some vnderstand the sinnes of their fore-fathers, so that heere is a prayer of the posteritie, intreating God not to punish them for the sinnes of their fathers. God in his law hath said that he will visite the sinnes *of the fathers vpon the children vnto the third and fourth generation of* these *that hate* him [Exod 20:5].

obiection

Heere it may be obiected and said, how can this be, seeing God him self hath said the contrarie? *The soule that sinneth* [. .

250

.] *shall die*, said the Lord. *The sonne shall not beare the iniquitie of the father, neither shall the father beare the iniquitie of the sonne* [Ezek 18:20]. How is it, then, that the psalmist heere desires God not to punish his people for the sinnes of their fore-fathers?

the answere

Indeede, if the children of ill fathers would doe well and studie to please God in all things, the Lord would neuer remember against them the iniquities of their parents. *Sed peccata cum offibus sepulti incerent*,[9] all their sinnes should be so burned with their bones that they should neuer be able to hurt any of the posteritie. But when the children followe the sinnes of their fathers and so approue all their ill actions, the guiltinesse, both of their fathers sinnes and also of their owne, cometh down vpon their pate. Christ clearly did signifie this to the Jewes of his time when he said vnto them, *fill yee vp the* [. . .] *measure of your fathers* [Matt 23:32] etc. *that vpon you may come all the righteous blood shed vpon the earth, from the blood of righteous Abel vnto the blood of Zacharias* [Matt 23:35].

The 1 Vse. Yee fathers and mothers beware to provoke God by your sinnes, for your ill actions will teach your children to doe as yee doe, to sweare as yee sweare, to drink as yee drink, to oppresse as yee oppresse, to deceiue as yee deceiue, to shed blood as yee doe, to commit filthinesse as yee doe, after that out shall come a diuine wrath like that flyeing roll of Zacharie, which shall eate vp your houses, not sparing either timber or stone.[10]

The 2 Vse. Yee who are children of ill parents learne heere not to approue the faults of your fathers and mothers. Mourne for them; seeke Gods mercie; tremble at Gods word; feare God; doe well and flie sinne; and the Lord shall neuer remember against you the sinnes of your fore-fathers.

Wee of this land have great neede to amend our life, for wee are the children of ill parents. Great sinnes & fearefull abominations haue beene committed in this land, cheefely blood and filthinesse. Wee presently haue many sinnes. Wee are a nation much subiect to lyeing and deceiving. Euery man hunteth his neighbour as with a net. He is accounted wise who can compasse his brother with a trick of law. Let vs beware that such and such sinnes bring not vpon vs the sinnes of former times, which, if they come, shall break the crowne, sword, and scepter of our kings into pieces, though in our kings house it be writen of them in letters of gold that which no nation in Europe can say, *nobis hac invicta dederunt centum six proan,* a hundreth and six kings haue borne our crowne, sword and scepter, whom no foraine enemie could be able wholy to subdue. The Amalekites were by God commanded to be rooted out for the faults of their fathers, wherein they also did walke. The blood of the prophets came vpon Jerusalem from Abel to Zacharias [Matt 23:35]. The sinnes of Jeroboam and of Ahab were punished in their posteritie that followed their sinnes, and shall the Lord spare vs if wee followe our fathers in their euill wayes? No not, but he will most seuerely punish vs, if, in so great a light of his gospell, wee followe the sinnes of these that sate in darkenesse and in the region of the shadow of death.

But, againe, if so be that wee will repent and returne vnfain-edly to the Lord our God, the iniquities of our fathers shall lye buried with their bones. As a sonne when his father is once dead needs not feare that euer his father come back againe to thrust him out of his possession, so likewise, if wee repent, wee neede not feare that the sinnes of our fathers euer be able to hurt vs, either spiritualy or temporaly.

Other interpreters of former iniquities heere vnderstand all these sinnes that haue beene comitted by vs from the beginning of our life, cheefely *the sinnes of* our *youth.* Dauid hath a notable prayer which may well be called the old mans prayer. O God, said he, *remember not the sinnes of my youth* [Ps 25:7]. So by former iniquities heere are vnderstood cheefely the iniquities of youth.

obiection

Heere some obiect and say, wherefore doeth the psalmist desire the Lord not to remember *the sinnes of* his *youth*? Were there no sinnes of old age to moue him to this prayer?

the answere

Some *estreme hac dici per extenuationem quic facile veniam mer-entur peccata inuentutis qui a ibi minus sapientia et plus ardoris et impetus ad malum,*[11] as if the prophet had said, because the sinnes of youth are more pardonable, because that age is an age of little wisedome subiect to furie and folie. One speakeing of youth saith very well, *inuentus atas lubrica et coeca carnis sequitur libidinem,*[12] youth is an age that is slipperie and blind, which followeth the swinge of the flesh. So youth, beeing both blind and rash, runne head longs into many sinnes.

But this can be no excuse for youth, as though *the sinnes of* [. . .] *youth* were of the smallest sorte. No not, it is a fearefull fault to giue the first fruits to the diuell. The first liquour which is powred into a vessel, if it be ill sauoured, hardly shall euer the taste thereof be cleane taken away.[13] It is not the custome of the godly, while they seeke mercy, to extenuate their faults. No not, but rather to aggrauate the same. So, by this reason, the faults of youth must be great ones, seeing the psalmist is thereby moued to cry heere, *O remember not against vs our former iniquities.*

Heere let all young men learne to take good heede to their life. Youth wantonly spent in sinne procures a sickly and a sorowfull old age. Let men of age heere learne a powerfull eiacalatorie prayer fit to be said at all times, *O remember not against vs our former iniquities.* Let this serue for reproofe to these old rotten ruffiens, who, in the presence of young men, will vaunt and bragge of their filthinesse. Others will boast of their drunkennesse, & they remember *the sinnes of* their *youth* and will not let God forget them. Such sport at this prayer, *O remember not against vs our former iniquities.*

Let all old men learne heere to teach their children how fearefull a thing it is to offend God. Say vnto them, yee who are fathers, Lemuel, Lemuel, my sonnes, my deare sonnes, *giue not* your *strength vnto women* [Prov 31:3], giue not your strength vnto wine, giue not your youth vnto the diuell. Beware to offend the Lord your God. If yee serue him well in your youth, it shall goe well with you in your old age. But much sorrowe and griefe shall come at last if yee spend your first yeeres in vnlawfull pleasures.

253

Let all parents heere learne to correct carefully the first faults of their children. Sinnes in youth are like the first small twigges which come out of trees easily nipped off at the first. O happy is that old man who can say to God, as the prophets widowe said to Elisha of her husband, *thou knowest that thy seruant did feare the Lord* [2 Kgs 4:1]. Happy is that old man whose youth hath beene holy. The Lord shall remember all his good things for to doe him good in the latter end. Also happy is that old man, who, repenting from his heart, can cry in the wordes of my text, *O remember not against* me *my former iniquities.*

2 Part
the second petition

The second petition is in these wordes, *let thy tender mercies speedily prevent vs.* Heere the psalmist seeketh foure things: first, mercies; secondly, *tender mercies*; thirdly, speedy mercies; fourthly, preventing mercies. *Let thy tender mercies speedily prevent vs.*

1. mercies

There be two sortes of mercies: mans mercies and Gods mercies. Mercie, as it is referred to man, is a greefe and sorrow of heart for other mens miseries, whereby, according to our power, wee are moued to help and pity them. In mans mercie, there be two things: the affection in the heart and the effect in the hand. According to this, the Samaritane that pitied and helped the man wounded betweene Jerusalem and Jericho is called the man *that shewed mercy on him* [Luke 10:37]. Againe, mercie, as it is referred to God, is the diuine essence inclining it selfe to pitty and releeue the miseries of all his creatures, particularly of his elected children. From this mercie, which is in God, flowe all the benefits of God, either spirituall or temporall, which are all called mercies because they flowe from the fountaine of Gods eternall mercie and euerlasting compassions. As for the spirituall as praedestination, vocation, iustification, sanctification, and glorification, they are all mercies floweing from mercie. *I*, said He, *will* haue *mercie on whom I will* haue *mercie*.[14] As for the temporall, as deliuerance from prison, from captiuitie, from pouertie and sicknesse, all such mercies receiued by the godly proceede from the same fountaine.

In this text, doubtlesse the psalmist cryeing for mercies seeketh, not onely temporall mercies like these worldlings who haue care of no thing, but of corne, wheate, and oyle [Ps 4:7]. Neither doeth he seeke onely spirituall mercies, but also temporall deliuerances. This is not against true Christianitie, for Christ, who did teach vs to pray for the forgiuenesse of our sinnes, commanded vs also to seeke from God our dayly bread [Matt 6:11-12].

Heere I obserue that mercie is a remedie for all sortes of afflictions. It is a salue for all sortes of sores. If a man be troubled in conscience, let him seeke mercy from the God of heauen. If a man be poore, let him seeke mercy and he shall find that, when *the* [. . .] *lions* shall *lacke and suffer hunger*, [. . .] *they shall not want any good thing* [Ps 34:10]. *A handfull of meele* with Gods mercie was a rich qirnell vnto that poore widowe [1 Kgs 17:12] all the time of the famine. Many sinnes make many troubles and cry for many iudgements, but Gods mercies will ouercome them all.

2. tender mercies

Now let vs see what sorte of mercies he prayeth heere for. It is for *tender mercies*, the mercies of a mother, heart mercies, which are from a fatherly loue. God, who is the God of mercies, hath some mercies for the wicked of this world. They are temporall mercies but not *tender mercies*. According to this, he gaue vnto profane Esau *the dew of heauen*.[15] He maketh his raine to fall as well vpon the wicked as the godly, and so likewise maketh his sunne to shine.[16] He will set crownes vpon the heads of the wicked as he did to Saul and Ahab. These be but temporall mercies which the Lord giueth vnto the wicked, as Abraham gaue gifts to the children of his concubines *and sent them away* [Gen 25:4]. But he giueth *tender mercies* to his owne, who are his heires, as Abraham gaue his heritage vnto Isaac, the sonne of the promise. This is mercy indeede which the psalmist heere calleth, *rehamecha*,[17] the mercies of a mother. The word is from *rehem vterus*, the place of the wombe, where the child is most tenderly wrapped.

This is our sute this day: that the Lord would most tenderly receiue vs within the bowels of his mercies. The bowels of Gods mercies are larger then bowels of fathers and mothers and friends. Mens mercies are but for seuen faults. *How oft*, said Peter, *shall my brother sinne against me, and I forgiue him? Till seuen times* [Matt 18:21]?[18] But there is no arithmeticien that can count the mercies of the Lord. He who hath commanded mans mercies to forgiue seuen times a day, yea *seuentie times seuen times* [Matt 18:22], hath mercies where of poore repenting sinners neede not either doubt or despaire.

Let all these who are troubled in conscience learne heere not to despaire. If the kings of Israel were mercifull kings, how much more mercifull is Christ Jesus, the true king of Israel. As he is called the king of kings, so may he be called the mercifull of mercifull. The sinnes against his iustice he will readily forgiue, but the sinnes against his mercy are of a higher eleuation. If a man sinne against the remedie of sinne, where-with shall his sinnes be remeded? Seeing Christ hath so many mercies for our miseries, wee should striue to haue mercies for the miseries of others.

Let vs therefore in matter of wrongs and iniuries euer set the example of Christ before vs. When wee are offended by any, by any sorte of offence, let vs reason a little within our selues, and say, what would Christ say or doe if now he were in my place? The Lord Jesus neuer rendered ill for ill. Well then, as yee desire mercie, showe mercie; as yee desire God to forgiue you, forgiue others. In all sortes of offences, remember this: art thou a railer? Remember, I pray thee to say, would Christ raile so? Is thy mouth defiled with filthie language? Thinke, I pray thee, if Christ would haue spoken so, while thou hast sleept at the preaching or turned in thy bed at preaching time. Say, would Christ haue done this? So, in steeling, in drinking, in scorning, in brawling, thinke if Christ would haue done so.

3. speedy mercies

We haue heard of one propertie of the mercies. The psalmist heere requires, viz *tender mercies*. Another propertie is that they be speedy mercies. *Let thy tender mercies speedily prevent vs.* When a man desires any thing earnestly, he desires to receiue it speedily. When your children are hungrie, they will weepe if yee giue them not meat speedily. As your children weepe for meat & crye for to get it speedily, so the children of God weepe for mercy and cry for to receiue it speedily. The cheefe reason wherefore Gods mercies are not so speedy in comeing to vs is because wee are slow to repent. If we would haue Gods mercies to come speedily to vs, let vs runne to God speedily by repentance.

4. preventing mercies

The last thing he requires of Gods mercies is that they be preventing mercies: *let thy tender mercies speedily prevent vs.* Heere the psalmist propounds in a maner Gods iudgement and his mercy. Running to come to vs like Peter and John, running to the graue [John 20:4], he, perceiuing this, cryeth, *let thy tender mercies speedily prevent vs*, that is Lord, let thy mercies come first vnto vs. *Let thy mercies* get the foregate. Let them out outstrife all thy iudgements, which are makeing great hast for to come and ouerthrowe vs.

Our God hath two sortes of preventing mercies: the one is for to keepe vs from sinne; the other is for to keepe vs from iudgement after wee haue sinned. It is a preventing mercie that hath kept vs many a time from doeing the ill wee haue desired to doe. Such was that mercie whereby God saued Abimelech from lyeing with Sarah, Abrahams wife. *I*, said the Lord, withhold *thee from sinning against me* [Gen 20:6]. It was a preventing mercie [1 Sam 25:32] that saued Dauid from the slaughter of Nabal. Againe, it is the Lords preventing mercie that hath saued vs from many iudgements which wee haue deserued. It was a preventing mercie that saued this land in the eightie eight yeere of God from that mightie armado.[19] It was a preventing mercie of God that saued our king and nobilitie from the powder blast, & our three kingdomes from an vniuersall combustion. For which deliuerance wee, his people, are oblished to extoll the might of his maiestie by an anniuersarie thankes.

3 Part
for wee are brought very lowe

In the last part of my text, wee haue a reason whereby the psalmist striueth to moue God to graunt him his petitions. The reason is in these wordes, *for wee are brought very lowe*. The Hebrew word *dalal*[20] signifieth *attenuatus, exhaustus, viribus*, that is made small, all the force and strength being exhausted.

Consider that the psalmist saith not heere, for wee are afflicted, but which is more, *attenuati exhausti*,[21] wee are altogether exhausted. What was said heere by the man of God may well be said by vs all in this fearfull day of dearth, wee are wonderfully exhausted. Our land is exhausted. The poor are exhausted by their masters who grind their face. Our cornes are exhausted. Our moneyes are exhausted. Onely one comfort rests, Gods mercies are not exhausted. If wee will repent and returne to the Lord our God, he and all his benefits will returne vnto vs. Turne vnto me, saith the Lord of hosts, and I will turne vnto you, saith the Lord of hostes. Wee haue all great neede to turne vnto him and cry for a speedy mercy, for, if his mercie tarie and linger but two yeeres in comeing to your cornes, the famine shall driue you as fast from your dwellings as mist before the wind. The best is before yee: be exhausted that great and small, rich and poore, young and old, come out and cry mightily vnto God for mercy. In other wordes of my text, *O remember not against vs our former iniquities. Let thy tender mercies speedily prevent vs, for wee are brought very lowe*; or, as it is in the old version, *for we are in great miserie*.[22]

The Doctrine. Obserue heere againe that God will suffer his people whiles to be brought to a great pinch. Behold heere his owne Israel in great miserie, almost exhausted. Heare them heere cryeing, *valde attenuati sumus*, wee are diminished and made very thinne, slender, and leane.

The Vse. Seeing this is often the portion of Gods children

258

heere on earth, let vs not despaire when the afflictions of dearth or death shall be sent vnto vs. When wee either feele or feare such plagues, let vs runne to God by prayer, cryeing in the wordes of my text, *O remember not against vs our former iniquities, [. . .] for wee are brought very lowe.*

The Doctrine. Againe, in the wordes of the iudgement in bringing them very lowe, I obserue a mercie. While they were in a good estate, they were insolently forgetting their dutie towards God by turning his grace into wantonnesse. But when he afflicted them, they powred out many prayers, where wee see that prosperitie, like pharaohs pompe, maketh men to forget God, or to say with pharaoh, *who is the Lord* [Exod 5:2]? But aduersitie is Malmad the god, which teacheth men discipline. The rod driueth folie out of the hautie heart. When Dauid had many people, he was proud and caused number them [2 Sam 24:1]. But so soone as God beganne to hewe them downe with the sword of pestilence, then *Dauids heart smot him* and he prayed vnto the Lord [2 Sam 24:10]. When wee had aboundance of cornes, seruants contemned their masters. The poore contemned Gods mercies. Plentie was called a plague.

But now consider the faces of the poore, and yee shall not see the plague of plentie, but the plague of this text in these wordes, *wee are brought very lowe*. Seeing God for our sinnes hath thus *brought* vs *very lowe*, let vs humble our selues before him, acknowledging our selues with the publican, not worthy to lift vp our eyes towards the heauens [Luke 18:13]. Happy is that loweness of miserie that moues vs to seeke Gods mercie. Such lowenesse that brings home to God is better then the highnesse that sends vs away like the proud forlorne, that would not tarie with his father, so long as he had a portion [Luke 15:12]. The Lord sanctifie so our afflictions this day that thereby wee all may be moued to returne to our God. To him be glory, praise, honour, and dominion, now and euermore, Amen.

The Sick Man His Svte

This sermon was made in the Church of Glasgow,
the sixt of Nouember, 1626, after a feuer in most mens
iudgements deadly.[1]

Remoue thy stroake [. . .] *from me,* for *I am consumed* with
the blowe of thine hand [Ps 39:10]. Solomon, speaking of the
vnderstanding king, saith that he *scattereth the wicked & bringeth
the wheele ouer them* [Prov 20:26], which is a forme of threshing,
whereby they are threshen out from among the chaffe of their
riches, honour, glory, & preferment, like wheat or corne put
out from among the straw by the rolling of a wheele, which
was the old forme of threshing. The wise king is Gods thresher
man.

But how is it that he can discerne the wicked from the godly
that his wheele runne not vpon the one as vpon the other?
Solomon telleth in the nixt verse how this is done, viz by a
wise spirit that God putteth in him, a spirit of discretion. *The
spirit of man,* saith he, *is the candle of the Lord searching all the
bowels of the belly* [Prov 20:27].

That which Solomon said of the wise king we may saye of
the godly man that is king ouer himselfe, & can command his
affections. He scattereth his vaine thoughts, his ill wordes, &
wicked workes. He bringeth the wheele ouer them, the wheele
of repentance whereby he thresheth them, so that the chaff he
separates there from the seede of grace. This is done, not by
any thing in nature that is in him, but by the good spirit, which
God putteth in him as a candle whereby he maye search & see
all the bowels of his belly.

King Dauid, the author of this psalme, haueing receiued this
candle from God, became wise both before God & man. As for
men that were wicked, he was ware[2] of them. He tooke heede
to his wayes; he was resolued to *keepe* his *mouth with a bridle
while* they were *before* him,[3] lest he should sinne with his tongue.
But at last, feeling such a gloweing heat within him, he was
forced to crye to his God, *deliuer me from all my transgressions.*[4]
He was in affliction. By the spirit, God his candle that was
within him, he knewe that his transgressions were the cause of
his affliction; and therefore most wisely, to be quite of his

afflictions, he dealeth with God for the remouing of his trans-gressions.

Hauing sought pardon in the eight verse, he seeketh delyu-erance in the tent verse following, which is our texte, *remoue thy stroake* [. . .] *from me* etc. This is the Christians methode: when God striketh a man, let him not first crye, Lord remoue this stroake. Let this be his first crye, *deliuer me from* [. . .] *my transgressions*. If the wicked misse the stroake, he careth not for his sinnes. From the godly, God will not remoue his stroake till they quite their sinnes. Gods custome is that he will not strike men without a cause. He striketh not till, with their sinnes, with heauy sinnes, they presse downe the Lord, *as a cart* [. . .] *pressed* downe with sheaues [Amos 2:13]. When they cast off him the heauy sheaues of their sinnes, he casteth off them the weighty sheaues of his iudgements. Till sinne be forgiuen, speake not of deliuerance. Let vs come to the words: *remoue thy stroake from me* for *I am consumed with the blowe of thine hand*.

In this verse, ye see cleerly two parts: 1. a prayer to God, 2. the reason of the prayer. The prayer is contained in these words, *remoue thy stroake* [. . .] *from me*. The reason is in these: for *I am consumed* with *the blowe of thine hand*.

1. Part
Remoue thy stroake from me

This is the prayer of a man of God who, being striken, hath recourse to the striker.

The Doctrine. Heere is the doctrine: when euer God stri-keth vs, let vs not spurre[5] against him. The voice cam from heauen to Paul after the hand of God had stricken him to the ground. *It is hard* [. . .] *to kick against the pricks* [Acts 9:5]. Let proud Julian spurre with spight; at last Christ shall cause him crye, *vicisti tandem Galilae*, thou hast ouercome me at last, O Jesus of Galilie.

Learne this in your prosperitie. When euer the Lord shall strike any of you with stroakes of pouertie, distresse, or sicknesse, powre out your prayers vnto God. Sigh for your sinnes. He is not like Baal that could not heare. Humble your selues vnder his hand; confesse that for one stripe ye deserue a thousand; laye downe your head vpon the hag stock; confesse your selues children of death. When Daniel & Israel were striken with captiuitie in that *strange land* [Ps 137:4], the prophet had his recourse vnto God by prayer. *O God my God, encline thine eare & heare. Open thine eyes & behold our desolations* etc. [Dan 9:18]. *O Lord heare; O Lord forgiue; O Lord hearken & doe* etc. [Dan 9:19]. When Christ him selfe was afflicted, he was affraide in the dayes of his flesh. What did he in this case? He prayed & he cryed to God in prayer. He, as it is writen, offered vp prayers & supplications with strong crying & teares [Job 5:7]. This is wryten for our example that in like case we maye seeke vnto our God. *Seeke the Lord*, said Amos, *and ye shall liue* [Amos 5:6]. This was Dauid, his waye. This was his song: in him alone all health & hope I see [Ps 62:1]. God is ready to helpe all these that hope in him. He hitteth no man on the teeth by disdainefull & angry refusals.

As for the wicked, the scripture brandeth them with this note, they call not vpon God. Nay, but in distresse, they flie from God & listen vnto Satan. They seeke vnto witches for helpe & for health. O foole, can the diuell remoue God his stroake? Darre he be a buckler betweene thee & the hand of the Almighty? Who darre be a ridder betweene thee, a worme, a gnat fighting against God with thy sinnes, & betweene the lord of armies fighting against thee with his plagues? Thou that hast sought to vnlawfull meanes in thy miserie, returne to thy God & seeke his mercy. *I flee from [. . .] my mistresse*, said Hagar vnto the angel [Gen 16:8]. *Returne to thy mistresse* [Gen 16:9], said the angel vnto Hagar. Thou that seekes Satans help, thou flees from thy master. O foole, returne to thy master; returne & runne to thy God.

Let this my preaching be to thee the sounding of a retire. None can helpe vs but he that hath plagued vs. None can heale vs but he that hath wounded vs. There is no salue; there is *no balme in Gilead* that can heale the wounds of God. God him selfe must be thy physician. The salue for the sore must be of his makeing. To him alone belongs this cure; to him alone we must haue recourse. He is most mercifull. Yea in him is a mine of mercy, more precious to a troubled soule than all the gold of Ophir.[6] In the most bitter of his iudgements, mercy may be found like the honey which Samson fond in the lyons iawes

[Judg 14:8]. If we had hearts to receiue, God is full of mercy. He is laden like a bee but often wants a hiue.

O fooles, flee from Satan. In your baptisme yee did renounce the diuell & all his workes. At all times, but chiefly in time of trouble, flee from Satan & turne vnto God. It is he whom we haue offended. It is he who woundeth vs with his stroake. It is he who onely can remoue his stroake from vs. *He hath torne; he will heale vs* [Hos 6:1]. If we seeke to vnlawfull meanes, he will consume vs with the blowe of his hand.

Let Saul be witnesse of this: because God answered him not at the first, he sought to Satan. He was too hasty: hast maketh wast.[7] O foole, though a king, he tooke the diuell to be his counseller. He hoped in his helpe; his helpe failed him. What was his reponse? Seeing God hath left thee, why cometh thou to me [1 Sam 28:16]? All his comfort ended in this, *to morrow shalt thou* be with me [1 Sam 28:19]. Jonah said well & wisely, *they that obserue lyeing vanitie forsake their owne mercy* [Jon 2:8]. Satan is but a lyeing vanitie, a vaine lyer, the father of lyes. They that seeke vnto him forsake their owne mercy. For a temporall toye, they losse that ioye which is in the face of their God. Such men be like these lingering courteours, who by their long onwaiting spend their cloake for a coate.

The Vse. Behold brethren, heere is the waye of remouing trouble: crye to God to remoue it. Make hast & hie thee as fast as thou can *vnto the throne of* his *grace* [Heb 4:16]. There call vpon him in time of thy trouble. *Be of good* courage, the master calleth thee [Mark 10:49]. Heare him. *Call vpon me in the daye of trouble*, saith he, and *I will deliuer thee* [Ps 50:15]. If thou saye he biddeth not such sinners as me, call vpon him. Heare the generall *whosoeuer shall call* vpon *the name of the Lord shall be saued* [Joel 2:32].[8] No other can be saued but these that call vpon the Lord. No other can saue but the Lord. *Saluation is of the Lord* [Jon 2:9]. Satan can sift, but can not saue.

Remoue thy stroake, saith Dauid vnto God. See how the man of God in the very time of stroakes turneth vnto God by prayer, the ambassadour of repentance. When a man repenteth, he sendeth vp vnto God a prayer as an ambassadour for peace. *Arise, call vpon thy God*, said the mariners, when their owne gods could not allaye the winds [Jon 1:6]. Thus they roused Jonah vnto prayer, which I may call the repenting hearts ambassadour. Prayer without repentance is but babeling, the wind of the mouth. Awaye with such men, whose workes crye for vengeance while their tongues crye for mercy. These be poisoned prayers. To these that are painefull in prayers, I will saye, your labour is not in vaine in the Lord. The spirit of God brandeth the wicked with this, they call not vpon God [1 Cor 15:18].⁹

The Doctrine. Obserue the doctrine heere: Dauid in trouble is earnest in prayer. So should we be. The s[c]hoole of affliction is the s[c]hoole of prayer. Enter into a grammer s[c]hoole, & ye shall heare a dinne of grammer. Euery one learning his owne lesson. Enter into the s[c]hoole of affliction, & yee shall heare a great dinne of prayer. There ye shall heare all Gods s[c]hollers at their prayers. There yee shall see them all vpon their knees heauing vp their hands to heauen & cryeing, God his mercy. *Doeth the wild asse braye when he hath grasse, or loweth the oxe ouer his fodder* [Job 6:5]? Can a man praye in prosperitie? Can he crye while he hath the grasse of health? Can he praye while he hath the fodder of wealth & worldly pleasures? No not, then he is wanton. But let the arrowes of the Almighty pierce his spirit & sappe him with the iuice of their poison; let the terrours of God set them selues in battell arraye against him, and yee shall heare him braye like an asse that wanteth grasse, & lowe like an oxe that wanteth fodder. I said *in my prosperitie* [. . .] *I shall neuer be moued* [Ps 30:6]. Who could saye that & praye? Well I see heere that it is good to be afflicted. *It is good for me that I haue beene afflicted* [Ps 119:71]. The spirit of man in prosperitie is like the drone bee ydle. It hath neuer laiser¹⁰ to praye. It is tyred before it begin, yea all his prayer is but an ydle buze. As is said of the echo, it is *vox, sonus, aura, nihil*, a voice, a sound, a breath, right nothing.

For to conclude this doctrine, I will saye that it is better to be in the house of fasting where faces are wrinkled with weeping than in the house of feasting. That house is blessed where men remember their end. Satan is seldome among mourners: he liketh most the laughters of these who can not saye with Sarah, the Lord *hath made me to laugh* [Gen 21:6]. *Remoue thy stroake* [. . .] *from me* etc, who is stricken heere? Wilt thou saye, it is Dauid, the man of God, his heart, Dauid that is beloued. *Is he not rightly named Jacob*, said Esau, *for he hath supplanted me*

264

[Gen 27:36]. Is he not rightly called Dauid? Maye I saye of Dauid: for God did loue him as the man of his heart, and yet behold heere how he striketh him though his dearly beloued.

The Doctrine. The lesson is this: take it not for a token of loue to be without trouble, neither for a token of hatred to be in trouble. No not, *the Lord seeth not as man seeth* [1 Sam 16:7]; neither iudgeth he as man iudgeth. *Whom* he *loueth, he chasteneth* [Heb 12:6]. As for these that are heated, they are often fatted vpon leasures. Fattest beasts are nearest the slaughter. They come soonest to the shambles. Who is so fat in the world as the wicked man who washeth his feete in butter? The wicked, saith Dauid, *hath no changes* [Ps 55:19]; and therefore *he couereth his face with* [. . .] *fatnesse, & maketh collops of fat on his flanks* [Job 15:27]. Such collops are kept for hels rosting yron. But as for the godly man whose face is grund small with afflictions, as with a grindstone, whose life is a mappe of miserie, his hell is heere, his heauen cometh after. *Many are the troubles of the righteous;*[11] behold his hell. *But the Lord deliuereth him out of them all* [Ps 34:19]; behold his heauen. Elias must heare a tempest before God come in the calme [1 Kgs 19:11].

The Vse. Make vse of this lesson. If yee would be blessed, informe your iudgement not to thinke ill of the afflicted. Blessed is he that iudgeth well of the afflicted or sicke [Ps 41:1]. When he him selfe shall be sicke, the Lord shall *make all his bedde in his sickenesse* [Ps 41:3]. That must be a well made bed which God maketh. Were thou neuer so sicke, if the Lord make thy bed, in it thou shall find rest to thy soule. If thou would lye vpon a bed which God hath made, iudge well of the afflicted.

But, if thou iudge rashly, Satan shall make thy bed, yea which is worse shall be thy bed-fallowe [1 Cor 5:5]. The apostle his lesson is worthy to be learned: iudge no thing before the time. The time of affliction is not the time of iudgement. Tarry till thou see the end. If he be a godly man, what euer his troubles haue beene, *the end of that man is peace* [Ps 37:37]. It is not so with the wicked. What euer their ioyes haue beene, they take all an ill end. That which Job said ignorantly of him selfe may rightly be saide of them: their *transgression is sealed vp in a bagge* [Job 14:17]. But tarry till this bagge be opened & than woe, woe, woe for euermore. Poets prattle meakill[12] of Pandoras

265

bagge,[13] wherein were all sortes of sorrowes. Fables, heere is the bagge wherein are sorrowes for euermore.

Let me be stricken with the righteous with stroakes that are moueable, of which I maye saye with Dauid heere, *remoue thy stroake* [. . .] *from me*, but God keepe me from the bagge. Let Judas & his mates take the bagge. Let it be so sealed heere Lord that afflictions winne not out vpon them. But thou will open it in the world to come. Than shall they mourne, world without end.

The Doctrine. The other lesson I obserue heere is in these wordes: *thy stroake*. It was Absalom that strooke him. It was the stroak of his owne sonne, and yet behold he calleth it *God his stroake*. He quiteth the stone & taketh him to the hand that cast it. Doubtlesse his greef was great. Yea it was so great that it let him not feele the cursing of Simei, the sonne of Jemini. As one greater paine will dazle the lesse, let him alone, said Dauid. *Behold* the *sonne* [. . .] *of my bowels seeketh my life* [2 Sam 16:11]; the man of my loines is become mine enemie. This was sore, and, yet passing by Absalom, this man of God, heere lookeing vnto God, calleth this affliction the Lord his stroake.

The lesson is this: what euer affliction cometh vnto vs, it cometh out of the hand of God. It is God his stroake, God his hand, &, as we saye, the send of God. When we are sore, & knowe not the second cause of our sore, we call our sore an income or the send of God. But surely euery affliction is an income which we may properly style the send of God.

The Vse. Heere is the patience of the saints & the cause of their patience. If a godly man knewe not this, he could not sit with a wrong. Who could beare with flesh, if there were no thing but flesh in the action? When we see God his hand in the stroake, it beckeneth vnto vs that we be patient. The ignorance of this point is the cause why men, like charets in the streete, iustle one against another. Behold heere a king pushing like a ramme *so that no beasts maye stand before him*. He is an oppressour. Men looke not vnto God. At last cometh out a goate [Dan 8:6], another king. What looketh he to? Not to God but to the ramme; and he runs at *him in the fury of his power* [Dan 8:6]. This is reuenge; this is the custome of the world. The ramme runs ouer the rest, and the goate runeth ouer the ramme. We rashly rush to reuenge because we see not the hand of our God.

266

Happy is the man afflicted by man that looketh not to man but to God. When Eli heard of the slaughter of his children which was to be done by men, he looked not to men. *It is the Lord,* said he, *let him doe what seemeth him good* [1 Sam 3:18]. This consideration is like Abigail to Dauid, a meanes from God to keepe vs from reuenge.

I wish brethren that both yee & I could practise this lesson: if there were any outcaste among vs, we should soone be friends. This wisdome friended Joseph & his brethren. It made him to forgiue & forget all their wrongs. *Be not grieued nor angry with your selues that ye sold me hither, for God did send me* hither *before you to preserue life* [Gen 45:5]. If Joseph had beene but a natural man, they had as deare bought him as euer they sold him. But O the power of grace. What euer euill they did to him, he calleth it the send of God. *God,* said he, *did send me before you* words worthy of euerlasting memorie. If men could thinke so & speake so, it would take awaye all feeds & ill will. The lake of this knowledge is the heauen of our life wherewith it is sowred. It is that miserable moth that eateth vp our loue. It is the feaster[14] of friendship, & the gall of bitternesse in this old & rustie age. Would men be so impatient at a wrong that man hath done if they could vnderstand what God is doeing?

There is not one of vs but we deserue more euill at God his hand than any mans hand or tongue can doe or saye. Seeing it is God that doeth or saith what euer is done or said to vs, were it neuer so euill, there is no thing done or said but that which iustly we deserue [Luke 23:41]. We are heere iustly, said the theefe to his companion. Learne at a theefe. What euer affliction yee fall into, were the instruments neuer so vniust, looke to God & saye with the theefe, we are heere iustly [Luke 23:41]. When Shimei cast stones at Dauid with cursing & railing [2 Sam 16:13], let him be, said Dauid to his captaine, because the Lord hath bidden him speake so. There was neuer a man that did there an ill turne but the Lord first bade him doe it. There was neuer a tongue said an ill worde against thee, but God first bad him saye it. Is there any euill in the city which *the Lord hath not done* [Amos 3:6]? Is there any ill word in the city which *the Lord hath not spoken?* *I make peace & create euill* [Isa 45:7], saith the Lord.

Heere is the patience of the saints in their greatest greefe.

This troublesome euill the Lord hath created it. Take patience O man & looke not to man. Affliction is a creation. *I create euill,* saith God. Can man create? Is man a creator? Can a creature be a creator? Affliction is God his creature. Man is but the messenger to fetch it vnto thee, or rather a rodde in his hand. But woe to the rodde when the child repenteth. It is broken & cast into the fire. Let dogges byte at clubbes, but, when thou is beaten, barke not at men, byte not at all. Looke vnto God with a repenting eye, & saye with Micah, *I will beare the indignation of the Lord,* for *I haue sinned against him* [Mic 7:9].

thy stroake

The Doctrine. The other doctrine I obserue is for our consolation. This is it: all the stroakes of tongue or of hand which we receiue from the wicked are God his stroakes. Heere ye see that Dauid calleth Absalom his wrongs, God his stroake. As it is of stroakes, so it is of wordes. Were they neuer so poisoned in the mouth of man with gall of bitternesse, they are from God. Simei could not haue stirred his tongue to curse Dauid if God had not bidden him. Absalom could not haue stricken at his father if God had not lent him a stroake.[15]

This is a great consolation that the wicked are so bridled that they can neither doe nor sail but at God his direction. It is wryten of Balaam that when he was goeing to curse God his people for a hyre,[16] the Lord mette him *& put a word in his mouth* [Num 23:16]. Marke the worde, a strange worde: the Lord *put a worde in his mouth,* frae.[17] Once God had *put* that *word in his mouth,* a good word for Israel, the lowne[18] could not speake out the ill word which was in his heart against Israel. Nay, but God put in his mouth a good word for Israel. As it is of the wordes of the tongue, so is it of the stroakes of the hand. He that put the word in the mouth of Balaam putteth the stroakes into the hands of the wicked, both in number & in measure, as he thinks best.

Heere is our comfort: where euer we fall, we fall into the hands of God. The wicked are cruell. Yea great is their crueltie, for *the* compassions *of the wicked are cruell* [Prov 12:10]. But God is not cruell and their stroake is his: they are the stone &

268

he is the arme, a mercifull arme, *for his mercies endureth for euer* [Ps 136:1]. Of all the louing & mercifull fathers, he is the most mercifull. *Fathers*, saith he, *prouoke not your children to wrath* [Eph 6:4] lest they be discouraged.

See how the heauenly father teacheth thy earthly father a lesson of mercy. Can he be cruell who teacheth fathers to be mercifull? Shall he be like the pharisees who teach and doe not? No not, mothers may for get the fruit of their wombe [Isa 49:15], but God printeth the godly *vpon the palmes of* his *hands* [Isa 49:16].[19] He neuer striketh them but with regret. If his worde could worke repentance in them, he would neuer come to stroakes. Full loath is he to strike till he be forced to stroakes. Such are the rumbling bowels of his compassions. Will yee heare him selfe speaking to his people? *O Ephraim, what shall I doe* to *thee? O Judah, what shall I doe to thee* [Hos 6:4]? See what wordes of loue. Heare him yet againe in the strife of loue. *How shall I giue thee vp Ephraim? How shall I deliuer thee, O Israel?* How shall I make thee as Admah? How shall I set thee as Zeboim? [Hos 11:8] Heare his boasting bowels in these foure interrogations.

But how concluds he? *Mine heart is turned within me. My repentings are kindled together* [Hos 11:8]. *I will not* [. . .] *destroye Ephraim* etc. [Hos 11:9], wordes worthy of letters of gold, wordes which vtter the very pith of God his mercy towards man. Heere I must crye with Dauid, O Lord, *what is man that thou* should be so *mindefull of him* [Ps 8:4]? But alas, O man, what is God that thou should so forget him?

What could God saye more to man to let him see that he taketh no pleasure to punish? God may strike his owne, but he is not a striker. The man of God should not be a striker. God will not haue a seruant that is giuen to stroakes. God can not be a striker, viz one that taketh pleasure in stroakes. *O thou preseruer of men* [Job 7:20], said Job. The diuell is a destroyer both in Greeke & Hebrewe, *Abaddon, Apollyon* [Rev 9:11]. He euer thirsteth for blood like a horseleach [Pro 30:15]. But God is *mercifull, slowe to anger, & of great kindnesse* [Jon 4:2]. There is nothing that can be done for the conuersion of a soule, but the Lord will doe it before he come to stroakes. He stealeth not a dint. Before he strike at men with his hand, he will hewe *them by his prophets* [Hos 6:5], that is by sharpe admonitions

269

wherewith, as with an axe or eache,[20] he maketh the spailes[21] of wickednesse flee from them that they may be made eauen & sound like timber fitted for a pretious building. Happy that soule that is hewen with the axe, & made sound with the plaine of God his word. We are all by nature knottie wood vnfit for such a building.

If by the heweing of the word, he can no preuaile with men, he will hide him self from them to moue them to amend. *I will goe*, saith he, *and returne to my place till they acknowledge their offence, & seeke my face* [Hos 5:15]. If none of these things can worke, if he can not preuaile neither by heweing nor hiding, at last he will come to stroakes. What shall the Lord doe with his stifnecked creature? Is it not time to strike, when neither wordes nor wyles can doe the turne? Is line come after line [Isa 28:13], commandement after commandement? *Heere a little & there a little* [Isa 28:13], hath it not wrought vpon thee?

Thou shalt not escape his hand. Stroakes are ready for thee. Shall man buffet God with his sinnes & not be scourged with his tawes?[22] Shall not God at last disdaine to be crossed with dust & ashes? When he hath shot his warning peeces, man should waken & repent. Shall the Lord hewe thee by his pro-phets in vaine? Shall the cock crowe & crowe againe while thou, with Peter, denyes him againe, againe & againe [Luke 22:34]? Wilt thou make three faults after two warnings? Darre thou curse thy selfe after the second crowe? Shall the Lord goe to his place & not be sought againe? For all this, will thou not seeke his face? The Lord at last shall muster all his plagues & bring them forth in battell araye against thee. If wordes will not worke, stroakes will doe his turne. Before they come, rather obeye his word the sooner the better. *To daye, if ye* [. . .] *heare his voice* [Ps 95:7], *harden not your hearts*.[23] Yee knowe not what shall be to morrow.

thy stroake

The Doctrine. In the stroake, marke the stubbornesse of our nature. We can not be reclaimed from our sinnes till we be striken. We are like Solomons yong child, in whose heart is such a folie that can not be driuen awaye but with the rodde of discipline [Prov 22:15]. Jonah must be weather beaten, yea put in prison, yea buried in a liuing tombe, before he can learne to goe whether the Lord commands him. Before that Peter can goe whether he should, he must be boasted that another shall cary him whether he would not [John 21:15]. The sharpe prickes keeped Paul from kicking. If God had not striken him to the ground, he had sunke to the hels. Had Dauid not beene striken, he had not beene so rich in penitentiall psalmes. Heare him selfe in this point. *Before I was afflicted, I went astraye* [Ps 119:67]. But now I learne thy statuts. See the stubbornesse of the very godly, who will not learne till they be striken. Then they learne. Better then than neuer.

The wicked will not learne. What euer the Lord threaten, like Hiel, they put neck in perrell [1 Kgs 16:34]. Jericho must be builded againe should the foundation thereof be laid in Abiram & the gates set vp in Segub. How often was Ahaz beaten? But what better was he? He is branded with this: that in *the time of his distresse, he did trespasse yet more against the Lord* [2 Chron 28:22]. This was strange, and therefore, immediately after these wordes, the finger of God pointeth him out as with a behold. *This is King Ahaz* [2 Chron 28:22].[24] It is best to obey God at his word. It is good also to amend at his stroakes. But in the very time of distresse to trespasse, *this is King Ahaz*, a wicked man.

thy stroake

Last of all in God his stroakes I see a consolation. The Lord striketh he thee? It is a fauour, a token. Thou are a childe, a token of his loue. Whom I loue, I chasten [Rev 3:19]. God can not cocker[25] his beloued, lest, beeing spared, they become spilt. Sometimes they are lethargick & therefore must be buffeted. If they slip with their faults, they will sleepe in their sinnes. The feuer is deadly except they be beaten. The stripes of God are for to hold them stirring & wakeing till they be cooled of their drowsie feuer.

This is all their cumber & their paine. They would sleepe pleasantly to death. But God will not let them; euery stroake of the Lord his hand cryeth vnto them, as the shipmaster cryed vnto Jonah, *what meenest thou, O sleeper? Arise, call vpon thy God* [Jon 1:6]. Seeing Lord I must die, let me not die nor drowne in my sleepe. Before my death, crye vpon this sleepy soule. Waken it with that shipmasters shoute, *arise call vpon thy God.* What are all our afflictions but warnings or wakenings? They all crye with one voice vnto vs, *what meenest thou, O sleeper?* They are the Lord his summons wherewith we are charged to returne to our God. They all crye vnto vs, *come* [. . .] *let vs returne vnto the Lord, for he hath torne, & he will heale vs: he hath smiten & he will bind vs vp* [Hos 6:1]. Behold the mercy of God, who healeth the part which he hath torne, as Christ healed Malcas his eare, which Peter hath cut off [John 18:10]. It is not onely a fauour that he healeth vs after he hath torne vs, but it is also kindnesse that he teareth vs that we maye returne. This is *the quyet fruite of righteousnesse* [Heb 12:11]. This much for the first part of the verse. Now let vs come to the second part in these wordes, *for I am consumed* with *the blowe of thine hand.*

2 Part
for I am consumed with the blowe of thine hand

In this second part, the reason is contained where by the prophet striueth to moue God to remoue his stroake from him. It is a reason of pitie, for, saith he, I am confused with *the blowe of thine hand.*

The Doctrine. Marke the lesson: all Dauid his reason is founded in his miserie that God maye pitie him. The papists with their loftie lookes will not be pitied. Woe to them if God pitie them not. They reason not with Dauid from pitie. The cheefe argument of their requeasts is from the worth of their works, which they call the price & payement of the most part of God his benefits. O phariseen, vpper browe stand & face the meiter.[26] Can thou merite? I can, saith he, not onely for my selfe, but also for others. Well, he that can doe so may boldly seeke his owne from God. The pharisee is little beholden vnto God. Nay, God is beholden vnto him. Fye on stinke; fye on the pride of life. It were more godly for papists to saye with Josephs brethren that they haue their corne for no thing, & their money too. Awaye stinking flesh. God chargeth his angels *with folie* [Job 4:18]. Awaye with the menstruous blood of thy righteousnesse. Goe to the s[c]hoole papists and learne the Lords prayer. Praye to God that yee maye vnderstand what ye saye when ye saye, forgiue vs our sinnes. But what neede we such reasons? They will not perswade. Yet this is our comfort: we would have cured Babylon but she would not.

The Vse. As for vs, it is our best when God is angry to crouch & to creepe to his feete. Let vs begge mercy; let papists craue their debts.

I am consumed with the blowe of thine hand

The Doctrine. Behold heere what God doeth vnto the man of his heart: he suffereth him not to goe awaye with his sinnes vnpunished. *If I sinne*, said Job, *then thou markest me* [Job 10:14]. What euer thou be, if thou sinne against God, thou shalt beare his markes. Fooles imagine a God of mercy without iustice. But as Christ said of mariage, so saye I of mercy & justice: let no man separate that which *God hath ioyned together* [Matt 19:6]. Mercy & iustice are ioyned in God. If thou doe well, shall it not be receiued there is mercy. But if thou doe ill, *sinne lyeth at the doore* [Gen 4:7]. There is justice. Fooles imagine that God is all made of mercy & that he can not strike. For this cause, they turne the grace of God into wantonnesse, singing into their hearts that badry song, let vs sinne that grace may abound [Rom 3:8]. Such wordes were inuented in hell. Speake the trueth & saye, let vs sinne that stroakes may abound. Fooles learne to be wise. Knowe that the Lord can strike, yea he can strike where man can not strike, euen vpon the spirit. The spirit of a couragious man will beare his infirmitie, *but* the *wounded spirit, who can beare it* [Prov 18:14]? This is the sadde stroake which maketh the sinner crye, *I am consumed* with *the blowe of thine hand*. This was Dauid his stroake.

Heere I see that God will not suffer his owne to runne riot in sinne. If they sinne, as he said of Solomon, he will chastise them *with the rod of men & with the stripes of the children of men* [2 Sam 7:14]. He will lode them with weighty afflictions. Deare shall they buy their folies, but his grace he will not take from them.

The wicked I confesse are often spaired heere: if men behold their outward estate with a carnall eye, they will thinke that God, like Iacob, hath crossed his hands & laide his right hand where he should haue laide his left, as if, by neglect, he had mistaken Ephraim for Manasses [Gen 48:14]. This was Dauid his thought. *Behold*, said he, *these are the vngodly, who prosper in the world; they incresse in riches* [Ps 73:12]. There is his right hand. All *the daye long have I been plagued, & chastened euery morning* [Ps 73:14]. There is God his left hand. What wrought this thought in Dauid? A beastly meditation. *Verily*, said he, *I haue cleansed my heart in vaine, &* washen *my hands in innocencie* [Ps 73:13]. This was his texte till he *went into the sanctuary of God. Then* and there he *vnderstood* [. . .] *their end.*[27] If the end be well, all is well. This is the lot of the wicked: they all take an ill end. God breaketh them with his tempest. But, as for the godly man, let his troubles be neuer so many & his stroakes neuer so sadde *the end of that man is peace* [Ps 37:37]. This blind Balam vnderstood whose prayer was *let me die the death of the righteous* [Num 23:10].

I am consumed

A sore word, the word consumption declaires the force of the blowe.

An obiection. Heere a doubt maye arise: how is it that Dauid did choose to fall into the hands of God, rather than into the hands of men? What could man his hand doe more vnto him than consume him?

The answere. I answere, he is not consumed that can crye he is consumed. He is not dead that can saye, he is dead. A dead man can not speake. *If a man die, shall he liue againe* [Job 14:14]? When there is little hope of life, yee will saye he is but a dead man though afterward he liue. All is not lost that is in perrell: (a) Ezechias was deadly sicke, & yet he liued [2 Chron 32:24]; (b) Moses was in the flags of the riuer & yet rescued [Exod 2:3]; (c) Iasaphat was fiercely assaulted but not killed [2 Chron 18:31]; (d) Sadrah & his fellowes were cast into a furnace [Dan 3:20], but were not consumed; (e) Daniel was cast into the lyons denne [Dan 6:16], but was not deuored; (f) Epaphroditus was sicke vnto death and yet did not die [Phil 2:27], which is more euen Paul in Asia [2 Cor 1:8]; (g) despaired of life and yet liued, which is most; (h) Lazarus was buried & againe behold him liuing in his winding sheete.[28] Heare him speaking in the place of silence. The sentence of death will be in many that will liue that they should not trust in themselues but in God who raiseth the dead.

Let neuer man despaire of life so long as he liueth. That which seemeth to man vnlikely is not with God impossible [Matt 19:26]. Yea mans extremitie is God his opportunitie. God amongst his owne is like the burning bush; he maye burne amongst them like a fire in a thorne, but he will not consume them. *The bush burned*, said Moses, but *was not consumed* [Exod 3:2]. This is the Lord his sluggorne,[29] mercifull & full of pitie. But *he reserueth wrath for his enemies* [Nah 1:2]; to them he *is a consumeing fire* [Heb 12:29].

I am consumed

These that are rotten within we call them consumed creatures. A sinner is rotten in heart. He truely may be called a consumed creature. Sinne is the cause of all our consumption; it is the worme that eateth vs. It maketh rottennesse in flesh & bones. Finds thou a stinke in the flesh of man? It is becaus it is sinfull flesh. Because there was not sinne in Christ his flesh, it could not be consumed in the graue. Thou will not *suffer* thy *holy one to see corruption* [Acts 2:27]. Because he was holy, his corruption could not be seene. O the sweet sauour of that holy body! O that perfume of holinesse better than the balme of Gilead [Jer 8:22]! It suffers no thing to rot; it is the salt of the earth & heauens conserue. There is no rottennesse where is perfect holinesse. Lazarus was but foure dayes in the graue & he stinked [John 11:39]. We are all but stinking creatures, because we are all but sinfull creatures. Sinne is our consumption, the matter of all our maladies. We are sickly because we are sinfull, because wee are sinfull by botches, by boyles, by feuers, by fluxes, by feasters.[30] God his armour bearers we are consumed; we rot & are wasted awaye.

Wherewith is this that he is consumed? *I am consumed*, saith he, with *the blowe of thine hand*.

The Doctrine. Let vs marke heere the great power of God who with a blowe, yea with a blast, can consume the most mighty. With *I am hee* [John 18:5], Christ made his armed enemies to goe backward to the ground. Who shall stand when God shall saye, *returne yee children of men* [Ps 90:3]? Who shall stand when a king doeth crye, *I am consumed* with *the blowe of thine hand*? Behold the power of God, who consumeth not with blowes but with one blowe. God neadeth not a second stroake. *Affliction*, saith Nahum, *shall not rise vp the second time* [Nah 1:9]. The philosopher his sayeing is heere true, *frustra fit per plura quod furi potest per pauciora*,[31] God needeth not to double his stroake, as he that is feeble fetcheth the second for the doeing of that which with the first he could not doe. God is not like Moses, who, instructing his power, *smote the rocke twice* [Numb 20:11]. God bade him smite it but once: *Thou shalt smite the rock* [Exod 17:6]. Once is enough for God, but man must double & triple. When Elisha was on his deathbedde, he badde Joash, king of Israel, *take* his *arrowes* & *smite vpon the ground*. The bowe being bent, the king *smote thrise & stayed* [2 Kgs 13:18]. Because he stayed at thrice, *the man of God was wroth. Thou shouldest*, said he, *haue smiten fiue or sixe times* [. . .]. *Then hadst thou smiten Syria till thou hadst consumed it* [2 Kgs 13:19]. The stroakes of men are like Joash his shots, one, two, three are not able to consume. But let the creator strike. The creature, were it neuer so strong, shall crye with this king at the first stroake, *I am consumed* with *the blowe of thine hand*.

with the blowe of thine hand

We must knowe that God hath two sortes of stroakes: there is one of consumption, the others are blowes of correction. The blowe of consumption cometh from the power of his wrath. *Who knoweth the power of thy wrath* [Ps 90:11]?[32] This is the stroake of his fourbished blade. This is the *affliction* that *riseth not vp the second time* [Nah 1:9]. Of this stroake, Elihu speaketh vnto Job by waye of counsell, *because there is wrath* [Job 36:18], *beware lest he take the awaye with his stroake* [Job 36:18]. This is the blowe of consumption which taketh a man awaye.

The stroakes of correction are many & of diuers sortes. Let the Lord but beckon & all his creatures shall runne vpon vs. They are all in readinesse &, as it were, lyeing in waite for vs to reuenge the Lord his quarrell, to helpe the Lord, to helpe the Lord against the mighty. *The starres in there courses* will fight for the Lord as sang Deborah [Judg 5:20]. All the plagues of Egypt, blood, haile, frogs, flies, lyce, death will all come out at his crye to help the Lord. The Lord is not like a bee which losseth her sting when she hath once stung, & can not sting no more. If at the first stroake, thou amend not, he shall plague thee & plague thee ouer againe were it till ten times. If thy stubburne heart can not be wrought to repentence by the fatherly stroakes of correction, he shall at last bring vpon thee the fearfull stroake of consumption. When the warnings of God can not moue thee, when the stroakes of his correction can not preuaile, it is a righteous thing with God to summon the eternall worme that dieth not, for to eate & consume thee with gapeing iawes.

I am consumed with the blowe of thine hand

Though Dauid saye heere that he was *consumed* with this *blowe*, we must not thinke that this blowe was a blowe of consumption. Not not, it was but a blowe of correction. And yet heare how he cryeth, *I am consumed* with *the blowe*.

The Doctrine. Heere obserue & marke the weaknesse of flesh. One stroake of God his hand is sufficient to consume a king for all his guard. King Dauid saith not heere that he was consumed with stroakes, but with the stroake in the singular number. A man is but a moth vnder the finger of God.

The Vse. Seeing it is so, let all flesh tremble before God; let no flesh be proud. Shall we be proud of that which at one stroake is consumed? Man in prosperitie can not dreame of this. When he is well heere, he thinks to bath him selfe in streames of blisse without any let. In health the strong man thinks he shall neuer be weakened. In wealth the rich man saith he shall neuer be impouerished. In honour the proud man saith he shall neuer be humbled. I said in my prosperitie, I shall neuer be moued. Awaye with such sayeings. One blowe of the Lord his fist will laye thy strength in the graue & thy honour in the dust. With one stroake, he will bring all thy health to maladie, & all thy wealth to miserie, to beggerie. *I haue seene the wicked in great power, & spreeding him selfe like a greene baye tree* [Ps 37:35] that is in great wealth & honour. *Yet he passed awaye, & loe he was not. Yea I sought him but I could not* find him [Ps 37:36]. What word of him then will yee saye? The prophet himselfe could not tell. *I sought him*, said he, *but I could not* find him. This is God his dealing with the wicked whereof there be many ey & eare witnesses, who maye saye, with the psalmist, *as we haue heard, so haue we seene* [Ps 48:8].

As for the perfect man and the vpright in his afflictions, he is like the burning bush which burnt but *was not consumed* [Exod 3:2]. Though he be bruised with blowes, all is for his well, *for the end of that man is peace* [Ps 37:37]. We saye well, if the end be well, all is well. The Lord grant vs such an end: to him be glory world without end, according to that *voice of great* [. . .] *rushing* [. . .] *blessed be the glory of the Lord from his place* [Ezek 3:12]. Amen, Amen. God his loue be with you all in Christ Jesus.

A Sermon Preached at the Excommunication[1] of a Rebellious Adulterer

the text

Jude v.22. *Haue compassion of some in putting difference.*
v. 23 *And others saue with feare, pulling* them *out of the fire; and hate euen the* very *garment spotted* with *the flesh.*[2]

In the two preceeding verses, the apostle hath shewen what euery godly man should doe for the well of him selfe. *But yee beloued*, saith he, *building vp your selues on your most holy faith praying in the holy Ghost, keepe your selues in the loue of God, lookeing for the mercy of our Lord Jesus Christ vnto eternall life* [Jude 20-21]. In the verses which I haue now read in your audience, he sheweth what the godly man should doe for the well of his neighbours: *haue compassion of some in putting difference, and others saue with feare pulling* them *out of the fire*; and hate the very garment spotted with the flesh.

the diuision of the text

In these wordes wee haue three precepts: 1. the first is a precept of mercy, *haue compassion of some in putting difference*; 2. the second is a precept of iustice *and others, saue with feare pulling them out of the fire*; 3. the third is a precept of chastitie, *and hate* [. . .] *the* very *garment spotted with the flesh.*

1 Part
Haue compassion on some etc.

Before I touch this first part & precept, obserue in generall that saue, saue, saue, is the cry of our God. Saue others by compassion; saue them by feare; saue thy selfe & others; & that so may be *hated* [. . .] *the* very *garment spotted* with *the flesh.*

The Doctrine. This is a faire doctrine of our Gods mercy. He hath sworne by his life that he delighteth not in the death of a sinner [Ezek 33:11]. No not, Gods soule is fully set vpon mans saluation. God hath so loued the world that for the saluation of the world he hath sent his loue for to losse his life. His name shall be called Jesus, *for he shall saue his people from their sinnes* [Matt 1:21].

The Vse. Let this encourage poore broken hearted sinners who hath gone at other times farre astray from their God. Let such come home againe to their God. Let them with that prodigall returne from their swinish huskes [Luke 15:16-17];[3] & I darre be bold to premise that the Lord, more mercifull then the father of that forlorne, shall come more then midde way for to meete them, who shall fall vpon their necks & kisse them & shall make all the heauens to reioice. For these my sonnes & daughters were dead, will he say, & are aliue againe. They were lost & now they are found againe.

It is a great folie for a man to sinne against God; it is a greater foly to continue in sinne. But of all folies this is the greatest after all, to despaire of Gods mercy & so to bound the holy one of Israel. This is blasphemie *against the Holy Ghost*[4] which shall neuer be forgiuen. If thy heart, O man, doubt of the mercies of thy God, yea of his eternall mercies, I will proue it vnto thee by most famous witnesses. In Gods word three witnesses or two at the fewest behoued to be had for the establishing of euery word [2 Cor 13:1]. But for to proue the eternall mercy of thy God, I shall produce to thee six & twentie witnesses in one psalme all saying one thing with out varieing in a syllabe. In that psalme, which I may call the mercifull psalme, six & twentie verse as many most famous witnesses constantly affirme, *for his mercy endureth for euer* [Ps 136:1]. Wherefore when euer wee find our selues in miserie, let vs runne to this God of mercy as Peter did on the waters cryeing, Lord saue me for I perish [Matt 14:30]. Now let vs come to the wordes.

The wordes of the first part & precept of my text are these, καὶ οὕς μέν ἐλεεῖτε διακρινόμενοι, *haue compassion of some in putting a difference*. The Greeke word which is turned heere *haue compassion* is a word of mercy from which is the word *eleemosyna*,[5] that is an almes, a gift giuen out of pitie to one that is in distresse. It is a great almes deede to giue meate to a hungrie man, to giue drinke to him that is athirst, & to cloath him that is naked; but it is a farre greater almes, a farre greater worke of mercy to be a meanes to saue a sinnefull soule, or to comfort a heart broken sinner. This worke of mercy is by the Lord enioined in the first part of this text.

The Doctrine. The doctrine I obserue is that first mention is made of mercy, & thereafter of iudgement. The precept of mercy, as yee see, taketh the foregate before iustice & iudgement. *I will*, said that royal musicien, *sing of mercy & of iudgement* [Ps 101:1], first *of mercy* & thereafter *of iudgement*. When mercy can not worke vpon the hard steele heart, the heart must be put into the fire of Gods anger; & there the preacher must blowe at these hote iuniper coales with the bellowes of iudgement, till the heart be so molten that, like waxe, it drop down for greefe within the bowels. Gods desire is with fairenesse & meekenesse & wordes of mercy, as with honied manna, to allure sinners in the wildernesse of their sinnes. But if they will not, he will hunt out vpon them the fierie serpents of his iudgements for to bite thru & burne them till they acknowledge their offences.

The Vse. Let vs learne mercy of the God of mercy. *Learne of me*, said mercy it selfe [Matt 11:29]. Let vs learne mercy, both of Gods precept & of his promise & of his practise. As for his precept, it is cleare: *be yee [. . .] mercifull as your Father is also mercifull* [Luke 6:36]. The promise: *blessed are the mercifull for they shall obtaine mercy* [Matt 5:7]. His practise was not contrarie to his precepts. He was not like the pharisees who said but did not. Lord, said Peter vnto him, *how oft shall my brother sinne against me, & I forgiue him? Till seuen times* [Matt 18:21]? What was the answere? *I say not vnto thee, vntill seuen times, but vntill seuentie times seuen* [Matt 18:22]. The Lords practise was to forgiue thousand times more. As capitall great letters which beginne a booke are greater & fairer then the rest,[6] so the mercies of Christ are great capitall mercies which so forgiue the sinnes of men that they take them quite away, makeing their red, bloody scarlet, crimsin abominations to change their colours & to become white like wool & snowe [Isa 1:18]. It is the practise of Christs mercies to call vpon all the wearied & ladened [Matt 11:28] with the weightie lead talents of sinne, & to ease them of their burden.

Why then from the precept & from the promise, but cheefely from the practise of our sauiour, let vs learne to be mercifull? After that the Lord had washen his apostles feete for to teach them to be humble, he tooke the cheefest argument of humilitie from his owne practise. *Yee call me*, said he, *Master & Lord & yee say well, for so I am. If I then, your Master & Lord,*[7] *haue washen your feete, yee also ought to wash one anothers feete* [John 13:13-14]. That where at I aime is this: God hath shewen vs mercy, & therefore wee should be mercifull one to another. God euer offreth mercy to a sinner before him in his iustice. This law of warre he gaue to his souldiers of Israel that, when they come before a city to beseege it, they should first make a proclamation of *peace vnto it* [Deut 20:10]. *If*, said the Lord, *it will make no peace with thee* [. . . ,] *then thou shalt beseege it* [Deut 20:12]. See how the Lord would haue a proclamed peace to be sent before a bloody warre, & that to the cities of his enemies. It is the Lords owne practise towards man who is the borne enemie of God. So soone as man cometh into this world, the Lord offereth vnto him conditions of peace. He giueth vnto him so many benefits that man can not deny but he practiseth this first precept of my text, viz *haue compassion*. This He doeth that man, by accepting of his mercy, may be exeemed[8] from the strange act of his iustice, so bent is he vnto mercy. Gods mercy and his iustice I confesse are euer in friendship & in such a loue that they continualy kisse one another. But O the mercies of God [Num 23:20], O the number! *Who*, said Balaam, *can count the dust of Jacob & the number of the fourth part of Israel* [Num 23:10]? But what is all the dust of Jacob & all the foure parts of Israel in number to the mercies of our God? Whereas his iudgements of iustice reach but to the *third & fourth generation* [Exod 20:5], his mercies are shewen *vnto thousands* [Exod 20:6]. What should all this teach vs but to be mercifull as our *Father is also mercifull* [Luke 6:36], & to haue compassion according to the precept of my text which I may call the mercifvill precept.

The 2 Vse. Let this serue for reproofe to all hard stonie hearted Nabals [1 Sam 25:20], who, while they feast like kings, will send no thing to Dauid in his neede, gluttons in whose dogges tongues greater workes of mercy are to be found then in their hands [Luke 16:21]. These be men who thinke that they are onely borne for themselues. If it goe well with their back & their belly, what care they who be cold or who be hungry? The word is trueth; *the* compassions *of the wicked are cruell.*[9] Well, but let them keepe their mercies to them selues; let all their compassions be spent vpon their owne pleasures. But heere is a knot. If men be not merciful, they shall find no mercy. When *I was* hungry, *yee gaue me no meate*; when *I was thirsty* [. . .] *yee gaue me no drinke* [Matt 25:42]; when I was naked yee gaue me no clothes [Matt 25:43]. Now keepe all your owne mercies to your selues, but yee shall get none of mine. *Depart from me* with the diuell & his angels.[10] Thus, as yee see, the wicked whose compassions are cruell shall one day meete with the rigour of a diuine wrath, which shall driue them away like chaffe before the wind [Ps 1:4].

on whom mercy should be had

Now let vs see on whom compassion should be had. *Haue compassion* on *some*, saith the Lord. On some then, yea, but not of all, no not. It is no almes to giue meat to young strong sturdy beggars that liue on other mens labours. It is likewise no mercy to shewe mercy to be a sinner not touched with a sense of his miserie. It is the Lords command that pearles be not cast before swine [Matt 7:6]. The fairest pearle of preaching is the preaching of mercy. An obstinate sinner is but a swine; & therefore the preacher must not cast the mercifvll pearle before such a vile person, who will treade it in that most filthie swinish puddle. Let vs *sinne that grace may abound* [Rom 6:1].

What then shall be done? *Haue* mercy *on some*, saith the spirit. Put on the bowels of compassion towards them; be tender ouer them. But who be these some on whom mercy must be had? These be they who faile by infirmitie, euen these who, as S. Paul saith, are *ouertaken in a fault* [Gal 6:1]. Wee must haue mercy on these I say, on these who haue either failed by infirmitie or are sory for their bygaine obstinacie, yea so at the very heart roots that they knowe not *wherewith* to *come before the Lord & bowe* them selues *before the high God* [Mic 6:6]. Such are they who in the greefe of their heart for offending God would *giue* their *first borne for* their *transgression & the fruite* of their *wombe for the sinne of* their *soule* [Mic 6:7]. To such in the musicke of mercy, wee must pipe the springs of pardon & remission of sinnes that their dolours[11] may be turned into dances.

The Doctrine. The doctrine I obserue heere: that great is the compassion of our God. His delight is not to destroye the children of men. If by any meanes they can be saued, the Lord will vse the same. The fathers of our flesh are mercifull, but such a mercy is no thing to Gods mercy. The mercies of a mother are wonderfull, yea so that it is said *can a mother forget her* [. . .] *child that she* haue not *compassion* on the fruite *of her wombe* [Isa 49:15]? Yet to such to forget is possible, & often the most louing mother hath become like *the ostriche, which leaueth her egges in the earth* [Job 39:13-14],[12] forgetting *that the foote may crush them, or that the wilde beast may breake them.*[13] *She is hardened against her yong ones as though they were not hers* [Job 39:16]. But O the Lord, the father of mercies, can neuer forget to be mercifull to heart broken sinners, for he hath printed them *vpon the palmes of* his *hands* [Isa 49:15]. His name & his nature is mercy so that he must as soone forget him selfe as to forget to be mercifull. *O Ephraim what shall I doe to thee? O Judah what shall I doe vnto thee* [Hos 6:4], *for I desired mercy & not sacrifice* [Hos 6:6]? In the wordes of my text is a precept of mercy, *haue* mercy *on some.*

The 1 Vse. The vse of this doctrine is first for these who are preachers. Where they see that the Lord, as is said in Hosea, desireth mercy, let them preach mercy [Hos 6:6]. To the heart broken sinners, the pipes of the preacher must play of no thing but of mercy. The mercifull spring of mercy must be tuned for such mourning Mordecais. The precept is plaine: restore such a one in the spirit of meekenesse.

The 2 Vse. Let this also serue for instruction to these who are in sorrowe. While mercy is preached vnto them, let them not refuse it. Hearken O heart broken sinner, & giue eare to that which I say. Is thy heart so pierced & pricked that for thy sinnes thou art forced to cry with these mourners in the Acts, *men & brethren, what shall I doe* [Acts 2:37]? I preach heere mercy to thy heart. I declare vnto thee that the Lord Jesus hath compassion on thee, & hath commanded mee this day to preach saluation to thy soule. And therefore see to thy selfe that Christ and his seruants haue not to say to thee one day with these little children sitting in the market places, *wee haue piped vnto you,* but *yee* would not dance [Matt 11:17]. If thy soule mourne for thy bygaine faults, be not like Rachel, who in her mourning *would not be comforted* [Matt 2:18]. Be rather like Hannah, good Samuels mother, a woman of a sorowfull spirit, indeede a woman who came to Gods house in great bitternesse of heart, but so soone as God offered her comfort she accepted of it. *So the woman went* away, saith the scripture, *& did eate & her countenance was no more sad* [1 Sam 1:18]. She was one of these some of my text to whom the preaching of compassion did belong. That which preacher Eli neglected, the Lord him selfe performed.

Now it may be that, in this sanctuary, there be of these some on whom compassion should be had. To you this day I preach Gods mercy, & I pray God that yee refuse not his mercy. What shall I say to thee, O wearied soule? Art thou sore burdened with sinne? *Cast thy burden vpon the Lord & he shall sustaine thee* [Ps 55:22]. Art thou pinched with pouertie? It is in mercy to thee for to keepe thee from presumptuous sinnes, the sicknes of the wealthy. Art thou weake in wit? Seest thou others who are subtile & crafty? Enuie them not, for it is for the most part *the foolish things of* this *world* whereof the Lord hath made choise [1 Cor 1:27]. Art thou troubled with an ill neighbour? Feare God & he shall giue thee a good neighbour, euen a good conscience, the best neighbour that euer man dwelt with. Is shame & disgrace come vpon thee? Repent thee of thy sinnes, & the Lord shall honour thee againe. Many looked that Mordecai should haue beene hanged, but he was exalted, & that Haman should haue beene exalted, but he was hanged.[14] What shall I say more? Art thou euill spoken of? Feare God, & such wordes shall be wordes of mercy for thee. I will tell thee a wonderfull word: all things, as if they tooke meate & wages from the godly man, worke to the best of all these that loue God. Finaly, for to end speaking of Gods comforts for particular troubles, is thy conscience so troubled that thou heares & sees no thing but like a day of battell, wherein no thing is to be seene but gapeing of wounded men & tumbling of garments into blood [Isa 9:5]? Heares thou nothing but the yelling of a wounded conscience strikeing thee with most fearefull knels[15] to the heart? Take courage, the Lord heere declares, that thou art of the number of these on whom the preacher is commanded to haue compassion, a most sure token of Gods owne mercy.

Oh can the tongues of angels or of men preach more of Gods

mercy then it is? No not, no creature is able sufficiently to declare how glade the Lord is to see a sinner sorrowfull for his sinnes comeing home againe from all his euill companie. The forlorne sonne returning from his whoores to his father was but a type & shadowe of a sinner returning from his sinnes to his God. The mercies of that father were but a figure of Gods compassions. Let me then this day cry an oyas[16] of mercy to all wearied soules. Mercy mercy, mercy, heere I proclaime this day to all repenting sinners. This day is a great almes day of mercy. This part of my text is a promise & a precept of mercy. Let the miserable soule blesse God that euer it heard of such a mercy. *To euery one that thirsteth come vnto the waters* [Isa 55:1]; come vnto the riuer of mercy *a riuer the streames whereof* [. . .] *make glade the citie of God* [Ps 46:4], a riuer which is the greatest riuer of the world. If all that drinke of Gods mercy should drinke of the Danube, of Tigeris, of the Tibre, or of Jordan, these riuers at last should be drunke dry. These riuers depend vpon the shoures of heauen, & wax & waine as weate or drougth come. These riuers haue borders & bounds & bottomes. But O the boundlesse, borderless, bottomelesse riuer, yea ocean of the mercies of our God whereunto all wearied sinners are inuited to come: *to euery one that thirsteth come* vnto *the waters*, which no finit thirst can for euer be able to drinke dry.

διακρινόμενοι
in putting a difference

Wee haue heard a preaching of mercy, but must this sweete mercy of God be preached vnto all alike? No not, there must be a vertue, διάκρισις, whereby the wisdome of the preacher must put a difference betweene the diuers humors of his auditors. In the French, it is *en vsant de discretion*,[17] which declareth that there must be great discretion in preaching of the word vnto a people.

The Doctrine. Great wisdome is required for him that is appointed to winne soules. He, saith the wise man, that winneth soules is wise. None but wise men who haue receiued from God this virtue of discretion can be able to saue soules. In all things, it is required that such men be discreete men but cheefely

286

in preaching the word. A preacher must see for his life that he preach not iudgement to a heart broken sinner.

The Vse. Let vs who are pastours study to be wise. Yee people pray for vs. S. Pauls prayer for Timothee was that God would giue him wisdome in all things [2 Tim 3:14-17]. What is said of pastours that I say of you all. Striue to be men of discretion who can make a difference. So long as wee haue vigour of body & spirit, let vs imploye it at the seruice of our God; & let vs striue to discerne things while wee haue adoe with God & man. Let vs striue to discerne while wee are in the dayes of discretion, euen in the age of wisdome before dotage of old age come.

What can a Barzillai doe when he beginneth to say, *I am this day fourescore yeeres old & can I discerne betweene good & euill* [2 Sam 19:35]. Old Moses indeede had the discerning spirit, for he in a particular maner was Moses, the man of God. While the idolaters were shouting & dancing about the golden calfe, young Joshuah heard the sound a farre. When he heard how the people shouted, he said vnto Moses, *there is a noise of warre in the camp* [Exod 32:17]. But O Joshuah had not the discerning spirit. But old Moses considering the difference said, *it is not the voice of them that shoute for mastery*, neither of these *that cry for beeing ouercome, but the noise of them that sing doe I heare* [Exod 32:18].

Alas the best of vs all faile much in this. Wee can not discerne, as wee should, the workeings of the spirit, & that which con-cerne the saluation of soules. Of too many may be said that which Christ said to the pharisees, *when it is euening, yee say it will be faire* [. . .], *for the skie is red* [. . .]. *In the morning, it will be foule weather, the day for the skie is red & louring. O yee hypocrites, yee can discerne the face of the skie, but yee can not discerne the signes of the times* [Matt 16:2-3].[18] That was for the doctors.

But what for the people? *And he said* [. . .] *to the people* [Luke 12:54], *when yee see the south wind blowe, yee say it will be heate; & it cometh to passe* [Luke 12:55]. And *when yee see a cloud rise out of the west, straight way yee say there cometh a showre; & so it is* [Luke 12:54]. But what is subioined? *Yee hypocrites, yee can discerne the face of the skie & of the earth, but how is it that yee doe not discerne this time* [Luke 12:56]? Let it be our prayer that the Lord our God would put this vertue of discretion into the hearts of preachers that they may rightly distinguish betweene offenders. Some the musicke of mercy will most easily perswade; others will not stirre till iustice arise & take the sceptre in her hand. Some care not, for the blessings of Mount Guerizim, but must be terrified with the curses of mount Teball. Some spirits obey best while they heare the songs of Sion; others are so lulled in the dangerous downes of securitie that they can not be wakened but by the thunders of Sinai. And this much for the first part of this verse, wherein is a precept of mercy, haue *compassion* on *some in putting difference.*

2 Part
others saue with feare pulling them out of the fire

In this second part, wee haue a precept of iustice, viz that others must be saued by another way then the way of mercy, euen by the way of rigour & of feare. The precept is that wee mourne vnto such that they may lament. *Others saue*, saith the Sauiour, & *saue with feare.* Happy is that feare that bringeth a man home to his God. Sweete are these gloumes that bring saluation to the soule.

Others saue. There is Christs precept, not destroye others with feare by the fearefull preachings of iudgement & sore threatinings; no not, but threaten & preach hell, & cry fire & vengeance against sinners that they may feare, & so with feare may be saued. But what be these others that he will heere to be saued with feare? They be dangerously diseased soules, viz hauty, proud, rebellious sinners to God & to his Church. Rebellion is the strongest poison of the diuell. It *is as the sinne of witchcraft* [1 Sam 15:23]; it is conspiracie & treason against the most high.

Such stubborne soules are ouercaried by the violent streame of their corruptions, like stifnecked & hard hearted pharoah, who in a maner durst darre the Lord him selfe. And *who is the Lord* [Exod 5:2], said the tyrant, as if a worme on earth could haue power to reuerse all the authoritie of heauen. Such sinners as pharoah, proud, hauty, & presumptuous, are these whom S. Jude calleth heere these others. What shall wee doe with them? The precept is that wee affright them, & put them in a feare, euen in feare of hells fire, in feare of the euerlasting burnings of a diuine wrath, in a feare S. Jude. But what will make such bold hearts to feare? What care they for our threatinings? These be men who, as the French prouerbe saith, *mangent des charettes ferrees*,[19] eat with their teeth chariots of yron. These be Ogs gyants, who lye in yron beds [Deut 3:11], men of might, men of hauty hearts, like that man of the gospell, who neither *feared* [. . .] *God* nor *regarded man* [Luke 18:2], who darre say that they trouble Israel? But who darre disobey the Lord who commandeth heere to saue them with feare?

The Doctrine. The doctrine I obserue heere is that wicked men who walke stubburnely in their sinnes must be gripped like nettles, not softly but hardly. As the godly take the kingdome of heauen by violence,[20] so must the wicked be taken by violence. Except the wedge be hard, it will not driue into a hard knot. A soft Eli is not fit for a Hophni and a Phineas hardened in knauerie. It is a cruell compassion to preach mercy to these who turne the grace of God into wantonnesse.

The Vse. While wee haue to doe with such proud contemners of God, let vs charge our sermons with iudgements till wee see them in a feare. Yea, if preachings worke not, let vs come to *extremum remedium*, the last remeede, euen by excommunication to deliuer them ouer into the diuels power. And now, after all lawfull meanes vsed toward a rebellious adulterer, wee are forced this day to pronounce a sentence full of horrour & terrour. Wee are for to deliuer him vp to Satan, & to cast him out of the society of Gods people. Wee are now for to hurle him out of Christs sheepefold that he may see the wolfe of hell comeing gapeing vpon him, that seeing that murthering monster he may shout & cry to Christ, master, *saue me*, for I perish [Matt 14:30]. Prophane men of a seared conscience peraduenture will account of excommunication as of paper shot. But *ecce clauaes*, behold the keyes. *Whatsoeuer*, saith the Lord, *yee shall bind on earth, shall be bound in heauen; and whatsoeuer yee shall loose on earth, shall be loosed in heauen* [Matt 18:18]. This is fast worke. Happy then is the man that feareth alwayes. A man that feares not God is the captaine of all foolehardis.

By all this yee see that a sanctified feare is a meanes of saluation. But who are these who are sent for to put such proud hauty rebelles into a feare? Euen the sillie things of this world, these who in carnall eyes seeme the very off scourings of the earth. Sillie simple Jacobs are sent forth for to affright the hoarie bold Esaus & and the bragging Lamechs, who boast that they will slay *a man to* their *wounding & a yong man to* their *hurt* [Gen 4:23].

The Doctrine. Great is the power of God & great is his maiestie, who by his little things maketh the loftiest hearts to feare & tremble. See how by wresting fingers he made the ioints of that tyrant Belshazzar to loose, & his knees for feare to smite *one against another* [Dan 5:6]. Though the faithfull preacher be neuer so weake in body, yet there is such a spirituall power in his preaching that it shall either put into the soule of his auditors a sauiur of life whereby they may be saued, or els a sauour of death whereby they shall be damned [2 Cor 2:15].

The Vse. Let this teach men who would not be saued by compassion while mercy was preached to seeke their saluation now with feare, while God is cryeing and others saue with feare. For this I will tell them that, though they had lyons hearts, if they will not now be saued by feare, the time is comeing that they shall so feare that they shall seeke a shelter vnder the rockes for to hide them from the face of the lamb that shall be a day of treading downe & of cryeing to the mountaines.[21] He who will not now be saued with feare shall be one day fearefully destroyed.

pulling them out of the fire

Now it followeth that wee heare how they must be saued by feare. It is set downe in these wordes as *pulling them out of the fire*. In the originall, it is ἐκ τοῦ πυρὸς ἁρπάζοντες, that is as if he had said *pulling them* with a hooke or cleeke *out of the fire*.

The word *harpago* properly signifieth a hooke or cleeke. This as yee see is *ultimium remedium*, the last remeede. When the word preached preuaileth not, when all admonitions are of none effect, when prayers for the rebellious man haue beene made & yet no appearance of repentance is to be seene, then the Church is commanded to take the hooke, & by violence drawe the rebellious sinner out of the diuels armes. If a man be fallen into a riuer where there is danger, his faithfull friend will doe all that he can for to grip him with his soft hand & to drawe him out without hurt. But before he losse him, if he hath a hooke or cleeke of yron into his hand, he will fasten it on his neck or on his shoulder, legge or thigh till the blood gush out. Such wounds of friendship are easily forgiuen. I neuer heard a plea for such sorte of wounds.

To come to the point in hand: there is a man among vs whom the diuell hath cast into the fire of adulterie & of fearefull rebellion. The Lord this day hath put into my hand the hooke or cleeke of excommunication for to saue him & pull him out of the fire, for to drawe him out of the diuels armes. Our God hath his hookes & the diuel hath his. The Lord hath hookes of mercy & of iudgement for the sauing of soules; the diuell, that great harpy of hell, hath his hookes, cleekes of crueltie for draweing of soules to damnation. Wee see in this same epistle how Michael & the diuell drewe with the hookes of a dispute who should get the body of Moses. But the Lord preuailed, & drewe vnto him the body of his seruant. Gods precept is heere that the sinner be pulled out of the fire. But yee will say, who cast this sinner into the fire? While the seruant did see the tares among the wheat, they said who did this [Matt 13:27]? The master answered, *an enemie hath done this* [Matt 13:27]. So say I that it is the enemie that cast this sinner into the fire. Heere God commands to pull him out.

The Doctrine. The doctrine I obserue is that the diuell casts men into the fire, & the Lord pulleth them out againe. *There come a certaine man* vnto Christ *kneeling downe* [. . .] *& saying, Lord haue mercy on my sonne for he is lunaticke & sore vexed, for oftentimes he falleth into the fire.*[22] It was the diuell that helped to cast him into the fire, & Christ tooke him out of the fire. It is Christs command heere that sinners be pulled out of the fire. The diuell is an Abaddon & Apollion [Rev 9:11], a destroyer, a murderer, whose precepts are precepts of destruction. *Cast thy selfe downe*, said he to Christ vpon the pinacle [Matt 4:6]. Cast thy selfe into the fire, saith he to him or her who are burning in their lusts. As his precept is, so is his practis to cast poore soules into the fire. But blessed be God for euer whose precept & practise is to pull out of the fire these whom the diuell hath cast into the fire.

291

The Vse. Let vs heere consider who is the best master, & to him that is best let vs adhere. Let vs giue our eare to be boared with an aule²³ by him whom wee thinke most worthy to be serued [Exod 21:6]. Would yee knowe what shall be the diuels wages & rewards? After that yee haue serued both in a moste vile & painefull drudgerie, he will cast your soules & bodies into the fire of hell. With his hells hooke, he will drawe you downe to that fierie dungeon of vnquencheable flammes. But as for the Lord your God, by the hand of his powerfull mercy & mercifull power, he shall pull you out of all the dangers of that fire & shall feede you to the full with these ioyes which are in his face, for in his face *is fulnesse of ioye* [Ps 16:11]. When Saul did goe about to drawe his seruants hearts from Dauid to him selfe, he said vnto them, *will the sonne of Jesse giue euery one of you fields & vineyards; & make you all captaines of thousands & captaines of hundreds* [1 Sam 22:7]? No not, would he say. It is the thing he neither will nor may doe. With how much greater reason may the Lord say to men & weemen, wherefore will yee leaue mee for to goe serue the diuell? Will the diuell giue eueryone of you kingdomes; will he giue you peace of conscience & ioye in the Holy Ghost? No not, all this wages & rewards shall be to cast both your soules & bodies into the fire. Let vs therefore all say this day, as Israel said to Joshuah, wee will serue the Lord for he is our God [Josh 24:31].

3 Part
and hate [. . .] the very garment spotted with the flesh

Now let vs come to the third & last part of our text in these wordes, and *hate* [. . .] *the very garment spotted* with *the flesh*, in which wordes wee haue a precept of hatred. In Gods word there be many precepts of loue with commands to shewe the same. *Simon, sonne of Jonah, louest thou me* [John 21:15], & againe *louest thou me*, and third time, *louest thou me*. In these three interrogations are subioined three precepts of loue, *feede my lambs, feede my sheepe*, & againe *feede my sheepe* [John 21:15-17], as if he had said, if thou louest me as thou sayest, be carefull that my sheepe & lambs want not meate, yea more I command *you that yee loue one another. By this shall all men knowe that yee are my disciples if yee [. . .] loue one [. . .] another.*²⁴ Loue as yee see is our Lords liuerie. It is the true Christians badge. It is on his breast like the *purseuants blason* or button vpon his breast. I neede not goe thorow all the precepts of loue. I will reduce them all to two great ones which, like two great captaines, command all the rest. The *first & greatest* is that wee *loue the Lord* our *God with all* our *heart,* [. . .] *with all* our *soule, & with* our whole strength; the second is that wee loue our neighbour as ourselues [Matt 19:19]. These be the two great commandements of loue. But alas oftentimes man hateth that which he should loue.

qui malefaciunt oderunt lucem²⁵

Ill doers hate the light which should be loued, as Ahab hated Elijah. But let vs see what wee are commanded to doe heere. Wee must heere obey a precept of hatred which enioineth vs to hate the harlots garments: *sordida eius vestimenta.*²⁶ The argument is from the lesse to the more that much more wee hate the sinnes of the harlot which are the spots of the garment.

Consider the originall word, it is μισοῦντες, which cometh from the word μῖσος, that is hatred. The learned philosopher,²⁷ speakeing of anger calleth ὀργὴν μόριον μίσους, *iram particulam odij,* anger, a parcell of hatred. Properly *ira inueterata est odium,* old rustie anger is hatred; let me yet speake more clearly. Anger is the father of hatred; *ira odium generat,* anger begets hatred. But it begets it as a pharisee begets a proselite whom he maketh *two fold more the child of hell then* himselfe [Matt 23:15]. This is true of sinnefull anger & of sinnefull hatred. But there is an anger that is not sinnefull. *Be* [. . .] *angry* but *sinne not* [Eph 4:26]. So there is an hatred that is not sinnefull, which the holy anger begets, &, like a spirituall proselite, maketh it two fold more holy then it selfe. This is the hatred of sinne which is heere commanded.

Obserue then O man that the Lord will not haue thee to be in anger against filthinesse, as fornication & adultrie, but he will haue thee to come to a hatred for to hate it with a strong old anger. As God hated Esau with a hatred from the wombe [Mal

1:3], so must wee hate sinnes from the wombe of concupiscence, wherein such monsters were conceiued. Wee must hate them as the wicked hate the godly, *odio violentia*; or, as Dauid said, that he hated these that hated God [Ps 139:21]. I, said he, haue *hated them with a perfect hatred* [Ps 139:22].

The Doctrine. The doctrine I obserue heere is that it is not enough to be angrie at sinne which maketh God to be angrie. No not, but wee must doe more. Wee must hate it, & that not with a partiall hatred, but with a perfect hatred. This hatred must not be like the discorde of little children, who will at the one houre discord & agree at the other. No not, but it must be without reconciliation. Where God hath commanded & proclaimed a warre, cursed be the peace maker. Israel must haue no truce with Lamalek. The seede of the woman & sinne, the seede of the serpent, are discharged to make friendship. The command is heere expresse[d] that wee hate [. . .] *the very garment spotted* with *the flesh*.

The Vse. The vse is for instruction: let vs beware to be friends with our lusts, which are spots in the soule. Let vs likewise beware to be friends to their friends, which are the back & the belly. As for the back, see what the Lord in Isaiah said to the daughters of Zion concerning the *brauery of their tinckling ornaments* [. . .] *& their caules & their round tyres like the moone* [Isa 3:18] & their *chaines* & their *bracelets, & their mufflers*[28] & a world of such vanities. The friends of fleshly lusts, which the soule of God did so hate, that instead of sweete smell, he sent a vile stinke & baldenesse [Isa 3:24] for their well set haire & burning for their beauty. As for the belly, it is the stinking kitching of fleshly lusts. Abundance of bread may be called sodomie. It was the sinne of Sodome. By this meanes especialy, the garments of Sodome were spotted with the flesh. O the filthy garments that were in Sodome, garments spotted with strange flesh which the soule of that righteous lot did hate with a sorte of vexation. Let vs therefore remember to learne first to be angrie at sinne.

Thereafter let vs continue in this holy anger. Let the sunne goe downe vpon it, yea, & let him rise vpon it againe. Let vs foster it in our breasts till it be *ira inuetrata*,[29] an old rustie anger turned into hatred. But let vs more particularly consider what it is that the apostle biddeth vs hate heere. *Hate*, saith he, [. . .]

294

the very garment spotted with *the flesh*. In the originall, it is τὸν ἀπὸ τῆς σαρκὸς ἐσπιλωμένον χιτῶνα, an hyperbolick speach taken from the forbidden things of the law which defiled him that but touched them.

The Doctrine. Heere first obserue that sinne is an vncleane & filthie thing, & that because it is of a spotting nature, yea so that it spotteth all where it cometh. Were it the stones of a house like that leprosie which infected the walls, it is like a freting canker which eateth out the very heart of all our best things. So adulterie by Job is called a consumption, which consumeth the whole substance of the vncleane persone.

The Vse. The vse is that, according to Gods precept heere, wee hate the defiled garments of vile fornicators & adulterers. When wee see a whoore, though clothed in silks, & satins, & pasmented with gold, let our soules abhorre her brauerie. Let vs in a godly hatred detest such a polluted harlot. All for beautie were it neuer so great is but like a gold ring on *a swines snoute* [Prov 11:22]. Likewise when thou see a whooremaster shakeing in his silks, let this soule abhorre him. Were he neuer so well clothed with his bootes & cleare spurres, if he be a man defiled with his lusts, if thou be Gods man, thou wilt hate these goodly garments because they are *spotted* with *the flesh*. Say in thy heart, O the vile man that feares not God. All that rich apparell will not saue them from the wrath of God. Were thy spurres neuer so cleare & sharpe, thou can not spurre so fast away from the Lord but his vengeance shall ouer take thee. In these & such meditations, command thy soule to abhorre him. Urge vpon it this thy Lords precept, *and hate* [. . .] *the very garment spotted* with *the flesh*.

The 2 Vse. The second vse of the preceeding doctrine is for reproofe to these who play the goodfellowes, sporting & feasting with these who are thus defiled. As spots are in the face, so are they spots in feasts, & these that feast with them shall hardly winne from them without a spot. It is hard to touch pitch & not be defiled. Let such knowe that their practise is against Gods precept, which commandeth vs *to hate* [. . .] *the very garment spotted* with *the flesh*. This precept was giuen out for to saue stubburne sinners, but such, by their carnall friendship & foolish familiaritie, goe about to make the commandement of God of none effect. Well, if such a sinner, whom Christ hath commanded to saue with feare, perishe in his sinnes, a part of his blood shall be vpon the heads of these who hardened him in his sinnes by countenanceing him & haunting his companie. Now fy vpon thee O man. Is not this the Lords precept, *and hate* [. . .] *the very garment spotted* with *the flesh*? Who darre say but this precept is good? Darre thou not say against it? How darre thou then practise against it? How can thou find in thine heart to be familiare with the man whose companie the Lord hath discharged thee to haunt? This is a sorte of excommunication whereby all true Nathaniels Israelities indeede are discharged to haunt the companie of vile men rotten in their lusts. And what is more plaine, as the spirit saith, *and hate* [. . .] *the very garment spotted* with *the flesh*?

Let such who loue the spotted sinners consider what Jehu, the sonne of Lanami the seer, said to Jehoshaphat because he tooke wicked King Ahabs part. *Shouldest thou*, said he, *helpe the vngodly, & loue them that hate the Lord? Therefore is wrath vpon thee from before the Lord* [2 Chron 19:2]. Let such men feare, lest after they, with such familiaritie, haue beene partakers of their sinnes, fall into the like condemnation with them. *Who is on my side, who?* said Jehu [2 Kgs 9:32]. So saith the Lord in all things that concerne his glory, *who is on my side, who? He that is not* for him *is against* him,[30] though the Lord for a space keepe silence so that a wicked man will thinke that he is altogether such a one as him selfe. Yet he at last will speake & *will reproue* him & will *set* all his sinnes *in order before* him [Ps 50:21]. He shall powre disgrace vpon him, & turne all his glory into shame, for O Lord, all *that depart from* thee *shall be written in the earth* [Jer 17:13].

The 3 Vse. Last of all is it so that wee must hate the garment of another made spotted with the flesh. Let vs then beware to spot our owne garments lest wee incurre the hatred of Gods soule & of all the godly who are commanded to hate such filthy garments. Certainely God hateth the filthie man, yea & his very garments; otherwise he had neuer giuen out this precept. Let vs therefore be persuaded that if wee defile our selues with fleshly lusts the Lords fearefull hatred will come out against vs like that flieing rolle in Zacharie which consumed the house of the theefe & of the sweerer.[31] It standeth vs therefore in hand to take good head that, while we hate the filthie garments of other men, wee be not clothed with filthie garments our selues. Dauid was very seuere against the man of the parable who had taken but a poore mans sheepe [2 Sam 12:3-5];[32] but he spared him selfe who had taken the poore mans wife, yea & the poore mans life, till his sinne was beaten back vpon his face with *thou art the man* [2 Sam 12:7]. He could neuer with a deepe sigh say, *I haue sinned against the Lord* [2 Sam 12:13].

So partiall is man towards him selfe, the not in another mans eye will offend him; & he will be tampering about it with much adoe, while in the meanetime there is a beame in his owne eye which greeueth him not. Many can straine the little gnats of other mens faults, but without paine swallow downe the great camels of their owne corruptions. But as for vs, if there be any spots vpon the garments of our conscience, let vs intreate the Lord to wash them awaye with the blood of his Sonne. Wash me, said Dauid, defiled with the flesh; *wash me & I shall be whiter then the snowe* [Ps 51:7]. After that wee are once washen with the blood of God & with the teares of vnfained repentance, let vs then fain the roots of our hearts *hate [euen] the very garment spotted* with *the flesh*. Fy on vs if wee againe defile the garment which the Lord hath washen with so deere a sope, euen the heart blood of his owne sonne.

The washing is too deare to Christ that wee should defile our soules againe; and therefore deare brethren, when the tempter shall come for to entise vs againe to be dogges & swine for to returne to the puddle & to our vomite againe,[33] let vs remember what Christ hath done to vs. Let vs say, Christ Jesus hath washen my soule, & how should I defile it againe? *I haue* washen *my feete*, said the spouse, & I will not *defile them* againe [Cant 5:3]. What are the feete to the soule? If one be so carefull not to defile his washen feete, how much more carefull should he be not to defile his washen soule? Though wee defile our feete, they may easily be washen againe. Let Rebecca runne to the well & drawe water. But shall Christs blood be as water spilt vpon the ground? O most vile sinner, after that he hath washen thee, one must his veines be opened againe for to let out more blood for to bath thy wilfull wounds & bloody blemishes. Tell me vile sinner, did Christ euery night gird him selfe with a towell for to wash his disciples feete? Thou wilt not find in all the holy scripture that euer he girded him selfe

297

with a towell [John 13:4] for that office. But once in his life, that which the apostle wrote to the Hebrewes is exceeding fearefull. *Let vs,* said he, *drawe neere with a true heart in* [. . .] *assurance of faith,* our hearts being pure *from an* ill *conscience* & washed in our bodies *with pure water* [Heb 10:22], yea with that which is purer then water, euen the purgeing & purifieing blood of Gods lamb. But what if wee defile & spot our selues wittingly & willingly after such a purgation? Let vs heare the testimonie of trueth which can not lie. *If wee sinne willingly,* thereafter *there remaineth no* [. . .] *sacrifice for sinne but a fearefull lookeing for of iudgement* & of violent fire [Heb 10:26-27].

It, as yee see then, standeth vs greatly in hand to keepe cleane that which the Lord hath once cleansed. When Christ came to his spouses doore knocking for to winne in, she said, *I haue washen my feete,* & I will not defile them againe. If so she answered her Lord knocking at her doore, what should wee answere when the filthie diuell cometh to the doore who euer maketh foule doores & defileth them? Likewise who arise for to let him in? I haue washen my feete & how should I *defile them* againe, said the spouse to her Christ knocking at her doore. But what shalt thou saye to Satan when he beginneth to knock? Say Christ Jesus hath washen my soule, & *how* should *I defile* it againe? The yong man, with his whoores sporting in his sinnes & spotting with sinne his soule & his conscience, little remembreth what it is to *hate* [. . .] *the very garment spotted* with *the flesh.* He little remembreth what it is to keepe his owne garments cleane till that dart of Solomon come & pierce him thorow the liuer [Prov 7:23]. Oh that men & women, before their filthie pleasures, could consider these fearefull paines, which followe such filthie folies hard at the heeles.

It is storied of a certaine chast damosell who after she had beene sought by a leacherous youth, & that with great importunitie, she yeelded vnto him at last, but vpon the condition that first he would doe her but one pleasure. The yong man desired to heare what it was. I, said she, desire but this one thing, that yee would hold for my sake your finger into the fire but for a space of an houre. While the yong man heard that, he shrinked saying that it was a paine which he was not able to suffer. Then the damosell wisely replyed, seeing that for my pleasure, yee are not able to suffer the paine of the fire in your finger but for the space of an houre, how would yee that I for your pleasure should suffer both in soule & body the vnquencheable fire of hell, not for an houre but for euer & euer? That heare the yong man, thinkeing shame of his sute, desisted to pursue her any more. Oh that wee all could well remember the fearefull paines which followe these filthy pleasures. O the shame & the disgrace both in this world & in the world to come that accompanie such carnall vncleanesse.

For to conclude the whole purpose in the name of Jesus, the spotlesse lamb, who is followed in heauen onely with these that haue washen their garments in his blood, I exhorte you all in the feare of God to wash away your bygaine spots that yee may appeare without blemish in his presence. I will tell you a fearefull word: the Lord God who is puritie itselfe will not be familiar with a soule defiled with filthie vice & spirituall spots. He will not reueale him selfe to that soule that delighteth in such companie. So long as the Egyptians were in the house, Joseph would not reueale him selfe to his brethren, but first of all, he caused the black Egyptians to the doore, that once done, he revealed him selfe to his brethren saying, *I am Joseph* [Gen 45:3], your brother. That done he embraced them & kissed all his brethren [Gen 45:15]. So before that the Lord Jesus, the great Joseph of heauen, will reueale him selfe to a sinnefull soule, he will first speak vnto vs like a stranger, but will not reueale him selfe vnto vs so long as the black Egyptians of its sinnes are within the chamber of the heart. So soone as they are put to the doore, then he will fall vpon the necke of the soule, & kisse it, & say, I am Joseph, I am Jesus thy Sauiour, & thy saluation to him, the Father of mercies & the Spirit of comfort, be glory & merciful dominion & power for euer, Amen.

After this sermon ended, the rebellious
adulterer beeing present was excommunicat, & deliuered
euer into the hands of the diuell

But (blessed, blessed) he a little after repented & confessed his fault & came home again.

Notes

OED   Oxford English Dictionary
CSD   Concise Scottish Dictionary
DOST   Dictionary of the Older Scottish Tongue
SND   Scottish National Dictionary
AV   Authorized Version
GB   Geneva Bible

An Exposition of the Epistle of S. Paul to the Hebrewes, Chapter 1

1. *bleinke* (ad), "obscuring"; from *blench*, "to deceive, obscure" (*OED*).
2. See Morris Palmer Tilley, *A Dictionary of the Proverbs in England in the Sixteenth and Seventeenth Centuries* (1950; rpt. Ann Arbor: The University of Michigan Press, 1966), L182: "Hot love is soon cold."
3. *meakill* (ad), "great"; also *mickle* (*OED*).
4. *foyson* (n), "plenty"; also *foison* (*OED*).
5. AV reads "thy."
6. See Tilley Y31: "It is too late to call again yesterday."
7. Boyd incorrectly identifies as Ps 95:7.
8. In the margin, Boyd writes, "Satan in his prophets did counterfeit God: Virgil, speaking of Sybilla, saith, *Non vultus non color vnus: non compto mansre coma*" (*Aeneidos*, VI, 47-48).
9. Boyd incorrectly identifies as Judg 6:8.
10. *dyted* (v), Scots for "to direct or instruct" (*DOST*).
11. Boyd's spelling varies; also *schollers*.
12. *badry* (ad), Scots variant of *bawdry* or *baudry* meaning "immorality, lewdness" (*DOST*).
13. *lowne* (ad), Scots for "to become calm, to die down" (*DOST*).
14. *difficile* (ad), "difficult" (*OED*).

Christ Ovr Righteovsnesse

1. Rom 10:1.
2. Rom 10:2.
3. Rom 10:2.

4. Rom 10:3.
5. Rom 10:6.
6. Rom 10:5.
7. Gk. ἐφφαθα.
8. Gk. Ταλιθα κουμ.
9. Matt 17:18.
10. Has no direct relevance in the text.
11. Christ as the beginning and end of all things.
12. See *The Godly Man His Confidence*, n.9, p. 313.
13. "Our Lord has come."
14. "namely an end to whom and an end for the sake of whom."
15. Jewish teaching, in distinguishing two kinds of Torah, affirms that moral definition is useless without expression in human behaviour. Observance of ceremonial law, as pertaining to festivals, sabbaths, sacrifice, ritual purity, etc., is as much an expression of Torah as are the great moral laws. In the context of Calvinist theology, observance of ceremonial law (baptism, communion) in true faith is an affirmation, not of one's conscious choosing of God, but of being called, through Grace, to the true Church.
16. Christianity presents the goat as a symbol of the damned in scenes of the Last Judgement, when the sheep or believers are separated from the goats or unbelievers (Matt 25:31–46).
17. Canticles or The Song of Solomon.
18. "We strive for what is forbidden."
19. GB.
20. Job 28:14.
21. This is Boyd's rendering of the proverb, derived from Aesop's fable on the dog and the shadow, of which another expression is "who but a silly Fop, as foolish as the Dog in the Fable, would not prefer the Substance before the Shadow?" (Oswald Dykes, *English Proverbs* [1709]). See *The Macmillan Book of Proverbs, Maxims, and Famous Phrases*, ed. Burton Stevenson (New York: Macmillan Co., 1948), p. 2079, No. 12.
22. Boyd incorrectly identifies as Luke 16:15.
23. Heb. אמן.
24. *aule* (n), variant of *awl*, a small tool, having a slender, cylindrical tapering, sharp-pointed blade, with which holes may be pierced (*OED*).
25. The "fiftieth year," or year following the seventh of seven successive sabbatical years, observed with the liberation of all Hebrew slaves and the return to original owners of all country and village lands. The land was to lie fallow as it had in the forty-ninth year (Lev 25:8–9).

26. *knat* (v), past tense of Scots for "to join with a knot, to tie up" (*DOST*).
27. Heb 11:4.
28. Heb 11:23.
29. Ps 19:10.
30. 2 Tim 4:7.

The Christian His Pilgrimage
preached the ninteene day of August 1627

1. Boyd's distinction of mind, will, and affections is commonplace in mediaeval and Renaissance psychology. One of the most thorough discussions of this "psychology" is in Perry Miller, *The New England Mind: the Seventeenth Century* (1939; rpt. Cambridge: Harvard University Press, 1954), pp. 239-279. While Miller focuses on the American Puritan experience, his discussion dwells at length on European antecedents.

2. This is an especially Calvinist view, in which the imagination is seen as unconfined by truth, unbound by the senses, and capable of forming images beyond what is natural. While reason was corrupted, it was far more trustworthy than either the emotions or the imagination. See "Introduction," p. xx .

3. 1 Cor 3:3.
4. Boyd incorrectly identifies as Luke 18:11.
5. GB.
6. *calmes* (n), Scots for "molds for casting bullets or other articles of metal" (*DOST*).
7. Matt 22:21.
8. See Tilley W136: "Soft wax will take any impression."
9. GB.
10. Phil 2:7.
11. Phil 2:8.
12. GB.
13. Incorrectly identified as 1 Tim 4:6.
14. Incorrectly identified as Jude 6.
15. *wilworship* (n), worship according to one's will or fancy, or imposed by human will, without divine authority (*OED*).
16. "the end at which one aims beyond which it is not permitted to go."
17. John 9:4.
18. *bonay* (ad), variant of Scots *bony* for "beautiful, handsome, pretty, nice" (*DOST*).
19. AV: "enuying."

20. *laiser* (n), Scots for leisure, "freedom or opportunity to do something specified or implied" (*DOST*).
21. *floure* (n), flower (*OED*).
22. *cumber* (n), variant of Scots *cummer*, "to harrass, to trouble, distress, or disturb severely" (*DOST*).
23. Boyd's reference is rather oblique: "Remember now thy Creator in the days of thy youth, while the evil days come not, nor the years draw nigh ..."
24. *spurre* (n), Scots for "spur" (*CSD*).
25. *wand* (n), Scots for "switch" (*CSD*).
26. 2 Tim 4:7.
27. 2 Tim 4:8.
28. Prov 26:13.

The Cleansing of the Temple

1. "the ear of corn must be rubbed."
2. Heb. פסח.
3. Heb. אתנים.
4. Likely Beza's recension of the Greek New Testament with Latin translation and commentary (1557), which went through many editions. Beza's text relies heavily on the notes of Henri Estienne. See Basil Hall, "Biblical Scholarship: Editions and Commentaries," *A Cambridge History of the Bible*, ed. S.L. Greenslade (Cambridge: University Press, 1963), pp. 61–62.
5. "a banker."
6. "when their religion had declined very considerably to covetousness; if this is true, or rather because it is true, we have every reason to be afraid, for our religion has declined to profit-seeking and covetousness." The identity of Boyd's "popish writer" is not known.
7. A standard criticism for the times: the Church is concerned more with the secular arm than with the spiritual one.
8. "May God block up the mouthes of such people."
9. Boyd's scriptural references are sometimes incomplete, as in this case where he mentions only Isa 6:6.
10. "words and whips."
11. *chires* (n), variant of Scots *chyar* and *chyre*, "shire" (*SND*).
12. Probably Titus (41–81 AD), whose legions sacked Jerusalem and destroyed the temple in 79 AD; Titus succeeded Vespasian as emperor in 79 AD.
13. "it was time for form to give way and truth to take its place."
14. "Rome has a price for everything including heaven."

15. *aliant* (n), "alien" (*OED*).
16. Boyd's reference (Isa 9:7) is incomplete.
17. Boyd's reference (Num 25:8) is incomplete.
18. Augustine, *In Joannis Evangelium Tractatus*, X (II:1-11), 9.

Mercy for Zion

1. "You will prepare yourself earnestly for this work."
2. Ps 66:18.
3. Jon 4:6-10.
4. Dagon, god of the Philistines.
5. Boyd's reference (Exod 14:19) is incomplete.
6. After Jacobus Arminius (c.1559-1609), Professor of Divinity at Leyden, who, while adopting predestination, insisted that grace could be resisted, and tied election to the human will to believe. Arminius' ideas had a significant impact on the English Church, but never threatened the Calvinism of the Scottish Church. Arminius' theology was condemned as "papist" by the Calvinists, who insisted human will plays no part in determining salvation. Boyd's remarks here are typically Calvinist.
7. Traditional home of the Samaritans.
8. GB.

Zions Teares

1. GB.
2. GB.
3. GB.
4. GB.
5. Reference to the French Huguenots, who were severely persecuted during the sixteenth and seventeenth centuries. While Louis XIII affirmed the freedom of conscience granted the Huguenots by Henry IV in the Edict of Nantes (1598), the Catholic Church continued in practice to deprive them of their rights. Forced conversion was commonplace.
6. GB.
7. *creple* (n), "cripple" (*OED*).
8. *lumpish* (ad), Scots for "to be lifeless or soulless" (*CSD*).
9. *lachryma*, reference to *Lachryma Christi*, "tears of Christ."
10. GB. Boyd misquotes; should read, "a time to weepe, and a time to laugh; a time to mourne, and a time to dance."
11. See n.5.

12. Species of acacia, from which was constructed the ark and other articles of Tabernacle furniture (Exod 25:5, 10, 13, 23, 28; Deut 10:3).
13. "belly gods," those whose sole commitment in life is to the satisfaction of worldly desires.
14. GB. Boyd's reference (Amos 6:4) is incomplete.
15. See Tilley H174: "To hang one's harp on the willow," from Ps 137:2 "We hanged our harps upon the willows in the midst thereof."
16. GB.
17. Boyd incorrectly identifies as Jer 4:21.
18. GB.
19. AV: "'to' the roofe."
20. GB.
21. GB.
22. GB.
23. *impuné* (Fr), variant of *impunité* (adv), "with impunity."
24. GB.
25. AV: "Manasseh."
26. AV: "tenth."
27. GB.

The Refvge of the Chvrch

1. GB.
2. GB.
3. The desire to keep in with both sides, as in "I meane not to run with the Hare and holde with the Hounde, to carye fire in the one hand and water in the other" (John Heywood, *Proverbs and Epigrams* [London: 1562]). See *The Macmillan Book of Proverbs, Maxims, and Famous Phrases*, p. 1077, No. 10.
4. Isa 3:18-23.
5. The 1588 revision of the *Bible de Genéve*, edited by Theodore Beza, which remained virtually unchanged until 1693.
6. *burrios* (n), Scots for "executioner, hangman" (*SND*).
7. Heb. תמעטני.
8. This association is Boyd's, drawing on Dan 2:35.
9. Acts 17:28.
10. Heb. גוים. : "the nations."
11. Heb. חמתך.
12. Rev 6:21.
13. Religious persecution in England: while much is made of Catholic persecution of Protestants during the reign of Mary I, as

well as Anglican persecution of Presbyterian, Congregational, and Separatist groups, there was little actual blood spilled, although there was from time to time a rigorous suppression of religious liberty.

14. Problems in Ireland were long standing. Unlike in England and Scotland, there was in Ireland no great disaffection with Catholicism, so that the efforts of Edward VI and particularly Elizabeth I to introduce Anglicanism met with severe resistance. The rebellions of Elizabeth's reign were as much revolts against the English as religious protests, and signalled the inextricable relationship between Catholicism and Irish patriotism. More directly relevant to Boyd's remarks is the alleged massacre of Protestants in Ireland in 1641. James I had initiated extensive English and Scottish colonization, particularly around Ulster, which had brought both Anglicans and Presbyterians to Ireland. Even so, the Irish Catholics maintained some hope that the Stuarts would tolerate Catholicism, even while the Stuarts, like the Tudors before them, had little tolerance for Ireland and saw it largely as a source of income. The shakiness of the Irish situation was exacerbated by the growing Irish fear of an English Parliament more and more dominated with specifically anti-Catholic designs. The result was the rebellion of 1641 in Ulster, in which thousands of English colonists were reputedly killed.

15. Drawn up by Alexander Henderson and Archibald Johnston, and first signed in February, 1638 in Greyfriars' Church, Edinburgh, the National Covenant brought together Scottish opposition to Charles' interference with the Scottish Church.

16. Signalling James' desire for extensive liturgical change, the "Five Articles of Perth" were introduced at the synod of Lothian in June, 1617, and affirmed at the Perth assembly in August, 1618. The "Five Articles" focused on "kneeling in the act of receiving the sacramentall elements of breade and wine at the Communion; observation of some holie dayes dedicate to Christ . . .; episcopal Confirmation or bishoping; private Baptisme; and private Communion." Acceptance of the Perth Articles varied. See Walter Roland Foster, *The Church Before the Covenants: The Church of Scotland, 1596-1638* (Edinburgh and London: Scottish Academic Press, 1975), pp. 183-192.

17. Boyd makes the common claim that the *Scottish Prayer Book*, written by the Scottish bishops on Charles' instruction, and introduced into Scotland in 1637-38, is largely the *Book of Common Prayer*, originally introduced into the English Church by Thomas Cranmer in 1549. While Charles contended that the two kingdoms should pray to God along more or less similar

lines, the two prayer books are far from the same, even though they generated similar criticism for their "popishness," and the *Scottish Prayer Book* was perceived as an "anglicanization" of the Scottish Church. It is true that Charles set limits beyond which the *Scottish Prayer Book* could not go, but its writers still made a "serious attempt . . . to incorporate existing Scottish usages or preferences and to conciliate Scottish prejudices." See Gordon Donaldson, *The Making of the Scottish Prayer Book of 1637* (Edinburgh: University Press, 1954); and William M'Millan, "The Anglican Book of Common Prayer in the Church of Scotland," *Records of the Scottish Church History Society* Vol. IV (1932), 138-149.

18. See n.14.
19. Boyd incorrectly identifies as 2 Kgs 19:14.

Scotlands Hallelviah

1. Montrose's defeat of Charles' forces at Newburne on Tyne in August, 1640, and the subsequent occupation of Newcastle, marks a high point for Scottish unity, although it proved to be shortlived in the face of renewed conflict among the Scottish nobles, as well as the Covenanters themselves.
2. *Scottish Prayer Book*; see n.16 for *The Refvge of the Chvrch.*
3. *fairded* (ad), variant of Scots *fard*, "painted" (*CSD*).
4. AV reads "The Lord gave, and the Lord hath taken away."
5. Boyd's rendering of "the dog which bites the stone that is hurled at him," as in "They resemble angry Dogges, which byte the stone not him that throweth it" (John Lyly, *Euphues: the Anatomy of Wit* [London, 1578]). See *The Macmillan Book of Proverbs, Maxims, and Famous Phrases*, p. 607, No. 3.
6. Heb. מצודה.
7. It is not clear whether Boyd refers to particular Scottish "strongholds" or whether this remark anticipates his reference to Sancerre and La Rochelle.
8. Located on a steep hill overlooking the Loire, the Huguenot fortress of Sancerre resisted assault for eight months from January 3 to August 19, 1573, succumbing in the end to famine.
9. The greatest of the Huguenot fortresses, La Rochelle resisted Richelieu's forces from September, 1627 to October, 1628.
10. AV: "afflictions."
11. Heb. מועקה.; Gk. θλίψεις; Lat. *tribulationes.*
12. *wherefra* (adv), "wherefrom" (*OED*).
13. Boyd tends to overstate his case, as Charles' Scottish military

efforts had very little success. Aberdeen fell to Hamilton's forces, but the city was quickly retaken by Montrose, and, while Charles crossed the Tweed at the end of May, 1639, his forces withdrew when faced with Leslie, who appeared on Duns Law on June 5.

14. Helen of Troy who laments the loss of Hector (*Illiad*, XXIV, 763).

15. Heb. **אנוש.**

16. *outgate* (n), "a passage or way out" (*OED*).

17. *promove* (v), Scots for "to move forward" from Latin *promovere* (*DOST*).

18. "the fisherman," reference to St. Peter.

19. Although Boyd quotes from the Geneva Bible from time to time, he quite clearly prefers the Authorized Version. This preference is confirmed in this statement that he would "rather follow the English version."

20. Used pejoratively by the Covenanters to refer to episcopal church government.

21. Boyd sometimes conflates Authorized and Geneva versions. In this case, "many" is from the AV and "troubles" is from the GB. Such confusion lends weight to the argument that Boyd quotes from memory.

22. See, *The Refvge of the Chvrch*, n. 6, p. 306.

23. Heb. **רויה.**

The Weapons of the Chvrch

1. Boyd's royalist sympathies and his support for the divine right of kings could hardly be clearer. While accepting that secular authority and religious authority rest in one person, Boyd insists that with authority goes responsibility. What the prince does, he does not do for himself but for God.

2. Heb. **שאל.**

3. Reference to the Spanish Armada, which sailed against England in July, 1588, and was defeated by the English in pitched battle from July 21 to July 30. It is estimated that half the Spanish fleet, some 63 ships, was lost.

4. Isa 9:6: "Prince of Peace" (Heb. **שׂר שלום**).

5. Philip II of Spain.

6. A more accurate reference is Num 23:9.

7. The Gunpowder Plot, supposedly masterminded by Guy Fawkes and a group of Catholic companions. The objective of the plot, ascertained by torture from the conspirators, was to

blow up the House of Lords when James I arrived to convene Parliament on November 5, 1605. Historians now doubt Fawkes' guilt, and suggest the plot was an elaborate scheme to discredit Catholics.

8. "peace the best of things; peace the road to triumphs; countless [petier]". The meaning of "petier" is unclear; perhaps Boyd means "prayers" or "petitions."

9. A more accurate transliteration is "*Shelayu*" (Heb. שׁליו).

10. Heb. שׁילה.

11. Ps 139:21-22.

12. 1 Cor 12:14-17.

13. GB.

14. Ps 109:15.

15. Julian the Apostate (331-363 A.D.), Emperor of Rome, while not overtly persecuting the early Christians, refused them the right to political office and disallowed them from teaching in the schools.

16. Ps 122:7-8.

The Trivmph of the Chvrch

1. Heb. צור.

2. "frequent sufferings."

3. "oxen feet and rotten herring guts"

4. Heb. נער.

5. Rev 12:4.

6. Reference (Luke 24:25) is incomplete.

7. "thick darkness."

8. *bootes* (n), variant of Scots *buits*, "instruments of torture" (*DOST*).

9. "follows his wagons."

10. *quiristers* (n), choristers (*OED*).

11. "prostrate animals."

12. "The doctrine of the gospel is more properly understood, and its promises and comforts more eagerly under a cross."

13. GB.

14. Heb. שׁמעי.

15. GB.

16. Heb. גם לא יכלו לי. (Ps 129:2).

17. Heb. עבות.

18. Ps 118:23.

19. "bonds"

20. Such remarks are typical for Boyd, who takes great care never

to criticise the king directly. That the king suffers from poor advice is an argument hardly original to Boyd.
21. One of the seven churches of Asia (Rev 1:4).
22. Rev 3:15-16.
23. Ps 107:8.
24. Boyd's praise of the "Nationall Assemblie" signals his agreement with the covenant and underlines the shortlived nature of his initial resistance.

A Sermon of Repentance

1. Heb. השליכו.
2. Heb. שלכת.
3. GB.
4. Acts 5:1-11.
5. *bund* (adv), Scots for "bound" or "limit" (*DOST*).
6. "insolvent."
7. Matt 18:3.
8. *farthin* (n), "farthing."
9. *ought* (v), Scots variants of *aught* for "owed" (*CSD*).
10. *peti* (ad), variant of Scots *petit* for "small" (*DOST*).

The Worldes Condemnation

1. Conflation of AV and GB.
2. Matt 26:24.
3. "spontaneously and as a favour."
4. Boyd incorrectly identifies as Cant 5:3.
5. 1 Kgs 21:20.
6. "that they may sin without sorrow, and with pleasure."
7. *stonechackers* (n), small bird inhabiting the heaths and commons of Britain (*OED*).
8. "with God as a leader preceding."
9. John 8:3.
10. Matt 5:16.

The Danger of Careless Examination

1. As in the sealing of a document by which it is made authentic; the unbroken seal gave assurance a document had not been opened (1 Kgs 21:8, Dan 12:4, Rev 5:1).

2. See Tilley D542: "Silly Dogs are more angry with the stone than with the hand that flung it."
3. GB.
4. See Tilley S257: "Seven at a feast, nine at a fray."
5. See Tilley S308: "One scabbed sheepman mars a whole flock."
6. Eph 1:6.
7. "weak, feeble, broken in strength, without strength."
8. "weak and sluggish."
9. The Authorized Version of James VI was never formally ratified in Scotland.
10. Reference (Luke 14:18) is incomplete.
11. Reference (Luke 14:18) is incomplete.
12. John 13:26-27.
13. Josh 10:12-14.
14. "He who grieves without witness has genuine grief."

The Safetie of the Chvrch

1. Heb. זבח.
2. Gen 43:11.
3. Gen 43:14.
4. "and without incense he will bring an acceptable offering."
5. "work done"; reference to the Catholic notion of justification by works.
6. GB.
7. 2 Cor 7:10.
8. Luke 1:29.
9. Mark 6:49.
10. Mark 6:50.
11. See Tilley R155: "Spare the rod and spoil the child."
12. Heb. היטיבה.
13. Heb. מה טבו.
14. The Hebrew text reads "*ketov lev*" (Heb. כתב לב).
15. See Tilley L140: "He trembles like an aspen leaf."
16. "the empty-handed traveller will sing in the presence of a robber."
17. Heb. שדי.
18. Matt 25:21.
19. Heb. ציון.
20. Ps 139:21.
21. "lamentable butcher's shop of Paris"; scholars are divided on the causes of the St. Bartholemew's Day Massacre (1572), which began in Paris and spread to the provinces, although historians

agree that Catherine de Medici was its author and instigator. Estimates of the Huguenot dead are also variable, ranging from a low of 1,000 to a high of 10,000.

22. Heb. בּרצונך.
23. Reference to the debate over justification by faith and justification by works.
24. John 8:24.
25. Ps 51:8.
26. Cicero, *Pro Rabirio*, II, 5.
27. "where someone mortal presides, not God, there is no escape there from evils."

The Godly Man His Confidence

1. Ps 57:8.
2. GB.
3. AV.
4. Ps 51:6.
5. See *The Safetie of the Chvrch*, n.5, p. 312.
6. *gadees* (n), plural variant of Scots *gaady*, a larger bead on a rosary (*CSD*).
7. "As if having conducted the exercise well."
8. Matt 6:16.
9. *anathema* (Gk. ἀνάθεμα) *maranatha* (Gk. Μαρὰνἀθἄ): *anathema* is used in the writings of Paul to signify "one accursed," later interpreted as excommunication; *anathema maranatha* signifies "one accursed until the coming of the Lord."
10. Boyd's reference (Rev 3:17) is incomplete.
11. Matt 16:24.
12. *bensell* (n), Scots for "a state of mental tension, excitement, or eagerness"; "a strong bent or inclination" (*DOST*).
13. See *The Safetie of the Chvrch*, n.17, p. 312.
14. See Tilley F162: "As wavering as feathers in the wind."
15. Ps 121:1.
16. " 'the soul keep silent' or 'the soul is silent.' "
17. Boyd's reference (1 Kgs 19:11) is incomplete.
18. *bund*; see *A Sermon of Repentance*, n.5, p. 311.
19. Drawing on the legend that the pelican pierces its breast to feed its young, Christian iconography represents the pelican as Christ's sacrifice on the cross through his love for humankind. The pelican is sometimes seen on top of the cross.
20. *propines* (n), Scots for "gifts" or "presents" (*DOST*).

21. *premme* (n), variation of *premie* or *premye*, "a reward, a gift" (*OED*).

22. GB.

A Sermon for a Fast

1. It is problematic whether Boyd is referring to a particular event or to what was a common problem during period of chronic food shortage.

2. A commonplace metaphor at least as old as Homer and popular with preachers of all persuasions.

3. *configuence* (n), "configuration" (*OED*).

4. AV: "prayer and fasting."

5. Boyd's reference (Joel 2) is incomplete.

6. "Pestilence," like "plague," was a generic term referring to all manner of diseases—bubonic plague, smallpox, measles, diptheria, influenza, whooping cough, etc. Scotland was plague free from 1631-1636, and therefore the outbreak of plague on the English side of the border in 1636 caused considerable consternation. The Scots Privy Council worked to keep pestilence out of Scotland by closing Scottish ports to colliers from Newcastle-on-Tyne, and by cancelling fairs at Roxburgh, North Berwick, and Selkirk, as well as a number of weekly markets. By May, 1636, the Council looked to shut down the border completely by prohibiting all markets and fairs in border towns. See J.F.D. Shrewsbury, *A History of Bubonic Plague in the British Isles* (Cambridge: The University Press, 1970), pp. 367-370.

7. *scandala* (n), "moral lapse," (*OED*).

8. Gen 9:21.

9. "But their sins should be burned with their bones and buried."

10. Zech 5:4.

11. "I have said this extreme thing by way of an extenuating example because the sins of youth easily deserve pardon--youth, a time when there is less wisdom and more passion and an impulse towards evil."

12. "Youth is an insecure and uncertain time of life which follows the appetite of the flesh."

13. See Tilley L333: "With what liquor a vessel is first seasoned, it will long keep the scent of it."

14. Exod 33:19.

15. Gen 27:28.

16. Matt 5:45.

17. Heb. רחמיך.

18. GB.
19. Spanish Armada; see *The Weapons of the Chvrch*, n.3.
20. Heb. דלל.
21. "weakened and exhausted."
22. GB.

The Sick Man His Svte

1. Written as a result of Boyd's serious illness in 1626.
2. *ware* (ad), "aware."
3. Ps 39:1.
4. Ps 39:8.
5. *spurre* (v), "spur" (*CSD*).
6. 1 Kgs 9:18.
7. See Tilley H189: "Haste makes waste."
8. GB.
9. No reference in text.
10. *laiser* (n), "leisure" (*OED*).
11. GB uses "troubles"; AV reads "afflictions."
12. *meakill* (adv), "much" (*OED*).
13. From Pandora's box, which Zeus forbad her to open, came all human sorrows and troubles. That Zeus knew Pandora would open the box suggests the inevitability of suffering in human existence.
14. *Feasters* (n), "festers" (*CSD*).
15. 2 Sam 16:11.
16. *hyre* (n), "wages" (*OED*).
17. *frae* (adv), Scots for "from the time that; as soon as" (*CSD*).
18. *lowne* (n), Scots for a "subdued person" (*DOST*).
19. Boyd incorrectly identifies as Isa 49:15.
20. *eache* (n), variant of "axe" (*OED*).
21. *spailes* (n), Scots for "a splinter, a fragment" (*CSD*).
22. *tawes* (n), Scots for "a whip with tails" (*CSD*).
23. Ps 97:8.
24. GB.
25. *cocker* (v), "to indulge, to pamper" (*OED*).
26. *meiter* (n), "matter" (*OED*).
27. Ps 73:17.
28. John 11:44.
29. *sluggorne* (n), variant of Scots *slughorne*, "slogan" (*CSD*).
30. See n.14.

31. "to no purpose is something achieved by several means when it can be achieved by fewer means."
32. GB.

A Sermon Preached at the Excommunication of a Rebellious Adulterer

1. The thrust of Boyd's sermon is consistent with basic Reform teaching that excommunication is to be used primarily for correction rather than punishment. Excommunication does not entail social ostracization, and therefore every attempt must be made, even after censure, to draw the person back into the Church. Calvin is explicit in this regard: "although excommunication . . . punishes the man, it does so in such a way that, by forewarning him of his future condemnation, it may call him back to salvation . . . though ecclesiastical discipline does not permit us to live familiarly or have intimate contact with excommunicated persons, we ought nevertheless to strive by whatever means we can in order that they may turn to a more virtuous life and may return to the society and unity of the church" (*Institutes of the Christian Religion*, IV, 12, 10).
2. GB.
3. Boyd's reference (Luke 15:17) is incomplete.
4. Mark 3:29.
5. Gk. ἐλεημοσυνη.
6. As is typical for the period.
7. AV: "Lord and Master."
8. *exeemed* (v), "exempted" (*OED*).
9. Prov 12:10.
10. Matt 25:41.
11. *dolours* (n), "pain, grief, anger" (*OED*).
12. Boyd's reference (Job 39:14) is incomplete.
13. Job 30:15.
14. Est 7:10.
15. *knels* (n), "strikes" (*OED*).
16. *oyas* (n), variant of *oyez*, "a call commanding attention" (*OED*).
17. "in wearing discretion."
18. Boyd's reference (Matt 16:2) is incomplete.
19. From French proverb, "avaleur de charrettes ferrés"; see Pierre Larousse, *Grand Dictionnaire Universel Du xix^c Siecle* (Genève-Paris: Slatkine, 1982), Deuxième partie, III, 1033.
20. Matt 11:12.
21. Rev 6:16.

22. Matt 17:14–15.
23. *aule*; see *Christ Ovr Righteousness*, n.24, p. 302.
24. John 13:34–5.
25. "Those who do wrong hate the light."
26. "Her dirty garments."
27. Boyd identifies Aristotle's *Politics* as his source. Other more likely sources are Horace, *Epistolae* I, 2, 62, "Ita furor brevis est: animum rege qui nisi paret / Imperat: hunc ferris, hunc tu compesce catena" ("Wrath is a short-lived madness; curb and bite / Your mind: 'twill rule you, if you rule not it"); and Seneca, *Medea*, 153, "Ira quae tegitus nocet; / Professa perdunt odia vindictae locum" ("Dangerous is wrath concealed; / Hatred proclaimed doth lose its chance of wreaking vengeance"). See Thomas Benfield Harbottle, *Dictionary of Classical Quotations* (New York: Frederick Ungar Publishing Co., n.d.), p. 111.
28. Isa 3:19.
29. "firmly rooted anger."
30. Matt 12:30.
31. Zech 5:1–5.
32. Boyd's reference (2 Sam 12:3) is incomplete.
33. See Tilley D455: "The dog returns to his vomit."